Kaye Liao
Sales & Editorial Representative
Higher Education - Social Sciences Specialist

Thomson Nelson
1120 Birchmount Road
Toronto, ON M1K 5G4

Tel (604) 999-9574 Fax (416) 750-3851
Toll Free 1-800-668-0671 Ext. 4477
kaye.liao@thomson.com
www.nelson.com

www.wadsworth.com

wadsworth.com is the World Wide Web site for Wadsworth and is your direct source to dozens of online resources.

At *wadsworth.com* you can find out about supplements, demonstration software, and student resources. You can also send email to many of our authors and preview new publications and exciting new technologies.

wadsworth.com
Changing the way the world learns®

Nazi Germany
and World War II

Second Edition

Nazi Germany and World War II

Second Edition

Donald D. Wall

Metropolitan State College of Denver

THOMSON

™

WADSWORTH

Australia • Canada • Mexico • Singapore • Spain
United Kingdom • United States

THOMSON

WADSWORTH™

Publisher/Executive Editor: Clark Baxter
Assistant Editor: Julie Iannacchino
Editorial Assistant: Jonathan Katz
Technology Project Manager: Steve Wainwright
Marketing Manager: Caroline Croley
Marketing Assistant: Mary Ho
Advertising Project Manager: Brian Chaffee
Project Manager, Editorial Production:
  Ray A. K. Crawford
Print/Media Buyer: Judy Inouye
Permissions Editor: Bob Kauser

Production Service: Johnstone Associates
Photo Researcher: Lindsay Kefauver
Copy Editor: Judith Johnstone
New maps on pp. 230, 269: Joseph Youst
Cover Designer: Devenish Design
Cover Image: Hulton Archive
Cover Printer: Transcontinental/
  Peterborough
Compositor: Pre-Press Company
Printer: Transcontinental/
  Peterborough

Printed in Canada
1 2 3 4 5 6 7 06 05 04 03 02

For more information about our products, contact us at:
Thomson Learning Academic Resource Center
1-800-423-0563
For permission to use material from this text, contact us by:
Phone: 1-800-730-2214
Fax: 1-800-730-2215
Web: http://www.thomsonrights.com

Wadsworth/Thomson Learning
10 Davis Drive
Belmont, CA 94002-3098
USA

Asia

Thomson Learning
5 Shenton Way #01-01
UIC Building
Singapore 068808

Australia

Nelson Thomson Learning
102 Dodds Street
South Melbourne, Victoria 3205
Australia

Canada

Nelson Thomson Learning
1120 Birchmount Road
Toronto, Ontario M1K 5G4
Canada

Europe/Middle East/Africa

Thomson Learning
High Holborn House
50/51 Bedford Row
London WC1R 4LR
United Kingdom

Latin America

Thomson Learning
Seneca, 53
Colonia Polanco
11560 Mexico D.F.
Mexico

Spain

Paraninfo Thomson Learning
Calle/Magallanes, 25
28015 Madrid, Spain

ISBN 0-534-60453-6

To Carrie, Matt, and Elizabeth
whose love and support made it possible

Contents

Preface

More than a half century after its destruction, the history of Nazi Germany has lost none of its power to enthrall and horrify readers and viewers throughout the world. Interest has been fed by a flood of films, oral histories, and printed material—a flood that shows no signs of subsiding. From my perspective as a college professor, a particularly gratifying measure of its popularity and relevance is the consistently high enrollment in my Nazi Germany course, offered every semester since 1972 at Metropolitan State College of Denver.

Over the years, my students—the topics they find to be particularly interesting, the questions they most frequently ask, and their comments and suggestions—have helped shape the course, and this book, around four central questions: Who was Adolf Hitler and how was he able to rise to such dizzying heights of power? How could Germany, a nation with such a brilliant record of achievement in all areas of human endeavor, succumb to, even enthusiastically support, Hitler's murderous rule? Why was World War II, "Hitler's war," the most destructive in human history? How could the Holocaust have happened? These questions have acquired a universal, and disturbing, significance. If such a malignancy could infect Germany, can any nation, any people, expect to remain permanently immune?

These questions provide the framework for my contribution to the vast, ever-expanding body of literature on Nazi Germany: a concise, comprehensive survey of the Third Reich based on current research findings. It is intended not for specialists but for students and general readers who want a deeper view of this period of German history and a sense of how it is relevant to their lives in the first decades of the twenty-first century. Although there is no formal division, the organization of the subject matter and the degree of coverage given each topic separate the book roughly into two parts. The first six chapters deal with Hitler's rise to power and his regime's policies up to the outbreak of war in 1939, while the last five chapters detail the war and the Holocaust, the final six years of the "thousand-year Reich" that lasted just over twelve years. As the title suggests, World War II, which is the logical outcome of Hitler's ideology and the central event of Nazi history (and of world history from 1939 to 1945) is given extensive coverage. The heart of the book is a narrative that emphasizes political history and war, but there is enough analytical material and coverage of cultural, economic, intellectual, and social topics to justify its description as a comprehensive survey.

The second edition gives me the opportunity to incorporate some of the most current research; suggestions from students, colleagues, reviewers, and other readers; a few new illustrations; and an updated bibliography. Most extensively revised is Chapter 10, which incorporates new and controversial interpretations of the Holocaust. New material on the nature of Nazi terror, and the degree of popular support for the regime and resistance to it, enriches Chapters 4, 5, and 9. I have added details to the war on the eastern front in Chapter 8 and have greatly expanded coverage of the last months of the war in Chapter 11, from the Normandy invasion, to the Battle of the Bulge, to the final destruction of the Third Reich. Excerpts from primary sources placed in text boxes—authentic, sometimes plaintive, voices from the period, some from well-known figures but more from ordinary people, including children—are a completely new feature of the second edition.

Acknowledgments

Several people have helped to make possible this revision of *Nazi Germany and World War II*. Executive history editor Clark Baxter got the project underway by suggesting that Wadsworth was interested in publishing a second edition. He assigned senior developmental editor Sue Gleason to supervise the first few chapters, and she, in turn, named Julie Iannacchino to be my editor for finishing the project. Production manager Judy Johnstone ably supervised the process and provided valuable editorial suggestions. Their competence, professionalism, support, and patience were much appreciated. They also selected several historians whose thoughtful reviews were sometimes critical, usually encouraging, and always helpful. They are: Hayward Farrar, Virginia Tech; Elliot Neaman, University of San Francisco; Robert W. Brown, University of North Carolina Pembroke; Peter Mellini, Sonoma State University; Wendell Mauter, Quincy University and Paul Vincent, Keene State College.

Closer to home, I am indebted to my colleague and department chair, Stephen Leonard. His masterful editing touch, which strengthened the first edition has not been lost in the second. I am grateful to my students and other readers, whose suggestions and enthusiastic reception of the book helped encourage me to write a second, and, I hope, improved edition. They reinforced my conviction that the story of Germany's descent into hell under the Hitler regime will always need to be told. Special thanks to my son Matt, whose computer skills, patience, and timely assistance frequently rescued me from electronic dilemmas as I was preparing the manuscript, to my daughter Elizabeth, whose editorial skills were most helpful, and to student assistant Denise Hull, who prepared the Infotrac® College Edition material for each chapter. Finally, I owe a debt of gratitude to my wife Carrie. Without her moral support and encouragement, as well as her assistance in preparing the manuscript, I could never have completed this project.

Germany and Hitler to 1919

In his opening statement to the International Military Tribunal in November 1945, Supreme Court Justice Robert Jackson, the chief American prosecutor, eloquently justified the trial: "The wrongs which we seek to condemn and punish have been so calculated, so malignant, and so devastating that civilization cannot tolerate their being ignored, because it cannot survive their being repeated."[1] In the dock were twenty-one defendants (one was being tried *in absentia*) accused of crimes ranging from conspiracy to wage aggressive war to genocide. Ironically, they belonged to the nation that, with its brilliant cultural heritage, had been a principal architect of modern European civilization—a civilization that was nearly destroyed by the war that Adolf Hitler unleashed in 1939.

World War II's predecessor broke out in August 1914. European civilization survived World War I, but the "war to end all wars," as it was popularly called in the United States, lasted over four years, consumed at least 10 million lives, and left millions of people on both sides embittered and disillusioned. It ushered in a new age of force and spawned new "isms," whose leaders used advanced technology to oppress, conquer, and murder on an unprecedented scale.

While the second global conflict may not have been entirely unexpected, World War I shocked the civilization to which Jackson referred. Europeans in 1914 reflected smugly on the preceding "century of progress," evidenced by rapid economic growth and industrialization, scientific advancement and technological innovation, and a culture admired and imitated throughout the world. Science and public humanitarianism had reduced the severity of age-old scourges of humankind, such as slavery, serfdom, epidemics, and mass starvation. At the same time, most Europeans did not consider war to be an uncivilized activity, and few recognized the potentially destructive force of popular ideologies, such as nationalism, racism, and anti-Semitism. The century of progress culminated in the "Great War," as barbaric a massacre as the world had ever seen.

Germany's bitter defeat in 1918 helped pave the way for Hitler's dictatorship and a second global conflict far more lethal than the first. This catastrophic turn of events—Hitler's rise to power and his conversion of the German nation into an instrument of death and destruction—was not the result of a peculiarly perverse national character. Nor did the German people deliberately choose a clearly marked path that inevitably led to the Nazi dictatorship. On the other hand, the Third Reich was neither an aberration nor an accident. It was a multi-causal phenomenon whose political, social, cultural, and intellectual antecedents can be divined in the period from the birth of the German Empire in 1871 to the outbreak of war in 1914. Historians can identify more precise roots in the debacle of World War I and more immediate causes in the collapse of the Weimar Republic and the Great Depression in the early 1930s. This chapter will provide an overview of German history from 1871 to 1919 and a biographical sketch of the young Hitler from his birth in 1889. Though Hitler's impact on German history before 1930 was minimal, his personality and ideas were shaped before and during World War I. Had he not undergone these experiences, elements already present on the German scene might never have mutated into the horrors of World War II.

Imperial Germany: Political and Economic Developments to 1914

In the Palace of Versailles, on January 18, 1871, Prussian Prime Minister Otto von Bismarck orchestrated the coronation of his sovereign, William I. For the first time in 600 years the German states were united under a single ruler. The formation of the Second Reich, successor to the Holy Roman Empire of the Middle Ages, was a proud moment in the history of a politically divided people often victimized by more powerful European states. The coronation of the new Kaiser took place several months before the end of the Franco-Prussian War, the third and bloodiest of Bismarck's wars of unification. Unlike the first two conflicts against Denmark and Austria, Prussia's war against France was a joint effort of all the German states.

Imperial Germany's constitution, which Bismarck designed, was a curious combination of authoritarian, federalist, and democratic principles. Elected by universal manhood suffrage, the parliament, or Reichstag, could vote only on legislation initiated by the Federal Council *(Bundesrat)*, a smaller body whose delegates represented the individual states. Prussia, which was larger and more powerful than all the other states combined, dominated the Council and dictated the Reichstag's agenda. Moreover, the chancellor and his cabinet, all of whom held identical positions in the Prussian government, were responsible only to the Kaiser, who was also the king of Prussia. If the Reichstag defeated government-sponsored legislation, the chancellor could dissolve it and call for new elections.

Legend:
GERMANY 1866–1918
— Extent of the North German Confederation
···· Extent of the German Empire
■ Kingdom of Prussia, 1862
▨ Prussian Acquisitions, 1866
▥ Additions to form the North German Confederation, 1867
▤ Additions to form the German Empire, 1871

Bismarck left an ambiguous legacy. He masterminded the unification of a nation that became a world power in less than two decades, but he also smothered the growth of democratic institutions and heightened political and social tensions. The domineering Bismarck intimidated and manipulated the Reichstag, the Federal Council, the Prussian government, and even his sovereign, Kaiser William I. The Iron Chancellor's policies strengthened his own position and reinforced the power of traditional elites, such as the army, upper-level civil servants, the judiciary, industrialists (a new elite with strong conservative tendencies), and his own class, the landowning aristocracy. In a dynamic society experiencing rapid industrialization, urbanization, and a population explosion, this was no small feat. To ease social tensions and to gain working class support, Bismarck sponsored one of the world's first health, accident, and retirement insurance programs, financed mostly by workers and employers. At the same time, his "anti-socialist" laws temporarily weakened the Social Democratic Party (SPD), whose advocacy of class warfare and Marxist revolution appealed to many workers and frightened the ruling classes. Bismarck also restricted the rights and privileges of the Catholic Church, which he believed was subject to the "foreign influence" of the Vatican in Rome. Thus, two large groups of citizens were openly discriminated against, with the support of the elites and with passive acceptance by the Protestant middle classes. Although anti-socialist and anti-Catholic restrictions were lifted before his retirement in 1890, Bismarck had set a precedent that would help make Nazi persecution of the Jews more acceptable to millions of Germans.

Despite these achievements, the new emperor, William II (1888–1918), grandson of the first Kaiser, forced Bismarck to resign in 1890. The young emperor saw himself as a dynamic, up-to-date ruler, but he had neither the temperament nor the skills to govern. William II and Bismarck's four successors could not guide the ship of state with the sure hand of their predecessor. Nor would the Reichstag, unable to escape the legacy of Bismarck's heavy-handed authoritarianism, accept the responsibility of leadership. Lacking a strong personality at the top, the government was often at the mercy of powerful pressure groups, such as the Pan German League, the Navy League, the Agrarian League (large landowners), and the Central Association of German Industrialists. All favored empire-building abroad and weakening the SPD and trade unions at home. Industrialists and landowners were particularly anti-democratic, and their associations lobbied aggressively against proposals to make government more responsive to the will of the people.

The demand for more popular participation in the political decision-making process was triggered by demographic change and economic growth. The Reich's population rose from 41 million in 1871 to 67 million in 1914 and shifted substantially to the large cities. By 1913 Germany's coal production, an excellent measure of industrial capacity, had quadrupled from 1870 levels, and its steel output was nearly three times greater than that of Great Britain.[2] Exports increased by 181 percent compared to Britain's 105 percent. Germany was Europe's undisputed leader in the "second industrial revolution," which was dominated by the production of high-grade steel, chemicals, and electrical equipment. Although the wealthy were the chief beneficiaries of industrial expansion, a slow trickle-down effect brought some relief to the poor. Real wages increased more than 50 percent from 1871 to 1914, and the standard of living rose markedly.[3] The government contributed to the well-being of the working classes by protecting trade unions, sponsoring vocational training, and expanding Bismarck's welfare system. Prosperity and democratic disunity helped the traditional elites ward off demands for political reform. The Social Democratic Party, democracy's largest advocate, was sharply divided over questions of ideology and tactics, and potential middle-class allies were wary of its Marxist rhetoric.

The Kaiser's "new course" in foreign policy neither eased social tensions nor enhanced the government's prestige. The Reich constructed a battle fleet to protect its large overseas empire and sought to dominate European diplomacy. Colonies and battleships stirred national pride, but the

Kaiser's erratic course helped to cement an alliance between France and Russia. The British, who saw Germany's warships as a challenge to their naval supremacy, abandoned their traditional "splendid isolation" in favor of friendly agreements with France and Russia. This dramatic shift in great-power relationships left the Reich with the weak Austrian Empire as its principal ally and filled millions of Germans with a growing sense of insecurity and fear.

Cultural and Intellectual Currents

Political ineptitude and social conflict did not impoverish culture. Public schools were open to all, and literacy was practically universal. Clubs were available to satisfy varied interests and groups, including women and the working classes. Local governments subsidized the performing arts, and composers such as Richard Wagner and Richard Strauss helped maintain Germany's musical pre-eminence. Literature and art flourished. Among the less refined, the violent, action-packed tales of the American wild west by Hitler's favorite novelist, Karl May, were popular. The early works of future Nobel prize winners Hermann Hesse and Thomas Mann were available for more cultivated tastes. Expressionist art, more abstract than the popular impressionism, made its first appearance in the early 1900s.

Social Darwinism, the idea that the strongest race or nation wins the struggle for survival and dominance, represented a darker side of late-nineteenth-century culture. It found especially fertile ground in Germany, whose impressive political, technological, and economic achievements seemed to prove that the Germans were the best of the Aryan race, which Europeans believed to be superior to all others. Historian Heinrich von Treitschke (1834–1896), a well-known lecturer and author, labeled Germans the "master race." He ranked other Germanic peoples, such as the Dutch, Scandinavians, and English, well below the Germans, but above the French and Italians, whom he dismissed as "hopelessly degenerate." At the bottom of Treitschke's racial hierarchy were the Jews, whom he denounced as "our political misfortune."[4]

As a result of the growing secularization of the nineteenth century, religious hatred of European Jews, once segregated and universally despised as "Christ killers," had cooled. Anti-Jewish sentiment, however, was still very much alive, and Social Darwinists helped perpetuate it by shifting the focus from religion to race. They classified the Jews as Semites, descendants of an ancient Mediterranean race, which by definition was "inferior." In 1879 German journalist Wilhelm Marr coined the term *anti-Semitism*, which immediately became synonymous with racial hatred of Jews. Treitschke blamed the Jews for socialism and democracy, which he believed were undermining his cherished authoritarian political institutions and hierarchical social order. Like many of his countrymen, Treitschke feared that traditional values and moral standards were being lost in the rush to industrialization and urbanization. Their unease found expression in the works of "folkish" writers (from *völkisch*, meaning of the *Volk*, or people, and suggestive of the people's racial pride and mystical powers), whose pessimistic "rhapsodies of irrationality"[5] blamed the "rootless" Jew for the "evils of modernization."

The composer Richard Wagner (1813–1883) exalted racial nationalism, denounced the Jews, and rejected democracy and socialism. Some of his operas, by celebrating heroes from German history and Germanic mythology, proclaim Aryan superiority. (Racist thinkers borrowed the linguistic term *Aryan* to name what they believed to be the originally pure white race.) Wagner's essays praised the people and his own works: "The Germans—what a magnificent folk! I am [the embodiment] of the German spirit. Ask the incomparable magic of my works!" About the Jews he wrote: "Emancipation from the yoke of Judaism appears to us the foremost necessity." Strength for the "war of liberation" will be nurtured by an "instinctive repugnance of the Jewish character."[6] Toward the end of his life Wagner spoke of a "grand solution" to the Jewish question, by which he meant the removal of Jews from western and central Europe. To his second wife Cosima (daughter of composer Franz Liszt), his children and a coterie of admiring disciples, including his English son-in-law, Houston Stewart Chamberlain, Wagner predicted that a great leader would rise from the *Volk* and restore Germany's racial purity.

Wagner's faithful followers revered him as a god-like figure, and millions of enraptured listeners wildly applauded his operas. His racist philosophy was transmitted by his disciples, most notably in Houston Stewart Chamberlain's *The Foundations of the Nineteenth Century*, published in 1899. Hitler idolized Wagner more than any historical figure except Frederick the Great. In 1923 he met the aged Cosima and Chamberlain, who were impressed by the rising young politician's flattery and unabashed admiration of the composer. Both agreed that Hitler was the great folk leader whom Wagner had prophesied. Later Hitler the dictator said that no one could understand National Socialism without understanding Wagner.

Although Friedrich Nietzsche (1844–1900), one of the most profound and influential thinkers of the pre–World War I era, denounced nationalism, racism, Wagner, and anti-Semitism ("the philosophy of those who feel cheated"), the Nazis claimed him as one of their own. Nietzsche envisioned a new order ruled by an artistic and intellectual elite of "supermen" (*Übermenschen*), often misinterpreted as political, military, or physical strongmen. His slashing attacks against Christianity, Judeo-Christian ethics, democracy, socialism, and bourgeois morality were popular, as was his call for the destruction of the existing order—with brutality and bloodshed if necessary. Nietzsche wrote: "The great politics will create a power strong enough to breed a . . . higher form of humanity . . . against the degenerate and parasitic."[7] Taken out of context, Nietzsche's hyperbole and aphorisms seemed to justify a police state governed oppressively by his supermen. He was widely read before the war, and copies of his sayings were issued to recruits in World War I.[8]

Social and Political Tensions Under William II

Never a Nietzschian *Übermensch*, a Wagnerian hero, a Bismarckian strong-man, or even a popular leader, William II narrowly escaped being stripped of his constitutional powers in 1908. Two close advisers, whom he promptly fired, were tried for sexual misconduct. His tactless remarks published in an interview in a London newspaper embarrassed his subjects and infuriated the British. Bowing to a flurry of angry criticism, the Kaiser promised to choose his words—and his chancellors—more carefully. He replaced the flamboyant Bernhard von Bülow, who had read the interview before it was published, with Theobald von Bethmann Hollweg, a colorless Prussian bureaucrat. In a speech marking the twenty-fifth anniversary of his coronation in 1913, William II lauded the fatherland's "great achievements" in intellectual and social life and its unprecedented economic growth. The Empire had "developed into a well-protected and friendly community for its inhabitants," said the Kaiser, and its desire for peace had dispelled "every cloud on the horizon."[9]

While William's glowing tribute was not without some basis in fact, for obvious reasons he did not mention current political and diplomatic crises. In the 1912 Reichstag election, the government received a stinging rebuke when one-third of the voters cast ballots for the SPD. Supported by the middle-class Progressive Party and the Catholic Center, the Socialists were in a position to lead an anti-government bloc in the Reichstag, but it never materialized. In foreign affairs, expansion of the battle fleet and clumsy attempts to split the Triple Entente (France, Russia, and Britain) strengthened anti-German sentiment across the Channel. Tensions were high in 1913, when the Reich's weak Austrian ally nearly came to blows with Serbia, whose expansionist aims in the Balkans enjoyed Russian support. A general European war would almost certainly pit Germany against France, Russia, and Great Britain.

The Kaiser's government and its conservative supporters had only themselves to blame for Germany's plight, according to modern historian Hans-Ulrich Wehler. He indicts the traditional elites, blaming their hunger for power and their opposition to social and political reforms for many of Germany's problems in the early twentieth century. The aggressive foreign policy and overseas expansion that they ardently supported neither diverted attention from the need for reform nor unified a divided society. In 1914 they "risked war rather than . . . making concessions" that would reduce their power. The elites of Imperial Germany, according to Wehler, provided continuity from the Second to the Third Reich. They served as "stirrup-holders for Hitler" in the early 1930s, hoping to use his popularity to destroy constitutional government. (The details are discussed in Chapter 3.) Most historians accept Wehler's contention that the irresponsible political behavior of the right played a critical role in the fall of Imperial Germany and the rise of the Third Reich.[10]

Hitler to 1914

In 1913, at the age of twenty-four, Adolf Hitler left his native Austria to take up residence in Munich. He saw Germany as a dynamic, militarily powerful, racially homogeneous nation that would lead the Aryan race to victory in the struggle against Jews and other "inferior breeds." By his own account, Hitler had become an anti-Semite while living in Vienna from 1907 to 1913. He blamed the Jews for his personal problems and for the decline of the multi-national, "mongrelized" Austrian Empire. Moving to Germany gave him the opportunity to participate in what he hoped would be the "glorious war of racial liberation." He also sought to avoid induction into the Austrian army.

That Germany's proud elites would act as "stirrup holders" for a lower-middle-class Austrian immigrant was a most implausible scenario in a class-conscious society. The contrast between origins, education, advantages, and connections could hardly have been more striking. Adolf Hitler was born on April 20, 1889, in Braunau, a town located on the Inn River, which forms the boundary between Austria and Bavaria. He was the fourth child, and the first to survive infancy, born to Klara (nee Pölzl) and Alois Hitler. Two other children followed. A brother Edmund died at the age of six in 1900; Paula, a sister born in 1896, survived to a healthy adulthood. Klara, twenty-three years younger than Alois, was his third wife and his second cousin. Alois had been born illegitimately in 1837 to a 42-year-old domestic servant, Maria Anna Schicklgruber, who later married the probable father, Georg Hiedler (the spelling of the name varied), a penniless drifter. (There is no solid evidence to support the contention that Alois's father—and hence Adolf's grandfather—was Jewish). Raised by Georg's

Hitler's mother, Klara Pölzl.   Hitler's father, Alois Hitler.

BUNDESARCHIV, KOBLENZ

Hitler as an infant.

brother, Johann Nepomuk Hiedler, Alois became a customs official for the Austrian government. In 1876 Alois legally changed his surname, and its spelling, to Hitler. With tongue in cheek, one of Hitler's biographers has observed that Adolf might not have prospered politically with his father's birth name: "It is a bit difficult to cry with fanatic intensity 'Heil Schicklgruber!'"[11]

The sparse documentation of Hitler's childhood reveals that he was an unhappy, lonely, and moody child. He may not have suffered the paternal physical abuse hinted at in *Mein Kampf,* but his father, who wanted his artistically inclined son to be a civil servant, undoubtedly neglected him. His indulgent mother did not provide emotional stability or instill self-discipline. He received high marks in elementary school, but he was a poor student in the *Realschule,* a mid-level secondary school emphasizing practical subjects. Hitler's teachers noted that he was a gifted underachiever and a moody, anti-social loner given to daydreaming. Two years after Alois's death in 1903, the family moved to Linz, which Adolf later claimed as his home town. At the age of 16, in 1905, a few weeks before graduation, Hitler dropped out of school. He never received a diploma.

Hitler spent most of the next two years visiting museums, attending operas, reading newspapers, devouring Karl May's novels, and dreaming of greatness in politics or the arts. In the spring of 1907, he decided to study art in Vienna. He traveled to the capital city with a friend, who was admitted to a conservatory of music. Although he passed the written portion of the entrance examination of the Vienna Academy of Fine Arts, Hitler was denied admission. The directors recognized a talent for architectural drawing, but his disproportional, lifeless depictions of human faces and figures did not meet the Academy's high standards. It was a shattering blow to Hitler's fragile ego, but something worse was to follow.

Informed that his mother was suffering from breast cancer, Hitler returned to Linz in the fall of 1907. Klara was under the care of the family's Jewish physician, Eduard Bloch, who recommended the topical application of gauze treated with a compound of iodine. Hitler consented to this untested procedure, which, he was told, might relieve his mother's pain and prolong her life. It did neither. Klara died a few days before Christmas at the age of 47. After settling her estate, Adolf returned to Vienna, only to be denied admission once again to the Academy. Failure at school, rejection by the Academy, and the death of the only person he loved were crushing blows to the rudderless 18-year-old.

Hitler spent the next five years living aimlessly in Vienna. Despite his later claim that he lived in dire poverty (he did live in a homeless shelter for several months), an orphan's benefit, a bequest from an aunt, and a small income from the sale of his water-color miniatures allowed him to live as a poor, but not destitute, vagabond. He frequently changed lodgings to avoid induction into the army. While living in the Austrian capital, Hitler first saw large numbers of Jews. Assimilated Viennese Jews looked Aryan, but those from poorer areas of the Empire were, in his view, repulsive. He also came to believe that Jews, especially from the eastern parts of the empire, were filthy, diseased sexual predators. In the works of obscure racists, such as Lanz von Liebenfels, Guido von List, and Theodor Fritsch, he found ample fodder to feed his anti-Semitic appetite. Liebenfels advocated sterilization of the "racially unfit," and List called for a war of annihilation against Jews led by a racially pure, militarily powerful Aryan state. Germany qualified, but Austria, whose "inferior" Slavic and Jewish populations outnumbered Germans 2 to 1, did not. Fritsch provided spurious documentation that the Jews were the cause of all of Germany's problems. He also wrote of the importance of Aryan symbols, such as the swastika, in the struggle against the Jew. Hitler later wrote that the anti-Semitism he acquired in Vienna became the "granite foundation" of his ideology and life.

Anti-Semitic politics, more popular in pre-war Austria than in Germany, played a role in Hitler's ideological education. The Aryan supremacist ideas of Georg Ritter von Schönerer's Pan-German League strengthened his hatred of Jews and Slavs, but the most enduring elements of the Austrian political leader's legacy were the *Heil* greeting, the title of *Führer*, and the total lack of democratic decision making in his movement.[12] The political skills of Vienna's mayor, Karl Lueger, made a deeper impression. Lueger was a superb orator whose orchestrated demonstrations and "Jew-baiting" speeches captivated huge crowds. The mayor's anti-Semitism was largely a political ploy, although Hitler may not have realized that. As leader of the Nazi Party under the Weimar Republic, he copied Lueger's style in organizing mass rallies and delivering fiery anti-Semitic speeches.

When Hitler arrived in Munich in 1913, major elements of his political ideology and personal philosophy had begun to form. He had acquired a deep and abiding hatred of Jews during his time in Vienna, blaming them for his rejection as an artist and other personal failures. Like other racial anti-Semites, he believed that Jews were largely responsible for the political decline of the Austrian Empire and that they posed a threat to the purity of the Aryan race. He had not yet rationalized his "visceral hatred into the fully-fledged world-view, with anti-Semitism as its core, that congealed in the early 1920s."[13] An integral part of this world-view was his conviction that the Jewish doctor's experimental treatment had defiled his mother's body and hastened her death. In Hitler's twisted mind, Dr. Bloch would become a symbol of the Jew as both crafty conspirator and biological despoiler of the Aryan race. Anti-Semitism explained his world and gave him a cause.

In Munich he continued to paint water colors and live in rooming houses, but he could not escape the army recruiters. He was arrested and turned over to Austrian authorities who, much to his relief, found him physically unfit for military service and allowed him to return to Munich. Hitler was jubilant when war broke out in 1914. In *Mein Kampf* he wrote: "I had fallen on my knees and thanked heaven out of my overflowing heart that it had been granted to me the good fortune of being allowed to live in these times."[14] He eagerly volunteered and was assigned to a combat unit as a "runner," whose job was to carry messages from battalion head-quarters to the front lines. Constantly exposed to fire, many runners died. The war and the adversity of his early years, however, had clearly proved one thing: Adolf Hitler was a survivor.

Outbreak of World War I

Hitler is clearly recognizable in a photograph of thousands of Müncheners cheering the announcement of Germany's declaration of war. Like their leaders, enthusiastic crowds throughout the Reich and Europe envisioned a short war, not the four-year slaughter that changed the face of Western Civilization. Governments did not "slither into war in 1914," a colorful phrase attributed to Britain's chancellor of the exchequer, David Lloyd

POPPERFOTO, LONDON

Hitler in a Munich crowd. This photo was taken at the Odeonsplatz on August 2, 1914.

George. A decade of diplomatic crises and rising military budgets had laid the psychological and military foundations for war when the heir to the Austrian throne, Archduke Francis Ferdinand, was assassinated in Sarajevo on June 28, 1914. Governments weighed the advantages and disadvantages of hostilities and decided that a short war was in their best interests. The French and British believed that Germany threatened their security. Austria feared that Serbia's expansion, supported by its Slavic "big brother," Russia, would spur other nationalities to demand autonomy or independence, which would destroy the Hapsburg Empire. France and Russia were committed to aid each other if attacked, and Britain could not tolerate Germany's naval and commercial challenge.

In Article 231 of the Treaty of Versailles, the victors held Germany responsible for causing "all the loss and damage" suffered by the Allies "as a consequence of the war imposed upon them by the aggression of Germany and her allies." The war-guilt clause humiliated a defeated nation and haunted the Weimar Republic. It also sparked a historiographical controversy that is still alive. Some scholars have accepted the treaty's verdict, while others have sought to apportion responsibility among the belligerents. Documents on the Reich's foreign policy published after World War II strengthened the case against Germany, but did not totally exonerate her opponents. The controversy took on new dimensions in 1961 when German historian Fritz Fischer published a book that confirmed the Versailles verdict and plumbed the reasons for his country's aggression. The German title, *Griff nach der Weltmacht* (literally, *Grasp for World Power*), clearly expresses Fischer's thesis: the traditional elites and Chancellor Bethmann Hollweg's government maneuvered the nation into war to strengthen the authoritarian order at home and extend German hegemony abroad.[15]

Similarities between the government's war aims, published in September 1914, and the traditional elites' pre-war expansionist goals in Europe and overseas strengthen Fischer's argument, but do not prove prior intent. His meticulously documented charges, however, are persuasive. Germany's leaders, underestimating their opponents' resolve and military capability and overestimating the power of their armed forces, plunged more recklessly into war than the other belligerents. After the Kaiser issued his "blank check" on July 5, reaffirming Germany's commitment to back Austria's Balkan policy, the General Staff in Berlin urged its counterpart in Vienna to invade Serbia immediately. Bethmann supported prompt military reprisals.

The dam burst on July 28 when Austria declared war on Serbia. Reports of Russia's partial mobilization against Austria prompted military chiefs in Berlin to activate the Schlieffen Plan, which called for the invasion of France by way of Belgium. Swift execution was essential to the plan's success; its makers had envisioned that France would capitulate in 4 to 6 weeks, after which the "ponderous Russian giant" could be destroyed. The tsar's proclamation of total mobilization on July 30 elicited an ultimatum from Bethmann, which Russia ignored. On August 1 Germany declared war on Russia, dispatched an ultimatum to France, and moved

THE SYSTEM OF ALLIANCES
■ Powers of the Triple Entente
▨ Central Powers
☐ Neutral Powers

troops toward the Belgian frontier. The Reich responded to France's non-committal reply by declaring war and invading Belgium.

Britain's declaration of war on August 4, preceded by a demand for Germany's immediate withdrawal from Belgium, ostensibly shocked the military and stunned Bethmann. The chancellor feigned bewilderment that the British would fight over a "scrap of paper," his inept description of the 1839 treaty guaranteeing Belgium's neutrality. That this was pure diplomatic posturing was revealed in 1973, when the diaries of Kurt Riezler, Bethmann's secretary and confidant, were published. The chancellor was quite certain, if the military was not, that Britain would enter the war if Germany violated Belgian neutrality. The diaries do not corroborate Fischer's charge of collusion between ruling elites and Bethmann, whose main concern was Germany's security. Riezler and Bethmann seemed resigned to an "unavoidable conflict" and confident that the *Volk* would triumph.[16]

The *Volk's* enthusiastic response to the declaration of war demonstrated a unity and national solidarity that was unprecedented in German history. The Kaiser recognized this unity when he addressed his *Volk* and promised that the war would resolve differences among classes, parties, creeds, and regions.[17] The Reichstag's vote to grant the government authority to issue bonds to finance the war was nearly unanimous. With the exception of a few of its more radical delegates, the SPD, which had never voted for military appropriations, supported the resolution. Caught up in the wave of nationalistic fervor, the Socialists believed that Germany was fighting a defensive war, that its cause was just. Urged on by a jingoist press and a flood of patriotic oratory, young men rose to the allure of war as wildly cheering crowds sent them on their way to the western front. Survivors of the carnage could scarcely imagine the incredible naïveté of such scenes.

The Course of the War

The course of the war from fall 1914 to spring 1918 was decided in early September. Belgian resistance slowed the German advance, and the transfer of several divisions to the eastern front weakened the drive into France. The French and British halted the German offensive at the Marne River east of Paris. As both sides tried to outflank each other, the front line spread from the Swiss border to the English Channel. On the eastern front, a small German force easily defeated a numerically superior Russian army, which had mobilized more quickly than expected. Field Marshal Paul von Hindenburg, called out of retirement to take command on the eastern front, did not need reinforcements from the west. For over three years, however, bloodied Russian forces tied down German divisions which might have tipped the balance in the Reich's favor on the western front.

The short-war illusion quickly gave way to the grim reality of World War I, a protracted conflict of attrition and unimaginable horror. Winston Churchill later described the new style of warfare: "Events passed very largely outside the scope of conscious choice. Governments and individuals conformed to the rhythm of the tragedy, and staggered forward in helpless violence, slaughtering and squandering on ever-increasing scales."[18] Both sides adopted the same tactics. Following artillery bombardment, the attacking army was ordered to go "over the top" (out of the trenches) into "no man's land" (the territory between the trenches), where they faced the enemy's withering machine-gun fire. Unable to achieve a breakthrough or capture territory, the major objective of an offensive was to kill as many of the enemy as possible. Generals could find no alternative to a stationary war of attrition. New weapons, such as the airplane (used mostly for reconnaissance), the tank (slow, easily immobilized), and poison gas (a tactical failure that condemned thousands to a slow, agonizing death), did not break the stalemate.

The population explosion of the nineteenth century, along with modern technology, helped governments prolong the mindless slaughter. They armed millions of men, produced vast amounts of war matériel, and mobilized, regimented, and indoctrinated civilian populations on an unprecedented scale. In the name of the war effort, the authorities changed dietary and work habits, relentlessly proclaimed their "just cause," and, for

The horrors of trench warfare were unprecedented. The living hardened themselves against the stench of decomposing bodies and the sight of mangled corpses.

the first time in European history, transferred millions of women from the home to the workplace. Sacrifice and austerity were the rule, especially in Germany, where the British blockade and a series of poor harvests caused severe shortages. In July 1916 the Reichstag passed the Patriotic Auxiliary Service Law, which empowered the War Office to regulate wages, production levels, and prices, and to restrict the free movement of labor. Although the legislation curtailed bargaining rights of labor unions, the exigencies of war forced the government to make concessions to labor unions and the SPD. Workers were allowed to look for better-paying jobs and to have representatives on factory councils.[19]

The Auxiliary Service Law helped maintain an adequate flow of supplies to the troops at the front, but civilians suffered. Survivors remembered with horror the "turnip winter" of 1916-1917, when the turnip, an unpleasant-tasting root vegetable normally fed to livestock, became the staple of a civilian diet of 1350 calories a day. Turnips were used for soup, coffee, the main course, and even dessert. A mother in Hamburg wrote to her son at the front: "The situation is very sad, already five weeks without

BUNDESARCHIV, KOBLENZ

Lance Corporal Hitler, seated at front left.

potatoes, flour and bread are scarce . . . we go to bed hungry and we wake up hungry . . . all there is is turnips, without potatoes, without meat, just cooked in water."[20] To compound the misery, coal was in short supply, and the winter of 1916–1917 turned out to be the coldest in memory. For all the hardships, however, most Germans continued to support the war effort, not with enthusiasm, but with a dogged determination "to see it through" (*Durchhalten*).

In the vain hope that new leadership might improve economic conditions at home and break the stalemate at the front, the Kaiser's government appointed Hindenburg as Supreme Commander in August 1916. His top aide and the architect of his victories over the Russians was the ambitious and politically astute Erich Ludendorff. In the absence of strong civilian leadership, he quickly seized the reins of power. In December 1916 Ludendorff expanded the Reich's list of war aims by demanding the independence of Poland and the Russian provinces of Lithuania, Latvia, and Estonia, which were to become German satellites. He also insisted on economic hegemony in the Balkans and the Ottoman Empire.

In January 1917 Ludendorff declared "unrestricted submarine warfare," a policy that authorized German vessels to fire torpedoes at any ship entering the zone around the British Isles. The objective was to reduce vital imports to a trickle, thereby forcing Britain to leave the war in six months. Ludendorff realized that the United States, Britain's chief supplier, would enter the war, but he was certain that significant numbers of American troops would not be combat-ready for at least a year. By that time, if the plan succeeded, the war would be over.

BOX 1.1 ■ ALL QUIET ON THE WESTERN FRONT

Erich Maria Remarque's *All Quiet on the Western Front,* first published in 1929, is one of the most uncompromising antiwar novels ever written It was widely read, and the American-made film version released in 1930 was highly acclaimed. Remarque's book was anathema to the Nazis, who were steeped in hate and war. They boycotted the Berlin premier of the film in 1930 (discussed in Chapter 3), and *All Quiet* was one of the first books to be thrown into the flames of the infamous book-burning ceremony in May 1933. The passage below, and many like it throughout the book, infuriated the Nazis:

> A man cannot realize that above such shattered bodies there are still human faces . . . And this is only one hospital, one single station; there are hundreds of thousands in Germany, hundreds of thousands in France, hundreds of thousands in Russia. How senseless is everything that can ever be written, done, or thought, when such things are possible. It must be all lies and of no account when the culture of a thousand years could not prevent this stream of blood being poured out, these torture chambers in their hundreds of thousands. A hospital alone shows what war is.
>
> . . . . I am twenty years old; yet I know nothing of life but despair, death, fear, and fatuous superficiality cast over an abyss of sorrow. I see how peoples are set against one another, and in silence, unknowingly, foolishly, obediently, innocently slay one another. I see the keenest brains of the world invent weapons and words to make it yet more refined and enduring. And all men of my age, here and over there, throughout the whole world see these things; all my generation is experiencing these things with me. What would our fathers do if we suddenly stood up and came before them and proffered our account? What do they expect of us if a time ever comes when the war is over? Through the years our business has been killing;—it was our first calling in life. Our knowledge of life is limited to death. What will happen afterwards? And what shall come out of us?

Erich Maria Remarque, *All Quiet on the Western Front* (New York: Fawcett World Library, 1958), pp. 228-29.

Ludendorff's plan failed. The publication of expansionist war aims strengthened the determination of the Allies and nullified President Woodrow Wilson's efforts to mediate. The United States, which entered the war in April 1917, did not field an army in France for over a year, but German submarines lacked the fire power to force Britain to its knees. Ludendorff also underestimated the reaction of his own people. As the military stalemate and downward economic spiral continued, there were massive labor strikes. In July 1917 the Reichstag passed a peace resolution, calling for immediate negotiations "on the basis of no reparations and no annexations."

Unmoved by the peace resolution and labor unrest, Ludendorff decided to launch a major offensive on the western front in March 1918. By that time he believed that Russia, ruled by Lenin and the Bolsheviks since the November 1917 revolution, would be out of the war. Rumors of the offensive did little for morale at the front. For hundreds of thousands trapped in the horrors of trench warfare, the war was no longer a national crusade. As portrayed in Erich Maria Remarque's *All Quiet on the Western Front*, the promises and patriotic rhetoric of 1914 rang hollow; soldiers fought for each other and for survival. But Remarque did not speak for the many equally war-weary combatants who continued to believe that Germany's cause was just and that her "righteous might" would bring victory. Adolf Hitler was one of them. For Hitler, the war provided a structured life, a sense of purpose, and close relationships that did not invade his privacy. He was a brave soldier, twice wounded and decorated. Ironically, he received the Reich's second-highest award, the Iron Cross First Class, on the recommendation of a Jewish officer. Another superior commended his bravery and intelligence, but observed that he was not "officer material" because of "anti-social tendencies." The war toughened Hitler and helped prepare him psychologically for future political struggles. "I set out for the front in 1914 with feelings of pure idealism," he wrote in *Mein Kampf*, but then "I saw men falling around me in the thousands. Thus I learned that life is a cruel struggle and has no other object but the preservation of the species."[21]

Devastated by economic collapse, millions of casualties, and revolutionary upheaval, Russia fulfilled Ludendorff's expectations by withdrawing from the war and signing the punitive Treaty of Brest-Litovsk with Germany on March 2, 1918. The former Russian empire lost most of its western territories as Lenin's regime was forced to recognize a new republic of Poland, the independence of Latvia, Lithuania, Estonia, and Finland, and the German annexation and occupation of the agriculturally rich Ukraine. The *Drang nach Osten* (drive to the east), held by some ardent nationalists, including Hitler, to be Germany's manifest destiny since the Middle Ages, was partly fulfilled. Russia's withdrawal created potential military advantages as well. Hundreds of thousands of troops no longer needed for combat in the east might have strengthened Ludendorff's offensive in the west. They were never transferred. The general kept most of them in the Ukraine to supervise the shipment of foodstuffs to Germany.

The final German offensive in the west began a few weeks after Brest-Litovsk; it ended three months later in bloody failure. With depleted human and material resources, Germany could not exploit French and British deficiencies. Fresh American troops helped the Allies resume the offensive in July. With their army in full retreat by early September, Hindenburg and Ludendorff realized that an invasion of Germany was imminent. On September 29 they advised the Kaiser to appoint a new chancellor whose government would be responsible to the Reichstag and would seek an immediate armistice. Liberal aristocrat Prince Max von Baden agreed to form such a government. Peace talks began on October 3 and ended five weeks later with Germany's surrender. Ludendorff's cynical prediction that "the politicians [by which he meant democrats and socialists] will have to eat the soup they've landed us in" came true.[22] Democracy would be saddled with the onus of defeat; the general staff and the Kaiser's government would escape blame for losing the war.

Revolution, Armistice, and the De Facto Republic

Germany's agony intensified during the armistice negotiations. At the front the bloodletting continued, for there was no ceasefire. Discipline broke down at the end of October with a sailors' mutiny in Kiel that was sparked by their officers' plan to embark on a dangerous mission to break the British blockade. Deserting soldiers and civilian strikers organized councils, patterned after the soviets of workers and soldiers formed during the Russian Revolution of 1917. In the German states, princely and monarchical rule was replaced by democratic and socialist governments. The economy was in shambles, with severe shortages of essentials, rising unemployment, and a steady decline in the unit of currency, the *Reichsmark*. By November 1 powerful Allied armies were approaching the German border and preparing to invade. The other Central Powers (Austria-Hungary, Bulgaria, and Turkey) had already laid down their arms.

The military collapse, social unrest, and pressure from the Allies, the Reichstag, and Hindenburg, prompted William II to flee to Holland on November 9. (He officially abdicated a few weeks later.) Prince Max's successor was SPD leader Friedrich Ebert, who formed the six-member Council of People's Plenipotentiaries (CPP), a provisional national government equally divided between moderate and radical Socialists. The next day, as uprisings in Berlin continued, a CPP member, Philipp Scheidemann, announced that Germany had become a republic. On November 11, 1918, a Reichstag delegation signed the armistice, without guarantees that Germany would be allowed to participate in the peace negotiations. The bloodiest war in European history, and the first phase of the "German Revolution of 1918–1919," ended simultaneously. Desperate political and economic crises tempered what might have been wild celebrations.

To restore order and maintain national unity, Ebert and the army struck a bargain: in return for political neutrality, the army would assist the CPP in maintaining order at home and administering the demobilization of troops at the front. Some radical Socialists, furious at this collusion between their moderate comrades and a hated symbol of the old order, joined the Spartacists, who were committed to a Marxist revolution. Together they formed the German Communist Party (KPD) on December 30, 1918. With the aid of disillusioned, anti-democratic veterans who formed vigilante groups known as *Freikorps* (free corps), the army suppressed workers' insurrections, culminating in an abortive Spartacist uprising in early January 1919. *Freikorps* gunmen murdered Spartacist leaders Karl Liebknecht and Rosa Luxemburg, but the German Communist Party, destined to play an important role in Hitler's rise to power, survived. With a semblance of order restored, Ebert scheduled elections for a constituent assembly later that month.

Germany's defeat and the establishment of a democratic republic further polarized a deeply divided society. Voicing the disillusionment of many who would support the new republic, Erich Remarque wrote of the traditional elites: "They stuffed [sic] out the word Patriotism ... with their desire for glory, their will to power, their false romanticism, their stupidity, their greed of business, and then paraded it before us as a shining ideal!"[23] Right-wing extremists blamed the nation's woes on the provisional government, branded as the "November Criminals." Elizabeth Förster Nietzsche, militant nationalist and guardian of her famous brother's literary legacy, voiced their anger in a letter to a friend in December 1918:

> That the German people themselves are destroying this magnificent fatherland is the most terrible tragedy. Our armies at the front were undefeated, but our stupid home guards, fools and children, have stabbed our brave soldiers in the back. The social democratic parties are behaving disgracefully and are throwing dirt on our best and greatest leaders. Germany offers a dreadful spectacle.[24]

By the end of 1918, the myth of the "stab-in-the-back" by the November Criminals had become an article of faith for the millions who came to oppose the Weimar Republic. By endless repetition of these inflammatory phrases, Hitler and other enemies of democracy would gain support.

When he heard the news of Germany's surrender, Hitler was in a military hospital recovering from temporary blindness suffered during a gas attack in late October. Shock and rage reinforced his conviction that he had been spared to carry out his "mission," which was to enter politics in order to avenge Germany's defeat, for which he blamed the Jews. He wrote in *Mein Kampf:* "There is no making pacts with Jews; there can only be the hard: either-or. I, for my part, decided to go into politics."[25] Although his conversion to political anti-Semitism may not have been so sudden and dramatic, blaming the Jews for Germany's defeat would become a principal theme of his propaganda in the 1920s. In the spring of 1919 he was posted to a Bavarian regiment in Munich as a political instructor charged with the task of inoculating new recruits "against contagion by socialist, pacifist, or democratic ideas."[26] He was also assigned to investigate the growing number of radical right-wing groups in the Bavarian capital. He attended a meeting of one of these, the German Workers Party, on September 12, 1919. A few days later he joined, thus making good on his decision to enter politics.

Conclusion

The war had politicized and radicalized German society. "The definitive measure of Germany's political future had now become the people, the great curbside republic of soldiers, workers, and consumers."[27] Politicians of all persuasions would have to reach out to the people and compete for votes. A variety of political parties participated in the first elections to the new Reichstag in the summer of 1920, and a vast majority of eligible voters cast ballots. The elections returned a democratic majority, but millions of conservative voters were deeply suspicious of the new constitution. What Ernst Jünger wrote about the impact of the war on the disillusioned right is particularly applicable to the Nazis and helps explain their rise to power:

> War, the father of all things, is also our father. It has hammered us, chis-eled us, and hardened us into what we are. And always, as long as the swirling wheeling of life revolves within us, this war will be the axis around which it will swirl. It has reared us for battle and we shall re-main fighters as long as we live. . . . This war is not the end but the new ascendancy of force. New forms will be filled with blood, and might will be seized with the hard fist."[28]

How Hitler and his followers fashioned their victory will be discussed in the next two chapters.

INFOTRAC® COLLEGE EDITION SEARCH TERMS

For additional reading go to Infotrac College Edition, your online research library at http://www.infotrac-college.com.

Enter the search term "history Germany industrial" using Keywords.

Enter the search term "Hitler, Adolph early life" using Subject Guide.

Enter the search term "Social Darwinism" using the Subject Guide.

Enter the search term "World War, 1914–1918" using the Subject Guide.

Enter the search term "trench warfare" using the Subject Guide.

Notes

1. Quoted in Robert E. Conot, *Justice at Nuremberg* (New York: Harper & Row, 1983), p. 105.

2. Volker R. Berghahn, *Modern Germany* (New York: Cambridge University Press, 1982), pp. 1–3, and pp. 254, 260–261.

3. Dietrich Orlow, *A History of Modern Germany* (Upper Saddle River, NJ: Prentice-Hall, 1999), p. 83.

4. Quoted in Gordon Craig, *Germany 1866–1945* (New York: Oxford University Press, 1978), p. 204.

5. Fritz Stern, *The Politics of Cultural Despair* (New York: Doubleday, 1965), p. 2.

6. Quoted in Hans Kohn, *The Mind of Germany* (New York: Harper & Row, 1960), pp. 202–204.

7. Quoted in Robert G. L. Waite, *The Psychopathic God Adolf Hitler* (New York: Basic Books, 1977), p. 276.

8. Ibid., p. 279.

9. Henry Cord Meyer, ed., *The Long Generation: Germany from Empire to Ruin, 1913–1945* (New York: Harper & Row, 1973), p. 41.

10. Hans-Ulrich Wehler, *The German Empire 1871–1918* (Dover, NH: Berg Publishers, 1985), pp. 245, 231; for a critique, see Holger H. Herwig,"Industry, Empire and the First World War," in Gordon Martel, ed., *Modern Germany Reconsidered, 1870–1945* (London: Routledge, 1992), pp. 60–61.

11. Waite, p. 126.

12. Ian Kershaw, *Hitler 1889–1936: Hubris* (New York: Norton, 1999), p. 34.

13. Ibid., p. 67.

14. Adolf Hitler, *Mein Kampf,* tr. by Ralph Manheim (Boston: Houghton Mifflin, 1962), p. 161.

15. Orlow, p. 73.

16. Wayne C. Thompson, "In the Eye of the Storm: Kurt Riezler," in Holger Herweg, ed., *The Outbreak of World War I* (Lexington, MA: Heath, 1991), p. 348.

17. Peter Fritzsche, *Germans into Nazis* (Cambridge: Harvard University Press, 1998), p. 29.

18. Winston S. Churchill, *The World Crisis, II* (New York: Scribner's, 1951), p. 1.

19. Fritzsche, p. 56.

20. Quoted in Fritzsche, p. 69.

21. *Mein Kampf,* p. 177.

22. Quoted in Wehler, p. 218.

23. Quoted in Koppel S. Pinson, *Modern Germany* (New York: MacMillan, 1966), p. 348.

24. Quoted in H.F. Peters, *Zarathustra's Sister* (New York: Crown Publishers, 1977), p. 205.

25. *Mein Kampf,* p. 206.

26. Alan Bullock, *Hitler: A Study in Tyranny* (New York: Harper & Row, 1964), p. 64.

27. Fritzsche, p. 82.

28. Quoted in Pinson, p. 349.

The Weimar Republic and Hitler

The accidental republic that filled the void left by the kaiser's abdication on November 9, 1918, became permanent on August 11, 1919, when Germany's first republican constitution was ratified. In a society deeply scarred by the wounds of a lost war, neither celebration nor counter-demonstration marked the occasion. To avoid unrest in Berlin and to associate the new regime with a brilliant cultural tradition, the National Assembly met in Weimar, once the residence of authors Johann von Goethe and Friedrich Schiller and composer J.S. Bach. The delegates elected Friedrich Ebert as president and Philipp Scheidemann as chancellor. Meeting in Versailles, the Allies recognized the new republic and, as the Assembly finished the constitution, completed the treaty. Incensed at its punitive provisions, Scheidemann resigned, and a majority of the delegates voted against it. Ebert, however, argued persuasively that rejecting the treaty would trigger a renewal of the war and the British blockade. On June 28, 1919, the fifth anniversary of Franz Ferdinand's assassination, Ebert's representatives signed the Treaty of Versailles. It was the infant republic's most damning act.

The promulgation of the Weimar Constitution ended the Revolution of 1918–1919. Although the Assembly failed to initiate social reform or create institutions loyal to the new regime,[1] the postwar upheaval had significantly altered Germany's political landscape. Monarchism was discredited, the traditional elites were less powerful, social democracy gained respectability, and the constitution guaranteed individual freedoms. Millions of men and newly enfranchised women voted for delegates to represent them in a sovereign parliament. Hundreds of thousands of Germans joined parties or pressure groups, most with narrow agendas reflecting particular economic, class, or regional interests.

One of many regional groups was the tiny, right-wing German Workers Party in Munich, which might have evaporated if Hitler had not attended a meeting on September 12, 1919. His stirring rebuttal to a member's call for Bavarian separatism was so impressive that he was invited to join the party and, a few days later, asked to become a member of the executive council. In the 1920s the impact of this party on national politics was minimal, but Hitler took full advantage of the republic's problems and the free rein that it gave to antidemocratic extremists to build up the party's strength. With the advent of the Great Depression in 1929, the party, which he had renamed the National Socialist German Workers Party, was strong enough to make a bid for power. At that point, Hitler's rise and the fall of the Weimar Republic became inseparable.

Rising from the ashes of military defeat, for which it was unjustly blamed, the republican government was forced to sign an unpopular treaty, for which it was never forgiven. The new democracy, though viewed by many Germans as a flawed system that embodied domestic disorder and international disgrace, proved remarkably resilient, but eventually succumbed to conservative opposition and economic crises. The demise of Weimar democracy, according to historian Mary Fulbrook, "has cast a shadow over interpretations of its [the republic's] course." However one assesses the validity of intellectual, cultural, political, and social links before 1914, "it is in the Weimar Republic that the immediate causation of Hitler's rise to power has to be sought."[2] The failure of democracy was critical to Hitler's success, and the reasons for that failure dominate studies of Weimar's history.

The Weimar Republic, 1919–1924

Delegates to the National Assembly labored under adverse conditions. Political unrest, attempted coups, and *Freikorps'* vigilante-style justice were common throughout Germany. Political turmoil was particularly acute in Bavaria, where anarchists and Communists established a short-lived Marxist regime in April 1919. It was crushed by the army and *Freikorps* volunteers, as were the uprisings elsewhere. Ebert's critics never forgave him for "selling out" to the army, but without military support the fledging republic—and democracy—may never have survived.

Critics of the Treaty of Versailles charge that the harsh terms it dictated to the vanquished left festering wounds that erupted twenty years later in a second global conflict. Others argue that if the settlement had been more punitive it might have prevented another world war by destroying the nation's capacity to wage war. Though the final draft was harsh enough to nurture a spirit of revenge, it left Germany's industrial base virtually intact. A modern German historian holds that the principal source of that spirit of revenge was the loss of the war "rather than the severe yet ultimately tolerable terms of the peace settlement."[3] A perceptive assessment, to be sure, but most Germans in 1919 would probably have put it differently. They felt they had been cheated out of victory, and what they regarded as the intolerable terms of the treaty heightened their desire for revenge.

The most inflammatory provisions were the war-guilt clause and mandatory reparations. A commission in 1921 decided that Germany should pay 132 billion gold marks, about $31 billion, to France, Belgium, Italy, and Great Britain, in partial compensation for Germany's "willful destruction of property and life." Though Germany's economy in 1919 had been weakened by the war, its industrial and economic potential was still greater than that of the victors; hence, the $31 billion reparations bill was probably affordable. The government and the public, however, perceived the issue differently. They believed that reparations payments would permanently block economic recovery. Germany's default in 1922 led to the French occupation of the Ruhr and the Great Inflation of 1923.

Other provisions of the treaty, as many Germans saw it, were nearly as grievous. The Allies disarmed their former enemy by capping the new volunteer army, called the *Reichswehr*, at 100,000, abolishing the general staff, prohibiting conscription and a military air force, and awarding most of the battle fleet to Britain. The victors transferred approximately 15 percent of the Reich's pre-war territory: Alsace-Lorraine to France, Eupen and Malmedy to Belgium, part of Schleswig to Denmark, and a large segment of what had been the Reich's eastern frontier to newly independent Poland. The latter award, called the "Polish Corridor," had been the ancient homeland for several million Germans and separated East Prussia from the rest of the country. It was the largest and most resented of the territorial losses; the promise of its return, which became a major theme of Hitler's foreign policy, enjoyed nearly unanimous support among the German people.

Other territorial adjustments were conditional. In the west, the Rhineland remained in German hands, but the French insisted that it should be a permanently demilitarized buffer zone, which their troops would occupy for at least ten years. The coal-rich province of Saarland was placed under French protection for fifteen years, after which a plebiscite would allow the people to choose either French or German sovereignty. In a plebiscite in the eastern province of Upper Silesia in 1921, the 65 percent of the residents who were German voted for annexation to the Weimar Republic. The remaining 35 percent were Polish, and their government immediately dispatched troops to occupy the territory. Upper Silesia remained under Polish jurisdiction until Hitler recaptured it in 1939. Some forty miles west of Cracow, near the German border of Upper Silesia, was the small town of Oswiecim. Its German name was Auschwitz.

Despite political unrest, economic depression, and the hostile reception of the treaty, the National Assembly produced a constitution that was democratic and workable. The Weimar Constitution applied universal democratic principles to particular German circumstances. The delegates chose to keep the imperial name, Reichstag, for the republican parliament while abolishing its Bismarckian limitations. The Reichstag was invested with absolute sovereignty; chancellors and their cabinets were to serve at its pleasure. The power of the state governments was also reduced. Although they would have jurisdiction in such areas as law enforcement, public health,

THE POSTWAR SETTLEMENTS

Territory lost by:

- Germany
- Austria and Hungary
- Russia
- Bulgaria
- From Turkey to Greece 1920, recovered 1923
- Frontiers of new or revived states

0   100 Miles
0   100 Kilometers

and education, the federal government was no longer financially dependent upon the states for its day-to-day operations. Constitutionally guaranteed human rights could not be suspended without due process of law, and any citizen who obtained the requisite number of signatures could petition the government to hold a referendum.

Electoral laws and presidential powers were especially controversial and ultimately detrimental to democracy. To affirm the republic's confidence in popular sovereignty, the constitution allowed one Reichstag delegate for every 60,000 votes cast for a political party. This principle, known as proportional representation, encouraged the proliferation of parties under the new regime, which was already burdened by the unwieldy multi-party system of its predecessor. Coalition building, essential to a smoothly functioning parliament with so many divergent interests, became much more difficult to achieve. To skeptical conservatives, the Reichstag's compromises and squabbling parties, as well as the high turnover of chancellors, proved that democracy would never work. Recognizing how fragile the republic was in 1919, the assembly empowered the popularly elected president, normally a ceremonial figurehead, to invoke a temporary state of emergency, during which he could dissolve the Reichstag, legislate by decree, and appoint and dismiss chancellors. While foreigners viewed this measure as evidence of Germany's habitual authoritarianism, supporters saw it as a means of protecting democracy in a hostile environment. Unfortunately, this article of the constitution would have exactly the opposite effect. While in force from 1930–1932 during the Great Depression, it helped destroy Weimar democracy and pave the way for Hitler's takeover. (How this happened is discussed in the following chapter.)

The political and economic environment was indeed hostile. There were assassinations of cabinet officers, abortive Communist coups at the state level, and a right-wing coup, or putsch, against the national government in March 1920. The Kapp Putsch, named after its leader Wolfgang Kapp, quickly collapsed, but not before forcing Ebert and his ministers to flee Berlin. The republic's prestige was tarnished, but a Reichstag election in June 1920 did not substantially reduce the democratic majority. Nevertheless, the already shaky political foundations were being threatened by high unemployment and declining industrial production, foreign trade, and national income. Though the potential for recovery existed, the government, industry, and the public blamed the Treaty of Versailles and the Allies for the slump. The republic made its first reparations payment in 1921, but the next year it defaulted. In January 1923 French and Belgian troops crossed the Rhine and occupied the heavily industrialized Ruhr district. Defiant trade unions organized a general strike, which the government supported by payments of currency without backing. This triggered the wildest inflationary spiral ever experienced by an industrialized nation.

Printing wagonloads of paper money twenty-four hours a day to finance passive resistance in the Ruhr caused the mark to plummet from 18,000 to the dollar in January to 4.2 trillion to the dollar the following November. By dramatizing its economic plight, Germany hoped to force the French and Belgians to withdraw from the Ruhr and renegotiate reparations payments. In spite of a breakdown in the delivery of goods and services by early summer, foreign troops remained on the east bank of the Rhine. In September Gustav Stresemann, a monarchist whose right-of-center People's Party (DVP) supported the republic, formed a new government. He ended the general strike and persuaded President Ebert to invoke an emergency decree to deal with the inflation and political unrest. (The emergency decree, which was lifted by the end of the year, had never been used; it was not activated again until 1930.) As the French and Belgians withdrew, the *Reichswehr* suppressed Communist coups at the state level. In early November the Stresemann government stabilized the currency by issuing a new mark backed by a mortgage on Germany's agricultural and industrial assets. The new mark, called the Rentenmark, was pegged at 4.2 trillion to the dollar and one trillion to one of the old Reichsmarks.

The nation staggered under the weight of the Great Inflation. Many thrifty middle-class citizens who supported the republic saw their lifetime savings vanish overnight. The experience of a saver with an account of 68,000 marks (about $16,000 in 1921) was typical. In the early summer of 1923, the bank, unable to service such a "tiny sum," returned the deposit with a 1-million-mark note, the smallest denomination available. On the envelope was a canceled stamp worth 5 million marks. Some blamed the democratic government for their losses and supported right-wing parties in the Reichstag election of May 1924, but once again the beleaguered republic survived. In the summer of 1924 a committee of fiscal experts from the Allied countries, chaired by American banker Charles Dawes, proposed restructuring the reparations payment schedule and priming the economic

UPI/BETTMANN/CORBIS

A woman uses worthless currency to light a fire in her cooking stove, summer 1923.

pump with substantial loans. The Germans accepted the Dawes Plan. Within months there were signs of economic recovery, and, under the leadership of Reichsbank president Hjalmar Schacht (a position he would hold under the Hitler regime), the currency stabilized, the gold standard was restored, and the Rentenmark was replaced by the traditional name, Reichsmark. These financial measures also strengthened democracy, as democratic parties recaptured middle-class support in Reichstag elections held in December 1924. Still facing numerous unsolved problems at the end of 1924, the republic had seemingly weathered its worst storms. Its supporters were guardedly optimistic.

Hitler and the Nazi Party, 1919–1924

In the fall of 1919 the German Workers Party (DAP) was one of several *völkisch* groups in Munich, where the political climate favored the radical right. Its leader was Anton Drexler, a railroad employee who appealed to workers and small property owners by blaming their economic woes on big business, foreigners, the Treaty of Versailles, and the Jews. After the collapse of the short-lived "red republic" in Munich in the spring of 1919, he added Communists to the enemies' list. Except for its working-class animus toward big business, the German Workers Party (DAP) and Hitler were ideologically compatible; however, that was not the principal reason for his decision to join. Hitler sensed that he could lead and shape this party more easily than other groups on the far right. Most of them, he believed, were flawed by elitism, weak organization, and an aversion to using street politics to win a mass following. Hitler quoted their racial and anti-Semitic diatribes and adopted one of their symbols, the swastika, as the new party's signature logo. He felt certain that the *völkisch* organizations would collapse without mass support and that the DAP under his leadership would flourish. He was right.

Hitler's resignation from the army several months after joining the German Workers Party marked the beginning of his full-time political career. Party members accepted his leadership, sensing that their group could not survive without his oratorical skills and keen political instincts. In February 1920 Hitler and Drexler wrote the party's 25-point program, which was essentially a list of standard right-wing themes that included pan-German nationalism, denunciation of Versailles, racial exclusiveness, rearmament, expansionism, and hostility toward big business. What most distinguished the DAP from other groups on the far right, however, was the power of Hitler's presentation of the program in a crowded beer hall and, in subsequent speeches, his passionate denunciation of the Treaty of Versailles and the "November Criminals," whom he linked to the Jews. His new name for the party, the National Socialist German Workers Party (NSDAP), was designed to broaden its appeal by uniting two popular nineteenth-century ideologies, nationalism and socialism. The familiar nickname "Nazi," formed by the first two letters of *national* (the German and

English are identical) and the second syllable, *zi*, of the German *sozialistische* (socialist), signified this ideological merger.

In the summer 1921 Hitler and the party faced a crisis over leadership, relations with other parties, and qualifications for membership. Bristling at the executive council's proposal to merge with other *völkisch* parties and to bar the upper middle class and aristocracy from membership, Hitler demanded, and received, absolute power. He promised to consult the executive council regularly, but it rarely met after 1921. He demanded to be addressed as the Führer (leader), a title earned by his charismatic oratory, inspirational leadership, and fund-raising skills. Under his command, the NSDAP prospered, recruiting persons with diverse backgrounds and qualifications, including women. Only Jews were excluded.

By the summer of 1922, the NSDAP had 6,000 members, a well-stocked treasury, strong leadership, a party newspaper titled the *Völkischer Beobachter*, and a paramilitary division known as the SA, or *Sturmabteilung* (storm troopers). Hermann Göring, a decorated combat flyer, organized the division and appointed former army captain Ernst Röhm to be its commanding officer. Members of the SA, recruited mostly from the *Freikorps* and the anti-democratic lower middle class, received rudimentary training in street fighting. They practiced their skills against hecklers and critics at public meetings. Hitler approved, sensing that SA intimidation would enhance the party's image of strength and demonstrate the loyalty of its members.

Hitler's insistence on a socially diverse membership paid dividends. While other political parties represented specific social classes, special interest groups, regions, or single issues, the Nazis claimed to champion the German people as a whole. It was a concept that complemented Hitler's charismatic leadership and helped sell the party to a diverse group of individuals who became leaders. Among the more prominent were the popular war hero Hermann Göring, the experienced police administrator Wilhelm Frick, the fanatical "Jew-baiter" and journalist Julius Streicher, the anti-Semitic poet and publisher Dietrich Eckart, and the wealthy socialite Max von Scheubner-Richter.

At the height of the Great Inflation in 1923, Hitler and his inner circle felt that the party had enough muscle and momentum to take advantage of the republic's vulnerability. A successful putsch against the Bavarian government, they believed, would attract a large enough following to march on Berlin and take over the national government. Hitler hoped to emulate Benito Mussolini, whose daring march on Rome a year earlier propelled the Fascist leader to the pinnacle of power in Italy. Like other extremist groups, the Nazis did not anticipate Ebert's declaration of a state of emergency on September 27. The republic's suppression of Communist coups against state governments made Hitler less confident than the SA and other restless followers who were "itching for a fight." Nevertheless, he promised to lead the putsch if Erich Ludendorff could be persuaded to march with the Nazis. The retired general, whose hatred of democracy exceeded his contempt for the lower-middle-class Austrian immigrant and his "low-life" followers, reluctantly agreed to participate. Confident of the popular support which Ludendorff would surely generate, Hitler gave little attention to tactical planning.

The Nazis did not act until early November. By that time the Stresemann government had suppressed short-lived Communist regimes in Saxony and Thuringia and set November 15 as the date for issuing the new mark. The Weimar Republic and Bavarian government were now much less vulnerable. On the evening of November 8, Hitler and his followers, looking much more formidable than they actually were, took over a beer hall where the head of Bavaria's government, Gustav von Kahr, and commander of the local branch of the Reichswehr, Otto von Lossow, were holding a rally. Hitler jumped on a table and fired a pistol into the air, shouting that the national revolution had begun. He accompanied Kahr, Lossow, and a highly ranked Munich police officer into a back room, where he outlined the Nazi plan. The Bavarian officials appeared to be impressed and pledged their full support. After leaving the beer hall, Hitler did not bother to follow up on the promise or to target for takeover key government buildings and centers of transportation and communication. The putsch was doomed to fail before it started.

Kahr and Lossow had no intention of backing the putsch. They stationed soldiers and state troopers along the proposed parade route on the morning of November 9, with orders to fire. The Nazi marchers drew many curious onlookers, but few supporters. As they approached a square in the inner city, they were met by a hail of bullets. Most of them fled in panic, but a few of the demonstrators returned the fire and killed four policemen. One of the sixteen Nazi fatalities was von Scheubner-Richter, shot dead while marching arm-in-arm with Hitler, who suffered a dislocated shoulder. The police arrested Hitler two days later. Göring sustained a painful wound in the groin, which eventually caused his addiction to morphine. The SA leader, Röhm, escaped to Austria. Unharmed and unfazed by the heavy fire, Ludendorff was taken into custody.

Ludendorff's role in the abortive Beer Hall Putsch drew reporters from all over Germany to cover the trial in March 1924. The old general rambled, but Hitler's performance was riveting. In the national spotlight for the first time, he defended himself skillfully and passionately. With a powerful boost from Bavarian prosecutors and judges, slightly further to the right than their colleagues in other states, he emerged from the trial as a national hero. Calling Hitler a "brave soldier and a gifted political leader," the prosecutor praised him for his fight against the November criminals, Marxism, and Jewry, and denied that the Nazi leader was a demagogue or an advocate of political violence. Against these charges, said the prosecutor, "he is protected by the sincerity of his beliefs, unselfish dedication to his chosen task," and an exemplary private life.[4] Hitler's image as the dedicated leader above the dirty politics and violence sometimes necessary to achieve his goals, had already been born.

BOX 2.1 ■ A COMPELLING IMAGE OF THE FÜHRER

In 1924 the Bavarian prosecutor unwittingly presented a compelling image
of the Führer that would prevail during the Weimar years, and, with some
variations, after 1933. Significantly, Marxism appears on the list of Hitler's
and Germany's enemies. Joseph Goebbels, who would become the Führer's
master "spin doctor," could not have said it better:

> Hitler came of a simple background; in the big war as a brave soldier he showed a
> German spirit, and afterward . . . he created the "National Socialist German
> Workers' Party," which is pledged to fighting international Marxism and Jewry, to
> settling accounts with the November criminals, and to disseminating the national
> idea among all layers of the population. . . . His honest endeavor to reawaken the
> German cause among an oppressed and disarmed people is most certainly to his
> credit. Here, helped by his unique oratorical gift, he has made a significant contri-
> bution. Even though the aggressive mood in the ranks of his followers led him
> into a one-sided position, it would be unfair to call him a demagogue; against this
> charge he is protected by the sincerity of his beliefs and the unselfish dedication
> to his chosen task. . . . His private life has always been clean, which deserves
> special approbation in view of the temptations which naturally came to him as a
> celebrated party leader. . . . Hitler is a highly gifted man who, coming out of a
> simple background, has, through serious and hard work, won for himself a re-
> spected place in public life. He dedicated himself to the ideas which inspired him
> to the point of self-sacrifice, and as a soldier he fulfilled his duty in the highest
> measure. He cannot be blamed for exploiting the position which he created for
> himself to his own purposes.

Quoted in Bracher, pp. 119–20.

In his concluding speech Hitler acknowledged that the judges would
find him guilty of high treason, but the judgement of the "eternal court of
history" was far more important. That court, said Hitler, will judge us as
"Germans who wanted the best for their people and their Fatherland, who
were willing to fight and to die." The "Goddess" who presides over that
court "will with a smile tear in pieces the charge of the Public Prosecutor
and the verdict of this court. For she acquits us."[5] A Bavarian police official
recommended deportation to Austria and warned that a short prison sentence would not end Hitler's threat to the security of the state. Unmoved
by the recommendation or the warning, the judges sentenced him to five
years of comfortable confinement in Landsberg prison near Munich. He
served less than ten months.

The Beer Hall Putsch was the central event of early Nazi history and
vital to Hitler's political education. The memory of the sixteen fallen "martyrs" who had sacrificed their lives for the fatherland inspired the party
faithful to persevere in what Hitler called the "holy struggle" against "reds,
reactionaries, democrats, and Jews." Hitler learned an important lesson
from the failure of the putsch: the NSDAP had to take power legally to win

the support of the army and the traditional elites. In the years ahead, his leadership skills would be tested by party radicals who favored the violent overthrow of the Weimar Republic. In Hitler's view, the army would have responded to a putsch with all the force at its disposal, thus ending the NSDAP's chances of ever ruling Germany. Fortunately for the Nazis—and unfortunately for Germany and the rest of the world—Hitler passed the test;. party radicals never attempted another putsch.

The Weimar Republic, 1924–1929

Between the implementation of the Dawes Plan in 1924 and the Wall Street stock market crash in 1929, the republic experienced a brief respite. This period was marked by relative political stability, a modest economic recovery, small diplomatic victories, and a brilliant cultural renaissance. The Reichstag was still sharply divided, but there was enough cooperation among the moderates to enact such controversial measures as an unemployment insurance fund. The strongest party of the right, the Nationalist People's Party (DNVP), did not abandon its opposition to the republic, but for many conservative swing voters democracy became acceptable, not because it was their preferred form of government, but because of improved economic conditions. Prosperity reduced popular support for the Nazis, Communists (KPD), and other extremist groups.

Despite the improvement, sluggish, uneven economic growth was one of the republic's most serious problems. Germany suffered from an unfavorable balance of trade, high interest rates for borrowers, and the over-production/under-consumption syndrome common throughout the industrialized world in the 1920s. Industrial production matched 1913 levels for the first time in 1927, followed by marginal increases in 1928 and 1929. Unemployment averaged 6.5 percent annually, climbing to 12 percent during the winter of 1928/1929. Real wages, or purchasing power, did not exceed the 1913 figure until 1928.[6] Fewer strikes in the late 1920s did not ease tensions between labor and management, as the promise of significantly increased social benefits and a more equitable distribution of wealth did not materialize.[7] Surpassing all other difficulties was dependence on American loans. Should that source of investment capital and cash flow diminish or dry up completely, the republic's economy would collapse. It was the worst-case scenario, and the Great Depression transformed it into frightening reality.

Heated debates over economic issues dominated sessions of the Reichstag. Moderates and conservatives were at odds over the level of public spending for social programs, the unions' demands for higher wages and a uniform eight-hour day, and tax reform to benefit the nonaffluent. From 1924 to 1930 the government ran an overall deficit of 1.3 billion marks. For many government employees, farmers, small-business men, and wage earners who found it increasingly difficult to make ends meet, public spending was too low and taxes were too high. The affluent, on the other hand, felt that the government's fiscal policies discouraged savings and investment, both of which were needed to strengthen the economy. According to a recent neo-Marxist interpretation, Germany did not produce enough wealth to stimulate growth or to finance the welfare state adequately. Hence, the gap between the rich and the poor widened, class conflict intensified, political parties proliferated, and the Reichstag became more fractious. An underfunded democracy could not withstand the Great Depression or counter the seductive appeal of Hitler's demagoguery.[8]

Democracy was tested at the polls twice during the economically troubled middle period. In the presidential election following Ebert's death in February 1925, the voters chose the candidate of the right, the 77-year-old field marshal, war hero, and symbol of vanished imperial glory, Paul von Hindenburg. He was one of the originators of the "stab-in-the-back" legend, a critic of the Weimar Constitution, and an avowed monarchist. A strong sense of duty, however, kept him from using his office to encourage right-wing extremists. As a ceremonial figurehead, he posed no immediate threat to democracy, but under an emergency decree (in effect from 1930 to early 1933), his extraordinary powers would be manipulated by anti-republican conspirators. Following the 1928 Reichstag election, the Social Democrats, scoring their biggest victory since 1920, formed a government. Other democratic parties did well, but enemies of the republic, such as the KPD on the left and the DNVP on the right, held their own. The NSDAP won enough popular votes to send twelve delegates to the Reichstag. Weimar democracy in 1929 was only slightly less fragile than it had been during the early years.

Under former chancellor Gustav Stresemann, who served as foreign minister from 1924 to 1929, the republic gained respect at home and improved its image abroad. In 1925 he signed the Locarno Treaty, formally recognizing territory lost to Belgium and France after the war. The following year Stresemann received the Nobel Peace Prize, and Germany became a member of the League of Nations. In 1929, when American banker Owen Young proposed reducing the amount of annual reparations payments and extending the period for paying the bill in full until 1988, the republic appeared to be on the verge of another diplomatic victory. Seeing an opportunity to discredit Weimar democracy, the radical right decided to sponsor a plebiscite on the Young Plan.

Alfred Hugenberg, a wealthy communications magnate who was elected head of the DNVP in 1928, led the fight against the Young Plan. He poured millions into the campaign and invited the Nazis to participate. Hitler's powerful oratory attracted large crowds, but the outcome of the plebiscite, held in the summer of 1929, disappointed its sponsors. Only 20 percent of the electorate voted against the Young Plan. The republic seemed to have won a vote of confidence, but time was not on its side. The plebiscite delayed Reichstag approval until March 1930, by which time the Great Depression was making itself felt. Meanwhile, the Nazis had received a powerful boost from the free publicity Hitler enjoyed and from their partnership with respectable conservatives. The republic suffered a great loss in October 1929 with the death of Gustav Stresemann, the only states- man with enough prestige, foresight, and courage to forge a coalition of the moderate right against Hitler.

Weimar Culture

While economic recovery and political stability proved to be short-lived, the glow of Weimar culture has endured. Increased public expenditures for education and the arts, as well as audiences hungering for something new and different, helped to produce an "intellectual and artistic hothouse atmosphere" where artists, writers, and other creative talents found encour- agement and mutual support.[9] Many welcomed new media and foreign in- fluences, such as motion pictures and American jazz, while others rejected traditional norms in favor of expressionism in the visual arts and atonal dis- sonance in classical music.

Weimar culture was also intensely political. Its creators were drawn into the struggle between the republic's supporters and its opponents. Many who were pro-republican believed that artistic innovation would provide the spiritual regeneration to restore the nation's pride and great- ness, while more conservative cultural figures saw modernism as evidence of decadence, permissiveness, Americanization, bolshevization, female emancipation, and elitism. No critics of Weimar culture were more strident or vulgar than the Nazis, who founded the *Kampfbund für deutsche Kultur* (literally, the league to fight for German culture) in 1928. In one of the league's first public lecture programs, Alfred Rosenberg, a prominent NSDAP propagandist, warned that "niggerized Americanism" from the west and "Mongolian waves of bolshevism" from the east threatened "the extermination of all German cultural values."[10]

Creative circles themselves were torn by deep political divisions. While conservatives denounced democracy, the more liberal members of the artistic community supported the republic. The most prominent was novelist Thomas Mann, who converted to democracy after the war and campaigned on its behalf. Still others were lukewarm republicans, who ap- preciated the government's protection of human rights and opposed groups that threatened free expression, but were often critical of "bour- geois values" and the greed of the rich. George Grosz's cartoon-like por- traits mercilessly satirized the "fat cats" of Weimar society, while Käthe Kollwitz sensitively portrayed the suffering of the poor. In 1928 playwright Bertolt Brecht and composer Kurt Weill gained international fame for Germany's first musical comedy, *The Three Penny Opera*. Behind the broad, farcical humor lay the author's serious commentary on what he perceived to be the inequality and social injustice of German society. *The Three Penny Opera*, Weimar's most celebrated and enduring theatrical work, established Brecht's reputation as its leading playwright and most brilliant Marxist critic. By not always distinguishing republicans from Weimar's enemies,

GEORGE GROSZ / VAGA

Artist George Grosz believed that corruption and greed defined big business, as shown in this 1926 depiction of Weimar's new ruling class.

Grosz, Brecht, and other antibourgeois critics helped to undermine confidence in the democratic system.[11]

Other artists and thinkers were less political. The Frankfurt School of Social and Psychological Research, which included several young scholars who would later gain fame in the United States, such as Erich Fromm, Erik Erikson, and Herbert Marcuse, developed new methodologies to study human behavior. Physicists Max Planck and Albert Einstein maintained the German tradition of excellence in their discipline. Mies van der Rohe and other Bauhaus architects produced "functional" designs that utilized modern technology. The dissonant music of composers Kurt Weill and Paul Hindemith reflected the uncertainty and pessimism of the "age of anxiety," as did several films produced by Weimar's innovative motion picture industry, such as *The Cabinet of Dr. Calagari* and *Metropolis*. With the exception of Kollwitz and Planck, all the persons mentioned here left Germany after Hitler's takeover. The Bauhaus and Frankfurt School were shut down, and most of the republic's creative filmmakers went into exile.

Thomas Mann and Oswald Spengler, two of Weimar's most famous authors, offer a study in political contrasts. Mann plumbed the fascist and liberal mentalities in his Nobel Prize–winning novel *The Magic Mountain*, published in 1924. The setting of the novel is in a Swiss tuberculosis sanatorium on the eve of World War I, where a dedicated liberal and a doctrinaire proto-fascist carry on lengthy philosophical discussions and compete for the conscience of a young, apolitical patient. The novel ends with the uncommitted youth leaving the sanatorium to fight in the war. In "Mario and the Magician," a chilling short story published in 1930, Mann warns how easily apolitical innocents can be seduced by the "magic" of a fanatical fascist. "Disorder and Early Sorrow" is about the generation gap, one of the most divisive social problems of the Weimar era. The young characters of the story have rejected their parents' conservative values, but have found nothing to take their place. Under the democratic regime, the young people sense a loss of purpose and order, as well as a lack of economic opportunity. They love their fatherland, but are uncertain as to which of the conflicting ideologies can best solve its problems. Hundreds of thousands of young people could relate to such conflicts. Mann feared that many would be easy prey for a fascist demagogue preaching hate and offering simplistic solutions.

Oswald Spengler, a former secondary school teacher, wrote *The Decline of the West*, which was published in 1918. His pessimistic philosophy of history compared civilizations to living organisms that grow, ripen, age, and die. He believed that Germany, the healthiest Western nation, could arrest the inevitable decline by adopting what he called "Prussian Socialism." To large audiences of mostly young people, he proposed the re-establishment of a hierarchical society governed by an enlightened despot like Frederick the Great. Unless the "conservative revolution" overthrew the Weimar Republic, Spengler warned, Western civilization would die. His gloomy prognosis and painful remedy struck a responsive chord among rudderless youth in search of a purpose and a cause. Like Nietzsche's slashing attacks against bourgeois values, Spengler's antidemocratic tirades made young minds more receptive to Nazi extremism. He was initially enthusiastic about Hitler's takeover in 1933, but had become thoroughly disenchanted by 1936 when he died. By that time many young "Spenglerians" had fallen under Hitler's spell.

That many young disciples of Spengler and other disenchanted Weimar youth became ardent Nazis would have come as no surprise to Thomas Mann and other defenders of the republic. As brilliant as Weimar culture was, it served as a tool for the Nazis to gain support by opposing modernity. Weimar culture confronted the disorientation of what to many was a vibrant new society, and the Nazis exploited German fears and anxieties by attacking the defenders of that new society. Those who were pro-democratic and "modern" knew that they would have no place in a Nazi society.

Hitler and the Nazi Party, 1924–1929

Hitler's imprisonment gave him time to reflect on his personal and public life and the future of the Nazi Party. He dictated his thoughts to Rudolf Hess, whose copious notes became the manuscript of *Mein Kampf*, published in 1925. Although the work is rambling, disorganized, and tedious, the central themes are clear. Hitler blasts the *völkisch* parties for their tactics and boasts that the NSDAP will succeed because of its skillful propaganda, diverse membership, and commitment to the "leadership principle", that is, unconditional obedience to the Führer and his appointees. *Mein Kampf* also contains autobiographical material, historical analysis derived mostly from Houston Stewart Chamberlain, and stinging attacks against the Weimar system and the Treaty of Versailles. Most important is the nucleus of a coherent *Weltanschauung* (world view), or ideology.[12]

The twin pillars of Hitler's *Weltanschauung* were anti-Semitism and living space (*Lebensraum*) in the east. He believed that Germany was locked in a deadly Darwinian struggle for survival and could best prove its "race value" by conquering territory. A nation or race that failed to do so was doomed to subjugation or, worse yet, extinction. Germany would win the battle for "world domination" if its "racially untainted young men" were trained to be ruthless, ideologically committed warriors. The Reich needed additional territory to maintain its power and to furnish space for its "sturdy sons," who in a century would produce "250 million Germans on this continent." The Reich's expansion was to be redirected toward the "heartland" of the Eurasian landmass: "We must terminate the colonial and trade policy of the pre-war period and direct our gaze towards the lands of the east." He specifically targeted "Russia and the border states subject to her," which were rich in material resources and populated by "inferior Slavic peoples," who would provide an unlimited supply of slave labor for the "master race."[13]

Hitler linked *Lebensraum* to anti-Semitism by blaming Jews for communism. The destruction of Soviet communism, he argued, would cripple the international Jewish conspiracy and give Germany the opportunity and resources to achieve his ultimate goal, the destruction of the Jewish race. He visualized a "struggle [that] would leave only victors and the annihilated. It meant a war of extermination."[14] It was a war that Germany had to win. "Should the Jew with the aid of his Marxist creed triumph," Hitler wrote in *Mein Kampf*, there would be no "human life on the planet." He believed that the Jews—rootless because they had no homeland—would use not only Marxism in their struggle to survive, but other "international" systems, such as democracy, pacifism, and capitalism. Their final goal was the "denationalization of the magnificent Aryan nations." On the biological level, he viewed them with alarm:

> The Jews woo confusion by the bastardization of other nations, lowering the racial level of the highest, and dominating this racial stew by exterminating the folkish intelligentsia and replacing them by members of his own race, always with the clear aim of ruining the hated white race, and himself rising to be its master. If physical beauty were today not forced entirely into the background by our foppish fashions, the seduction of hundreds of thousands of Aryan girls by bow-legged, repulsive Jewish bastards would not be possible.[15]

Hitler took a giant step toward the completion of his *Lebensraum* plan when his legions invaded the Soviet Union on June 22, 1941. It was no coincidence that at virtually the same time his special forces began the systematic murder of Russian Jews.

Hitler elaborated on foreign-policy issues in speeches and an unpublished manuscript written in 1928. (It was discovered in the U.S. National Archives in 1961 and published under the title *Hitler's Secret Book.*) He advocated an alliance with Italy, a Mediterranean power, and an entente with Britain and its vast overseas empire. Their spheres of influence lay outside of his vision for the moment. He was confident that Italy and Britain would not block his "drive to the east" and that they would support his short-range goals, such as the annexation of Austria and neighboring German-speaking territories, voiding the Treaty of Versailles, and "settling accounts" with France. Publicly, Hitler emphasized the short-range goals, which he claimed could be achieved without war.

Upon his release from prison in December 1924, Hitler encouraged his dispirited followers to adopt new tactics for the political struggle that lay ahead: "Instead of . . . armed conspiracy, we shall have to hold our noses and enter the Reichstag against the Catholic and Marxist deputies. If outvoting them takes longer than outshooting them, at least the results will be guaranteed by their own constitution."[16]

The only condition attached to his parole, a ban on public speaking, was no obstacle to reestablishing total control of the party and breathing new life into an organization that nearly collapsed in his absence. By the end of 1925, with membership still below pre-putsch levels, the NSDAP was no longer a regional party. Recruitment outside of Bavaria was spear-headed by Gregor Strasser, a Munich pharmacist, and Joseph Goebbels, the editor of Strasser's fortnightly party newsletter. Their populist agenda, which enjoyed considerable support among the party faithful, was uncompromising in its identification with the working class and opposition to big business and bourgeois political parties.

Although pleased with the national recruitment effort, Hitler feared the political consequences of alienating the affluent or any party in the Reichstag that might be useful. In February 1926 Nazi leaders met to resolve the crisis. Strasser and his allies pledged their loyalty to Hitler and agreed to support his overtures to big business and the Reichstag's bourgeois parties. They endorsed his sole leadership of the NSDAP as a *Volkspartei*, a political movement for all the people. Goebbels became one of Hitler's most ardent disciples and eagerly accepted his new post as Gauleiter (district leader) of "Red Berlin," a stronghold of the SPD and the KPD. The "little doctor," so-called because of his stature and his doctorate in literature, wrote, spoke, and fought against the left, gaining some working-class converts. Strasser continued to serve Hitler faithfully, but never abandoned his populist convictions or his identification with the party's left wing.

With the crisis of 1926 behind them, Hitler and his lieutenants recruited more aggressively, broadened the party's appeal and streamlined the organizational structure. Membership rose from 27,000 in 1925 to 108,000 in 1929. Formations, or affiliated organizations, were established for specific groups, such as youth, university students, teachers, lawyers, physicians, and women. Membership in the SA, largest of the formations, rose to nearly 100,000. One of its small branches was the SS, or *Schutzstaffeln* (protection squad), which had originated as Hitler's personal bodyguard. Early in 1929 the Führer charged Heinrich Himmler, one of Strasser's former associates, with transforming the SS into an elite "palace guard." Hitler approved an administrative plan to divide the nation into forty-five districts (*Gaue*), each with a Gauleiter directly appointed by the Führer. The districts were subdivided into circles (*Kreise*), with smaller jurisdictions under a Kreisleiter appointed by lesser party officials. Hitler also established a "shadow government" of party leaders who would become cabinet officers in the event of a Nazi takeover.

The NSDAP was eager to plunge into partisan politics in the 1928 Reichstag election. Most of the states had lifted the ban on Hitler's public speaking, and the Nazi propaganda machine, buoyed by the success of the first *Parteitag* (party rally) at Nuremberg the previous year, was in high gear. Hitler and other powerful speakers, such as Göring, Goebbels, Strasser, and Hess, sounded the central themes: the republic was crumbling because of democracy's failure, the Treaty of Versailles, Communist plots, and capitalist exploitation. In the Nazi view, both the "red menace" and corporate greed were Jewish inspired. Promises were vague. Hitler's charismatic leadership would deal with the troublemakers, restore national pride, strengthen the armed forces, and establish a *Volksgemeinschaft* (racial community) from

Hitler is showered with flowers by SA men at the first Nuremberg party rally in 1927.

which non-Aryans would be excluded. On the strength of 800,000 popular votes, the NSDAP sent twelve delegates to the Reichstag. Because the
Nazis did poorly in larger cities outside of Bavaria, Hitler ordered the party
to aim its heaviest guns at rural areas and small towns, with the exception
of Berlin, where Goebbels was to redouble his efforts.

Despite an unimpressive showing at the polls, the NSDAP attracted
new members and contributors. Though still representing a cross-section
of society, the party's social composition was changing slightly. The upper
classes (university-trained, salaried, and affluent), teachers, and the petit
bourgeoisie (artisans, shopkeepers, and lower-level white-collar workers)
were still overrepresented, but by 1929 farmers and the working classes,
previously underrepresented, were joining in larger numbers.[17] Both members and leaders were still somewhat younger than the nation as a whole
and, except for the KPD, much younger than the leadership of other parties. The Nazis' youthful image was an invaluable asset.

Female membership declined from 10 percent in 1921 to less than 5
percent in 1929. Hitler was not concerned, and his antifeminist views never
changed. The democratic parties supported women's rights and campaigned for female votes, but Hitler insisted on the "absolute exclusion of
women from any responsibility in his movement."[18] Moreover, Nazi propagandists attacked the republic's emancipation of women and attributed
Weimar society's "lust for pleasure" and the widespread "indulgence of
every possible sensual and sensory titillation up to the most refined sadism"
to a "feminine-determined civilization process."[19] Nevertheless, many

women would shift their allegiance to the Nazis under the impact of the Great Depression.

On the eve of the Great Depression in 1929, as the SPD-led democratic coalition was beginning to unravel, the Nazi Party was gathering strength. Hitler's campaign against the Young Plan and his temporary alliance with Hugenberg's DNVP gained respectability for what had been perceived to be a motley crew of lower-middle-class south Germans led by a colorful but unstable Austrian immigrant. No party leader could match Hitler's charisma, which inspired commitment and aroused passions on an unprecedented scale. His followers were united by common attitudes, a sense of purpose, a firm belief in their destiny, and an unshakable loyalty to their Führer. Goebbels, one of twelve Nazis to serve in the 1928 Reichstag, gave voice to the party's fanatical determination: "We acquire the weapons of democracy to paralyze it with its own assistance. . . . We'll take any legal means to revolutionize the existing situation. We come as enemies, like the wolf tearing into a flock of sheep."[20]

Conclusion

The Weimar Republic was born under a cloud from which it could never escape. It staggered under the burden of one life-threatening crisis after the other, and it lacked time to resolve these crises fully. Defeat in World War I, the perceived injustices of the treaty, economic decline, political instability, class conflict, and formidable right-wing opposition inflicted deep wounds on the infant republic. Yet the democracy despised by millions of conservative citizens proved sufficiently resilient to survive the crises of the early years. From 1924 to 1929 the republic, basking in the glow of prosperity and political stability, enjoyed a brief honeymoon. That stability and prosperity, like the democratic majority in the Reichstag, rested on unsteady foundations. An unseasoned and, for many, an unwanted democracy took a few faltering steps toward permanence, but solutions were partial and healing was superficial. The republic needed time, much more time, to sink healthy roots into the German earth. The Great Depression stole the time Weimar required and opened a window of opportunity for the Nazis and other extremists.

INFOTRAC® COLLEGE EDITION SEARCH TERMS

For additional reading go to Infotrac College Edition, your online research library at http://www.infotrac-college.com.

Enter the search term "Treaty of Versailles" using the Subject Guide.

Enter the search term "Weimar Germany" using Keywords.

Enter the search term "Hitler, Adolph philosophy" using the Subject Guide.

Enter the search term "Great Inflation" using Keywords.

Enter the search term "beerhall putsch" using the Subject Guide.

Notes

1. A.J. Nicholls, *Weimar and the Rise of Hitler* (New York: St. Martin's Press, 1991), p. 143.

2. Mary Fulbrook, *A Concise History of Germany* (Cambridge: University Press, 1990), p. 155.

3. Detlev Peukert, *The Weimar Republic: The Crisis of Classical Modernity* (New York: Hill and Wang, 1991), p. 278.

4. Quoted in Karl D. Bracher, *The German Dictatorship* (New York: Praeger Publishers, 1970), pp. 119–120.

5. Louis L. Snyder, *National Socialist Germany* (Malibar, FL: Robert Krieger Publishing Co., 1984), p. 85.

6. Volker R. Berghahn, *Modern Germany* (New York: Cambridge University Press, 1982), pp. 258, 266, 272.

7. Ibid., pp. 106–107.

8. Peukert, pp. 278–79.

9. Dietrich Orlow, *A History of Modern Germany* (Englewood Cliffs, NJ: Prentice-Hall, 1995), p. 161.

10. Quoted in Alan E. Steinweis, "Weimar Culture and the Rise of National Socialism," *Central European History* 24 (1991): 408.

11. Orlow, p. 164.

12. Eberhard Jäckel, *Hitler's Weltanschauung* (Middleton, CT: Wesleyan University Press, 1972), p. 27 ff.

13. Adolf Hitler, *Mein Kampf*, trans. by Ralph Manheim (Boston: Houghton Mifflin, 1962), p. 65.

14. Ian Kershaw, *Hitler 1889–1936: Hubris* (New York: Norton, 1999), p. 245.

15. *Mein Kampf*, p. 562.

16. Quoted in Jane Caplan, "The Rise of National Socialism," in Gordon Martel, ed., *Modern Germany Revisited*, 1870–1945 (London: Routledge, 1992), p. 122.

17. Michael Kater, *The Nazi Party: A Social Profile of Members and Leaders* (Cambridge: Harvard University Press, 1983), p. 242.

18. Claudia Koonz, "The Fascist Solution to the Women Question in Italy and Germany," in Renate Bridenthal, Claudia Koonz, and Susan Stuard, eds., *Becoming Visible: Women in European History* (Boston: Houghton Mifflin, 1987), p. 514.

19. Quoted in Steinweis, p. 410.

20. Quoted in Bracher, p. 141.

Collapse of the Weimar Republic and the Nazi Seizure of Power, 1929–1933

Gustav Stresemann, the republic's foreign minister since 1924, died at age 54 on October 3, 1929. Three weeks later, "Black Thursday" on Wall Street, investors lost billions as the value of securities on the New York Stock Exchange plummeted. Within months the German economy declined precipitously. As chancellor, Stresemann's bold initiatives helped end the Great Inflation in 1923, but the republic was powerless to prevent the Great Depression. Had he lived, Weimar's most celebrated statesman might have rallied the moderate right against Nazis, Communists, and other enemies of democracy. Unfortunately, there was no one of Stresemann's stature or courage to defend the republic in the hour of its greatest peril.

Grim statistics reveal the dimensions of the Great Depression. Industrial production, measured at 100 in 1929, dropped to 82.4 the following year, 69 in 1931, and 66 in 1932. From 1929 to 1933, exports, a principal source of national income, fell by two-thirds. The recall of U.S. loans and bank closures forced many businesses to cut back or shut down. Unemployment soared from 1.5 million in 1929, to 3 million in 1930, to 4.5 million in 1931. By the spring of 1932, the 6 million unemployed—over 30 percent of the work force—was the highest in the industrialized world. Millions more were underemployed, had stopped looking for work, or feared that their names might appear on the next "reduction in force" list.

Politically, the Depression made itself felt in March 1930, when Chancellor Hermann Müller, a Social Democrat, resigned. He had failed to achieve a compromise between conservatives and radical socialists who differed on the means of financing the deficit-ridden unemployment insurance fund. Müller's resignation marked the collapse of the republic's last democratic coalition. His successor was Heinrich Brüning, a member of the Center Party whose political and economic views were acceptable to the right. The Reichstag rejected the new chancellor's request to grant the president emergency powers, but it was too polarized to pass legislation to address the worsening economic crisis. After several months of gridlock, Brüning dissolved the Reichstag and scheduled elections for September 1930. The new Reichstag was even more divided, but the delegates approved a new emergency decree that gave the president sole power to appoint and dismiss chancellors. This decree was never revoked. By surrendering its legislative powers to what historians call the "presidential dictatorship," the Reichstag became little more than a contentious debating society.

Weimar's Fall and Hitler's Rise

Burdened by the consequences of a lost war and a humiliating treaty, a fractious parliament, inept leaders, powerful conservative opposition, class conflict, and economic crises, the republic was ill-equipped to deal with the Depression. As it worsened, the Social Democratic Party (SPD), Weimar's largest party and democracy's staunchest defender, put the narrow interests of constituents above preservation of the republic. The Müller government's resignation fatally wounded parliamentary democracy. Although some young militants took to the streets to fight for social democracy, the party's leaders and most of its members lacked the foresight, courage, and will to defend the republic against extremists.

The KPD was disciplined, united, and committed to the violent overthrow of the republic. Its fatal mistake was to follow Moscow's misguided directive to make war against the SPD, which it branded as "social fascists" and traitors to communism. The popularity of Hitler's movement, the German Communists were told, was a symptom of decadent capitalism and, like the creaky economic system it represented, would soon wither away. The Communist International (Comintern) instructed its German comrades to work with the NSDAP in bringing down the republic. A few perceptive members saw the Nazis as their mortal enemy, but KPD leaders ignored their warning and followed Moscow's orders. By so doing, the Communists guaranteed their own destruction. An SPD/KPD coalition of the left might have been powerful enough to stop Hitler and the Nazis, or at least to impede their progress.

More grievous than the left's sin of omission was the traditional elites' pact with the Nazis. Led by the aggressive wing of the Nationalist People's Party (DNVP), these self-styled "New Conservatives" were committed to the destruction of democracy. So firm was their determination to topple the republic that they invited the Nazis to join their conspiracy to scrap the constitution and establish an authoritarian regime. The New Conservatives were clever enough to see the republic's vulnerability, honest enough to acknowledge their own unpopularity, and foolish enough to believe they could tame Hitler. They planned to restore the monarchy, or to write a Bismarckian-style constitution, or, if civil war seemed imminent, to install a military dictatorship. With the Nazis on their side, the New Conservatives were confident that their agenda would placate the masses and make Germany permanently safe for authoritarianism.

Recent historical interpretations of the collapse of the Weimar Republic and the Nazis' success highlight the differences between structuralists and intentionalists. Structuralist historians see external forces rather than individuals as the principal catalysts of change. They hold that Germany's depressed economy and faltering democracy created a mass electorate receptive to Hitler's program. Without the crises of the early 1930s, his movement would have remained "an insignificant minority on the lunatic fringes of the political system."[1] The Depression contributed to "an atmosphere of doom" and provided the New Conservatives with a stage on which to deliver the fatal blow. Hence, the republic was dead before Hitler took over: "He merely stripped . . . [its killers] . . . of their power." The old elites were strong enough to destroy democracy, but too feeble to restore the prewar order. They handed the keys of power to Hitler.[2]

BOX 3.1 ■ THE DEPRESSION ATTRACTS NEW MEMBERS TO THE NAZI PARTY

A disillusioned blue-collar worker, who joined the party for economic and political reasons, wrote:

> The terrible burden of the breakdown threatened to bring all economic life to a standstill. Thousands of factories closed their doors. Hunger was the daily companion of the German working man. Added to this was the artificial whip of scarcity, wielded by the Jews, which sent working men scurrying from their homes to beg for food from the farmers. . . . The government carried its measures against the public so far that many an honest working man had to resort to theft to obtain food. . . . All fellow citizens, with the exception of the Communists, yearned for better times. As for me, like many another, I had lost all I possessed through adverse economic conditions. And so, early in 1930, I joined the National Socialist party.

A small retailer, who lost his business in 1926, was more bitter, as well as more ideologically oriented:

> When we consider that on the one hand the policies of the Red government (the Republic), particularly the inflation and taxes, deprived me of all means of livelihood, while on the other hand we soldiers of the front were being ruled by a gang of exploiters ready to stoop to any means to seize the starvation wages of our suffering, duped comrades, it will become clear why a number of us welcomed the activities of patriotic groups, particularly those of the Hitler movement. The combination of patriotic aims along with social reform led many an old soldier and idealist under the banner of the National Socialist German Workers' Party.

Theodore Abel, *The Nazi Movement* (New York: Atherton Press, 1966), pp. 126–27.

While not minimizing circumstances and impersonal forces, intentionalist historians argue that only a leader with Hitler's extraordinary qualities could have translated the Great Depression, obtuse politicians on the left, and willing accomplices on the right into a stunning electoral victory. His instincts, charisma, sense of timing, and indomitable will were indispensable to Nazi success. Equally important was control of his own movement. If Hitler had not prevailed over the party's anti–big business wing, the New Conservatives' partnership might not have materialized. If he had lost control of his belligerent comrades who favored an armed takeover, the army almost certainly would have crushed them.

The Depression and Weimar's impotence swelled extremists' audiences and undermined a rational resistance to radical solutions. The Nazis capitalized on this opportunity to present themselves as a dynamic party of the people, with no ties to a particular class or interest group. Their promise of a quick fix for Germany's ills attracted millions of voters. Hitler's appeal, however, ran deeper. He and his movement were the inheritors and beneficiaries of "deep and ill-hidden strains of anti-Semitism, antimodernism," and hatred of social democracy, all of which had "nurtured *völkisch* movements since the 1890s."[3] The lost war, the humiliation of Versailles, and the republic's ineptitude transformed these attitudes into obsessions. Hitler knew exactly how, when, and for which group to strike these dissonant chords and how to link them to contemporary problems.

The 1930 Reichstag Election

Brüning's austerity agenda—cutting social programs and sharply reducing government spending—was endorsed by fiscal experts in Germany and abroad. He viewed the Great Depression as the inevitable consequence of an overheated economy and believed that, with the aid of a balanced budget and a stable currency, it would eventually correct itself. The chancellor rejected deficit spending, public works projects to reduce unemployment, and tax incentives for the private sector. To balance the budget, Brüning cut civil servants' salaries by 20 percent and pressured employers and businessmen to reduce wages and prices by 10 percent. As the Depression tightened its grip and revenues declined, the government raised excise and income taxes and, for the first time, levied a regressive head tax on every adult citizen. Austerity and unequal sacrifice did not work. The deficit and unemployment rose, while industrial production and foreign trade fell.

Brüning was quickly dubbed *der Hungerkanzler*, the "Chancellor of Hunger." Although not oblivious to the rising misery index, he vetoed even modest increases in welfare payments. Without the backing of the president's emergency powers, a Reichstag vote of no confidence would have compelled Brüning to resign, but as long as the New Conservatives and President Hindenburg's advisers supported his policies, the chancellor's job was secure. Even union leaders, who shared conservatives' fear of deficit

A well-dressed Hitler addresses a group of mostly upper-class university students in Berlin, 1930. His appearance as a well-bred gentleman pleased such audiences, but his charisma and passion impressed them more.

spending, initially endorsed Brüning's austerity program. They did not propose public works projects until early 1932, when the unemployed numbered nearly 6 million.

The Reichstag election on September 14, 1930, took place in an atmosphere of deepening gloom. Political unrest and a bleak economic outlook did not bode well for consensus-building or majority rule. Normally, France's decision to withdraw troops from the Rhineland, plus reports that U.S. president Herbert Hoover intended to propose a moratorium on reparations and war debts, would have been good news for the government, but domestic crises held center stage in 1930. The ballots cast by 82 percent of the electorate, up from the 75 percent who went to the polls in 1928, registered dissatisfaction, not with democratic principles, but with the breakdown of Weimar's parliamentary system, Brüning's counterproductive economic policies, and the proliferation of political parties. Hitler mercilessly lampooned the latter in a filmed campaign speech, slowly enumerating the thirty-four political parties on the ballot in 1930.

The Nazis and Communists were the chief beneficiaries of voter discontent in 1930. With 18 percent of the popular vote, just over 6 million, the Nazi delegation in the Reichstag rose from 12 to 107. The NSDAP had become the second largest party, trailing the Socialists by only 36. The KPD ran a respectable third, increasing its representation from 54 to 77. Among other major parties that supported the republic, the Catholic Center, the Democratic Party (DDP), and Stresemann's People's Party (DVP)

BOX 3.2 ■ NAZI CAMPAIGN RHETORIC

The first selection is a passage from "The Common Interest Before Self-Interest," a pamphlet first written by Joseph Goebbels in 1926 and frequently reprinted. It stresses commitment to the national community:

> What is the first commandment of every National Socialist? Love Germany more than anything, and your fellow Germans more than yourself! What is the aim of the National Socialist idea of liberty? To create the national community of all honestly creative Germans! What is the content of that national community? Freedom and bread for every German! Who is a fellow German, a racial comrade? Every honestly creative German is, provided his blood, his customs, his culture are German, and provided he speaks the German tongue! What is the basic economic principle with which National Socialism wishes to replace the present economic warfare of all against all? The Common Interest Before Self-Interest!

Hitler was always portrayed as the magnificent, indispensable leader, as illustrated by an excerpt from the party's official appeal to the voters for the March 1932 presidential election:

> The National Socialist movement assembled at this hour as a fighting squad around its leader, . . . calls on the entire German people to join its ranks, and to lead Germany to freedom! . . . Hitler is the word of deliverance for millions, for they are in despair, and see only in this name a path to new life and creativity. . . .
>
> Hitler is the furious will of Germany's youth, which, in the midst of a tired generation, is fighting for new forms, and neither can nor will abandon its faith in a better German future. Hence Hitler is the password and the flaming signal of all who wish for a German future.

Joachim Remak, ed., *The Nazi Years: A Documentary History* (Prospect Heights, IL: Waveland Press, 1990), pp. 39, 42.

lost ground, but not as drastically as the conservative DNVP, which dropped 33 seats. Its loss was not necessarily democracy's gain. Some of the DNVP's constituents, as well as many swing voters on the right, cast ballots for the NSDAP. The election convinced several DNVP leaders that the salvation of their party rested on a coalition with the Nazis.

In their first national campaign, the Nazis generated unprecedented excitement. Their energy, showmanship, and attention to detail persuaded many to vote for the NSDAP and impressed the millions who did not. Hitler was the first politician to travel by air to small towns whose residents had never seen a nationally known party leader. He and other Nazi speakers trained to imitate his style and to emphasize what particular audiences wanted to hear, attacked the Weimar system, the Treaty of Versailles, communism, Jews, and big business. Vague on details, they promised economic recovery, rearmament, a government based on the "leadership principle," and the creation of an exclusively Aryan *Volksgemeinschaft* (racial or national community). There was something for almost everyone, and the Nazi style made the message more compelling. Among the opposition parties, the KPD ran the strongest campaign, but commitment to a Marxist revolution limited their appeal.

The election results polarized the Reichstag as never before. The Nazis resorted to disruptive tactics orchestrated by Hermann Göring; often supported by the Communists, they reduced parliamentary debates to shouting matches and name-calling. The Reichstag's performance made a mockery of the democratic process and ensured the continuation of legislation by decree, which is exactly what Hitler wanted. He sensed that a long-term presidential dictatorship would stall economic recovery and condition the public to dictatorial solutions. The New Conservatives were also pleased. They believed that prolonged governmental paralysis and a steadily deteriorating economy would hasten the republic's demise and their accession to power. Puzzled by a worsening depression and pressured by the New Conservatives, Brüning continued his program. The "Chancellor of Hunger" had become a tool of the radical right; he may always have been one of them.

Nazi Campaign Tactics

The Nazis never stopped campaigning. Since another election before Hindenburg's term expired in February 1932 was unlikely, Hitler and Goebbels had time to refine campaign practices. No detail was overlooked in planning demonstrations, speaking engagements, rallies, parades, and mass meetings. The SA's rough treatment of hecklers and counter-demonstrators enhanced the party's image of strength, while the high visibility of young people suggested that Nazism was the wave of the future. Dramatic spectacles captivated audiences and made them more attentive to speakers emulating their Führer and the party's second-best orator, Joseph Goebbels. Both were also skilled actors, able to mask cynical attitudes which, if widely known, might have alienated thousands of voters. Hitler and Goebbels, who wrote that the "elective majority is always stupid . . . [and] easily seduced by loudmouths and political charlatans,"[4] instructed speakers to repeat a few simple slogans, buzzwords, catch phrases, and lies. Equally cynical about the "small intelligence" of the masses, Hitler believed that they were particularly gullible at night. He reveled in spectacular nocturnal demonstrations, capturing the attention of weary audiences who were "more likely to believe the big lie" and more easily aroused by emotion.

By 1930 the swastika, displayed on banners, flags, and armbands, was widely recognized as the logo of the NSDAP. Goebbels, aware of his countrymen's love of music, felt that the Nazis needed a signature song, whose "chords would ring out on the barricades of freedom." Early in 1930 he found it among the effects of Horst Wessel, a slain storm trooper who had lived with a former prostitute in the slums of Berlin. Wessel was a pimp who was probably murdered by rivals. Goebbels sensed that Wessel's marching song, which included Nazi slogans set to music borrowed from familiar tunes, would become the NSDAP's theme song. The party faithful immediately identified with the "Horst Wessel Song," and their enthusiastic renditions made a favorable impression on the general public. Disguising the sordid circumstances of his murder, Goebbels elevated Wessel to the status of national hero and Nazi martyr, shot down either by the "Red Front" or "Reaction," words which appear in the first verse of the song.[5]

The Nazis demonstrated their versatility as propagandists and tested their expanded influence in December 1930. Goebbels ordered his staff to disrupt the Berlin premier of *All Quiet on the Western Front*, the American film based on Remarque's novel. It turned into a riot, as Nazis invaded the theater, threw stink bombs, and released thousands of white mice. The audience was terrorized by a fanatical mob under the leadership of a "club-footed psychopath" (a reference to Goebbels's physical disability), wrote critic Carl von Ossietzky, and then the movie was "quashed by obscure censorship officials," who lamely argued that it was "really a very bad film." Banning the antiwar movie, according to Ossietzky, signified that Germans preferred war to peace. Fascism, which "can be beaten only in the streets," has scored another victory, and "liberal cowardice, which stays home in moments of trouble, is now bankrupt."[6] Equally ominous, in retrospect, was Goebbels's target. He chose *All Quiet on the Western Front*, not because of the Aryan Remarque's politics but because he feared that the film's "war is hell" theme would promote pacifism. To the Nazis, war was the supreme virtue and pacifism the cardinal sin; their ultimate goals could not be achieved without war.

The SA specialized in physical terror. Its first commander, Ernst Röhm, returned to Germany in time to participate in the 1930 election campaign. (Röhm served as a military consultant to the Bolivian government from 1925 to 1930). His strong leadership and aggressive recruitment swelled membership rolls to over 500,000 by the end of 1931. Like Goebbels's propaganda, the storm troopers' contribution to the NSDAP's electoral success was vital. Hitler ordered Röhm's "brown shirts" to attack Communists and Socialists and to avoid confrontation with the police, the military, and conservative organizations. Several hundred people died in street battles from 1930 to 1933. Remarkably, the authorities and the press accepted spurious Nazi claims that the KPD and the SPD were responsible for the bloodshed and mayhem.[7] To the New Conservatives, Hitler portrayed SA violence as the opening round in what they feared might become a civil war or a Communist revolution. He assured them that SA troopers were front-line soldiers in the struggle against the "Reds" and that a Nazi government would end violence and unrest. It was outrageous political blackmail, a testimony to Hitler's duplicity and the gullibility of the New Conservatives.

The growth of the Nazi Party during the Depression did not substantially alter its diverse social composition. The affluent and well-educated, the lower middle class, teachers, farmers, small-town residents, and young people were still overrepresented. Blue-collar workers in larger cities remained

Nazis and Communists clash on a Berlin street in 1930. From 1930 to 1933 hundreds of people were killed or injured in political warfare, usually initiated by the SA. Hitler's promise to crush the Communists and end political violence won him the support of conservatives.

underrepresented, and Protestants continued to outnumber Catholics, most of whom remained loyal to the Center Party.[8] Female membership did not vary, but Nazi women, largely ignored by their male leaders, became more active. They formed their own intraparty organizations that quietly campaigned to small groups and set up community services such as soup kitchens. By offsetting "the brutal masculine type exalted by Hitler," their image of loving womanhood made a vital contribution to the party's success.[9]

Nazis and Conservatives

Until the fall of 1931, Nazi progress appeared unstoppable. Thousands of newcomers joined the party, audiences grew larger and more enthusiastic, and vigorous campaigning won pluralities in local elections, enabling the NSDAP to control several state governments. Hitler sought to strengthen the party financially and politically by courting the affluent right more aggressively. Most business leaders, wary of the NSDAP's anticapitalist rhetoric and appalled by SA violence, had not been generous contributors. He persuaded a few to open their pocketbooks, but the majority remained skeptical. Politically, he was more successful. In August DNVP leader Hugenberg invited Hitler to attend a meeting in Harzburg, a small town in the state of Brunswick.

Hugenberg did not admire Hitler, but he and Hjalmar Schacht, a financial expert and president of the Reichsbank from 1925 to 1930, had decided to form a partnership of expediency with the Nazis. Some DNVP members agreed, but many wanted no association with what they regarded as the Nazi rabble and their unstable leader. Despite these reservations, a majority of the party's executive committee voted in favor of a coalition. Joining the DNVP were leaders of another powerful New Conservative group, the *Stahlhelm* (steel helmet), a large veterans' organization. Together with Hitler and his lieutenants they formed the Harzburg Front, which would command up to 30 percent of the Reichstag vote. The Nazis thus gained more respect from traditional elites and more generous contributions from the business community. For the New Conservatives the alliance was an admission that their goals were unattainable without Nazi support.

A month after the Harzburg Front was formed, a bizarre incident in Munich briefly slowed the party's momentum and threatened to jeopardize Hitler's skyrocketing career. On September 19, 1931, the body of his 23-year-old niece and live-in companion, Geli Raubal (the daughter of his widowed half-sister Angela), was found in her apartment with a gaping wound in her chest and Hitler's pistol in her hand. The report in the anti-Nazi *Munich Post* implied that her death was related to a "violent lovers' quarrel," possibly over her affair with his chauffeur, and noted her broken nose and "other serious injuries." A few days later, the same newspaper published a letter from Hitler, denying that he and Geli had ever quarreled, but acknowledging that she "was tormented with worry" over her debut as a vocal soloist in Vienna. He gave a similar statement to the Munich police.

Hitler relaxes under the adoring gaze of his niece, Geli Raubal. Her suicide ended the only close relationship he had had with anyone other than his mother. Hitler's mood became somber after Geli's death in 1931.

Seeking to counteract lurid rumors about the incident, Nazi Party head-quarters issued a press release, giving the reason for Geli's suicide as "unsatisfied artistic achievement."[10] This became the official explanation of her death. Bavarian minister of justice Franz Gürtner, a high-ranking party member who would become the Third Reich's minister of justice, pressured the Munich police to forgo an autopsy and ship the body to Vienna for burial.

Hitler appeared to be genuinely distraught over the death of his niece. He went into seclusion, and, according to Rudolf Hess, contemplated suicide. Other members of his circle reported that he seriously considered resigning his post as party leader and that he vowed never again to touch meat or alcohol. At the Nuremberg trials, Göring testified that Hitler became increasingly suspicious and plunged into long periods of isolation and depression following his niece's suicide. The circumstances surrounding Geli Raubal's death may remain a mystery, but one thing is certain: the party's successful cover-up insulated Hitler from what could have become a career-ending scandal. Within weeks, he was again campaigning and, with the presidential election only months away, planning strategy for winning the nation's highest elective office. Geli's death seemed to reinvigorate him and reinforce his sense of mission.

By the end of 1931, Hindenburg, now eighty-four years old and physically and emotionally exhausted, longed to retire to his estate in eastern Germany. He was comfortable as a figurehead, but the presidential dictatorship was burdensome. Unswayed by pressure from the New Conservatives and members of his circle, Hindenburg announced that he would not run for a second term. There was a dearth of moderate candidates with enough stature to defeat the extremists. Ernst Thälmann, head of the KPD, could not win, but party loyalists would deliver at least 15 percent of the popular vote. Without Hindenburg in the race, Hitler was reasonably certain of victory. In January 1932 he received an offer that bolstered his confidence. Steel magnate Fritz Thyssen, a rarity among the superrich because of his consistent support of the Nazis, invited Hitler to address the Industry Club of Düsseldorf.

Hitler brilliantly tailored his message and delivery to appeal to the Rhineland industrialists. With strong conviction, controlled emotion, and carefully reasoned arguments, he denounced Versailles, warned of the Communist menace, attacked democracy, and made an impassioned plea for Germany's rebirth under strong, dedicated leaders. He spoke of the need for unity and the willingness of all "to fight for the national colors." He did not solicit money or votes, but declared that the industrialists' moral support would improve his chances for victory, which would be "the starting-point for German recovery." There could be no recovery, Hitler said, without the kind of sacrifice his followers demonstrated: "SA and SS men mount their trucks, protect meetings, undertake marches [and] then return to [work] or, as jobless, take the pittance of a dole."[11] The response to the two-and-a-half-hour speech was polite but not enthusiastic. The industrialists were impressed by his sincerity and strong convictions, but their contributions to the party did not substantially increase.

By early 1932 the number of citizens on the dole had risen alarmingly. One of every two families felt the immediate shock of unemployment or underemployment. Lower wages, business failures, and bank closures compounded the financial woes of the thrifty middle class. Foreign trade continued its downward slide as the United States and other industrialized nations raised tariffs. The Great Depression, already one of the longest in history, was setting records for progressively steeper declines. For governments, financial experts, and the vast majority of citizens, prospects for recovery were bleak. Few Germans believed that the presidential and Reichstag elections would improve the economy or ease political tensions.

Elections: Spring and Summer, 1932

A few weeks before the March 10 presidential election, Hindenburg reluctantly agreed to run as the candidate of every faction between the NSDAP and the KPD; he had been persuaded by his circle of advisers, especially his son Oskar and General Kurt von Schleicher. Like all New Conservatives, they hoped to suspend the Weimar constitution, but respected the old general's wish to end the presidential dictatorship and curb political violence. Neither a closet constitutionalist nor a convert to democracy, Hindenburg believed that the moderate right could gain control of the Reichstag and solve the nation's problems. Ironically, the democratic parties, unable to find a candidate who could outpoll the extremists, supported the old field marshal.

If Hitler's confidence was shaken by Hindenburg's decision, it was not evident in the ensuing campaign. Backed by Goebbels's well-oiled propaganda machine, Hitler's charisma drew large, enthusiastic crowds and attracted extensive press coverage. Hindenburg, who delivered only one brief public address, relied on the unpopular chancellor to speak on his behalf. Chancellor Brüning, who proved to be a surprisingly effective campaigner, accused Hitler of demagoguery and exposed the emptiness of Nazi promises. The NSDAP's coalition partners, whom Hitler and his campaign managers ignored, ran Theodor Düsterberg, deputy chief of the *Stahlhelm*. Neither he nor KPD leader Thälmann was a formidable contender. Hitler clearly out-campaigned his opponents, but in the final tally his 30 percent was a distant second to Hindenburg's 49.6 percent. Thälmann and Düsterberg received 13 and 6.8 percent, respectively.

Since no candidate received a majority, a run-off among the top three was held on April 10. Hindenburg was reelected, with 53 percent of the vote. With an assist from his coalition partners, Hitler won 13.5 million popular votes, about 37 percent of the total. Thälmann trailed far behind with 10 percent. Hitler was disappointed, but not surprised. His strong showing elevated his standing as a popular leader whose party Hindenburg's circle could no longer ignore. Some presidential advisers believed

A Nazi campaign poster for the July 1932 Reichstag election. Showing Hindenburg and Hitler together implied solidarity between traditional conservatism and Nazi radicalism. The inscription accuses the SPD of disloyalty to the German fatherland.

that the time was right to offer Hitler a cabinet post. Brüning, on the other hand, was beginning to see the Nazis for what they really were. Three days after the run-off election, the chancellor issued an executive order banning public demonstrations of the SA and SS. This rare display of political courage and insight backfired. Hindenburg's advisers pressured the police to enforce the ban unevenly and began plotting Brüning's ouster.

Told that the chancellor was supporting Communist trade-union activities and infuriated by his proposal to subdivide insolvent estates in eastern Germany that were owned by aristocratic friends, Hindenburg forced Brüning to resign on May 30. His successor was Schleicher's choice, newcomer Franz von Papen. This vain, ambitious Catholic aristocrat and member of the Prussian Diet, who was known for obsequious flattery and love of intrigue, had ingratiated himself with powerful New Conservatives. Hindenburg was impressed by Papen's pleasant personality and confident assurance that a Reichstag majority of the right was attainable.

As minister of defense, Schleicher intended to run the government and make Papen a "salesman" of the New Conservatives' program. The minister underestimated the chancellor. Papen, who easily persuaded Hindenburg to dissolve the Reichstag, scheduled elections for July 31. On June 16, in an ill-advised attempt to gain Nazi support, Papen lifted the ban on the SA and SS. Within hours NSDAP paramilitary legions and Communists were engaged in the bloodiest civil conflict since the end of the war. Rather than employing extraordinary measures to reduce the violence, Papen dismissed Prussia's Social Democratic premier on the pretext that he could not maintain order. This unconstitutional act exacerbated violence in Prussia and heightened tensions throughout the country. At the same time, economic indicators sank to their lowest level. Confident of victory, optimistic Nazis predicted that their party would be the first in the republic's history to win an absolute parliamentary majority.

The Nazis' campaign was a political extravaganza unparalleled in German history. Spectators were enthralled by mass demonstrations, choreographed rituals, and huge parades featuring a sea of banners by day and countless torches by night. They flooded the country with posters and pamphlets and, emulating an American practice, staged motorcades and rallies during the lunch hour. The Nazis found most U.S. campaign tactics to be unsuitable, however. Hitler preferred long speeches, avoided interviews, and, flanked by SA men at all public appearances, did not normally "work the crowds." Singing and band music were much more common, and humor was conspicuously absent. Germans were not accustomed to politics as entertainment. Unlike Franklin Roosevelt, running for president in 1932, no German politician would have allowed himself to be publicly "roasted" by a comedian like Will Rogers. The most striking difference, however, lay in the message. Roosevelt criticized Herbert Hoover's policies and offered a program that was significantly different, but he did not attack his opponent personally. Hitler and his lieutenants preached hatred and fear, and they practiced violence.

The NSDAP's 13.7 million votes, about 37.5 percent of the electorate, was more than any of the republic's parties had ever received. Their Reichstag delegation more than doubled, to 230. Although optimistic projections of 15 to 16 million popular votes and a Nazi/DNVP parliamentary majority did not materialize, it was an impressive showing. With the DNVP's thirty-seven seats, down four from 1930, the Harzburg Front commanded 267 votes. Had there been a left coalition of the SPD's 133, down ten, and the KPD's 89, up twelve, it could have mustered only 222 votes in the Reichstag. The Center Party, which had drifted to the right since the Depression, gained six seats, from 69 to 75. The other major parties fell far behind, while many smaller ones failed to win the 60,000-vote minimum. The Nazis were the clear winners. A Hitler-led government seemed imminent.

Nazi Voters

Hitler's insistence on maintaining the party's broad constituency was indispensable to the Nazis' electoral success in the summer of 1932. The reliable support of the lower middle class—small farmers, shopkeepers, poorly paid white-collar workers, and independent artisans—was reinforced by voters from other classes and from all regions. Recent studies have confirmed these familiar trends, but have revised the common belief that most new Nazi voters were unemployed. Analysis of election returns from small towns, rural areas, and particular districts of large cities reveals that the affluent, blue-collar workers, older citizens, pensioners, and Catholics voted for the NSDAP in larger numbers than previously supposed. The Nazis attracted more women, and, in areas where votes were tabulated by gender, females outnumbered male voters for the first time.[12]

Since exit polls did not exist in the early 1930s, modern researchers can only draw inferences about the motivation of Nazi voters. So much has been made of Hitler's charisma, enhanced by the party's flair for showmanship, that it is easy to ignore the astute and cynical politician in him. His powerful appeal derived from a combination of calculation and fanaticism, together with his keen understanding of the German voter and his practical experience of politics, gained not in the Chancellery or Reichstag, but in the streets.[13] Most Nazi voters, including women, were won over by a combination of his charisma, the promise of an orderly *Volksgemeinschaft*, and an economic program that, for all its vagueness, offered hope. Hitler and his lieutenants played on the fears of industrial modernization, seen by the lower middle class as a threat to its livelihood and perceived by the affluent upper classes as an agent of social leveling. The NSDAP promised jobs, an authoritarian government, and destruction of the KPD, whose commitment to proletarian revolution terrified both groups.

Ever the astute politician, Hitler sensed what modern research has confirmed—that most Germans did not share his murderous hatred of the Jews or see them as poisoners of the Aryan race. The Depression, however, enabled the Nazis to exploit social and economic anti-Semitism, while downplaying its role as the "radical racial doctrine that formed the true core" of their ideology.[14] Their strategy was to link Jews to modernization, advanced capitalism, and bolshevization. Nazi speakers claimed that high interest rates and more department stores were evidence of a Jewish plot to destroy Aryan shopkeepers and artisans. Blaming Jews for the spread of communism, however, was the Nazis' most effective ploy. By arousing the latent anti-Semitism of millions of citizens from all classes who dreaded the economic and social consequences of bolshevization, Hitler and his lieutenants won popular support for what would become their racial war against the Jews.

Nazis, Communists, and the DNVP were the principal beneficiaries of the electorate's frustrations and fears, compounded by a worsening depression, political gridlock, and more incidents of violence. The three parties committed to authoritarian rule received at least 55 percent of the popular vote in the summer of 1932. A majority had repudiated the Weimar system, but not necessarily its underlying democratic principles. Many of the swing voters among the 55 percent, along with the 45 percent who voted for moderate parties, probably opposed the abolition of constitutionally guaranteed human rights, which were still in place despite two years of the presidential dictatorship. With strong leadership, constitutional government might have survived.

The November Reichstag Election and Its Consequences

There were no able leaders outside the Nazi camp. Chancellor Papen was as stubborn as he was inept. In the face of the voters' stinging rebuke of his policies, he refused to resign. Normally, the president would ask the head of the largest party (in this case, Hitler) to form a new government. Extraordinary circumstances, however, dictated a compromise. Hindenburg despised the "Bohemian lance-corporal," and the New Conservatives feared that Hitler as chancellor would be more difficult to control. Papen and Schleicher offered him the vice-chancellorship, and Hindenburg promised a high-ranking cabinet position. Hitler held out for the chancellorship. Without "unequivocal leadership of the government," he said, the Nazis would accept neither power nor responsibility. The president was equally adamant and admonished Hitler to "conduct himself properly."[15]

Hitler now found himself in an unenviable position. If a popular vote of 37.5% did not open the door to the chancellorship, it was unlikely that anything less than a 55 to 60 percent landslide would move the Hindenburg circle to rethink its position. Hitler knew that a victory of that magnitude was impossible. In fact, he and Goebbels were beginning to sense that Nazi popularity had peaked. Röhm and the radicals argued more forcefully than ever for a putsch. Hitler, as always, vetoed their plan; he was still convinced that his destiny would be fulfilled by legal means. Nevertheless, Röhm's brown shirts, frustrated by their Führer's refusal to accept the vice-chancellorship, began to attack groups on the right, such as the *Stahlhelm*.

Although he did not yet realize it, Papen also faced an uncertain future. Unable to form a majority of the right, he called for a vote of confidence in the Reichstag, losing by more than 500 to 55. Most heads of parliamentary governments suffering such an embarrassing defeat would have resigned immediately, but not Papen. He stubbornly clung to power, denied his unpopularity and incompetence, and brushed aside Hindenburg's growing displeasure. Contrary to Schleicher's advice, he dissolved the Reichstag and scheduled elections for November 6.

A change in the political and economic climate made the Nazis less optimistic. Contributions from big business had dropped off sharply as the industrialists worried about SA violence against right-wing groups. They feared that Hitler was losing control of his storm troopers. What was good news for the public—the Depression had bottomed out and economic indicators were inching upward—was bad news for the NSDAP. To mollify the restless storm troopers, Hitler allowed them to collaborate with the Communists in an election-eve transport strike in Berlin. There were numerous acts of violence and sabotage. Wealthy sympathizers and middle-class supporters were unmoved by Hitler's explanation that the SA would become uncontrollable if its violence was curbed. He claimed that it was necessary to destabilize the republic and hasten its demise.

Just under 80 percent of the electorate went to the polls on November 6. It was the fourth national election in nine months and the first time since 1928 that the Nazis faltered. Losing more than 2 million votes, their percentage fell from 37.5 to 33.1, while their Reichstag delegation dropped from 230 to 196. The SPD and Center lost votes, but the DNVP, cutting into Nazi support, jumped from 37 to 52. The KPD's 100-man delegation, up from 89 in July, was a record high for the Communists. The election, which proved that the Nazi tide could be stopped, was a depressing experience for a party accustomed to victory. In an unusually pessimistic mood Goebbels wrote: "The future looks dark and gloomy. All chances and hopes have quite disappeared." He seemed to have accepted the radicals' argument that a putsch was the only remaining option. In a diary entry a few days later, however, he expressed confidence in Hitler's ability to "pull it off." Goebbels wrote: "Something has to happen . . . if we are to come to power [legally] in the near future."[16]

Hitler viewed the November election as a setback that might delay the legal takeover, but he was certain that something or someone would make it possible. He persuaded a majority of his dispirited followers that Providence, time, and circumstances were on their side. Fortuitously for the Nazis, Hindenburg set the machinery in motion on November 17 when he asked for Papen's resignation. The angry ex-chancellor began plotting against Schleicher, whom he blamed (quite rightly) for his dismissal. Hitler would soon become a key figure in Papen's conspiracy to regain power. On December 5, 1932, under strong pressure from Hindenburg and his advisers, General Kurt von Schleicher reluctantly accepted the top post. He was to be the republic's last chancellor.

The Final Act: The Nazi Seizure of Power

The November election cost the NSDAP more than momentum, popularity, and financial support. To the New Conservatives who had so shamelessly courted Hitler, the Nazi movement, while still formidable and potentially useful, no longer seemed indispensable to the fulfillment of their goals. Hitler found himself in an uncharacteristically passive role, waiting for something to happen, but the NSDAP was still a force to be reckoned with. A third of the population, "all potential or real devotees of the Führer cult," still saw in Hitler the only hope for Germany's future.[17] They and millions of others benefited little from small gains in the economy; the Great Depression, as they saw it, retained its grip on the nation. At the same time, SA violence, which had fed conservatives' fear of civil war since the 1930 election, continued unabated. There was enough hope, enough despair, and enough fear to keep the Nazis politically alive.

A public opinion poll about prospects for the future at the end of 1932 would almost certainly have been negative. In the arts the prevailing mood of pessimism was reflected in Fritz Lang's *M*, a popular film about a child murderer, portrayed by Peter Lorre, and *Mahagonny*, a bitterly satirical musical by Bertolt Brecht and Kurt Weill. Hans Fallada's *Little Man, What Now?*, a novel about an unemployed white-collar worker, was a bestseller. Economic hopelessness, an uncaring bureaucracy, and the violent confusion of election campaigns conspired to crush the novel's bewildered clerk and his family. Millions of Germans could identify with the plight of Fallada's "little man." Christopher Isherwood, the British author of *The Berlin Stories*, wrote of the despair and sense of foreboding that could be felt throughout the city in the early 1930s: "The dead cold grips the town in utter silence . . . Berlin is a skeleton which aches in the cold. . . . The iron throbs and shrinks, the stone and the bricks ache dully, the plaster is numb."[18] His stories allude to SA/Communist violence, anti-Semitism, the powerful attraction of Nazism for the young, the decadence of Berlin night life, and the cabarets' biting political satire and black humor. In one of the opening scenes of *Cabaret*, a film based on Isherwood's *Goodbye to Berlin*, a young uniformed Nazi trying to collect money from the patrons of the cabaret is forcibly ejected. As the camera silently pans the audience in a memorable closing scene that takes place shortly before Hitler's takeover, many of the patrons are wearing swastika armbands.

General Schleicher, as charming as Papen but politically more astute, was under no illusions about the difficulties he faced. The people's confidence in the government had never been lower, and economic improvement was barely perceptible. Schleicher's penchant for behind-the-scenes maneuvering had alienated powerful figures in the president's circle and the Reichstag. Hindenburg himself, however, trusted his chancellor and supported most of his initiatives, one of which was to offer a cabinet post to Gregor Strasser. This bold move was designed to split the NSDAP, reduce Hitler's influence, and win support of the party's left wing. Over Hitler's objection, Strasser met with Schleicher in the chancellery. Though he was tempted, Strasser declined. Accepting the chancellor's offer, he decided, would constitute a betrayal of the Führer and the party. This meeting, symptomatic of Schleicher's unsuccessful efforts to form a majority in the Reichstag, would ultimately cost both men their lives.

Schleicher also sought to win over the Socialists. To provide jobs for the unemployed, he proposed public works projects, partially financed by a sharp reduction of government subsidies to insolvent estates in eastern Germany. The SPD refused to cooperate. Hindenburg, whose estate was on the list, was not pleased, but he still held Schleicher in high regard. In a Christmas greeting the president addressed the chancellor as his "young friend" and thanked him for creating an atmosphere of calm.

No one was more delighted by Schleicher's distress than Franz von Papen. By the beginning of the new year, he had devised a scheme to unseat the republic's only military chancellor and regain power. On January 4, 1933, Papen chaired a meeting attended by Hitler and prominent conservatives in the home of Kurt von Schröder, a wealthy Cologne banker. The former chancellor unveiled his plan to form a government that would bypass the Reichstag and abolish the Weimar constitution. As a figurehead chancellor, Hitler's popularity would legitimize and strengthen unconstitutional government, while Papen as vice chancellor and minister-president of Prussia would appoint a majority of the cabinet ministers and run the government.

Hitler accepted Papen's plan without reservations or conditions. Satisfied with only one Nazi in the cabinet, he named Wilhelm Frick as minister of the interior, whose jurisdiction included personnel matters and police work. This modest request reinforced the New Conservatives' perception of the Nazi leader as reasonable, cooperative, and, most important, manageable. They urged him to name another Nazi to the cabinet. Hitler nominated Hermann Göring as minister without portfolio and Prussian minister of the interior. The former title was honorific; the latter empowered Göring to command the political police force of Germany's largest state. Papen, Hugenberg, and the other New Conservative cabinet members were blind to the implications of Hitler's choice of positions. The head of the DNVP boasted that they had the Nazi leader "boxed in," while Papen assured his colleagues that he would push Hitler into a corner so hard he would be squeaking.

Neither of the conspirators dreamed that their plan would materialize so quickly. Hindenburg's hatred of Hitler and the NSDAP's sagging popularity were obstacles, but the old general was beginning to lose confidence in Schleicher, and he was still fond of his *Fränzchen* (the affectionate diminutive of Franz). Moreover, Hitler could boast of an upsurge in Nazi popularity, as evidenced by a mid-January electoral victory in the tiny state of Lippe. Papen persuaded worried members of the president's circle that he could manage Hitler and that the Nazis' propaganda machine could be harnessed to win grassroots support for authoritarian government. Hindenburg, however, refused to budge until the end of the month. On January 28 Schleicher, acknowledging that he could not deliver on his promise to form a majority government, asked for, and was refused, authorization to dissolve the Reichstag. To the president, this request lent credibility to Papen's fabricated story about Schleicher's plot to install a military dictatorship. For Hindenburg there were no other choices. He dismissed Schleicher and accepted Papen's plan. Two days later Hitler took the chancellor's oath of office. The Nazis celebrated with a massive torchlight parade, witnessed by their Führer from a balcony of the Reich chancellery.

Conclusion

Hitler's chancellorship was avoidable. Six months earlier he might have been swept into office by popular demand or by a call from powerful constituencies to save a nation teetering on the brink of civil war. In January 1933, however, political and economic crises were slightly less threatening, and the Nazi movement had temporarily lost momentum. Hitler's appointment was the outcome of petty intrigues and secret plotting initiated by the unfortunate republic's most vain and inept chancellor. Papen was no different from other right-wing politicians in miscalculating Nazi intentions or underestimating their leader, but he was more easily duped into thinking that, as vice chancellor backed by his hand-picked cabinet, he could control Hitler. The KPD, the SPD, the Center, and the moderate right all contributed to the Nazi victory, but the New Conservatives top the list of unwitting accomplices. By destroying the Weimar Republic they made Hitler's dictatorship possible.

Hitler was lucky. Without external factors—the Great Depression, the dearth of strong leaders, the obtuse behavior of opposition parties, the presidency of a superannuated monarchist, and the arrogant blundering of Franz von Papen—the NSDAP might have continued to lose popular support. With disastrous results, Hitler's contemporaries underestimated him. Recent research and decades of chronological distance, however, enable the student of Nazi Germany to avoid that mistake. Hitler was a political genius obsessed by a self-appointed mission to lead a national revolution, create a new Germanic empire, and wreak vengeance on the Jews. A modern historian concludes that Hitler had mobilized "enormous energies and profound expectations for a new beginning, reimagining the nation as a new, fiercely nationalistic body politic."[19] If Papen's scheme had not materialized, there would almost certainly have been another time, another opportunity, for a legal takeover.

For the time being the electorate outside the ranks of Nazi followers was prepared to support the new chancellor, who promised swift action to end the economic crisis and curb political violence. Few Germans had read

Mein Kampf, and few of its readers believed that Hitler meant what he wrote. Many were lulled into acquiescence by the legality of his appointment, as he suspected they would be. There would have been less support for the Nazi Führer if his SA brawlers had taken power by force. One retired public figure, well qualified to pass judgment, was not deceived by the "legality" of Hitler's takeover or his glib promises. In a telegram to Hindenburg two days after the installation of the Papen-Hitler government, General Ludendorff foresaw an escalation of Nazi terror with horrible consequences. He wrote: "By naming Hitler Reich Chancellor, you have delivered our holy German fatherland to the greatest demagogue of all time. I can assure you that this evil man will plunge our Reich into the abyss and bring to our nation unparalleled misery."[20]

Had Ludendorff's warning been widely circulated, most people would probably have ignored it. In any case, it was too late. The fate of 70 million Germans was now in the hands of a fanatical *Realschule* dropout from Austria. His rise to power, one of the great political success stories of the twentieth century, temporarily masked destructive impulses that, when unleashed during the war, would cost millions of lives.

INFOTRAC® COLLEGE EDITION SEARCH TERMS

For additional reading go to Infotrac College Edition, your online research library at http://www.infotrac-college.com.

Enter the search term "Germany Great Depression" using Keywords.

Enter the search term "Hindenburg, Paul von" using the Subject Guide.

Enter the search term "Hitler, Adolph" using the Subject Guide.

Enter the search term "Reichstag" using the Subject Guide.

Enter the search term "National Socialist German Workers Party" using the Subject Guide.

Notes

1. Ian Kershaw, *Hitler* (London: Longman, 1991), p. 52.
2. Sebastian Haffner, *The Meaning of Hitler* (New York: MacMillan, 1979), p. 61; Detlev Peukert, *The Weimar Republic: The Crisis of Classical Modernity* (New York: Hill & Wang, 1991), p. 280.
3. Dietrich Orlow, *A History of Modern Germany* (Upper Saddle River, NJ: Prentice-Hall, 1999), p. 154.
4. Quoted in Helmut Heiber, *Goebbels* (New York: Hawthorn Books, 1972), p. 106.
5. Louis L. Snyder, *The Weimar Republic* (New York: D. Van Nostrand, 1966), pp. 204–205.

6. Quoted in Peter Gay, *Weimar Culture* (New York: Harper & Row, 1968), p. 137.

7. Thomas Childers and Eugene Weiss, "Voters and Violence: Political Violence and the Limits of National Socialist Mass Mobilization," in *German Studies Review* (October 1990): 481.

8. Thomas Childers, *The Nazi Voter* (Chapel Hill: University of North Carolina Press, 1983), pp. 188–190.

9. Claudia Koonz, "The Fascist Solution to the Women Question in Italy and Germany," in Renate Bridenthal, Claudia Koonz, and Susan Stuard, eds., *Becoming Visible: Women in European History* (Boston: Houghton Mifflin, 1987), p. 515.

10. Ron Rosenbaum, *Explaining Hitler: The Search for the Origins of His Evil* (New York: Random House, 1998), pp. 100–102, 108; Alan Bullock, *Hitler and Stalin: Parallel Lives* (New York: Alfred A. Knopf, 1992), p. 377.

11. Snyder, p. 210.

12. Childers, *The Nazi Voter*, p. 260.

13. Alan Bullock, *Hitler* (New York: Harper & Row, 1962), p. 375.

14. Ian Kershaw, "The Persecution of the Jews and German Popular Opinion in the Third Reich," in *Leo Baeck Institute Year Book* 26, 1981, pp. 24–26; Childers, *The Nazi Voter*, p. 267.

15. Quoted in Snyder, p. 211.

16. Quoted in Otto Friedrich, *Before the Deluge* (New York: Harper & Row, 1972), p. 378.

17. Ian Kershaw, *Hitler 1889–1936: Hubris* (New York: Norton, 1999), p. 412.

18. Quoted in Friedrich, p. 351.

19. Peter Fritzsche, *Germans into Nazis* (Cambridge: Harvard University Press, 1998), p. 214.

20. Quoted in *Gutachten des Instituts für Zeitgeschichte,* vol. 1 (Munich: Institut für Zeitgeschichte, 1958), p. 367.

CHAPTER FOUR

Nazi Germany, 1933–1939: Political and Economic Affairs

Hitler's appointment as chancellor on January 30, 1933, which the Nazis called the *Machtergreifung* (seizure of power), was the first act in the tragedy of Hitler's triumph over the German nation. In the next stages he consolidated his power and presided over a sustained economic recovery. The consolidation of power happened so quickly and so thoroughly that it appeared to follow a precise blueprint. Although economic recovery took longer and was less thorough, it too seemed to bear the mark of advanced planning. In fact, though, Hitler had no grand design; the Nazis were simply successful and often-lucky improvisers. Before the *Machtergreifung,* Hitler offered neither a precise blueprint for the Nazi state nor a detailed plan for the economy. He pledged little more specific than replacing democracy with the "leadership principle," tearing up the Treaty of Versailles "page by page," and silencing Communists and other foes of the "new order." He promised jobs and an end to the Depression, but said almost nothing about how he would achieve these goals. Essentially, he asked the German people to trust him and the instincts that had catapulted him to the leadership of the country's most dynamic and popular political party.

Hitler's dictatorship bore little resemblance to the traditional authoritarian regime—efficient, conservative, and benevolent—that most Germans hoped for. Whether they had voted for the Nazis or for other parties before 1933, citizens were astounded at the speed and terrified by the ruthlessness with which Hitler smashed potential opponents and forced the "alignment," or *Gleichschaltung* (literally, putting into the same gear), of institutions and organizations he deemed of value to his regime. No group was more shocked than the New Conservatives, whose conspiracy to destroy the republic paved the way for Hitler's takeover. Though applauding the arrest of Communists and the abolition of labor unions, they were stunned by the use of terror against all individuals and institutions that impeded his course.

Within a few months Hitler, making a mockery of Franz von Papen's earlier boast, had pushed the traditional elites "squeaking into a corner." Conservatives and other interest groups soon discovered that the new chancellor was the master manipulator and controller, beholden to no one.

Recently, scholars have suggested that Hitler, hamstrung by bureaucratic tangles, chaotic administration, inept management, and poor planning, was actually a "weak dictator."[1] But in 1933 millions saw the Führer and his lieutenants as efficient, decisive, and utterly ruthless. The lack of planning, disorderly bureaucratic structure, and capricious decision making were apparent from the beginning, but nothing could disguise what quickly unfolded as the frightening reality of Hitler's government: the citizens of a once-democratic republic were transformed into subjects of a "total state" (a term the Nazis were fond of using), ruled by a dictatorship that was arbitrary, radical, and violent.

Consolidation of Power, 1933

On the day he took the oath of office, Hitler persuaded his cabinet to agree to the dissolution of the Reichstag. An election was scheduled for the first week in March. Throughout February, Hitler and his lieutenants conducted the campaign with elaborate showmanship and unprecedented violence. An estimated two hundred persons, mostly Communists, were killed in Berlin alone. At the same time, Hermann Göring, the new head of the Prussian Ministry of the Interior, reorganized and expanded the political police force of Germany's largest state. Staffed by Nazi loyalists, Göring transformed the Prussian political police into a squad of brutal terrorists, which formed the nucleus of the infamous Gestapo. This pseudo-legal instrument of state power arrested thousands of Communists and other opponents of the regime.

The most spectacular event of Hitler's first months in office was the Reichstag fire. Set ablaze during the night of February 27–28, 1933, the massive, ornate headquarters of Germany's parliament was left a smoking shell. Marinus van der Lubbe, a young, mentally deranged Dutch Communist who may have been the arsonist, or one of the arsonists, was arrested in the ruins of the building. He was tried, convicted, and beheaded. Several other Communists were charged with complicity in the crime and were tried by a Prussian court, which acquitted them. A case can be made, based on circumstantial evidence, that certain Nazi leaders, especially Göring, were responsible for the fire; however, their complicity will probably never be proved conclusively. More important was Hitler's use of this incident. The next day, February 28, citing the Reichstag fire as evidence of an attempted Communist coup, he issued an emergency decree, the Presidential Law for the Protection of State and People. This decree suspended the civil liberties of all citizens. Despite Hitler's assurance that it was temporary, the decree was never revoked. As in the past, he used the "Communist menace" to his advantage. On February 28, 1933, it provided a pseudo-legal basis for a twelve-year reign of terror.

On Sunday, March 5, the German people went to the polls for the
fifth time in twelve months. Election weariness had not set in. Nearly 40
million people, 90 percent of the electorate, cast ballots. Remarkably, in an
election that saw much harassment of opposing candidates, nearly 19 million Germans voted for political parties other than the Nazis (NSDAP) and
their allies. Nevertheless, the Nazis received more than 17 million votes,
43.9 percent of the total, giving them 288 seats in the Reichstag. With the
fifty-three seats won by the Nationalist People's Party (DNVP), Hitler's
conservative coalition partners, the NSDAP commanded a bare majority
in the 647-member Reichstag. Hitler proclaimed victory and immediately
made plans to end constitutional government altogether. Subsequently, intimidation, terror, and false promises were employed to secure the required
two-thirds majority to amend the constitution.

The new Reichstag opened on March 21 with an elaborate ceremony
in the Garrison Church at Potsdam, the site of Frederick the Great's tomb.
It was skillfully staged by Joseph Goebbels, whom Hitler had appointed to
head the newly created ministry of propaganda and public enlightenment.
Obsequiously paying homage to the authoritarian Prussian tradition, Hitler
assured the civilian and military dignitaries that President Hindenburg
would preside over Germany's revival. Two days later the Reichstag met in
an opera house, surrounded by SS men. Inside the building, hundreds of
SA troopers provided an intimidating presence. All Communist delegates
had been arrested, and 26 Social Democrats were not permitted to attend.
Hitler proposed the Enabling Act, which would empower him to make

Hitler, Göring, and Röhm lead the procession behind Hindenburg to open the new Reichstag
on March 21, 1933. Public deference to the old field marshal during Hitler's first weeks in
office lulled conservatives into thinking that Hitler was one of them.

laws without the Reichstag's approval for the next four years. Only ninety-four delegates, less than one-sixth of the total, voted against the bill. They were all Social Democrats. Among the majority voting for the act were delegates of the Center Party. Its leaders had been bought off by Hitler's promise to respect the legal status and traditional privileges of the Catholic church. Hitler was now a legal dictator, "created by democracy and appointed by parliament."[2]

On April 7 Hitler brought the bureaucracy into line by promulgating the Law for the Restoration of the Professional Civil Service, which eliminated tenure, the right of appeal, and other legal safeguards. At least 10 percent of all state employees were purged, with Prussia suffering a much higher rate of attrition than other German states. Jewish officials fell victim to this law, as did those whom Minister of the Interior Wilhelm Frick judged to be incompetent or to have democratic tendencies. Some civil servants became "March violets," citizens who thought it expedient to join the party after passage of the Enabling Act; all were required to sign a loyalty oath to the regime, an obligation made mandatory for all public employees later in the year. Hitler knew that a highly qualified bureaucracy was essential to fulfilling his goals. Over the objections of party radicals, he insisted that professionalism rather than ideological conformity was to be the chief criterion in deciding which bureaucrats would keep their jobs and which applicants would fill vacancies and new positions. It was a principle more honored in the breach than in the observance, but the bureaucracy never entirely lost its autonomy. In the end, it made little difference. Civil servants, even those who harbored misgivings about the Nazi regime, served Hitler's state faithfully.[3]

The *Gleichschaltung* of state governments began in February. As Prussian minister of the interior, Göring assumed the de facto authority of Reich commissioner, the chief executive of Germany's largest state. In the weeks following the emergency decree, Frick appointed commissioners in other states, claiming that their governments could not maintain order. In most cases, the disorder was staged by SA and SS men. The commissioners' power over the legislatures and elected officials was also backed by the SA and SS. By mid-April permanent commissioners, often local Gauleiters, had been installed. The *Gleichschaltung* of the states was complete in January 1934, when the legislatures and the Reichsrat, the constitutional body representing the states at the national level, were abolished outright. For the first time in modern German history, the federal principle was replaced, in theory, by a supreme central authority.

Without the protection of state governments and the support of political parties in the Reichstag, Germany's labor unions were in a precarious position. Hoping to ensure their survival, they severed their ties with a longstanding ally, the Social Democratic Party (SPD). It was to no avail. Following a gigantic, government-sponsored rally on May 1, all labor unions were abolished. The SA and SS closed union headquarters, confiscated funds and property, and arrested officials who resisted. This audacious show of force eliminated a source of political opposition and fulfilled Hitler's promise to big business that he would "deal with the unions." On May 6 the Führer announced the formation of the German Labor Front (*Deutsche Arbeitsfront*, the DAF) to be led by Robert Ley, a Gauleiter, head of the party's political organization and Gregor Strasser's successor as the NSDAP's chief of administration. All workers were required to join and pay dues; strikes and collective bargaining were strictly forbidden. The DAF, which excluded Jews, would eventually number 25 million members, making it the largest single mass organization in the Third Reich. Membership in the Labor Front became a prerequisite for employment.

With the abolition of the labor unions, other political leaders realized that the Nazis intended to establish a one-party state. For all practical purposes, the Communist Party had ceased to exist after the Enabling Act was passed. By the end of June, the State Party (formerly the Democratic Party), Gustav Stresemann's German People's Party, and smaller regional and special-interest parties had dissolved themselves. Attempts to merge with the Nazis having failed, Alfred Hugenberg's Nationalist Party disbanded on June 27, the day after its leader resigned his ministerial posts, one in economics, the other in agriculture. The SPD's executive council was divided between those who favored an accommodation with the Nazis and those who wished to transfer party headquarters to Prague, from which city they hoped to mount Socialist opposition against Hitler's regime. The debate ended on June 23, when the government forbade all SPD activity, closed the party's offices, confiscated its property, and arrested any leaders who did not cooperate.[4]

At the beginning of July, when only the Center Party and its Bavarian branch remained intact, Hitler announced his intention to negotiate an agreement with the papacy. In return for a written guarantee of traditional rights, such as maintaining schools, youth organizations, and religious publications, the Nazis demanded that Catholic clergymen give up all political activity. With the approval of the bishops, who wanted to believe that the regime would honor a written agreement, the executive council dissolved the Center Party on July 5. Germany's last independent political party, often a staunch supporter of democracy, passed peacefully out of existence. Acting as Hitler's personal representative, Franz von Papen signed the Concordat on July 20, pledging that the government would guarantee all traditional rights and religious activities of the Catholic Church. Eugenio Pacelli, former Papal Nuncio in Germany who became Vatican Secretary of State in 1930, signed the Concordat. He would become Pope Pius XII in 1939.

On July 14 Hitler proclaimed that the NSDAP was Germany's sole political party. The following November, there was a Reichstag election with only NSDAP candidates on the ballot. Hitler convened the all-Nazi Reichstag occasionally to serve as an approving audience for propaganda speeches and policy statements. As for other political activity, Hitler decreed that any attempt to found a new party or to work within the shell of an old one would be punishable by imprisonment. The Gestapo enforced the decree, but the regime never succeeded in eradicating all opposition before the outbreak of war. Kept under constant Gestapo surveillance, leaders of the Center and the State Party were silent, but the Socialists and Communists were more active. Several SPD leaders did go to Prague, where they published reports on life under the Third Reich. Party members inside Germany supplied the information and circulated the reports throughout the country.[5] The Communists, left leaderless by the arrest or flight of party officials, distributed anti-Nazi leaflets and tried to mobilize discontent among the workers. Both groups were high on the Gestapo's list, and eventually nearly all of them were arrested. Socialist and Communist opposition was real and persistent, but it never constituted a meaningful threat to Hitler's power.

The Nazis had cause to celebrate Hitler's first nine months in office. He had abolished the labor unions and political parties, and the *Gleichschaltung* of the state was virtually complete. Terror, as evidenced by thousands of dissidents languishing in newly erected concentration camps, and propaganda, skillfully directed and relentlessly delivered by Goebbels's ministry, had been, and would continue to be, essential to the Führer's success. In November 1933 Hitler staged his first plebiscite, another means of political manipulation. Nearly 90 percent of the electorate voted *Ja*, approving Germany's withdrawal from the Geneva Disarmament Conference and the League of Nations. Hitler interpreted the vote as an enthusiastic endorsement of his leadership, which, for the most part, it was. He ignored nearly 3 million voters who expressed their disapproval by marking their ballots improperly (there was no "against" square on the ballot). A courageous action to be sure, but it was hardly more than a ripple on the surface of Hitler's road to total power. Shortly after the plebiscite, Franz von Papen, speaking on behalf of the government, congratulated Hitler: "In nine months, the genius of your leadership and the ideals which you have newly placed before us have succeeded in creating, from a people inwardly torn apart and without hope, a united Reich."[6]

Consolidation of Power: 1934

After a year in office, two important institutions had eluded Hitler's total control. They were the SA, the party's paramilitary arm of over 4 million increasingly restless storm troopers, and the army, which had not been subjected to *Gleichschaltung*. Ernst Röhm and other SA leaders held that the "Nazi Revolution," the establishment of Hitler's dictatorship, was incomplete. They favored a second revolution that would bring the bureaucracy, big business, and the army under party control. To Röhm, only the latter seemed attainable by the spring of 1934. The army enthusiastically supported Hitler's authoritarian rule and his commitment to rearmament, but the generals were uncertain about his attitude toward the SA. Consequently, they feared Röhm's avowed intention to combine the regular army and the SA into a "people's army," with himself as supreme commander.

Aware of unrest within SA ranks and genuinely grateful for what they had contributed to his success, Hitler sought to mollify Röhm and his followers. In December 1933 he appointed the SA leader to the cabinet as minister without portfolio and promulgated the Law for Securing the Unity of Party and State. Neither the appointment nor the law, which declared that the party was the pillar of the German state, "indissolubly linked to it" and theoretically dominant in all matters of state, satisfied Röhm. Nor was he moved by a 1934 New Year's greeting from Hitler, thanking the SA for its "imperishable services" to the party, but reminding its leader that a second revolution was both unnecessary and unwise. Responding in print a few weeks later, Röhm argued that the Nazi movement would wither away without a permanent revolutionary dynamic. "Adolf is rotten," he said to friends. "He's betraying all of us . . . to military and business reactionaries."[7] As a further embarrassment to Hitler, Röhm and several SA leaders continued to flaunt their homosexuality.

Hitler's dilemma was acute. On the one hand, he was reluctant to discipline the insubordinate, but still loyal, SA leader. On the other hand, the military's expertise and cooperation were essential to the fulfillment of his goals, and trusted lieutenants Göring and Heinrich Himmler reminded the Führer that he could not tolerate their archrival's "insubordination." Pressure from the military forced him to decide that the storm troopers were expendable. In April 1934 Hitler met with the generals and promised that the army would always be the "sole bearer of arms for the nation" and the SA would be "reduced to insignificance." The military chiefs agreed to swear an oath to his person when he succeeded Hindenburg, whose health was failing. With Hitler's approval, Göring and Himmler began laying plans for a blood purge of the SA.

Hitler had only to give the order for the purge to be carried out, but he took no action for another six weeks. On June 4 he ordered Röhm and the SA unit commanders to go on one month's leave. They complied, vigorously affirming their loyalty and denying rumors that the SA was planning a putsch. On June 17, while Hitler was still procrastinating, Vice Chancellor Papen attacked party radicals in a speech at the University of Marburg. He claimed that the SA, the violent "Marxist wing" of the party, was conspiring to overthrow the government. The speech was an indirect criticism of Hitler's leadership and implicitly challenged him to discipline Röhm and his lieutenants. A few days later, after he had threatened to resign, the vice chancellor received an ovation at a public appearance in Hamburg. Shortly thereafter, Hindenburg warned Hitler of the dangers of civil unrest and hinted at martial law.

On June 29 Hitler finally gave the order to implement the purge. The next morning, he flew to Munich where SS troops, furnished with transportation and weapons by the army, had already begun their work. In a resort hotel near the Bavarian capital, they shot several SA leaders in their rooms, one of them in bed with his male lover. Others were taken to a prison in the city and murdered. Hitler personally confronted Röhm in the

---

BOX 4.1   ■   A SPOKESMAN FOR THE REICH CABINET JUSTIFIES THE PURGE

At the meeting of the Reich Cabinet on Tuesday, July 3, the Reich chancellor, Adolf Hitler, began by giving a detailed account of the origin and suppression of the high treason plot. The Reich chancellor stressed that lightning action had been necessary, that otherwise many thousands of people would have been in danger of being wiped out.

Defense Minister General von Blomberg thanked the Führer in the name of the Reich Cabinet and the army for his determined and courageous action, by which he had saved the German people from civil war. The Führer had shown greatness as a statesman and soldier. This had aroused in the hearts of the members of the Cabinet and of the whole German people a vow of service, devotion, and loyalty in this grave hour.

The Reich Cabinet then approved a law on measures for the self-defense of the State. Its single paragraph reads:

> The measures taken on June 30 and July 1 and 2 to suppress the acts of high treason are legal, being necessary for the self-defense of the State.

Reich Minister of Justice Dr. Gürtner commented that measures of self-defense taken before the imminent occurrence of a treasonable action should be considered not only legal but also the duty of a statesman.

Jeremy Noakes and Geoffrey Pridham, *Documents on Nazism, 1919–1945* (New York: The Viking Press, 1975), p. 217.

---

hotel, accused him of treason, and urged him to take his own life. Röhm refused. SS men took him to a Munich prison and shot him several days later. Göring and Himmler directed the purge in Berlin. Some prominent victims were not associated with the SA, such as former chancellor Kurt von Schleicher and his aide, General Kurt von Bredow, Gustav von Kahr (Hitler had never forgotten Kahr's refusal to support the 1923 Beer Hall Putsch), and Gregor Strasser. Papen was placed under house arrest, but the author of his Marburg speech and his press secretary were murdered. For Hitler, the purge, called the Night of the Long Knives, was also a means of settling old scores.

In a radio address a few days later, Hitler announced that seventy-seven persons, all involved in a conspiracy to overthrow the government, had been liquidated. The death toll was probably much higher, although the exact figure will never be known. From official Germany there was nothing but praise for Hitler's "courageous action." Both Hindenburg and the minister of defense, General Werner von Blomberg, congratulated the Führer on behalf of the German people and the armed forces. The murder of two generals did not seem to disturb Blomberg, who, along with most civilians, breathed a sigh of relief. Hitler had crushed the Communists and the SA, thought to be the principal perpetrators of political violence. The people did not necessarily condone the murders, but they believed, or wanted to believe, that the Führer's blood purge was necessary to maintain law and order. Unencumbered by the revolutionary wing of the party, he was now free to establish a traditional authoritarian regime that would allow ordinary people to be comfortably apolitical. The people's silence gave consent, but fear of the Gestapo and SS also stifled protest.

For Hitler, Hindenburg's death on August 2 at age eighty-six, was perfectly timed. Shortly after delivering the eulogy at the state funeral, he issued a proclamation merging the offices of chancellor and president. Out of deference to the late field marshal, Hitler stated, he was to be addressed as Führer and Reich chancellor, never as president. A few days later the military fulfilled their part of the agreement: "I swear by God this holy oath that I will give unlimited obedience to the Führer of the German Reich, Adolf Hitler, the supreme commander of the Wehrmacht, and, as a brave soldier, will be ready at any time to lay down my life for this oath."[9] In a letter to Blomberg, Hitler repeated his assurance that only the army would bear arms for the nation. That promise blinded the military to the implications of the oath. By pledging obedience to the person of the Führer, they committed themselves to his murderous ideology. That was precisely what Hitler wanted. The army had become his accomplice.

In a plebiscite held on August 19, approximately 85 percent of the electorate voted in favor of merging the nation's two highest offices. Ignoring the nearly 6 million improperly marked ballots, Hitler declared: "Beginning with the highest office of the Reich through the entire administration down to the leadership of the smallest village, the German Reich is today in the hands of the National Socialist Party. The fight for governmental power has ceased as of this day."[9] The army had capitulated, and the insubordinate party leaders Strasser and Röhm were dead. Hindenburg's death, Schleicher's murder, and Papen's ambassadorial appointments to Austria in 1936 and Turkey in 1939 had virtually eliminated the leadership of the right. Hitler was the master of Germany with more real power over people's lives than any strongman in history, with the exception of his fellow totalitarian dictator, Josef Stalin.

The purge of the SA, the *Gleichschaltung* of the army, and the death of Hindenburg marked the end of a nineteen-month period of consolidation. No serious challenges to Hitler would be mounted until the abortive assassination plot of July 20, 1944. No further sweeping policy changes or purges were needed to enhance his power, which, according to Nazi theorist Ernst R. Huber, writing shortly after the August 1934 plebiscite, was "comprehensive and total." That power united in itself "all the instruments of political organization," extended to all areas of the people's life, and "comprehended all members of the community, who are obliged to give loyalty and obedience to the Führer."[10] The title of Führer charged his leadership with a unique legitimacy. His authority was supra-legal and nearly transcendent, resting on a self-appointed mission to lead Germany's drive to European supremacy and the claim that he embodied the people's racial will. This claim was the theoretical basis for the cult of the leader, the essence of Hitler's totalitarian power. In the 1930s it was unique. Unlike Stalin, whose predecessor left him both a power structure and an ideology, Hitler had largely himself to thank—through his charisma, fanaticism, political genius, and indomitable will—for his incredible success.

The Nazi State

Hitler the charismatic leader was also Germany's supreme policy maker and legislator. While assuming an active role in foreign policy, he practiced a more detached style of leadership in the domestic sphere. He allowed his loyal subordinates a good deal of latitude in managing political and economic affairs, but they worked in an atmosphere in which the only certainty was the Führer's supremacy. Hitler did not attach a high priority to efficiency, tradition, and orderly procedure. New appointments and offices led to duplication and overlapping jurisdictions, while lack of communication and coordination among government agencies, the rise and decline of individual empire builders, and vicious infighting among subordinates were normal. Hitler did not discourage his underlings from engaging in "brass knuckles" politics, for, as supreme arbiter, his personal power was enhanced in disputes. At worst, the Third Reich's administration was "chaotic."[11] At best, it was subject to constant improvisation, though it was never totally devoid of competent administrators.

A major source of political and administrative uncertainty was the relationship between party and state. Before January 30, 1933, the party's mission was to do whatever was necessary to install Hitler as chancellor. After the *Machtergreifung*, he appointed a handful of favorites to new and existing positions in the Reich government. At the local level, only the most astute and ambitious party leaders captured jobs, such as state commissioners and administrators, mayors, and rural district executives. Those Nazis were under no illusions about the political role of the NSDAP in the new regime. The party would never dominate the state as the Communist Party did in the Soviet Union. Loyalty, service, and sacrifice would not be automatically rewarded. Hitler's Law for Securing the Unity of Party and State, identifying the party as the pillar of the state and "indissolubly linked to it," established a theoretical principle, but meant little in practice. The SS bullets on the Night of the Long Knives offered convincing proof that an SA takeover of the army and party control of other institutions were never on the Führer's agenda.

Hitler's announcement on August 19, 1934, that the Reich was in the hands of the Nazi Party was only a rhetorical flourish. The levers of power were actually manipulated by the leader of the "movement," as Hitler liked to call it, supported by both Nazi and unaffiliated officeholders. While the NSDAP as such was not in charge, it had not lost its political influence. By the end of 1935, the party had more than 4 million members, about one-fourth of whom were "old fighters" who had joined in the 1920s. With 25,000 full-time employees, its own system of courts, and a well-stocked treasury, the party was a formidable political force.

In theory, Rudolf Hess, the head of the Party Chancellery, the Führer's deputy, and a cabinet minister, was the chief executive officer of the NSDAP. He was also one of fifteen Reichsleiters, the title given to the highest ranking officials of the party. Approximately forty Gauleiters and 920 Kreisleiters, all appointed directly by Hitler, presided over regional and district functions. Affiliated organizations for such groups as lawyers, judges, doctors, professors, teachers, students, and women, expanded their membership after the *Machtergreifung*. Sometimes these organizations could be the stepping-stones to real power. Hans Frank, head of the Nazi Lawyers' League, became one of Hitler's principal legal advisers; in October 1939 he was appointed governor general of occupied Poland.

At the Nuremberg party rally in 1935, Hitler addressed the still-confused relationship between party and state. The NSDAP as the "sole representative of the state" was to establish authority, discipline, and the general validity of the leadership principle. In its "educational and propagandistic role," said the Führer, the party was to serve as the "political selection organization" for the regime. He charged the state with the "continuation of the historic and developed administration of governmental agencies." Though not exactly a model of clarity and precision, this statement, with the operative words "educational and propagandistic," gave a sense of purpose to the millions of party members who had not become full-time employees of the state. With Hitler's blessing they would serve as propagandists and educators of the "Nazi state idea." In countless meetings and training sessions and by means of numerous political tracts, they explained government policies and taught the principles of Nazism to the masses. Without the work of the party faithful at the local level, Goebbels's high-powered propaganda machine would have been much less effective. These political tasks were of no small importance to the regime.

The party did serve as a "political selection organization." Nazi loyalists who had captured important positions were the principal practitioners of power in the regime. With few exceptions, no unaffiliated office holder or appointee was a major political force. Hitler needed and used professionals, but he never trusted them. Career bureaucrats staffed cabinet ministries and state and local government agencies, but the Führer usually appointed Nazi loyalists to positions of leadership. By 1936 the heads of most new agencies and a majority of cabinet chiefs were old fighters, often in jurisdictional conflict with qualified officials who were late joiners. An example of the latter was Franz Seldte, the minister of labor, whose authority was usurped by the German Labor Front. Although Robert Ley was an inept administrator and an alcoholic (nicknamed the "Reichboozer"), his swollen bureaucracy of party loyalists and SS men and the sheer size of the DAF "empire" simply made the ministry of labor redundant. Göring, a more able administrator, was another trusted lieutenant whose power ex-

Goebbels was fond of being photographed with his children, whose appearance, unlike that of their father, was identifiably Aryan.

panded at the expense of the professionals. Career military officers resented his appointment as head of the Luftwaffe in 1935. They were incensed when Hitler promoted Göring to the newly created rank of Reich Marshal. No general had ever attained such a lofty title.

It would have been difficult to write a manual on how to succeed in the Nazi regime. Luck, skill, ruthlessness, hard work, opportunism, and Hitler's support at the right time, under the right circumstances, and in the right combinations figured into the formula. All played a role in the success of Joseph Goebbels. Minister of propaganda and public enlightenment, Reichsleiter, and Gauleiter of Berlin, he was one of Hitler's most powerful lieutenants. Able and energetic, Goebbels overshadowed Alfred Rosenberg, the party's inept "supervisor of ideological instruction," whose reputation as a propagandist rested on the lip service Hitler paid to his limited talents as racial ideologue and party theoretician. Rosenberg was also chief of the

NSDAP foreign affairs bureau, but it could not compete with a rival party agency, the "Ribbentrop Bureau for Foreign Policy." Joachim von Ribbentrop, a former champagne salesman, impressed the Führer and eventually succeeded career diplomat Konstantin von Neurath as foreign minister.

Martin Bormann's case was exceptional. He was a Reichsleiter, largely because he married the daughter of a prominent, older Nazi. Bormann was Hess's top aide in the party chancellery, but he never held, nor did he seek, a government position. More than any individual in the hierarchy, Bormann gained influence and power by ingratiating himself with Hitler. Although the most ostentatiously obsequious of the Führer's followers, he was no mere flatterer. By skillfully managing the royalties from sales of *Mein Kampf* and other sources of income, he made Hitler a modestly wealthy man. Bormann also supervised the construction of the Berghof, the Führer's new Alpine residence near Berchtesgaden. Taking advantage of Hitler's confidence and Hess's inattentiveness to detail and noncombative personality, Bormann gradually assumed control of party personnel. He secured promotions for some of his cronies and found jobs in the state administration for others. By the outbreak of war in 1939, Bormann was closer than ever to Hitler and had become the de facto head of the NSDAP.

The SS and Nazi Terror

The most successful of Hitler's lieutenants was Heinrich Himmler. In less than a decade, he converted what originally had been a small branch of the SA into a powerful empire. Although no one could have imagined the enormous scope of the wartime SS—a state within a state of 900,000 men engaged in combat, managing concentration camps, and operating profitable civilian and military enterprises—Himmler had laid solid foundations before 1939. His bland, colorless personality and unassuming manner belied his ruthless ambition, administrative skill, and racial fanaticism. The Röhm purge had demonstrated the unconditional loyalty of the well-trained SS forces and their willingness to serve the Führer in any capacity. The rewards were substantial. In replacing the SA as the regime's exclusive paramilitary arm, the SS took control of all concentration camps. Shortly before the Night of the Long Knives, Göring, in return for Himmler's support in what might have become a prolonged internal power struggle, relinquished control of the Prussian political police. With Hitler's approval, the SS leader took charge of political police forces across Germany. Soon after the Röhm purge, they were consolidated into a national secret police, the Gestapo (an acronym for *Geheime Staatspolizei*, secret state police).

Himmler's meteoric rise continued. In June 1936 Hitler placed all police services under his jurisdiction and bestowed upon him the unique title of "Reich Leader SS and Chief of the German Police." Typical of the administrative inconsistency of the Third Reich, Himmler's decisions in both capacities had ministerial authority, even though he was not a cabinet officer. As chief of the German police, he reported to the minister of the interior; however, Frick's authority was nominal. As Reich Leader SS, Himmler answered only to Hitler, who trusted the "loyal Heinrich" implicitly and gave him a free hand to build the SS into the racially elite vanguard of the Nazi movement.

Fond of fantasizing about Germany's medieval past, Himmler likened the SS to a crusading order that offered masculine comradeship, discipline, and a sense of mission. While standards were high for all members, only the most intellectually, physically, and racially fit were permitted to attend SS leadership schools, where they received rigorous physical training and racial indoctrination. Graduating as officers, these young men, mostly from middle- and upper-class backgrounds, saw themselves as the new Nazi elite, the very embodiment of Hitler's ideology. In 1937 a young officer told Austrian writer Eugen Kogon that it was the mission of the SS to "exterminate all racially and biologically inferior elements" and to remove totally all "incorrigible political opposition . . . to the National Socialist state." Within ten years the SS would "dictate the law of Adolf Hitler to Europe, put a halt to the inevitable decay of the continent, and build a true community of nations, with Germany as the leading power."[12] If such radical goals were to be achieved, total identification with the new order was essential. All SS officers were required to sever religious and family ties, prove 100 percent Aryan ancestry as far back as 1750, and marry only women who were considered racially fit. Some officers fathered children out of wedlock with suitable Aryan partners, who were paid for their contribution to the Reich. In such cases, both children and mothers received care in *Lebensborn* (fount of life) institutions, which Himmler established in 1936.

Himmler never doubted that the SS would be the vanguard of Germany's master race and ruler of the new order. It was a romantic and cruel fantasy, but he was never out of touch with the reality of the regime's power struggles. Over the objections of high party officials in 1938, the SS Security Service (*Sicherheitsdienst*, SD), which had been reporting on public opinion since 1933, won the right to become the chief reporting agency for both party and state. The SD agents spied on party and government officials as well as ordinary people, and, in the absence of a free press, the Nazi leadership welcomed their candid public-opinion reports. Under the command of Reinhard Heydrich, a tall, blond, blue-eyed former naval officer, SD agents compiled incriminating dossiers on thousands of citizens, including those in Hitler's inner circle. In 1938 Himmler won yet another victory: the Führer granted him permission to arm a *Verfügungstruppe*, or special unit, of the SS. The formation of a combat unit, which became the nucleus of the Waffen SS (not so-called until 1940), broke Hitler's promise to the army that it would always be the sole bearer of arms for the German nation.

In June 1936 Himmler combined the Gestapo and the Ministry of the Interior's Criminal Police to form the two major branches of the Security Police, a new SS division commanded by Heydrich. The Gestapo, the most powerful of the new Nazi police agencies, had been under SS supervision before Himmler's appointment as the nation's police chief in 1936. Its well-deserved reputation for brutal efficiency was due in no small part to SS training. Recent research has shown that the Gestapo had less manpower than previously supposed; nevertheless, it became in 1933, and remained until 1945, the leading organ of terror and chief enforcer of racial doctrine, political conformity, and social policy under the Nazi regime. It was staffed by "capable and cruel officers" who applied "barbaric torture to disarm and destroy the regime's targeted enemies."[13] Heading the Gestapo's list of enemies were Communists, Socialists, Jews, and individuals suspected of political subversion, but other categories of prisoners in the concentration camps, such as homosexuals, Jehovah's Witnesses, and "asocials" (a designation for those who did not conform to the Nazi work ethic or social norms), were not spared. As the chief enforcer of Nazi terror, the Gestapo received support from a host of ordinary citizens who acted as informers and from other surveillance and policing divisions of the regime, such as the Criminal Police, party officials, the regular police, the SD, and other branches of the SS. Harsh treatment of targeted groups had the support of the great majority of people, who were neither interrogated nor arrested, but the Gestapo and its helpers created an atmosphere of terror in which no one had immunity from police brutality. "Fear made everybody suspicious of one another, thereby reinforcing the security system."[14]

Two systems of criminal justice operated in the Third Reich. Courts that existed before the Nazi takeover continued to function and to hand down verdicts in accordance with established civil and criminal law. In cases involving Nazi doctrine, the regime's officials pressured judges to convict persons who did not conform to new political, social, or racial standards. A second system was created by the Nazis. Special Courts (*Sondergerichte*), set up after the Reichstag fire to deal with politically suspicious persons, were under the jurisdiction of local, pro-Nazi state prosecutors. They usually found in the Gestapo's favor. Other arrestees were turned over to the party's People's Court, established in 1934. Some were "tried" by arresting Gestapo officers; many received no trial at all. Enforcement was uneven and sentences varied, but the eventual fate of many of the defendants was the concentration camp.

A celebrated case in 1938 illustrates how both systems worked. Pastor Martin Niemöller, the outspoken leader of a group of dissenting Protestant clergymen called the Confessing Church, was arrested in 1937 for violating the Insidious Acts Law, which defined criticism of party and state officials as a crime. Several months later a regular court pronounced him guilty, but released him on the grounds that he had served his sentence while awaiting trial in prison. Within hours he was seized by the Gestapo on Hitler's order (Niemöller had criticized the Führer to his face in an earlier meeting) and taken to the Sachsenhausen concentration camp. Later the outspoken pastor was transferred to Dachau, where he languished until the end of the war.

BOX 4.2 ■ **DISCIPLINE AT THE DACHAU CONCENTRATION CAMP**

Nazi administration may have been unsystematic, but punitive regulations for the Dachau camp were precise, detailed, specific, and chilling:

> The following are punishable with two weeks' solitary confinement: Anyone exchanging by his own volition . . . the quarters to which he is assigned, or insti-gating his fellow prisoners to do so. Anyone enclosing or hiding forbidden articles or articles produced in the camp in outgoing laundry bundles, or sewing them into pieces of laundry. Anyone entering or leaving barracks, shelters, or other buildings by other than authorized entrances, or creeping through windows or other openings. Anyone smoking in shelters, toilets and places which are fire haz-ards, or keeping or depositing flammable objects in such places. If a fire results from neglect of this prohibition, it will be considered as an act of sabotage [for which prisoners were sometimes hanged].
>
> [Solitary] confinement will be in a cell, with a hard bed, and with bread and wa-ter. The prisoner will receive warm food every four days. Punitive work consists of severe or particularly dirty work, performed under close supervision. Incidental punishments are: drilling, beatings, withholding of mail and food, hard rest, tying to stakes, reprimands and warnings.

Offenders considered as agitators were to be hanged. This included dis-cussing politics, forming cliques, collecting "true or false information about the concentration camp" and trying to smuggle this information to the out-side world. Agitators who tried to "seek contact with the outside world by giving light or other signals" or who sought to induce "others to escape or commit a crime" would suffer the death penalty.

Noakes and Pridham, pp. 285–86.

The SS Death's Head units (*Totenkopfverbände*) managed a network of concentration camps housing thousands of prisoners. The camps were laboratories where various forms of physical and emotional cruelty were practiced in order to achieve maximum dehumanization of the inmates. Color-coded triangles sewn to their clothing identified each prisoner's of-fense or association: red for political prisoners, green for common criminals, black for the work-shy and asocials (also called shiftless elements), yellow for Jews, purple for Jehovah's Witnesses, and pink for homosexuals. All prisoners lived together in crowded, extremely uncomfortable barracks, which they were required to keep impeccably neat. They were overworked, undernour-ished, and cruelly punished at random or for alleged infractions of camp rules. Some were hanged or shot; others died from the effects of torture or prolonged exposure to the inhuman conditions of the camp. Released prisoners were threatened with re-arrest if they disclosed details of their captivity. Nevertheless, the general public heard rumors about these cham-bers of horror, and all citizens knew that they were potential victims. The concentration camps, police brutality, and informers created a heightened sense of insecurity and, not coincidentally, a more compliant population.

Hitler's regime substantially altered the political landscape of Germany. The destruction of the form and substance of Weimar democracy, the abolition or realignment of established institutions, and the ruthless enforcement of harsh social and racial codes were radical, if not revolutionary, developments. The irony of an inefficient bureaucracy replacing the alleged disorder of the Weimar Republic was not lost on perceptive citizens. (For obvious reasons, it was risky to express that irony.) Germans were accustomed to dealing with a variety of officious bureaucrats, but the labyrinth of Nazi administration surpassed anything previously experienced. The people had to fill out longer forms, carry larger packets of identity papers, and deal with a host of authorities and agencies, often with overlapping jurisdictions. They were also required to attend numerous meetings and to listen to speeches. Everyone lived in the shadow of an arbitrary lawlessness, which made terror one of the hallmarks of the Third Reich. Hitler's capricious will constituted the supreme law, and ultimately the only law and political principle, in a society accustomed to order.

The Nazi Economy

Neither terror nor bureaucratic confusion stalled an economic recovery that lifted the nation out of the depths of the Great Depression. To the German people, it was one of the Führer's greatest achievements. Hitler's economic instincts were less acute than his brilliant political intuition, but he knew what he wanted: full employment to solidify popular support and industrial expansion to sustain a massive rearmament program. To achieve these goals, he favored almost any program or policy that would work, short of communist-style collectivization and confiscation. His instincts and economic advisers told him that, with the proper political guidance, the existing free-enterprise system was best suited to his purpose. He also rejected such sweeping measures as the nationalization of big business and the banking system and the breakup of large retail establishments, a pet idea of party radicals.

As in the political sphere, the Nazis' management of the economy was characterized by intense rivalry, duplication, overlapping jurisdictions, and lack of central direction. Industrialists, bankers, small businesses, and state agencies, including the military, engaged in wasteful, counter-productive, and bitter competition. Without Hjalmar Schacht there would have been even more mismanagement. Reichsbank president under the Weimar Republic and an internationally recognized financial expert with strong ties to the business community, Schacht believed that economic recovery depended on a fruitful partnership between government and the private sector, with the government establishing basic policy. Recognizing the urgent need for a consummate professional in the complex areas of economics and finance, the Führer reappointed Schacht to his old post at the Reichsbank and entrusted him with the key position of minister of economics.

From the beginning, rearmament was Hitler's highest priority. As early as February 1933, he revealed to his inner circle that Germany would defy the Treaty of Versailles and launch a major rearmament program. His military advisers and the foreign office were fearful of diplomatic repercussions, however, and Schacht suggested that a depressed economy could not sustain an extensive arms buildup. Hitler agreed to a less ambitious rearmament program, deficit spending, and a four-year plan of economic recovery, with reduction of unemployment to be given top priority. The government pumped funds into public works projects and provided tax incentives, low-interest loans, and subsidies for job-creating investments in the private sector. Like all Nazi programs, the four-year plan was accompanied by intensive propaganda, which in this instance stressed the will to triumph over economic difficulties, the common good over individual welfare (*Gemeinnutz vor Eigennutz*), and hard work. The latter was reinforced by the dismissal of shirkers and the arrest of the work-shy, whom authorities charged with deliberately refusing gainful employment. Nazi officialdom was quite consistent in enforcing a stringent work ethic.

By the end of 1935, economic recovery and a renewed sense of vitality, purpose, and community were apparent. More tangibly, the economy was producing impressive statistics. Unemployment fell by almost two-thirds, from a Depression high of nearly 6 million to 2.15 million. By comparison with its base of 100 points in 1928 (the last full year before the Depression), the index of industrial production rose from 66 in 1933 to 96 in 1935. In the same period, the gross national product (GNP) increased from 59 billion to 74 billion marks. Military expenditures expanded more rapidly, from 1.9 billion marks or 3 percent of the GNP in 1933 to 6 billion marks or 8 percent of the GNP in 1935.[15] The number of white-collar workers in government and business rose substantially, while services recorded more modest increases.

Highly visible public works projects provided employment for hundreds of thousands. The Third Reich experienced a construction boom, including new housing, remodeling and repair of existing facilities, public buildings, bridges, roads, and land reclamation projects. Some of the workers were young men between the ages of 18 and 25 who were fulfilling the Reich Labor Service's requirement to perform six months of manual labor. (The Reich Labor Service was a branch of the DAF.) The most spectacular and expensive public works project was a network of *autobahns* (superhighways) built under the able leadership of an old Nazi engineer, Fritz Todt. His empire, called "Organization Todt," completed the first controlled-access highway system in the world. It did not matter to Hitler that few citizens could afford to own a car. The autobahns provided jobs (52,000, with 100,000 employed in related industries, according to Todt's speech at the 1934 party rally), stirred German pride, impressed foreign visitors, and, most important, made splendid roadways for military vehicles.

Statistically, Germany was out of the Great Depression at the end of 1936, when unemployed workers totaled 1.6 million, and the index of

NATIONAL ARCHIVES

Hitler breaks ground for a new autobahn. The autobahns were the centerpiece of the Nazis' public works program.

industrial production registered 107, surpassing 1928 levels for the first time. The economic recovery was due in no small part to the self-discipline, skill, and hard work of the German people. Government policy played a significant role, but its contribution is impossible to measure precisely. Indeed, Nazi economic policy did not lend itself easily to classification at the time and does not do so in retrospect. The government did not nationalize big business, but it imposed strict controls on production, labor relations, pricing and marketing policies, investments, foreign trade, and the use of foreign currency. For most industries, the regime rejected the fascist "corporate state" model (Mussolini's highly touted government/private sector corporations, twenty-two in all), but in agriculture the Reich

Autobahns were designed to accommodate both military vehicles and civilian traffic, though the latter never materialized under the Third Reich.

Nutrition Estate, to which all landowners, tenants, processors, and whole-sale and retail distributors were required to belong, fixed prices, regulated supplies, and prescribed charges for every phase of food processing.

For Hitler, Germany's economic progress—for strategic and ideological reasons—was too slow. To achieve its expansionist goals and prepare itself for what he believed to be an inevitable conflict with Bolshevism, the Reich needed to increase industrial growth and the production of war matériel. Against the advice of Schacht, who favored a slower pace of rearmament and strengthening the domestic economy, Hitler opted for a more radical approach. Speaking at the 1936 party rally, he announced his decision to launch a second four-year plan. Its goal was clear: "The German Army must be operational in four years. The German economy must be fit for war within four years."[16] Such an outcome was necessary, Hitler declared, because the world was moving toward a conflict with Bolshevism, whose essence and aim . . . is solely the elimination of those strata of mankind (i.e., the Aryan race) and their replacement by world-wide Jewry." Bolshevism's victory would result in the "annihilation of the German people."[17] To defeat this enemy, Hitler asserted, the Reich's army would have to be the world's best equipped, the most rigorously trained, and the most ideologically motivated.

Hitler offered few details about achieving economic growth. He did cite the importance of hard work, sacrifice, strong political leadership, and territorial expansion, but the task of administering the program was assigned to Hermann Göring, whose appointment as head of the four-year plan marked the end of Hjalmar Schacht's influence and ultimately his resignation as minister of economics and president of the Reichsbank. Göring announced that industry was to become self-sufficient in strategic materials, such as rubber, oil, iron ore, aluminum, and nonferrous metals used in the manufacture of high-grade steel. Autarky, or economic self-sufficiency, was an ambitious goal and, given the Reich's supply of raw materials, a totally unrealistic one.

The four-year plan's only unqualified success was synthetic rubber, which was produced in sufficient quantities for export by the giant chemical firm, I.G. Farben. Several coal gasification plants were erected, but they produced only enough fuel to supply 20 percent of Germany's needs during the war. Despite Hitler's threats ("businessmen will perish if they fail"), steel magnates Krupp and Thyssen refused to develop extensive deposits of low-grade iron ore in northern Germany on the grounds that the cost would be prohibitive. The government therefore financed the construction of the huge "Hermann Göring Works" in order to exploit these deposits. This quasi-socialist enterprise produced about one-fourth of its projected goal of 8 million tons of pig iron and steel annually. By the outbreak of war in 1939, the Hermann Göring Works, along with expropriated Austrian and Czech steel mills, met less than one-third of Germany's requirements. For most of its iron-ore needs, and for virtually all aluminum, natural petroleum, and nonferrous metals, Germany had to rely on imports.

To guarantee the flow of strategic materials, the government imposed tight restrictions on foreign trade and currency. In spite of a propaganda barrage against eating "un-German" foods, most foreign-currency reserves were used to pay for imported foodstuffs, which amounted to about 20 percent of total consumption. Bilateral trade agreements were negotiated with Yugoslavia and Hungary, whereby both would ship aluminum ore in return for German manufactured goods of roughly the same value. Romanian oil and Spanish tungsten were acquired through similar barter arrangements. To increase foreign-currency reserves, the government lowered the price of German goods to countries whose businesses and governments agreed to pay with their own currencies. Though the Reich fell far short of autarky, through various arrangements it did provide sufficient quantities of strategic materials to fuel the war machine.

Economic recovery continued its uneven course under the four-year plan. Including the Reich Labor Service's six-month compulsory service and the hundreds of thousands of military conscripts temporarily withdrawn from the workforce (the draft was reinstituted in 1935), the government reported full employment by the end of 1938. There were actually shortages of highly skilled workers in the arms industry. Total industrial output was 25 percent greater than in 1928, and the GNP reached 105 billion marks. Production of capital goods, including war matériel, rose by 44 percent, while consumer goods showed an increase of 16 percent. Despite government controls and higher taxes, big business fared better than smaller enterprises. Public works projects and construction continued to flourish, but there was a shortage of adequate housing in the heavily industrialized cities, whose populations were swelled by an influx of workers. Government spending rose to

35 percent of the national income in 1938 (compared to 24 percent in Great Britain and 11 percent in the United States), and the national debt of 12 billion marks in 1933 had quadrupled by 1939. Both contributed to short-term economic growth, though neither was a sign of a healthy economy.[18]

Several sectors of the economy did not surpass their 1928 levels. The total volume of foreign trade in 1939 was only 50 percent of the pre-Depression high. Commerce with industrialized nations dropped off sharply, while trade with underdeveloped areas rose during the late 1930s. Retail trade at the peak of the Reich's peacetime economy was somewhat healthier, but reached only 85 percent of the 1928 volume. Farmers harvested more potatoes and sugar beets, but total food production and farm income barely exceeded 1933 levels. Despite lower taxes, declining interest rates, and propaganda glorifying the peasant, more than 700,000 farmers had left the land by 1939.[19]

Göring's oft-quoted phrase, "guns instead of butter," was partly true. Guns had top priority, but austerity was never part of the Nazi plan. With the notable exception of the Jews, the standard of living for nearly all Germans in 1939 exceeded Depression levels. While the affluent minority was considerably better off, even those who fared relatively less well, such as small businessmen, craftsmen, farmers, and semi-skilled and unskilled workers, obtained at least small rewards from the nation's economic recovery. Real wages, or purchasing power, rose slightly, but the total amount of wages declined from 62 percent of the national income in 1928 to 57 percent ten years later. There were no sharp tax increases for wage-earners, and the government maintained health and retirement insurance plans at their pre-1933 levels. As an inducement to have more children, the regime increased the family allowance, a nontaxable stipend for each child.

For nonaffluent citizens, however, economic gains did not compensate fully for losses. Many small businesses recorded reduced profits because government price controls favored large corporations. Labor lost the right to strike and bargain collectively, and labor-management councils of the German Labor Front usually settled disputes in favor of management. Some workers were involuntarily moved to other job locations, where they often lived in substandard housing. Except for highly skilled workers employed by firms manufacturing war matériel, wages were frozen at 1932 levels. This meant that ordinary wage-earners could increase their take-home pay only by working longer hours. Many were forced to do so to make up for higher taxes and insurance payments and such new payroll deductions as dues for the German Labor Front, fees for party membership, and "contributions" to Winter Relief, a Depression welfare program that was no longer needed in 1938. Increased purchasing power did not necessarily result in higher living standards.[20] By 1938 the SD reported widespread complaints about spot rationing, shortages, and poor quality of consumer goods. For millions of hard-working citizens, there was no economic miracle under the Third Reich.

BOX 4.3 ■ WAGES AND EARNING POWER IN THE
THIRD REICH

A government report for the first quarter of 1937 is generally optimistic, but
does admit to a few problems:

> Hourly wages have generally increased. This time, owing to seasonal factors, only
> the consumer goods industries have had no share in this increase. The production
> goods industries, above all the trades indirectly or directly involved in armaments,
> are almost entirely responsible for the increase in wages here mentioned. Thus,
> hourly wages in the spring of 1937 are approximately 8 percent (December 1936:
> 7.3 percent), [and] weekly earnings approximately 19 percent above the level of
> autumn 1933. In assessing these figures, however, it must be borne in mind that
> only averages are given here, which include . . . higher wage increases as well as
> those of lower increases or even wage decreases. Thus 2.5 billion of the increase in
> total earnings . . . from approximately 12 billion in 1933 to 18 billion in 1936
> consists of increases in hourly wages and increased earnings due to a longer work-
> ing week. . . .

Noakes and Pridham, pp, 447–48.

Writing in 1982, author Bernt Engelmann, who was involved in anti-Nazi
activities, recalls a 1939 conversation in Berlin with a friend, who, like millions of workers, was struggling to make ends meet.

> "Where are you working?"

> "At the electrical equipment plant in the S-division. S for secret. They have us
> working so hard you'd think the war was starting next week. My brother works in
> Wittenau, north of the city, at a branch of Düren Metals where all they make is
> airplane parts. They're even worse off than we are. They're up to twelve hours a
> day now, and they're constantly being forced to increase their output—all for 35
> marks a week. And half of that gets deducted for dues, food, and contributions.
> I make 24 marks a week, but I take home only 15. You can't live on that. If we
> didn't have the garden, we'd starve."

Engelmann, p. 157.

Conclusion

Hitler's popularity was at its peak on April 28, 1939, eight days after his
fiftieth birthday, when he delivered a speech taking full credit for the
regime's political and economic achievements:

> I overcame chaos in Germany, restored order, and enormously raised
> production in all fields of our national economy. I succeeded in com-
> pletely resettling in useful production those seven million unemployed
> who so touched all our hearts. I have not only politically united Ger-
> many, but rearmed it militarily.[21]

Most Germans accepted Hitler's claim to be the architect of material progress, political unity, and military strength. Concentration camps, shortages of consumer goods, and other political and economic problems were blamed on subordinates. If allowed to speak freely, the few who would have denounced Gestapo terror, bureaucratic inefficiency, regimentation in the workplace, and an uneven economic recovery probably would have hailed

This poster with the "Ein Volk, Ein Reich, Ein Führer" caption bore Hitler's most popular formal portrait.

Hitler as a great statesman. Only a handful would have realized that, for their Führer, political unity and economic recovery were only means to an end. Germany had been "rearmed militarily," and for Hitler that was all that mattered.

Hitler's Germany was a totalitarian state. The violence and terror, political oppression, cult of the leader, intensive propaganda, and demand for total allegiance to an official ideology defined the Nazi regime. Hitler was the supreme head of the government and leader of the nation. Neither his subordinates nor the German people mistook a detached executive style and inefficient administration for weakness. There was also an immoral dimension to Hitler's new order. Totalitarianism has been aptly described as a "system of mass conscription into complicity with evil."[22] Many were conscripted willingly, some passively, and a few involuntarily, but most were ultimately drawn into a web of deceit, brutality, and finally murder. This process of politicization was unprecedented in German history. It was difficult to avoid participation in a regime in which evil was the rule rather than the exception.

INFOTRAC® COLLEGE EDITION SEARCH TERMS

For additional reading go to Infotrac College Edition, your online research library at http://www.infotrac-college.com.

Enter the search term "concentration camps Germany" using Keywords.

Enter the search term "Goebbels, Joseph" using the Subject Guide.

Enter the search term "Goering, Hermann" using the Subject Guide.

Enter the search term "Himmler, Heinrich" using the Subject Guide.

Notes

1. Ian Kershaw, *The Nazi Dictatorship* (London: Edward Arnold, 1989), p. 62. Hans Mommsen, a prominent German historian, characterized Hitler as a "weak dictator" in the 1960s.

2. Konrad Heiden, *The Fuehrer* (Boston: Houghton Mifflin, 1944), p. 579.

3. Mary Fulbrook, *The Divided Nation* (New York: Oxford University Press, 1992), p. 694.

4. Gordon Craig, *Germany 1866–1945* (New York: Oxford University Press, 1978), p. 590.

5. Detlev Peukert, *Inside Nazi Germany* (London: Bratsford, 1987), p. 49.

6. Quoted in Ian Kershaw, *Hitler 1889–1936: Hubris* (New York: Norton, 1999), p. 429.

7. Quoted in Joachim Fest, *Hitler* (Harcourt Brace Jovanovich, 1973), p. 451.

8. Quoted in Craig, p. 589.

9. Quoted in Karl D. Bracher, *The German Dictatorship* (New York: Praeger Publishers, 1970), p. 246.

10. Quoted in Craig, p. 590.

11. Kershaw, *The Nazi Dictatorship*, pp. 65–67; Fulbrook, pp. 73–74.

12. Eugen Kogon, *The Theory and Practice of Hell* (London: Secker and Warburg, 1950), p. 15.

13. Eric A. Johnson, *Nazi Terror: The Gestapo, Jews, and Ordinary Germans* (New York: Basic Books, 1999), p. 485.

14. Jeremy Noakes and Geoffrey Pridham, eds., *Documents on Nazism, 1919–1945* (New York: Viking Press, 1975), p. 291. Widespread popular support for Gestapo terror and the regime's repressive racist policies form the central thesis of Robert Gellately, *Backing Hitler: Consent and Coercion in Nazi Germany* (Oxford University Press, 2001).

15. Volker R. Berghahn, *Modern Germany* (New York: Cambridge University Press, 1982), p. 146; John Hiden, *Germany and Europe, 1919–1939* (London: Longman, 1993), p. 211.

16. *Documents on German Foreign Policy* (Washington, DC, 1966), Series C, 5: 862.

17. Ian Kershaw, *Hitler 1936–1945: Nemesis* (New York: W. W. Norton, 2000), pp. 19–20.

18. Hajo Holborn, *A History of Modern Germany, 1840–1945* (New York: Alfred A. Knopf, 1969), pp. 751, 755.

19. David Schoenbaum, *Hitler's Social Revolution* (New York: Doubleday, 1966), p. 150.

20. Bernt Engelmann, *In Hitler's Germany* (New York: Schocken Books, 1986), p. 157.

21. Quoted in Sebastian Haffner, *The Meaning of Hitler* (New York: MacMillan, 1979), p. 32.

22. George F. Will, "Public Television Curls Up with a Good Book," *Rocky Mountain News*, February 17, 1989, p. 53.

Nazi Germany, 1933–1939:
Culture and Society

The Nazis had established a totalitarian state and achieved economic recovery, but they had promised more. German society was to be transformed into a *Volksgemeinschaft*, a national or racial community. That task was still unfinished, as Hitler acknowledged in August 1934 when he stated that "the fight for our precious people continues." To win the hearts and minds of the uncommitted, without which a *Volksgemeinschaft* could not exist, the propaganda ministry, the party, and the SS would have to intensify their efforts to radicalize the nation's cultural, intellectual, and social life. The goal was a society without traditional class distinctions, populated by "folk comrades"—that is, Aryans who were racially, physically, mentally, and ideologically sound. Since the primary test for membership was racial purity, Jews and Gypsies, who were classified as non-Aryans, were disqualified. The regime also excluded an ever-widening range of "unfit" persons, such as criminals, vagrants, asocials, unproductive workers, homosexuals, Jehovah's Witnesses, the mentally and physically handicapped, and anyone who re-fused to conform to prescribed social and political norms.[1] In theory, all folk comrades were equal, but in practice the leadership principle, as in the political sphere, separated the leaders from the followers.

Historians debate the extent of cultural, ideological, and social change during the first six years of the Third Reich. Some detect the emergence of a distinctive culture, the establishment of an official ideol-ogy, and a leveling of society. Others hold that the Nazis' vaunted "cultural revolution" was superficial, their ideology hollow, and the talk of *Volksge-meinschaft* mere rhetoric. This chapter will focus on the Strength-through-Joy program, the Nuremberg party rallies, the Reich Chambers of Cul-ture, education, youth, women, the family, the churches, and persecution of the "racially unfit." Discussion and analysis of these aspects of the cul-tural, intellectual, and social history of the Third Reich show that Nazi leaders often had clear ideas that they vigorously pursued. Bureaucratic ineptitude, lukewarm support from many, and opposition from a few slowed, but never seriously threatened, their march toward the racial community. By the outbreak of war in 1939, the foundations of the *Volksgemeinschaft* were firmly in place.

Ideological Programs and Symbols

Nazi ideology consisted of a set of propositions rather than systematic doctrine. Three of the principal themes were the idea of struggle, racialism, and the Führer mystique. Struggle for supremacy over individuals, nations, and races, one of Hitler's favorite touchstones, buttressed the leadership principle and the Nazi war ethos. Aryan racial superiority provided the ideological foundation for the *Volksgemeinschaft*. The person of the Führer, his unique role as charismatic leader and his sense of mission, was an indispensable component of Nazi ideology. It ignited an emotional spark and aroused religious fervor. When Hitler spoke, Goebbels wrote, "one had the feeling that Germany had been transformed into a single great church . . . into which its intercessor stepped before the throne of the Almighty to bear witness."[2] These ideological themes and their variations gave rise to a host of programs, policies, and symbols.

Strength-through-Joy was representative of the new programs designed to build the *Volksgemeinschaft*. Inaugurated in the fall of 1933 under the auspices of the German Labor Front, it aimed to promote a sense of community and to enhance the enjoyment of life. Generously funded and highly popular, the program supplied discounted tickets to plays, concerts, and operas to citizens who previously could not afford to attend cultural events. Strength-through-Joy arranged inexpensive vacation trips to places previously beyond the means of ordinary wage-earners, such as the Norwegian coast and Mediterranean islands. It had a fleet of ships, owned a resort hotel on a Baltic island, and provided a two-week vacation in the Alps for $15 per person.

Strength-through-Joy promoted the Volkswagen, the "people's car." Hitler helped design it and wanted to name it the "Strength-through-Joy car." (He reluctantly approved the name Volkswagen, inadvertently contributing to the automaker's success after World War II.) In August 1938 German Labor Front chief Robert Ley announced that a payment of five marks a week would guarantee ownership of a Volkswagen after an unspecified period of time. The total cost of the car was 990 marks, the equivalent of $235. A few Volkswagens were built, but none were delivered to the thousands who made their payments every week until the end of the war. From the outset, the Volkswagen factory at Wolfsburg manufactured military vehicles.

Ley's touting of the Volkswagen expressed the philosophy of Strength-through-Joy. He pointed out that the purchase of a Volkswagen,

This poster was published before the "KdF-Wagen" (Strength-through-Joy car) was re-named "Volkswagen." It reads: "If you want to drive your own car, you need to save only five marks a week." The caption below reads: "Information about the purchase price and method of payment is available at Strength-through-Joy offices in the Munich area."

now possible for each German "without distinction of class, profession, or property," would be a "powerful step forward in the development of the German people" and a way of "saying thank you to the Führer."[3] To the millions who participated, the Strength-through-Joy program delivered the culture and amenities of what appeared to be the Führer's dynamic *Volksgemeinschaft.* Along with joy, it promoted egalitarianism. "There was democracy in Nazism and it was real," said a rank-and-file party member after the war. "We simple working class men stood side by side with the upper classes in the programs of the Labor Front. We had something in common."[4]

While Strength-through-Joy was attempting to weld the German people into a community, the Propaganda Ministry was working to ensure that the community would be a Nazi one by nationalizing Nazi symbols and festivals. The swastika banner became the flag of the German Reich in March 1933, and soon after, the "Horst Wessel Song" took its place beside "Deutschland über Alles" as a second national anthem. Nazi anniversaries became legal holidays. January 30 and February 24, respectively, marked the seizure of power in 1933 and the first proclamation of the party program in 1920. Hitler's birthday on April 20 was celebrated with pomp appropriate to the founder of the "thousand-year Reich." An October harvest festival praised the peasant as the embodiment of the "blood and soil" of the racial community. The people honored the "martyrs" of the 1923 Beer Hall Putsch and paid tribute to the old fighters of the

At the Nuremberg rallies, uniformed masses standing at attention and marching for their Führer provided an awesome visual display of the Nazi regime's power.

movement's early years on November 9, the most solemn day of the Nazi year. Other holidays, such as Heroes' Memorial Day and Christmas, were Nazified, the latter without much success. Most Germans continued to observe Christmas in the traditional way. Participation in holiday ceremonies was compulsory for members of the party and affiliated organizations. Others were encouraged to witness demonstrations and parades, to attend party gatherings, and to listen to the Führer, either in person or on the radio.

The Nuremberg party rally, held annually during the second week of September, dwarfed all other Nazi festivals. Held in a gigantic stadium designed to direct all eyes to Hitler's rostrum, it enthralled both Germans and foreign visitors. Masses of uniformed men, the army, the SS and SA, the Hitler Youth, and work battalions marched in close-order drill and stood in symmetrical ranks to cheer the Führer. Spirited band music accompanied parades and demonstrations, with participants often serving as the chorus. By directing hundreds of searchlight beams skyward, Hitler's architect Albert Speer created a spectacle so fantastic that the British ambassador called it a "cathedral of light." The grand finale, also taking place after dark, was Hitler's principal address to the party faithful.

Hitler was the star of the show. "It was the Führer who was celebrated at Nuremberg, not Nazism as an idea or the party as an organization," wrote Hans Frank in his Nuremberg prison cell in 1946. "The crowd burned with fervor around Hitler, the Savior, Creator, and Defender of the German fatherland."[5] To foreign visitors, the fervor was contagious. The French ambassador, Francois-Poncet, observed: "Many visitors, dazzled by Nazi display, were infected by the virus of Nazism. They returned home convinced by the doctrine and filled with admiration for the performance."[6] At one of the rallies several foreign correspondents, caught up in the excitement of the moment, rose to their feet and with arms outstretched in the Hitler salute joined the German crowd in singing "Deutschland, Deutschland über Alles."

Hitler's agenda at each of the rallies was carefully planned weeks in advance. No detail was overlooked. Upon landing at the Nuremberg airport, he was conveyed to a hotel by a motorcade while thousands cheered. Later he reviewed his marching followers, greeted groups, and delivered long speeches to the party leadership and members of affiliated organizations. Besides propaganda and pep talks, Hitler addressed specific issues at each of the rallies. In 1934 he explained to the SA and SS that the Röhm purge had strengthened and unified the movement. Germany's Jews were the target of his wrath in 1935, as he proclaimed the first of the Nuremberg laws, which stripped Jews of their citizenship. Two weeks before the Munich Agreement in 1938, the Czech government felt the fury of a Hitler tirade, including ominous threats of war. It was the last party rally; they had served their purpose well. No other forum of Nazi propaganda glorified the Führer so magnificently.

The Reich Chambers of Culture

The mission of "total propaganda," according to Goebbels, was to influence all sectors of public life. To convert existing cultural institutions into agencies of the propaganda ministry, he established the Reich Chamber of Culture in the fall of 1933. It quickly burgeoned into a large bureaucracy, with seven subchambers: press, radio, literature, theater, film, fine arts, and music. The regime required all persons involved in the creation, reproduction, processing, dissemination, or circulation of any form of the media to join the chambers. The net was a wide one, snaring editors, writers, printers, retailers, artists, musicians, directors, announcers, engineers, and technicians. Nothing could be printed, broadcast, displayed, or performed without the approval of the chambers. Individuals whose pre-1933 work did not conform to new racial or ideological standards (Jews, leftists, democrats) did not qualify for membership. Others were expelled after Hitler seized power, and book publishers and newspapers were shut down. Nonmembers suffered exile, financial hardship, or imprisonment.

The Reich Chamber of the Press was the largest, and it faced the formidable task of capturing the nation's press. Germans read newspapers avidly; at least 4,700 papers were being published in January 1933. Max Amann, head of the Press Chamber and the party's publisher, controlled about 2.5 percent of all newspapers at that time, including the leading Nazi daily, the *Völkischer Beobachter*. Under Amann's direction, frequent press conferences at the Propaganda Ministry, government-controlled news services, and rigorously enforced standards for content, style, and format, became the rule for all newspapers and periodicals. Editors were propagandists, according to Goebbels, and were held responsible for what they printed and for making their newspapers toe the party line. So strictly enforced were the standards that hundreds of newspapers were shut down each year. By 1942 only 977 publications remained, and Amann controlled 80 percent of them.[7] It was a captive press, offering censored news, ideologically correct editorials, and innocuous features.

Already a government monopoly by 1928, the radio was relatively easy to manage. Shortly after Hitler took over, the Propaganda Ministry acquired all shares of the National Broadcasting Company and controlling interest in all regional companies. The Radio Chamber not only dictated the programming schedule, but also pressured manufacturers to produce affordable radios, called *Volksempfänger* (people's receivers). Each was equipped with a device that could jam foreign broadcasts. By 1936 at least 30 million people could be reached over the radio, not including those subjected to broadcasts through public loudspeakers on the streets or in restaurants. The Radio Chamber even scheduled special music for factories and "inspirational messages" to be aired during work breaks. Stations broadcast managed news, presented political programs, and, with carefully selected music and cultural programming, "shaped leisure evening hours."[8] Best of all, from the Nazi point of view, the radio served as an effective medium for the Führer's oratorical talents. Making full use of the new medium, Hitler became one of the world's first political mass communicators.

No other cultural event of the Third Reich is more firmly etched in historical memory than the book burnings. On May 10, 1933, members of Goebbels's staff ignited these highly publicized bonfires in public squares and university towns all over the country. Consigned to the flames were the works of such well-known Jews as Karl Marx, Sigmund Freud, and the poet Heinrich Heine. (A century earlier, Heine had warned that, where books are burned, sooner or later people would be burned.) Aryan authors classified as leftist or democratic, such as Thomas Mann, Hermann Hesse, Bertolt Brecht, and Erich Maria Remarque, fared no better. "The past is lying in flames," said Goebbels, and "the future will rise from the flames in our hearts . . . . Brightened by these flames our vow shall be: the Reich and the Nation and our Führer. Adolf Hitler: Heil! Heil! Heil!"[9]

The Literature Chamber followed up on the literary conflagration by purging libraries and bookstores, shutting down publishing houses, supervising the publication of new books, and issuing blacklists. Remarque's anti-war novel *All Quiet on the Western Front* was an obvious choice, but the chamber also blacklisted obscure science fiction works, such as *War with the Newts*, denounced for its "attempt to ridicule the racial idea, and Germany's defensive battle against the Jews." Showing the regime's puritanical streak, the chamber classified as undesirable a novel dealing with "erotic relationships of young girls." In deference to Hitler's ally Mussolini, a book titled *Mountain Fate* was attacked for making "foul comments about Italian mountain guides."[10]

Nevertheless, there was no dearth of reading material in Nazi Germany. Sentimental love stories and romantic peasant novels sold well, as did novels about officially approved heroes, historical events, mysteries, and adventures. In the latter category, tales of the American wild west by Hitler's favorite author, Karl May, sold briskly. Among classics, Shakespeare and Goethe were considered safe, but Schiller, whose dramas "criticized political authority," was not recommended. Not surprisingly, works by prominent Nazis, such as Rosenberg's *Myth of the Twentieth Century* and Goebbels's romantic novel *Michael*, appeared on bookshelves all over the country. *Mein Kampf* became a bestseller, though not necessarily the most widely read book in Germany.

Some respected literary figures preferred exile to conformity. Joining the exodus were the Mann brothers and Thomas's son Klaus, Stefan and Arnold Zweig, and Alfred Döblin. Among the well-known authors who remained to defend Nazism were the playwright Gerhard Hauptmann, an aging, politically flexible relic, and the poet Gottfried Benn. In responding to an attack by Klaus Mann, Benn offered a rationale for an intellectual's support of Nazism. Mann had pointed out that Benn and others like him were too sympathetic to the irrational: "Then suddenly one has arrived at the cult of violence, and then one is with Adolf Hitler." In his reply Benn wrote of a "change in the direction of German history," based on a "conception of human nature which is mythical and profound." He boasted of his commitment to National Socialism, "because it is my people who are making themselves a new destiny."[11]

Building on such sentiments, Goebbels molded the theater and the movies into forums for entertainment and propaganda. The Theater Chamber closed few theaters, but forced into exile nonconformist luminaries such as Berthold Brecht, Kurt Weill, and director Max Reinhardt. As in literature, all Jewish works and plays with social criticism or politically incorrect content were banned. Light operas, comedies, historical dramas, and new plays with a political message dominated the playbills. Goebbels invented "art observation" to replace criticism. "Observers" were allowed only to praise, and in the case of boring ideological dramas, they were required to do so. The new artistic standards dismayed critics in exile, but attendance at German theaters, swelled by the lower classes with their Strength-through-Joy tickets, was greater than ever.

The innovation, creativity, and vitality of the Weimar Republic's film industry died in 1933. Keenly interested in movies, Goebbels quickly seized control of the industry. The Film Chamber banned most films made before the *Machtergreifung*, dictated the subject matter of new productions, and gradually acquired controlling interest in all movie studios. Goebbels had a hand in producing at least 100 of the approximately 1,000 feature films made from 1933 to 1945. Several were explicitly ideological, such as the spectacular wartime epic *Kolberg* (about a north German town's heroic resistance to the French invasion in 1806), but most were not. Goebbels preferred comedies, love stories, sentimental family tales, and escapist adventures. Much of the propaganda in the well-attended movie theaters was provided by highly slanted newsreels. Like their literary counterparts, talented filmmakers and actors fled. Fritz Lang, a director with an international reputation, escaped to Holland. Two prominent performers, Marlene Dietrich and Peter Lorre, gained fame in the United States.

Ironically, Goebbels did little more than approve the two most famous and enduring Nazi films, *Triumph of the Will* and *Olympia*. Both were produced by Leni Riefenstahl, a former dancer and actress who had directed a film in 1932. Hitler liked her first effort and asked her to make a film of the 1934 party rally that was visually artistic rather than heavy-handed political propaganda. He suggested the title. Stressing the "ein Volk, ein Reich, ein Führer" theme, *Triumph of the Will* is a masterful portrayal of Hitler's charisma and the effect it had on his audiences, as well as the pageantry and showmanship that were on display at every party rally. While *Olympia* offers comprehensive coverage of the events of the 1936 Olympic Games in Berlin, its central themes are the glorification of Aryan athletic prowess and the celebration of renewed German vitality under Hitler's leadership. Both films are documentaries, transformed into powerful works of propaganda art by Riefenstahl's skillful editing and imaginative photography.

The Nazis' cultural perspective also made itself felt in the fine arts. Speaking at a party congress in 1933, Hitler denounced all expressionist and modernist art as Jewish, un-German, and decadent, and insisted that all art of the Third Reich should have a "racial bias." The Art Chamber purged museums and arranged displays of "decadent art" (expressionist and modernist) in Munich and Berlin in 1937. Despite its cramped quarters, the Munich exhibition was viewed by far more people than a simultaneous showing of Nazi works in the House of German Art, a spacious new structure. Embarrassed chamber directors removed the modern paintings and either stored, sold, or destroyed them.

Artists responded to Hitler's charge with realistic paintings of nude young Aryans, portraits of the Führer and other Nazi dignitaries, idyllic scenes of Teutonic peasant families, and monumental sculptures of party comrades in various poses. Captioned posters with stiff, stylized figures depicting such themes as work, comradeship, struggle, and sacrifice were particularly prevalent. Following the chamber's directives, artists did not strive to elevate popular tastes or express themselves. They simply portrayed the aesthetic values and the "race and blood" ideology of the Third Reich and its leader. There was no room for the social satire of the famous Weimar artist George Grosz, who went into exile. Nor could the abstract expressionist paintings of Emil Nolde, a prominent artist who joined the party and offered his services to the regime, satisfy the arbiters of Nazi taste.

According to Albert Speer, the Third Reich's most famous architect, there was no official Nazi style. New buildings reflected a variety of regional and functional designs. Yet Hitler, who retained an active interest in architecture before the war, was quite specific as to what he liked and disliked. The modern international style of the famous Bauhaus school was banned. The grandiose, massive, and monumental neoclassical style, represented by the new Reich Chancellery in Berlin and the House of German Art in Munich, was encouraged. These structures and the gigantic speakers' rostrum on the grounds of the Nuremberg party rallies were the prototypes of what would have become an official Nazi style. It was to symbolize the totalitarian power and racial strength of the thousand-year Reich. Hitler commissioned Speer and his staff to draft plans for a new imperial capital complex in Berlin, including buildings, boulevards, esplanades, fountains, and squares, all on a monumental scale. These plans, Speer wrote retrospectively, "were marked by excessive ornamentation, a passion for pomp, and total decadence. And not only the style but the excessive size of these buildings plainly revealed Hitler's intentions."[12]

Presided over by Germany's most famous living composer, Richard Strauss, the Music Chamber sought to eliminate Jewish and modernist influences. It prohibited the performance of works by Jewish composers, such as Felix Mendelssohn (whose conversion to Christianity did not remove the racial taint), Gustav Mahler, and Arnold Schönberg, who was also a modernist. As part of the Reich Music Festival, which was held in Düsseldorf in 1938, Goebbels's ministry staged the "Exhibition of Degenerate

Music." Included on the program were works of Jewish composers and the world-renowned Aryan modernist, Paul Hindemith. Strauss, who had fallen out of favor with Goebbels and resigned from the chamber in 1935, conducted two of his compositions at the Reich Music Festival, but had nothing to do with showcasing the "degenerate music." Shortly after this incident, Hindemith, whom Strauss had earlier defended, fled to Switzerland. In 1940 he settled in the United States.[13]

There was still a great deal of music to be heard, though, and more opportunity to hear it than ever before. In crowded concert halls and opera houses, the works of Beethoven, Brahms, Schumann, Wagner, and Johann Strauss were performed, but Mozart's music was rarely played because of his association with the Freemasons, an international organization scorned by the Nazis. The light operas of Franz Lehar were especially popular. The chamber approved of most German folk and popular music and some foreign "hits," but frowned on American jazz and swing music. Some years later, Russian composer Dimitri Shostakovitch wrote a symphony honoring the people of Leningrad under siege by the Germans in World War II. No event or personality of the Third Reich inspired anything comparable in stature to the "Leningrad" Symphony. Nazism contributed nothing to Germany's rich musical heritage.

Some Nazis, including Göring, who reportedly "reached for his revolver" when he heard the word *culture*, were proud to be labeled barbarians. The culture of the Third Reich, though, was not so much barbaric as totalitarian. Except for the light-hearted, escapist fare, much of what was produced was heavy, repetitious, and dull. Far less variety was offered than during the Weimar period, but the Nazis could boast of increased availability. Approved literature and art sold well; attendance at cinemas, theaters, concerts, operas, and museums rose; millions listened to the radio for the first time; and newspaper readership remained constant. Neither uplifting nor thought-provoking, the culture of the Third Reich was ideologically sound and politically safe. Its role was to strengthen the bond between the "folk comrades" and their leaders.

Education, Youth, Women, and the Family

The Nazis targeted Germany's schools for an early and complete takeover. It was not difficult. For university professors, most of whom were conservative nationalists, adjusting to the Nazi philosophy of education was relatively simple. The regime could also count on the support of a majority of elementary and secondary teachers who were either party members or ideologically compatible. Nevertheless, most of the administrative and curricular reforms envisioned by the Nazis were not realized due to bureaucratic infighting and the ineptitude of Bernhard Rust, who was appointed Reich minister of education in 1934. Significant changes occurred, however, and they made the schools far more effective instruments of propaganda than they otherwise would have been.

In the universities the leadership principle replaced the democratic process. The regime appointed the rectors, the top administrative officials traditionally elected by the faculty. By 1934, 1,100 professors, about 15 percent of the total, had resigned or lost their positions. Among them were all the Jewish faculty members, including Albert Einstein and five other Nobel Prize–winning scientists. Some positions were filled by less-qualified Nazi sympathizers; others remained vacant. No programs, however, were abolished. The universities continued to offer courses and degrees in all traditional disciplines and professional fields, including theology. By 1936 four universities were offering a doctorate in racial science, the Third Reich's only new academic program.

The content of the university curriculum did not change markedly, but students were subjected to vulgar interpretations. The struggles and ultimate triumph of the Aryans became the dominant theme of historical study. In his 1933 inaugural lecture at the University of Cologne, respected political scientist Carl Schmitt articulated a new principle of legal education: Adolf Hitler was the source of all German law. Professors of physics and chemistry ridiculed the work of Jewish scientists, and only the needs of rearmament and war saved "Jewish science" from oblivion. One of the world's leading nuclear physicists, Werner Heisenberg, drew upon all available theories and discoveries as he directed Germany's atomic-bomb research and development during the war.

Racism and anti-intellectualism were responsible for the most dramatic change in university life, the sharp decline in enrollment. It was down 50 percent by 1939. All Jewish students were excluded, and before the war Aryan women were discouraged from attending. Compulsory labor service and military training made it difficult for young men to fit the university into their lives. The best and the brightest were aggressively recruited by SS schools, where they were taught that they would replace university graduates as the nation's elite. Julius Streicher expressed the Nazis' profound anti-intellectualism: "If the brains of all university professors were put at one end of the scale, and the brains of the Führer at the other, which end do you think would tip?" If Streicher had been more thoughtful, he would certainly have softened his criticism of one professor, the existentialist philosopher Martin Heidegger, who proclaimed: "Not theses and ideas are the laws of your being! The Führer himself and he alone is Germany's reality and law today and in the future."[14]

The Nazis found a host of collaborators at the elementary and secondary levels. Some teachers were dismissed, but proportionately fewer than in higher education. Even those teachers who were not ardent Nazis adapted easily to the new style. There was little opposition to a 1933 decree restricting the enrollment of Jewish children to no more than 1.5 percent of the total. (By 1938 that percentage had been reduced to zero.) All classes began with the Hitler salute, and many teachers read from *Mein Kampf* or other Nazi literature as part of an opening devotion. Although some new textbooks were introduced, the regime could rely on most

BOX 5.1 ■ THE HITLER YOUTH: FROM YOUNG BOYS TO
TRUE BELIEVERS

Ten-year-old Alfons Heck joined the *Jungvolk* on April 20, 1938. Fifty years later, he recalled his feelings:

> All these [physical] activities were designed to make us fit according to our motto: swift as greyhounds, tough as leather and hard as the steel of Krupp. In that, the Hitler Youth succeeded. . . . Our prewar activities resembled those of the Boy Scouts, but with much more emphasis on discipline and political indoctrination. The paraphernalia, the parades, the flags and symbols, the soul-stirring music and the pomp and mysticism were very close in feeling to religious rituals. At the induction ceremony, my spine tingled in the conviction that I now belonged to something both majestic and threatened by bitter enemies. It was Deutsch-land. . . . As the final act of the induction ceremony, we were handed the dagger with the Swastika inlaid in the handle and the inscription "Blood and Honor" on its blade. . . . I accepted the two basic tenets of the Nazi creed: belief in the innate superiority of the Germanic-Nordic race, and the conviction that total submis-sion to Germany and to the Führer was our first duty.

A few months later, Heck was invited to attend the Nuremberg party rally. Hitler's closing speech reinforced his growing conviction that "we Germans were indeed the superior race." He vividly recalls the powerful impact of that speech:

> His right fist punctuated the air in a staccato of short, powerful jabs as he roared out a promise and an irresistible enticement of power already proven to the world. "You, my youth," he shouted, with his eyes seemingly fixed only on me, "are des-tined to be the leaders of a glorious new world order under the supremacy of National Socialism." From that moment on, I belonged to Adolf Hitler body and soul.

Alfons Heck, *The Burden of Hitler's Legacy* (Frederick, CO: Renaissance House, 1988), pp. 57–58.

teachers to give a Nazi interpretation to existing materials in courses in history, anthropology, sociology, the humanities, the sciences, and religion. New requirements included "racial biology" and more rigorous physical training. While the degree of ideological indoctrination varied, all schools impressed upon children the importance of their commitment to the Führer and the racial community.

The Nazis did not leave the vital task of converting the young entirely to educators. The Führer assigned to the Hitler Youth the primary respon-sibility for indoctrinating Germany's young people. Its leader, Baldur von Schirach, a young, self-styled poet who had three American grandparents, reported directly to Hitler. Under Schirach's leadership, the Hitler Youth expanded to embrace virtually all German youngsters from the ages of ten to eighteen. By 1936 all other youth organizations, religious or political, had been abolished, and in 1939 membership in the Hitler Youth was made mandatory. The few who refused to join were barred from the German Labor Front, which usually resulted in unemployment. At the age of ten, boys and girls entered the *Jungvolk* and *Jungmädel*, respectively, and at the age of fourteen, boys were promoted to the Hitler Youth, a term designating both the entire organization and older teenage boys; girls graduated to the *Bund deutscher Mädel* (League of German Girls). Schirach also organized training programs for thousands of local youth leaders.

All Hitler Youth activities centered on fulfillment of its mission, which, according to Schirach, was "to see that new members of the National Socialist movement will grow up in the same spirit through which the party achieved greatness."[15] There were hikes, sporting events, demonstrations, physical training, and, the heart of the program, ideological education. Events were scheduled for evenings and weekends so that school children, as well as those members who were employed, could attend. All activities stressed discipline, loyalty, courage, self-sacrifice, and obedience. Young people were trained to prepare themselves for service to the fatherland, leadership in the racial community, and above all, total commitment to the Führer.

That commitment, and the youth's formal initiation into the *Volksgemeinschaft*, were celebrated and solemnized on Youth Pledge Day, the ceremony marking completion of the first four years of membership. It was an elaborate ritual with music, flags, speeches, and readings from *Mein Kampf*.

Girls of the Hitler Youth underwent training in the domestic arts.

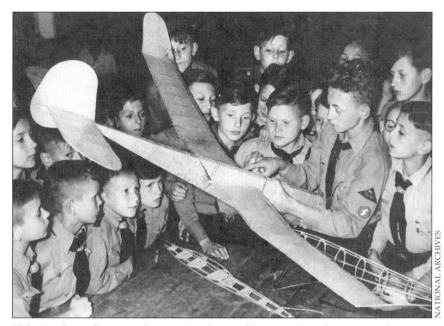

NATIONAL ARCHIVES

Hitler Youth usually engaged in activities that would prepare them for service to the Reich. For example, building and studying model airplanes provided these Hitler Youth boys with a form of pre-military training.

The climax occurred when the youths recited a confession and took an oath. The confession read: "The will of the Führer is our will, his faith is our faith, and with his words we confess: my faith is rooted in my people, I will serve my people with my will, I will give my life for my people." The participants then swore to do their duty "in love and loyalty to the Führer and our flag."[16]

Teenagers in the Hitler Youth received prevocational training along with more intensive ideological education. Girls were encouraged to prepare for motherhood and given practice in tasks befitting the woman's role in the *Volksgemeinschaft*. Physical training for boys had taken on a pronounced military character by 1939, although Schirach denied it at his Nuremberg trial. He also denied that the Hitler Youth was anti-Christian. Yet, many activities were scheduled for Sunday morning, and Schirach's own poetry, written expressly for his young charges, discredited the church and deified Hitler. The prosecutor at Nuremberg read a sample: "We are the happy Hitler Youth, we need no Christian virtue, for our leader is Adolf Hitler. He is our savior and redeemer. No pastor . . . can take from us the feeling we have as Hitler's children."[17] Schirach accomplished his mission. Over 90 percent of "Hitler's children," according to a modern historian of the Hitler Youth, "remained faithful to the cause even beyond Stalingrad."[18]

Schirach insisted that the Hitler Youth strengthened the "sacred bonds of family." It could be argued, however, that the Nazi youth program had exactly the opposite effect. After-hours activities took time that might have been spent with the family. A few zealous members, while not explicitly ordered to spy on their parents, actually did report their less-dedicated elders to Nazi authorities. Nevertheless, traditional family ties did not markedly deteriorate under the Third Reich. Both the divorce rate and juvenile crime declined after 1933, although the latter increased during the war. The Nazis sought to strengthen each family's commitment to Hitler and the *Volksgemeinschaft*. To achieve this goal, they supported traditional German patriarchy and sought to persuade women that they had a special role in strengthening the bonds of the family.

The Nazi attitude toward women was clear: they were to stay home, serve and support their husbands, have babies, and teach their children the values of the racial community. According to Rudolf Hess, the ideal German woman stood at her husband's side and made the world "richer and more beautiful in content for him." German women have babies, Hess maintained, not simply because their husbands and the state so desire, but because "they are proud to bring healthy children into the world, to bring them up for the nation, and in this way to do their part in the preservation of the life of their Volk."[19] Speaking to a group of women, Hitler was more blunt: "You ask me what I have done for the women of Germany. Well, my answer is this: in my new army I have provided you the finest fathers of children in the world."[20]

Ideological platitudes were reinforced by financial inducements. These included low-interest loans to women who quit their jobs upon marriage, with an automatic reduction of the principal for each child born, a tax exemption that doubled for each dependent child, and family allowances that increased geometrically with the number of children. The propaganda ministry ceaselessly extolled the dignity and patriotism of motherhood and bestowed the Mother's Cross upon mothers of five children. Those who gave birth to eight children were awarded the Mother's Cross in gold.

Under the leadership of Gertrud Scholtz-Klink, widow of an NSDAP official and mother of four, the Nazi Women's League (*NS-Frauenschaft*), the party's principal women's organization, placed itself at the regime's disposal. Scholtz-Klink recruited thousands of new members to the Women's League and integrated all non-Socialist and non-Communist associations, including those affiliated with the churches, into the newly formed *Frauenwerk* (Women's Bureau). By 1938 this network had 8 million members, including thousands of former fighters for women's rights, who were welcome as long as they had no Jewish ancestors or ties with Marxist groups. Although normally in harmony with the regime, the Women's Bureau was not always acquiescent. Its members protested against the expulsion of women from high-ranking state jobs and discrimination against married women in the workplace. Religious members did not hide their displeasure at the regime's "anti-church" propaganda and policies. Nevertheless, the Nazi women's organizations were an asset to the *Volksgemeinschaft*, especially before the war.[21]

BOX 5.2 ■ HITLER ON THE TASKS OF WOMEN

The first excerpt is from a speech to the Nazi Women's League in 1936:

> . . . . So long as we possess a healthy manly race—and we National Socialists will attend to that—we will form no female mortar battalions and no female sharp-shooters corps. For that is not equality of rights, but a diminution of the rights of woman. . . .
>
> An unlimited range of work opportunities exists for women. For us the woman has always been man's most loyal comrade in work and in life. I am often told: You want to drive women out of the professions. Not at all. I wish only to create the broadest measure of possibility for her to co-found her own family and to be able to have children, because by so doing she most benefits our *Volk!*
>
> If today a female jurist accomplishes ever so much and next door there lives a mother with five, six, seven children, who are all healthy and well-brought up, then I would like to say: From the standpoint of the eternal value of our people the woman who has given birth to children and raised them and who thereby has given back our people life for the future has accomplished more and does more!

In 1935 Hitler addressed the National Socialist Women's Congress on the subject of women's rights:

> The so-called granting of equal rights to women, which Marxism demands, in reality does not grant equal rights but constitutes a deprivation of rights, since it draws the woman into an area in which she will necessarily be inferior. It places the woman in situations that cannot strengthen her position—vis-a-vis both man and society—but only weaken it. . . .
>
> I would be ashamed to be a German man if in the event of a war even only one woman had to go to the front. The woman has her own battlefield. With every child that she brings into the world, she fights her battle for the nation. The man stands up for the *Volk*, exactly as the woman stands up for the family.

George Mosse, ed., *Nazi Culture* (New York: Grosset & Dunlap, 1966), pp. 39–40.

Most women did not complain about their subordinate status, loss of rights, or exclusion from public life. On the contrary, many expressed satisfaction with their role as wives, mothers, and homemakers in the *Volksgemeinschaft*. An increase in the birthrate was particularly gratifying to the regime. There were 1,410,000 births recorded in 1939, up from 971,000 in 1933. In the same period, the number of births per 1,000 women of childbearing age rose from 58.9 to 84.8.[22] In the job market, Nazi policy was less successful, but hardly a dismal failure. The number of working women rose to 5.8 million in 1939, up from 4.2 million in 1933. Even though they were paid less than men and had fewer opportunities for advancement, women worked side by side with men in a variety of jobs in trade and industry. Some unmarried women under the age of 25 were required by the Labor Service to work for a year in agriculture or domestic service.

With the inscription, "you also belong to the Führer," this poster was meant to assure young girls that they, too, had an important place in Hitler's new order.

The regime initially forced professional women to resign if their husbands could support them, but the numbers of women in universities, teaching, social work, medicine, and the civil service reached pre-1933 levels after the outbreak of war. In Germany, as in other industrialized nations, long-term patterns of women's employment continued.

The Churches

According to an old German saying, the three words *Kirche, Kinder, Küche* (church, children, kitchen) sum up a woman's duties. The Nazis, untraditionally, rejected the first. Publicly, Hitler professed neutrality toward the churches, but he promised retribution against "political clergymen" who criticized the regime. Privately, he was contemptuous: "The Evangelical [Protestant] clergy are insignificant little people, submissive as dogs, with a laughable religion." Envisioning the future of Catholicism, he said: "In St. Peter's chair a senile officiant; facing him a few sinister old women as gaga and poor in spirit as anyone could wish. The young and healthy are on our side."[23] Hitler intended to "settle accounts" with dissenting clergymen after the war and watch the institutional church wither away through natural attrition. In the meantime, he was content to avoid confrontation and allow the churches administrative autonomy, so long as the clergy engaged only in "religious activities." Hitler knew that the churches were no threat to the state and that even politically minded clergymen were loyal to the fatherland and conscience-bound to obey the duly constituted authority of their nation.

Hitler's desire to avoid conflict did not spare the church from persecution. The existence of an institution that claimed the total allegiance of its followers offended the ideological sensibilities of men like Heydrich, Himmler, and Bormann. If given free rein, their anti-Christian sentiments would have inspired an even harsher persecution. As it was, the Gestapo, Criminal Police, and regular police arrested hundreds of clergymen, usually for violating the Insidious Acts Law. Those incarcerated, about 3 percent of all clergymen, were usually released after brief periods of detention and were relatively well treated. Before the war, however, at least two individuals died from the effects of torture. Restrictions on speaking and travel were lighter punishments, usually imposed by pro-Nazi church administrators. More Protestant than Catholic clergy were arrested, but the trials of several priests on morals charges received more publicity. From time to time the SS newspaper, *Das Schwarze Korps*, published scurrilous attacks against the clergy of both churches. Because its members were free to make their own decisions, the Protestant church suffered a higher rate of attrition. Most of those who dropped their church membership before the war—about 3 percent of the population—were Protestants. (There were tangible benefits to dropping out: the church tax was waived for nonmembers, and their children were not required to attend public school religion classes.)

Despite harassment, surveillance, restrictions, arrests, and the Nazis' anti-Christian ideology, the churches carried on. Worship services were held on schedule, the sacraments were administered regularly, religious festivals were observed, and religious education continued at all levels. Youth organizations were abolished, but the regime did not interfere with the rite of confirmation. Only mild restrictions were placed on the religious press and broadcasting. The government continued to collect and distribute the church tax, the churches' major source of funding. (The church tax was a surcharge levied on the income tax of all citizens who retained their membership.) In a speech to the Reichstag in January 1939, Hitler boasted of his generous financial support for an "unappreciative church."

Hitler's reference to an unappreciative church had some basis in fact. Among established institutions, only the churches resisted Nazism. There was more acquiescence than protest, but resistance—limited, qualified, and timid though it may have been—was real. The Protestant clergy, ministering to nearly 60 percent of all Germans (nominal membership for most), were sharply divided. About 15 percent were Nazi sympathizers, and they held most of the top administrative positions in the twenty-eight regional churches. At the other extreme were the dissenters who belonged to the Confessing Church, which at its peak attracted 25 percent of all Protestant clergymen. In several meetings before the war, this group adopted resolutions condemning policies of pro-Nazi church administrators and attacking Rosenberg's muddled racial philosophy as "neo-paganism."

The Confessing Church thwarted the efforts of the Ministry of Religious Affairs, which Hitler established in 1935, to centralize the administration and force all regional bodies to submit to the authority of a "Reich Bishop." Only once did the dissenting pastors address the real evils of National Socialism. In a memorandum to Hitler in 1936, Martin Niemöller and nine other clergymen denounced the Gestapo and concentration camps, racism and anti-Semitism, and the propaganda ministry's deification of the Führer. After 1937 there was little protest of any kind from the Confessing Church, which had been demoralized by Niemöller's imprisonment, the arrest of some of its members, and internal dissension. Accommodation with the regime became the rule, and the church's leaders pledged their support to the Führer when German armies invaded Poland in 1939.

The failure of the Confessing Church to stand by victims of Nazi persecution was reflected in an oft-quoted statement attributed to Niemöller after the war:

> When they arrested the Communists, I said I am not a Communist, so I did nothing. When they attacked the trade unions, I said I am not a unionist, so I did nothing. When they persecuted the Catholics, I said I am not a Catholic, so I did nothing. When they rounded up the Jews, I said I am not a Jew, so I did nothing. When they came for me, there was no one left to stand up for anyone.[24]

One of the most famous members of the Confessing Church was forsaken by his colleagues. Dietrich Bonhoeffer, who died at the hands of a Nazi hangman a month before the end of the war, was unique among protesting clergymen in that he recognized as early as 1933 that anti-Semitism was the principal evil, the very essence of Nazism. After the Gestapo closed his underground seminary for Confessing Church theology students, he joined the Resistance Movement. Bonhoeffer had strong theological and moral reservations about associating with a group whose goal was the forcible removal, possibly even the assassination, of Hitler. When he joined the Resistance Movement in 1938, however, he had concluded that Hitler and Nazism were so evil that violence and treason were justified. Bonhoeffer once remarked that it was his duty, not simply to shout a warning to pedestrians, but to stop a madman driving a car down a narrow, crowded street. Confessing Church clergy regularly prayed for Niemöller during their worship services, but they never once uttered Bonhoeffer's name. His resistance, they claimed, was political.

Resistance in the hierarchical Roman Catholic Church took a different form than in the divided Protestant Church. The bishops' criticism of Nazism before the *Machtergreifung* gave way to guarded cooperation following the Concordat. Repeated violations of that agreement, along with falsely accused nuns and priests whose trials received lurid publicity, convinced the bishops to act. They urged Pope Pius XI to speak out on behalf of Germany's 27 million Roman Catholics. He did so in March 1937 in the widely distributed encyclical, titled *With Burning Sorrow*. Restrictions on youth work and religious education, the "idolatrous cult of race," and the arrest and trial of clerical personnel came under attack. Hitler, who never canceled his membership in the Catholic Church, was furious. He ordered the confiscation of all copies of the encyclical and the arrest of anyone caught distributing it. The trials, which had been suspended because of the Olympic Games, resumed, and anti-Catholic propaganda was intensified. German Catholics were further demoralized by the harsh persecution of their co-religionists in Austria after the annexation in 1938. In March 1939 the German bishops encouraged the newly invested Pope Pius XII to send a friendly message to Hitler, expressing hope for improvement in German-Vatican relations. As in the Confessing Church, accommodation with the regime had become a high priority, and the bishops, like their Protestant counterparts, proclaimed their support for Hitler's war in 1939.

More boldly than any other religious or secular organization, the Jehovah's Witnesses, numbering approximately 20,000, resisted Nazi tyranny. The Hitler salute, oaths, and military service were violations of their strict religious code. Moreover, they openly labeled Hitler the anti-Christ and condemned the immorality of his regime. Eventually, over 6,000 Jehovah's Witnesses, or *Ernste Bibelforscher* (serious Bible scholars) as they were also called, were arrested; one-third of them perished in concentration camps. Himmler, who admired their zeal and commitment, ordered their release if they denied their faith and took an oath of loyalty to the *Volksgemeinschaft*. None of them did so.[25] Rarely mentioned in Gestapo records and SD reports were the other sects (tiny, self-supporting religious groups) such as Baptists, Methodists, and Mormons. Unlike the defiant Jehovah's Witnesses, they did not resist; like most Catholics and Protestants, they cooperated without losing their identity.

Aliens, Dissenters, and Outcasts

Hitler believed that one of the main causes of Germany's defeat in 1918 was the disintegration of the home front "sapped by biological decline, which was the result of ignoring principles of race and eugenics."[26] Determined to reverse that decline, in July 1933 the regime promulgated the Law for the Prevention of Hereditarily Diseased Progeny. The law called for the sterilization of persons not of "German blood and Nordic race," those not "four-square in body and soul," social nonconformists, and "evaders of German hard work."[27] Germany's 20,000 Gypsies were guilty on all four counts. Those arrested from 1933 to 1935 were classified as criminals or work-shy in the concentration camps. The Nuremberg race laws of 1935 declared Gypsies, like Jews, to be of "alien type." More arrests followed the decree of the Prussian Ministry of the Interior in 1937, which put Gypsies into the asocial category, defined as persons having a hereditary tendency toward, or being chronically guilty of, deviant behavior. When the police ordered the arrest of all Gypsies in Germany shortly after the outbreak of war, more than half were already in camps or prisons; a relatively smaller number had been sterilized. Deportations to Poland began in early 1940.

Except for mass deportation, Aryan outcasts were treated equally harshly. Homosexuals, whose refusal to procreate violated the regime's demographic policy, were by definition neither four-square in body and soul nor socially conformist. (Lesbians, who were biologically capable of bearing children, were treated less harshly.) Habitual criminals, work evaders, vagrants, prostitutes, drunkards, and persons with contagious diseases, especially sexually transmitted ones, were categorized as either genetically or chronically asocial. Police decrees and the Institute of Criminal Biology, founded by a reputable neurologist, furnished definitions. Individuals within these categories were either imprisoned or sterilized.

The mentally ill and physically handicapped were also to be prevented from producing "diseased progeny." The law sanctioned the compulsory sterilization of allegedly hereditary diseases, such as feeblemindedness, schizophrenia, manic depression, epilepsy, Huntington's Chorea, blindness, deafness, and "serious physical malformation." Ardent racists in the medical and legal communities, who had been advocating sterilization of "social misfits," the mentally retarded, and physically handicapped long before 1933, eagerly served on hundreds of hereditary health courts, each consisting of a judge and two physicians. These courts, assisted by the police, private citizens, and hospital and asylum medical staffs, identified thousands of "diseased persons," and in virtually every instance decreed sterilization. The most common procedures, normally carried out in clinics and hospitals under the supervision of licensed physicians, were tubal ligations and X-ray treatment for women and vasectomies and castration for men. Hundreds of patients did not survive the treatment, and most of those who did were left with permanent physical disabilities and emotional scars. Between

1933 and 1945 an estimated total of 400,000 people—including Gypsies, asocials, mentally retarded Aryans, and all other "diseased persons" specified in the law—were sterilized, approximately 1% of the population capable of producing children.[28] The sterilization program also established precedents for systematic euthanasia, a far more radical and brutal program that began in 1939 (discussed in Chapter 10).

From the party's earliest days, Hitler and Nazi propaganda branded the Jews as "alien to the community." Given the intensity of that propaganda, numerous incidents of SA violence, and the Führer's unconcealed hatred, it was clear that persecution of Jews would be high on the Nazis' agenda. In the first years after 1933, however, that persecution was unsystematic and sporadic. As was typical in the Third Reich, several government and party agencies were involved in formulating and administering policy. Hitler articulated the goals and occasionally made public statements, but rarely issued explicit directives. Up to 1939, no one was really in charge of the "Jewish question."

The SA was one of the most fervently anti-Semitic branches of the Nazi movement. To satisfy those old fighters and test the anti-Semitic fervor of the people, Hitler approved, and may even have initiated, the highly publicized SA boycott of Jewish shops in April 1933. It was not a success, as many Aryans crossed, or tried to cross, the picket lines. Lack of popular support may have dictated a more cautious and less systematic policy, but Hitler did not abandon his goals. For the short term, Germany was to be *Judenfrei*, that is, free of Jews. The ultimate goal, as he had declared in the early 1920s, was "the elimination of the Jews altogether."

Hitler preferred "rational anti-Semitism," which would lead to the "systematic legal fight," as opposed to the emotional variety, which found "its ultimate expression in the form of pogroms." There were no pogroms until 1938, but the SA, SS, and Gestapo routinely brutalized and arrested thousands of Jews. Reducing the Jewish population in the civil service and the schools was part of the "legal fight," as was the sterilization of hundreds of mentally defective Jews. Emigration was a much more humane option. Under Reinhard Heydrich's direction, thousands of Jews emigrated before 1936; most of them went to Palestine. The United States readily granted permanent visas to celebrities, such as Albert Einstein and symphony orchestra conductor Bruno Walter, but admitted few ordinary Jews.

Hitler chose the 1935 party rally as the forum for proclaiming the Nuremberg race laws. The first of these, the Law for the Protection of German Blood and Honor, intensified his systematic legal fight against the Jews (no longer called non-Aryans). The law prohibited marriages and extramarital intercourse between Jews and Germans, the employment of German females under the age of forty-five in Jewish households, and any display of the swastika flag by Jews. Successive laws promulgated by the ministry of justice used both race and religion to define Jews. A person descended from three or four Jewish grandparents (a three-quarter or full Jew) or the offspring of a union involving one three-quarter or full Jewish parent was classified as a Jew regardless of religious affiliation. A person descended from two Jewish grandparents, but not belonging to a Jewish religious community or not married to a Jew, was a *Mischling*, or half-Jew, not necessarily a Jew legally, but also not a bona fide Aryan. The status of the grandparents was determined by their membership in a Jewish religious community. Neither cancellation of religious membership nor conversion to Christianity removed the disabilities of the three-quarter or full Jew.

By classifying Jews as aliens, the Nuremberg race laws deprived them of citizenship. The irony of these laws was that the Nazis, whose propaganda depicted the Jew as a physically repulsive racial type, had to use religion, to which they were indifferent, to help segregate Germany's assimilated Jewish community. Despite the implicit admission that Jews looked very much like Aryans, Goebbels's ministry, the propaganda organs of the party, SS publications, and Julius Streicher's lurid anti-Semitic newspaper *Der Stürmer*, continued to portray them as physically repulsive and diseased specimens who were a biological menace to the *Volksgemeinschaft*. Nor did the Nazis neglect the alleged threat of the Jews to the nation's economic, political, and cultural well-being. The Nazis' anti-Semitic policy may have been unsystematic, but their vicious propaganda campaign was well-organized, extensive, and relentless. If this effort did not always instill murderous hatred among the people, it depersonalized the Jews and desensitized the public to harsh measures against them.

The legal fight, which was nothing more than a euphemism for persecution, was intensified after the Nuremberg laws were passed. The Jews were gradually expelled from regular schools, public accommodations, the professions, and corporate boards of directors. By 1939, their exclusion was total. They could still engage in retail trade and own property, but the new "Aryanization" law forced them to sell their property to Aryans at far below market value. In April 1938 the regime enacted a law requiring all Jewish men and women to add "Israel" and "Sarah," respectively, to their legal names. Immigration policy was both cruel and illogical. While still paying lip service to the idea of a *Judenfrei* Germany, the government made it increasingly difficult for Jews to obtain passports. At the same time, those who were able to emigrate found doors closing throughout the world. At a conference held in Evian, France, in September 1938, delegates from the United States and other western nations offered sympathy but refused to ease restrictions. They confirmed Goebbels's cynical contention that no one really wanted Germany's Jews. In 1938 the Nazis deported to Poland several thousand resident Jews whose native citizenship had been revoked by the Polish government. The next year the British government, yielding to pressure from Arab residents, blocked further Jewish immigration to Palestine.

The pogrom of November 9–10, 1938, called Crystal Night (*Kristallnacht*) because so much glass was broken, was the only incident of organized violence against the Jews before the war. Goebbels, still smarting from Hitler's public rebuke of his affair with a Czech actress, desperately

UPI/BETTMANN/CORBIS

Passersby in Berlin examine a Jewish-owned store, the windows of which were broken on Crystal Night. Though the first pogrom in western Europe in hundreds of years was widely publicized in the foreign press, it aroused little sympathy for the Jews.

wanted to recapture his standing in the hierarchy. On November 9 a young Jew, seeking revenge for the deportation of his parents, murdered a German diplomat in Paris. Seizing upon this incident, Goebbels urged all "decent Germans" to retaliate against the Reich's Jews. Actually, the pogrom was executed by SA and SS men in street clothes. They destroyed thousands of Jewish shops, burned all synagogues, killed nearly 200 Jews, and arrested 40,000, most of whom were subsequently deported to Poland. A few days later, Göring fined the Jews 1 billion marks for property damage and ordered all their insurance compensation to be confiscated. Forced labor was introduced shortly after Crystal Night, and emigration became all but impossible. For 250,000 impoverished Jews who could not leave, Germany had become a prison.

The people's reaction to Crystal Night was varied and muted. A few residents of smaller towns joined the SA's rampage, but the vast majority of citizens remained passive. Some, including party members, felt that the destructiveness and savagery were excessive, but many, like Melita Maschmann (see text box), were able to rationalize the brutality. They believed that some kind of official violence, however gratuitous, was needed to teach the Jews a lesson. Those who were shocked by the wanton destruction of property were gratified by the government's prompt imposition of fines and seizure of insurance compensation. Though the numbers were relatively small, the regime could hardly have been pleased by folk comrades who expressed sympathy for the beaten and terrorized victims

---

BOX 5.3 ■ CRYSTAL NIGHT: A PARTY MEMBER'S REACTION

Melita Maschmann, a young party member, retrospectively analyzes her reaction to the events of that night in Berlin, which a policeman described to
her the following morning. She concludes with a remarkable admission:

> But almost at once I switched over to accepting what had happened as over and
> done with and avoiding critical reflection. I said to myself: The Jews are the ene-
> mies of the New Germany. Last night they had a taste of what that means. Let us
> hope that World Jewry, which has resolved to hinder Germany's "new steps toward
> greatness," will take the events of last night as a warning. If the Jews sow hatred
> against us all over the world, they must learn that we have hostages for them in
> our hands.
>
> With these and similar thoughts I constructed for myself a justification of the
> pogrom. But in any case I forced the memory of it out of my consciousness as
> quickly as possible. As the years went by I grew better and better at switching off
> quickly in this manner on similar occasions. It was the only way . . . to prevent the
> onset of doubts about the rightness of what had happened. I probably knew . . . that
> serious doubts would have torn away the basis of my existence from under me. Not
> in the economic but in the existential sense. I had totally identified myself with Na-
> tional Socialism. The moment of horror became more and more dangerous to me as
> the years went by. For this reason it had to become shorter and shorter. On the
> "Night of Broken Glass" our feelings were not yet hardened to the sight of human
> suffering as they were later during the war. Perhaps if I had met one of the perse-
> cuted and oppressed, an old man with the fear of death in his face, perhaps, . . .

Jeremy Noakes and Geoffrey Pridham, eds., *Documents on Nazism, 1919–1945* (New
York: Viking Press, 1975), p. 476.

---

and sought to protect their Jewish neighbors from the fury of the SA and
SS.[29] A tiny band of ordinary citizens in the Rhineland who had formed a
network to help political prisoners and Jews to escape intensified their efforts. The Gestapo arrested individuals involved in this dangerous activity,
but the rescue missions continued.[30] Some individual Christians were
among those citizens who protected Jews, but only one clergyman in all of
Germany issued a public protest. Julius van Jan, pastor of a small Protestant
parish in Württemberg, condemned Crystal Night in a sermon on November 13; he was subsequently beaten by a gang of Nazi toughs and imprisoned.[31] Such retribution was a formidable deterrent to organized moral
protest on behalf of the Jews. For those who were appalled by the violence,
fear was more powerful than moral indignation. Crystal Night taught a
powerful lesson to all Germans. Alfons Heck writes: "No German old
enough to walk could ever plead ignorance to the persecution of the Jews,
and no Jew could harbor any delusion that Hitler wanted Germany anything but *judenrein*, clean of Jews."[32]

Until 1939 Hitler said nothing publicly that hinted at the ultimate
fate of the Jews. Speaking to the Reichstag on January 30, the sixth an-

niversary of the *Machtergreifung* and less than three months after Crystal Night, he was explicit: "If international finance Jewry within Europe and abroad should succeed once more in plunging the peoples into a world war, then the consequence will be not the bolshevization of the world and therewith a victory of Jewry, but, on the contrary, the destruction of the Jewish race in Europe." He was less guarded in a private meeting with the Czech foreign minister nine days earlier: "We are going to destroy the Jews. They are not going to get away with what they did on November 9, 1918. The day of reckoning has come."[33] While not necessarily proving that Hitler had already decided to exterminate the Jews of Europe, these statements suggest that he was contemplating more radical solutions to the Jewish question in the event of war. They confirmed what the eminent Swiss theologian, Karl Barth, wrote several weeks after Crystal Night: "National Socialism lives, moves, and has its being in anti-Semitism."[34]

Conclusion

By the outbreak of war in 1939, the Nazis had laid the foundations of the *Volksgemeinschaft*. Goebbels's propaganda machine, reinforced by terror, had imposed a degree of cultural and intellectual uniformity unprecedented in German history. The Reich Chamber of Culture had put an identifiably Nazi stamp on what was produced in all aspects of German culture. At the same time, the chamber banned all pre- and post-1933 works judged to be offensive to "folk comrades." The roles of family, women, children, educators, and, to a lesser extent, clergymen had been redefined. Dissenters were imprisoned or isolated, and aliens and outcasts were being purged, with the prospect of even harsher measures to follow. Social tensions still existed, but programs such as Strength-through-Joy and the Hitler Youth were eroding traditional class distinctions. Studies of public opinion in the Third Reich and postwar oral history projects reveal that the majority of Germans may not have fully adopted the values of the *Volksgemeinschaft*, but 80 to 90 percent of the population remained committed to Hitler until he began to lose the war in Russia.[35]

INFOTRAC® COLLEGE EDITION SEARCH TERMS

For additional reading go to Infotrac College Edition, your online research library at http://www.infotrac-college.com.

Enter the search term "Nuremburg" using Keywords.

Enter the search term "Hitler Youth" using Keywords.

Enter the search term "German history education" using Keywords.

Enter the search term "German History women" using Keywords.

Enter the search term "Kristallnacht" using Keywords.

Notes

1. Thomas Saunders, "Nazism and Social Revolution," in Gordon Martel, ed., *Modern Germany Reconsidered, 1870–1945* (London: Routledge, 1992), pp. 166–67.

2. Quoted in Ian Kershaw, *The Hitler Myth* (New York: Oxford University Press, 1987), p. 79.

3. Joachim Remak, ed. *The Nazi Years: A Documentary History* (Prospect Heights, IL: Waveland Press, 1990), pp. 76–77.

4. Quoted in Milton Mayer, *They Thought They Were Free* (Chicago: University of Chicago Press, 1955), p. 105.

5. Quoted in John S. Conway, *The Nazi Persecution of the Churches* (London: Weidenfeld and Nicolson, 1968), p. 142.

6. Jackson J. Spielvogel, *Hitler and Nazi Germany* (Upper Saddle River, NJ: Prentice-Hall, 2001), p. 149.

7. Gordon Craig, *Germany, 1866–1945* (New York: Oxford University Press, 1978), p. 658.

8. George Mosse, *Nazi Culture* (New York: Grosset & Dunlap, 1966), pp. 139, 191.

9. Quoted in David Welch, *The Third Reich: Politics and Propaganda* (London and New York, 1993), p. 28.

10. Remak, pp. 85–86.

11. Quoted in Craig, pp. 645, 664.

12. Albert Speer, *Inside the Third Reich* (New York: MacMillan, 1970), p. 160.

13. Michael H. Kater, *Composers of the Nazi Era* (New York: Oxford University Press, 2000), p. 249.

14. Streicher and Heidegger are quoted in Karl D. Bracher, *The German Dictatorship* (New York: Praeger Publishers, 1970), pp. 272, 268.

15. Mosse, p. 294.

16. NSDAP Hauptkulturamt der Reichspropagandaleitung, *Die neue Gemeinschaft* (Berlin, 1940–1944), March 1940, pp. 1–3.

17. Quoted in Hans Müller, "Der pseudo-religiöse Charakter der nationalsozialistischen Weltanschauung," *Geschichte in Wissenschaft und Unterricht* (June, 1961), p. 341.

18. Gerhard Rempel, *Hitler's Children* (Chapel Hill: The University of North Carolina Press, 1989), p. 256.

19. Mosse, p. 41.

20. Quoted in T.L. Jarman, *The Rise and Fall of Nazi Germany* (New York: New American Library, 1956), p. 181.

21. Claudia Koonz, "The Fascist Solution to the Women Question in Italy and Germany," in Renate Bridenthal, Claudia Koonz, and Susan Stuard, eds.,

Becoming Visible: Women in European History (Boston: Houghton Mifflin, 1987), pp. 519–20.

22. Craig, p. 630.

23. Norman Cameron and R. H. Stevens, eds., *Hitler's Secret Conversations, 1941–1944* (New York: New American Library, 1961), p. 449. The German *evangelische Kirche*, literally the evangelical church, was and is the name of the tax-supported church body to which all Lutheran and Reformed Christians (over 50 percent of the population) belong. To avoid confusion with the more specific American meaning of evangelical, it is best translated as Protestant.

24. Quoted in John S. Conway, "The Political Theology of Martin Niemöller," *German Studies Review*, October 1986, pp. 539–40.

25. Michael H. Kater, "Die Ernsten Bibelforscher im Dritten Reich," *Viertel-jahrshefte für Zeitgeschichte* (April 1969), p. 190.

26. Jeremy Noakes, "Social Outcasts in the Third Reich," in Richard Bessel, ed., *Life in the Third Reich* (New York: Oxford University Press, 1987), p. 83.

27. Quoted in Detlev Peukert, *Inside Nazi Germany* (London: Bratsford, 1987), p. 208.

28. Noakes, p. 86; Koonz, p. 521; Michael Burleigh, *Death and Deliverance: "Euthanasia" in Germany c. 1900–1945* (Cambridge University Press, 1994), pp. 55–56.

29. Daniel Jonah Goldhagen, *Hitler's Willing Executioners* (New York: Alfred A. Knopf, 1996), p. 101; Ian Kershaw, *Popular Opinion and Political Dissent in the Third Reich: Bavaria, 1933–1945* (Oxford: Clarendon Press, 1983), pp. 267–71.

30. Bernt Engelmann, *In Hitler's Germany* (New York: Schocken Books, 1986), pp. 142–44. The author articipated in one of these groups.

31. Conway, *The Nazi Persecution of the Churches*, p. 373.

32. Alfons Heck, *The Burden of Hitler's Legacy* (Frederick, CO: Renaissance House, 1988), p. 62.

33. Quoted in Craig, p. 637.

34. Karl Barth, *The Church and the Political Problem of Our Day* (New York: Scribner's, 1939), p. 149.

35. Saunders, p. 172; Rempel, p. 256.

Hitler's Foreign Policy

World War II began before dawn on September 1, 1939, when German forces invaded Poland. Hitler did not formally declare war, but two days later the British and French proclaimed that "a state of war existed" between their countries and Germany. A second global conflict had broken out less than twenty-one years after the end of the first. Unlike its predecessor in 1914, responsibility for the outbreak of World War II has never sparked a controversy. Virtually all historians have accepted the verdict of the judges at the Nuremberg trials in 1946: Hitler and his lieutenants planned and waged an aggressive war. With access to abundant documentation and a wide variety of sources in the postwar decades, scholars have assessed the Nuremberg verdict and found it to be valid. In his exhaustive study of the diplomatic prelude to the war, published in 1989, historian Donald Cameron Watt concludes: "What is so extraordinary . . . is that Hitler's will for war was able to overcome the reluctance with which virtually everybody else approached it. Hitler willed, desired, [and] lusted after war."[1]

In 1961 British historian A. J. P. Taylor challenged the Nuremberg verdict in his *Origins of the Second World War*. It was, and still is, the only revisionist work to be taken seriously. Taylor admits that Hitler's invasion of Soviet Russia in 1941 was premeditated, but "it is unlikely that he intended the actual war against Great Britain and France in 1939."[2] Taylor argues that Hitler planned to destroy the Treaty of Versailles and annex neighboring territories inhabited by German-speaking peoples. He achieved these goals without bloodshed but not without the threat of force. To avoid another conflict with Germany, the British and French adopted what Taylor calls the "misguided policy of appeasement." It failed, Hitler invaded Poland, and the Reich's previous antagonists declared war. Most historians now agree with Taylor that the Nazis did not expect Britain and France to declare war in September 1939, but there is ample documentation to prove that Hitler was plotting aggressive action before the invasion of Poland. The Nuremberg verdict still stands, but Taylor's thesis has been a catalyst for more critical and analytical studies of the origins of the war.

Hitler's Goals

Hitler's ultimate objectives, first articulated in the 1920s, drove the foreign policy of the Third Reich. At the conclusion of *Mein Kampf* he wrote: "A state which in this age of racial poisoning dedicates itself to the care of its best racial elements must some day become lord of the earth."[3] Hitler was convinced that the past and future of human civilization depended on the Aryans and "therefore they alone among the peoples of the earth deserve to live and prosper."[4] Hitler never doubted that Germany was the only Aryan nation fit to lead the struggle against the "race poisoners" of the world. To ensure the Aryan victory in the war for "world domination," Germany would have to train its "racially untainted young men" to be ruthless, ideologically committed warriors. Imperial Germany's defeat in World War I, Hitler believed, was due in part to a shortage of racially pure, ideologically dedicated soldiers. Hence, the racial cleansing of the Third Reich, which included the elimination of aliens (chiefly the Jews and Gypsies) and of mentally and physically disabled Aryans, became an essential racial component of Hitler's foreign policy.

The territorial policy of the Third Reich was shaped by Hitler's conviction that the British blockade, which strangled the Second Reich's overseas trade during World War I, was one of the principal reasons for the defeat in 1918. In *Mein Kampf* he wrote that Germany must redirect its expansion toward the heartland of the Eurasian land mass, specifically "Russia and the border states subject to her." Hitler believed that the conquest of eastern Europe would provide an inexhaustible supply of foodstuffs for the "thousand year Reich." He was also convinced that a "nation's strategic security was in direct proportion to its territorial dimensions."[5] Hence, the Third Reich's staying power required a vast continental landmass. In Hitler's view, it was the narrow geopolitical vision of its leaders that irreparably damaged the Kaiser's Reich.

The subjugation of the Soviet Union would also fulfill Hitler's specific racial and political objectives. He believed that the "Slavic hordes" and their communist masters could be subdued by conventional warfare, but they could threaten German rule by sheer weight of numbers. Consequently, the entire area would have to be "Germanized," which meant the enslavement, resettlement, or extermination of indigenous populations. To Hitler, Russia was the breeding ground of Jewish "bacilli," which he held responsible for the Bolshevik Revolution in 1917. He saw the Bolshevik takeover as a victory for world Jewry, and the Soviet Union as the center from which the danger of a global communist revolution and the rule of Jewry radiated. This possibility, according to Hitler, was particularly dangerous to the Aryan race and its German core. His obsession with racial purity became so inextricably linked with the destruction of the Soviet Union—his central political objective—that "Russia's defeat and the extermination of the Jews were—in theory as later in practice—inseparable for him."[6]

Before he could achieve his long-term goals, Hitler had to fulfill his immediate objectives, also formulated in the 1920s. These included rearming Germany, abolishing the Treaty of Versailles, neutralizing France, and acquiring neighboring German-speaking territories. Hitler's diplomacy—sometimes aggressive, often risky, always skillful—was remarkably successful. By the summer of 1939 Germany's economy and war machine were ready for a limited war, the Treaty of Versailles was a dead letter, France was diplomatically isolated and militarily vulnerable, and Hitler seemed on the verge of peacefully acquiring the mostly German-speaking Polish corridor. The Reich had increased its Germanic population base by annexing Austria and the German-speaking Czechoslovakian region of the Sudetenland in 1938. In March 1939 the occupation of the rest of Czechoslovakia, an industrialized nation whose citizens were Slavic speakers, expanded Germany's productive capacity.

Hitler was only partly successful in meeting two other immediate objectives: alliances with Italy and Britain. Since neither of those nations was interested in expansion into eastern Europe, Hitler believed that both would be willing to help protect Germany's western frontier against France, thereby improving his chances of victory in the east. As an inducement to form the Rome–Berlin Axis in 1936, Hitler agreed to support Mussolini's imperial aspirations in the Mediterranean and North Africa. The alliance with Britain never materialized, however, even though Hitler was prepared to guarantee the security of Britain's overseas empire. This concession was not enough; the British viewed his plans for continental expansion as a grave threat to their security and commercial interests.

The realization of Hitler's grandiose, murderous vision dictated a future totally dedicated to the needs of war. In 1934 Hitler told Hermann Rauschning, a party official who later defected to the West and wrote about the dangers of Nazism, that war was essential and permanent: "War is a constant; war is everywhere. There is no beginning, there is no conclusion of peace. War is life. All struggle is war. War is the primal condition."[7] Yet he repeatedly claimed that his goals could be attained peacefully and promised that there would be no war. It was Hitler's biggest lie, but most Germans and many foreigners believed it, or wanted to believe it. This deception worked to Hitler's advantage as he became the prime mover in European diplomacy from 1933 to 1939.

Hitler's Diplomacy, 1933–1936

Hitler's decision to launch a full-scale rearmament program early in 1933 signaled the beginning of a new era in German foreign policy. Strengthening the armed forces, which were unprepared to wage war on even one smaller neighbor, was essential to the attainment of his goals. But rearmament also offered immediate political and economic benefits. Bold diplomatic initiatives, such as challenging the arms limitation provisions of the Treaty of Versailles, would solidify the support of the traditional elites, especially the military and industrialists. Such moves would be impossible if the army remained within the 100,000-man limit set by the treaty. By the end of 1933, the army was larger and better equipped, and the military air force, expressly prohibited in the treaty, had expanded. To pay for the programs, military appropriations rose from 800 million Reichsmarks (RM) in 1932, only 1 percent of the GNP, to 1.9 billion RM in 1933, 3 percent of a slightly larger GNP. The rearmament program's modest contribution to Germany's economic recovery pleased the industrialists.[8]

In October 1933 the French provided Hitler with his first opportunity to challenge the Treaty of Versailles. At the Geneva Disarmament Conference, which had reconvened on the day after Hitler's appointment to the chancellorship, the British offered to allow Germany to achieve parity in manpower and weapons with other European states within five years. Since the other powers had ignored the treaty's mandate for a "general limitation of the armaments of all nations," Hitler countered by proposing an end to all arms controls. The French refused, and insisted on retaining the limits for an eight-year period in which Germany could prove its good faith and clearly indicate the scope of its long-range rearmament goals. Adopted in October 1933, the French plan gave Hitler a pretext for leaving the Geneva Conference and the League of Nations simultaneously. He proclaimed his peaceful intentions and protested against the "obvious aim to discriminate against Germany."[9] Hitler had won his first diplomatic victory by making demands that he sensed his opponents would reject, a tactic that would prove successful in later negotiations. Withdrawal from the Geneva Conference and the League of Nations also enhanced his popularity at home and his diplomatic reputation abroad.

By the end of 1934 Germany's rearmament was in full swing, with the enthusiastic approval of the army, big business, and the general public. Defense spending rose to 4.1 billion RM, 6 percent of a GNP that had increased by 8 billion RM. The armed forces were significantly stronger, but Germany was still diplomatically vulnerable. In January 1934 Hitler concluded a nonaggression pact with Poland, the first in a series of bilateral agreements that were generally more beneficial to Germany than the other signatory. Hitler and his generals feared that their eastern neighbor, a participant in France's "collective security" network of alliances and agreements among eastern European nations, might attack the Reich's weakly defended eastern border. The nonaggression pact temporarily eased tensions and gave Poland a false sense of security, which served Hitler's purposes admirably. This bilateral agreement, which he had no intention of honoring, weakened France's effort to create a system of anti-German alliances in eastern Europe.

Because his army was not combat-ready in 1934, Hitler responded cautiously to an incident involving Austria and Italy. Internal unrest in Austria

led to the establishment of a quasi-fascist dictatorship under Chancellor
Engelbert Dollfuss in February 1934. Austrian Nazis, with Hitler's approval,
instigated riots and created so much disorder that Mussolini, who feared that
his northern neighbor's instability might endanger Italy's security, sent angry
protests to Berlin. Following a visit to Venice in June, Hitler mistakenly believed that Mussolini was prepared to withdraw his protection from Dollfuss.
He therefore urged the Austrian Nazis to increase the tempo of unrest,
which culminated in an abortive putsch in July and the assassination of Dollfuss. Mussolini, whose army was much larger than Hitler's, sent several Italian
divisions in battle dress to the Brenner Pass. Hitler denied complicity in the
failed putsch and urged the Austrian Nazis to support the new chancellor,
Kurt von Schuschnigg. The Italian dictator withdrew his troops from the
Austrian frontier and the crisis passed. For Hitler the lesson was clear: the
Reich's armed forces were not yet strong enough to risk confrontation with
a well-armed state. Moreover, he did not wish to alienate a potential ally.

The year 1935 was a successful one for Hitler. It began with a previously scheduled plebiscite in the Saar, a tiny coal-rich German province
that had been under French occupation since 1919. Given the choice between France and Germany, the Saarlanders voted overwhelmingly to join
the Reich. Buoyed by the plebiscite, Hitler shunned an Anglo-French offer
of eventual equality in armaments, readmission to the League of Nations,
and a reciprocal regional agreement against air attack. In early March he
announced the formation of the Luftwaffe and the reestablishment of universal conscription to raise an army of thirty-six divisions, approximately
550,000 men. (Under the *Wehrgesetz* [defense law] that Hitler issued in
May 1935, the term Reichswehr, used to designate the Weimar Republic's
100,000-man army, was replaced by Wehrmacht.) Both measures violated
the military provisions of the Treaty of Versailles. A month later, representatives of the French, British, and Italian governments met at Stresa in northern Italy to formulate a response. They issued a declaration of solidarity,
condemned Hitler's breach of the treaty, and intimated that they would
stand firm against further violations.

Within weeks the solidarity of the "Stresa Front" was crumbling. In
June 1935 the British, seeking to avoid a costly arms buildup and wary of
becoming entangled in the continent's collective security system, concluded a naval pact with Germany without consulting France. Hitler's delegate, Joachim von Ribbentrop, agreed that the Reich would voluntarily
limit its naval tonnage to 35 percent of Britain's total, while the British
conceded equal submarine tonnage to Germany. The naval pact showed
that the British preferred direct negotiations with Germany and, as Hitler
hoped, had not ruled out the possibility of an Anglo-German entente.

The Stresa Front evaporated completely in October 1935 when Mussolini invaded Ethiopia in an act of unprovoked and brutal aggression. The
Italians bombed civilian populations and used mustard gas against the
troops of the poorly armed African nation. The League of Nations voted

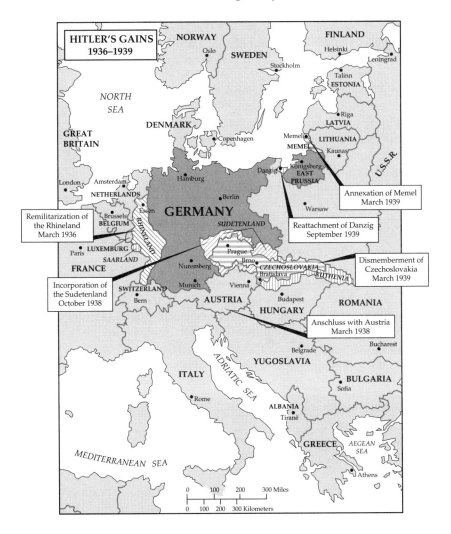

to impose sanctions on Italy, but under the League's rules such a vote meant only that the member nations voluntarily agreed to curtail the export of all strategic materials, except oil, to the resource-poor aggressor. League delegates politely applauded the Ethiopian emperor Haile Selassie's eloquent warning of the grave dangers to the West if Italian aggression went unpunished, but the sanctions were ignored. To Hitler, it was clear that democratic nations, including the United States, which also ignored the sanctions, lacked the will to penalize fascist aggression. He was much more optimistic about the success of his next and most audacious challenge to the Treaty of Versailles, the militarization of the Rhineland.

Although he was quite certain that the French would not block the passage of German troops, Hitler proceeded cautiously. He secured Italy's consent from Mussolini, a signatory of the 1925 Locarno Treaty in which Germany pledged to honor the territorial adjustments to its western frontier. He then announced that the demilitarization of the Rhineland had been invalidated by the formation of a new Franco-Soviet alliance on February 11, 1936. Hitler issued the order for troop deployment on March 2 and set the date for it to be carried out on the following Saturday, March 7, hoping that no counteraction would be taken until the weekend was over. As it turned out, there was no resistance. German forces, numbering 22,000 troops and 14,000 local policemen, crossed the river on schedule to the cheers of thousands of Rhinelanders.

The militarization of the Rhineland was Hitler's greatest triumph to date, but also, as he later admitted, the most "nerve-racking" time of his life. "If the French had . . . marched we would have had to withdraw with our tails between our legs." Germany had only one division, and that "would have been wholly inadequate for even a moderate resistance." Years later he congratulated himself: "Anyone you can care to mention would have lost his nerve. . . . What saved us was my unshakable obstinacy and my amazing aplomb."[10] Hitler's "amazing aplomb" was greeted with unprecedented national acclaim. Socialist observers' public opinion reports (sent regularly to the SPD leadership in Prague) noted that the mood of joy was infectious and that Hitler's defiance of the west, the attack on Versailles, and the peaceful restoration of sovereignty over German territory had aroused a "new admiration" for the Führer. A middle-class housewife from Hamburg, Luise Smoltz, wrote in her diary: "I was totally . . . overjoyed at the entry march of our soldiers, at the greatness of Hitler and the power of his speech, the force of the man."[11] Hitler's plebiscite on March 29 showed massive popular support for the Rhineland venture: 98.8 percent.

The militarization of the Rhineland was a watershed in the diplomatic history of the 1930s. It invalidated the Locarno Pact, nullified the Treaty of Versailles, and dealt a fatal blow to France's collective security arrangements in eastern Europe. The French, whose army was far larger than the Wehrmacht, greatly overestimated the number of German occupation forces in the Rhineland. They refused to take counter measures without British support. The latter was not forthcoming. Britain responded by issuing a written protest to Hitler's action. In retrospect, it appears that Britain and France had missed their last best chance to block Nazi aggression without bloodshed. Had the French dispatched even a single division into the Rhineland, they would have dealt a severe, perhaps fatal, blow to Hitler's prestige in Germany.

By not taking the offensive, the French exposed the exclusively defensive nature of their strategic thinking. They assumed that their highly touted Maginot Line, a sophisticated network of permanent fortifications under construction since 1930, would enable them to beat back a German invasion. Before the year was out, the Belgians, fearful of endangering their neutral status, withdrew their support for the proposed extension of the Maginot Line along the Franco-Belgian border to the English Channel. The

This cartoon, published in *The Nation* in the fall of 1936, exposed Hitler's duplicity. While claiming to be a man of peace, as represented by the dove and the olive branch, Hitler was arming Germany.

British, no longer encumbered by the Treaty of Versailles or French collective security, were convinced that European peace depended on their ability to meet Hitler's demands. The Führer exulted in his diplomatic triumph, but he would have to wait at least two years for another spectacular victory.

The outbreak of the Spanish Civil War in July 1936 allowed Hitler to test new equipment in combat, strike a blow at communism (Soviet agents and local communists eventually took over the Spanish government in the war), and reach an agreement with Mussolini. The *Duce*, whose prestige always needed bolstering, dispatched several well-equipped divisions to aid a fellow Fascist, General Francisco Franco, leader of powerful right-wing forces seeking to overthrow Spain's leftist, democratic government. Hitler sent 16,000 troops armed with newly manufactured planes, tanks, and artillery. For the first time in Europe, aircraft deliberately bombed civilian populations. The German raid over the Basque city of Guernica in 1937 was immortalized by Pablo Picasso's *Guernica*, a huge canvas that graphically depicted the effects of terror bombing in mournful blacks, whites, and grays. Once again the West's desultory response appeared to reward fascist aggression. Fearing air raids over Paris and London in the event of war with Germany, the French and British kept the peace by yielding to Hitler. Meanwhile, German participation in the war, which Franco's forces won after two-and-a-half years of bloody fighting, strengthened Hitler's diplomatic and economic position. The Reich's armed forces performed well, and their military cooperation with Italy culminated in the formation of the Rome–Berlin Axis on October 25, 1936.

The first step following the formation of the Rome-Berlin-Tokyo Axis took place on November 25, 1936, when Ribbentrop concluded the Anti-Comintern Pact with Japan. Ostensibly designed to fight Bolshevism, the principal feature of the agreement was the promise of benevolent neutrality if either power went to war against the Soviet Union. Stalin's army was not an immediate threat, but Hitler felt that the Reich needed additional moral and, if necessary, military support against the spread of communism. Earlier in 1936 Stalin, finally recognizing fascism as a mortal enemy, ordered communists throughout the world to form an anti-fascist "popular front" with all parties of the left. The Anti-Comintern Pact was designed not only to diminish the Soviet threat but also to pressure Britain into an agreement with Germany. It encouraged the Japanese to escalate their war against China, which increased the risk of confrontation with the great sea powers, Britain and the United States.[12] The Anti-Comintern Pact, which Italy signed in November 1937, foreshadowed the alignment of belligerents in the war: the three Axis powers against the three Allies, Britain, the Soviet Union, and the United States.

Interlude, 1936–1938

Europe experienced a diplomatic respite from the end of 1936 to March 1938. Hitler believed that Germany was economically and militarily unprepared for territorial expansion at that time. Industrial production and employment continued to rise, but rapid rearmament had unwelcome side effects, such as shortages of consumer goods, massive deficit spending, and an unfavorable balance of trade. To solve these problems, Hjalmar Schacht, minister of economics and president of the Reichsbank, proposed slowing the pace of rearmament, devaluing the Reichsmark to bring it in line with the dollar and the pound, increasing trade with industrialized nations, and demanding the return of the Reich's overseas colonies. (Some of Germany's colonies had become League of Nations mandates; others were transferred to the Allied nations.) It was a conservative program that enjoyed considerable support among the business community and the military. Nevertheless, Hitler rejected Schacht's proposals and appointed Göring to head the four-year plan in September 1936. Its provisions for autarky, tighter government controls, and increased expenditures for rearmament, were exactly the opposite of what Schacht and other traditional elites believed to be in Germany's best interests.

The ultimate solution to Germany's economic problems, Hitler believed, lay in the conquest of living space (*Lebensraum*) in the east, which would create an economically self-sufficient continental empire. By exploiting this vast region's natural resources, the Reich could finance its arms buildup and relieve shortages of consumer goods without increased deficit spending or raising taxes.[13] The promise of a future empire in the east could not solve Germany's immediate economic problems, especially the high cost of Hitler's insistence on accelerating the rearmament program. Nor could the Führer's grandiose vision dispel the undercurrent of dissatisfaction among the military, the foreign ministry, and some industrialists.

On November 5, 1937, Hitler summoned high-ranking military and government officials to a meeting in the Reich Chancellery to discuss expansion, rearmament, and economic growth. In attendance were Werner von Blomberg, minister of war and supreme commander of the Wehrmacht (the term referred to all three branches of the armed forces collectively); Werner von Fritsch, commander-in-chief of the army; Erich Raeder, chief of naval operations; Hermann Göring, head of the Luftwaffe; Foreign Minister Konstantin von Neurath; and Hitler's military adjutant, Colonel Friedrich Hossbach. His account of the meeting, the Hossbach Memorandum, or Protocol, became one of the most famous documents of Third Reich diplomacy.

The central theme of Hitler's four-hour monologue was the conquest of living space in the east, without which the thousand-year Reich would never materialize. He had made an "immutable decision" to employ force as the solution to the "space problem," and Germany had to be prepared to use it no later than 1943–1945. By that time the Reich's enemies—France, the Soviet Union, and Britain, whose refusal to endorse his continental imperialism had made an Anglo-German entente impossible—would be sufficiently armed to halt the Reich's expansion. Hitler predicted that British and French intervention in the Spanish Civil War, which could lead to war with Italy (because of Mussolini's substantial commitment of troops and matériel to Franco's forces), would allow Germany to launch its drive to the east as early as 1938. This drive would begin with the "lightning defeat" of Czechoslovakia and Austria. Blomberg, Fritsch, and Neurath questioned the likelihood of full-scale war in the Mediterranean and argued that Britain and France, together with a powerful Czech army, could easily block Germany's eastward expansion. A few months later, all three had lost their jobs.

To the Nuremberg prosecutors, the Hossbach Memorandum was a "blueprint for war," offering conclusive proof that Hitler and his lieutenants were plotting aggression nearly two years before the invasion of Poland. With the exception of A. J. P. Taylor, historians agree that the Hossbach Memorandum, in which Hitler also addressed domestic problems, provides clear evidence for the Nazi regime's aggressive intent. Taylor argues that the conference was not designed to present a blueprint for conquest, but was simply a "maneuver in domestic affairs" to discredit Schacht and other conservatives who opposed rapid rearmament. Taylor writes: "The memorandum tells us what we knew already, that Hitler (like every

BOX 6.1 ■ THE HOSSBACH MEMORANDUM: EXCERPTS

The Hossbach Memorandum may not exactly have been a "blueprint for war," but it clearly signaled Hitler's intention to pursue a more aggressive foreign policy and underscored the centrality of living space in the Reich's strategic planning. The text is based partly on memory and partly on Hossbach's notes taken at the conference.

> The aim of German policy was to make secure and to preserve the racial community and to enlarge it. It was therefore a question of space. The German racial community comprised over 85 million people and, because of their number and the narrow limits of habitable space in Europe, constituted a tightly packed racial core such as was not to be met in any other country and such as implied the right to a greater living space than in the case of other peoples. . . . The space necessary to insure it (the security of our food situation) can only be sought in Europe, not . . . in the exploitation of colonies. . . . Moreover, areas producing raw materials can be more usefully sought in Europe in immediate proximity to the Reich, than overseas.

In the Memorandum, Hitler targets Austria and Czechoslovakia for forcible "incorporation" and discusses the attitude of Russia and Poland.

> The incorporation of . . . [Czechoslovakia and Austria] with Germany . . . would mean shorter and better frontiers . . . and creating new units up to a level of about 12 divisions. . . .

> The degree of surprise and the swiftness of our action were decisive factors for Poland's attitude. Poland—with Russia at her rear—will have little inclination to engage in war against a victorious Germany. Military intervention by Russia must be countered by the swiftness of our operations; however, whether such an intervention was a practical contingency at all was, in view of Japan's attitude, more than doubtful.

Although not at the conclusion of the Memorandum, Hitler's most warlike statement reads:

> Germany's problem could only be solved by means of force and this was never without attendant risk.

Louis L. Snyder, *National Socialist Germany: Twelve Years That Shook the World* (Malabar, FL: Krieger, 1984), pp. 137–43.

other German statesman) intended Germany to become the dominant power in Europe." Taylor dismisses Hitler's references to conquering living space in the east as "speculations on how this [German hegemony in Europe] might happen." The speculations were "mistaken," and they "bear hardly any relation to the actual outbreak of war in 1939."[14] Yet, Hitler's remarks were more than speculations. On December 22, 1937, Hitler ordered the general staff to begin planning "Operation Green," the code name for an invasion of Czechoslovakia.

Hitler's belief that Germany must abandon its former colonial and trade policy in favor of an economically self-sufficient empire in the east had become the undisputed centerpiece of the Third Reich's foreign policy. For the traditional elites and the nation as a whole, there was no turning back. Personnel changes following the Hossbach Conference reflected Hitler's determination to silence conservative critics. He targeted the Foreign Ministry, which had traditionally been a preserve of the old aristocracy. The Reich's ambassador to Great Britain, Joachim von Ribbentrop, replaced Neurath as foreign minister. Impressed by Ribbentrop's role in negotiating the Anglo-German naval agreement and the Anti-Comintern Pact with Japan, Hitler had appointed him to the ambassadorial post in 1936. Once in London, Ribbentrop's tactless diplomacy helped convince the British that a mutual assistance pact with Germany was not in their best interests. Fortunately for Ribbentrop, the British were still open to bilateral talks with the Reich. Hitler was willing to overlook his ambassador's bungling and to "kick him upstairs," where he could do less damage. The Führer wanted his foreign minister to be little more than an errand boy, a task for which Ribbentrop was ideally suited.

Hitler's top priority was tightening his hold over the army. In late January 1938 Blomberg, embarrassed by the highly publicized disclosure of his wife's previous police record as a prostitute, resigned. The disclosure had been instigated by Göring, who had hoped to replace Blomberg. Hitler, however, had decided to dissolve the ministry of war and himself assume the powers of commander-in-chief of the Wehrmacht. A few days earlier, Reinhard Heydrich produced a police dossier of a homosexual whose name happened to be Werner Fritsch. The general was not a homosexual, as Heydrich later admitted, but, aware of Hitler's displeasure, Fritsch resigned. His replacement was the more malleable Walther von Brauchitsch. Fearing Hitler's wrath, Brauchitsch and other generals did not rise to the defense of their colleagues.

In place of the war ministry, Hitler established the *Oberkommando der Wehrmacht* (High Command of the Armed Forces), or OKW. To head the new command structure, he selected the obsequious General Wilhelm Keitel. Hitler's takeover of the army was now complete. His generals either had to comply or resign. The only one to choose the latter was Chief-of-Staff Ludwig Beck, who resigned in August 1938. A resistance movement formed around Beck, giving dissenting officers a third option: clandestine opposition while still in uniform.

The Road to War, 1938–1939

By March 1938 Hitler felt that both the domestic and foreign situations were ripe for the union (*Anschluss*) of Austria and the Reich. He was more popular than ever, the army and business community were supportive, arms production was rising, and economic indicators were inching upward.

Britain had not intervened in the Spanish Civil War, but Foreign Secretary Lord Halifax, reflecting the views of the new prime minister Neville Chamberlain, told Hitler in November 1937 that Danzig, Austria, and Czechoslovakia were "questions which fall into the category of possible alterations in the European order." He added that Britain's interest was "to see that any alterations [by which he meant Hitler's annexation of some neighboring German-speaking territories] should come through the course of peaceful evolution."[15] Civil war had not broken out in France, as Hitler had predicted at the Hossbach Conference, but political turmoil had reached crisis proportions. Diplomatically, the French could do little more than follow Britain's lead. Meanwhile Austrian Nazis under orders from Berlin were undermining Chancellor Schuschnigg's government by persistent internal agitation.

The prelude to the *Anschluss* took place on February 12, 1938, in the Berghof, Hitler's new home near Berchtesgaden. He berated Schuschnigg for hours, demanding sweeping concessions for Austrian Nazis, including the appointment of one of their leaders, Arthur Seyss-Inquart, as minister of the interior and security. This amounted to a Nazi takeover of the Austrian government, as Schuschnigg well knew. On March 9 the Austrian chancellor announced that a plebiscite on Hitler's demands would be held on March 13. Hitler was furious. On March 10 he issued a directive for an invasion, which was carried out bloodlessly two days later. Most Austrians welcomed their Germanic cousins from the Reich, especially their former compatriot, whose tumultuous reception in Linz convinced him to abandon his initial idea of a satellite government under Seyss-Inquart in favor of immediate *Anschluss*. Most of Hitler's former countrymen approved when Austria was formally annexed to the "Greater German Reich."

Hitler's first territorial acquisition was an unmitigated triumph. In his final plebiscite, held shortly after his return from Vienna, 98 percent of the German electorate voted in favor of the *Anschluss*. Economic benefits included valuable ores, additional steel capacity, and over 44 million Reichsmarks in foreign exchange reserves, all of which helped to maintain the tempo of rearmament.[16] Mussolini telephoned his approval, while the British fatalistically accepted the *Anschluss* as a "family affair." Strategically, Germany was now in a stronger position to take action against Czechoslovakia, the other nation named in the Hossbach Memorandum. To most Europeans, Hitler's initial demand—autonomy for the 3 million German-speaking inhabitants of the border province of Sudetenland—appeared reasonable. Nor did the peace of Europe seem threatened when he ordered the Sudeten Nazis to agitate more vigorously and to make demands so sweeping that the Prague government would have to refuse them.

Tensions heightened in May 1938 when both Czechs and Germans made military decisions. Responding to false rumors of German troop movements, the Czech government partially mobilized its armed forces. Several days later Hitler approved the final draft of Operation Green, which included a reference to his "unalterable decision to smash Czechoslovakia by military action in the near future." This call for aggression replaced an earlier draft by Keitel, which stated that Germany "would not smash Czechoslovakia without provocation in the near future through military action."[17] Hitler's explicit invasion directive, which included a deadline of October 1, 1938, removed all doubt that he planned and wanted war before 1939.

Throughout the summer of 1938 Hitler and Czechoslovakia's western advocates, Britain and France, engaged in a diplomatic tug-of-war. As the Sudeten Nazis demonstrated, rioted, and demanded autonomy, the Czech government, which had maintained correct, if not always friendly, relations with its minorities, imposed tighter restrictions. If the Czechs were forced to give up the heavily fortified Sudetenland, they could not defend themselves against a German attack. Moreover, the loss of one minority group was likely to spur demands from Hungarian, Polish, and Slovak minorities for autonomy or independence.

The French had pledged earlier to defend Czechoslovakia, but because of their domestic political strife, they were content to let the British, who had no treaty obligations in eastern Europe, take the initiative. Hitler's assessment was correct: Britain was opposed to Germany's continental expansion, but would not risk war to prevent it. On the other hand, Chamberlain, who wanted to be remembered as a peacemaker, was reluctant to give the Reich a free hand in eastern Europe. He therefore sought agreements with Hitler that would simultaneously preserve Britain's honor and the peace of Europe.

The crisis reached a critical phase in early September. In a speech at the last Nuremberg party rally on September 12, 1938, Hitler lashed out at the Czech government, which had just declared martial law in the riot-torn Sudetenland. He demanded annexation as the only "just and lasting solution" to the crisis, which, he claimed, had cost the lives of more than 300 Germans. Prepared to arrange for the peaceful transfer of the Sudetenland, Chamberlain flew to Berchtesgaden on September 15 for the first of two face-to-face meetings. Hitler said that he would rather risk another world war than allow "Czech atrocities" to continue. Nevertheless, he was willing to discuss the matter further at another meeting on German soil, and he reiterated an earlier pledge that the Reich had no further territorial claims.

A week later, at Bad Godesberg, Hitler shocked Chamberlain by demanding that Germany be allowed to occupy the Sudetenland on October 1 and that the grievances of the Polish and Hungarian minorities be immediately resolved. By rejecting the peaceful transfer of the Sudetenland, Hitler revealed his intention to crush Czechoslovakia even if it meant war with Britain and France. The meeting ended in an impasse, and no further talks were scheduled. On September 27, as Chamberlain and French premier Edouard Daladier reluctantly ordered mobilization, Hitler staged a demonstration of motorized units in Berlin. Like their counterparts in Britain and France, the German public showed little enthusiasm for war.

Still favoring a military solution to the Czech crisis, the Führer did not revise his timetable.

On September 28 Hitler abruptly changed his mind. Italy's unwillingness to go to war, the mobilization of the French and British, the apathy of the German people, and his generals' gloomy assessment of the Wehrmacht's offensive capability persuaded him to postpone the invasion. Mussolini rescued Hitler from an embarrassing dilemma by proposing a four-power conference to work out the details of the Reich's takeover of Czech territory. The Munich summit conference, attended by the Italian dictator, Hitler, Chamberlain, and Daladier, took place on September 29–30. It marked the culmination of British and French appeasement, as the western leaders sanctioned Germany's occupation and annexation of the Sudetenland on October 1. The four principals agreed to guarantee Czechoslovakia's territorial integrity once the Polish and Hungarian border issues were settled. Not on the agenda was a private meeting between Chamberlain and Hitler that resulted in a pledge to consult each other if future crises threatened the peace of Europe. The Führer assured the prime minister that the Reich was interested only in incorporating neighboring German-speaking regions and had no further territorial demands.

Millions of Europeans acclaimed the signatories as great statesmen who had averted war. Motion-picture cameras recorded Chamberlain's return from Munich and his pronouncement of having achieved "peace in our time," as he waved the draft of his private agreement with Hitler. The film is a powerful visual reminder of a universally discredited policy. Yet

This oft-shown still from motion picture footage shows Chamberlain returning from the Munich Conference. Chamberlain said that the agreement signed by "Herr Hitler" would guarantee "peace in our time"; in retrospect it signified the folly of appeasement.

both he and Daladier received enthusiastic receptions. For the German people, Munich seemed to confirm the propaganda image of their Führer as a man of peace. They did not know that Hitler regarded Munich as a flawed triumph: "That fellow Chamberlain has spoiled my entry into Prague," he said to his SS guards in the Reich Chancellery upon his return from Munich.[18] The Führer felt "trapped into settling for what he had publicly claimed rather than what he really wanted," which was a war to destroy Czechoslovakia. To the last days of his life, Hitler regretted his change of plans in 1938. The western powers, he complained to Bormann in his Berlin bunker in February 1945, had deprived him of war on its most "favorable date."[19]

Britain's most formidable opponent of appeasement, Winston Churchill, blasted the Munich Agreement: "Instead of snatching the victuals from the table, [Hitler] has been content to have them served to him course by course. We are in the presence of a disaster of the first magnitude."[20] Few historians would argue against the proposition that appeasement was the wrong policy at the wrong time. The Munich Agreement reinforced Hitler's view that the British and French, whom he contemptuously characterized as "small fry," had given him a free hand in eastern Europe. Czechoslovakia, deprived of its frontier fortifications in the Sudetenland and the territories that it would be forced to cede to Poland and Hungary, was vulnerable to a Nazi takeover. To Josef Stalin, whose belated offer to aid the Czechs may have been disingenuous, the Munich Agreement signaled the western powers' intention to direct the Reich's expansionist impulse eastward. The suspicious Soviet dictator therefore embarked on a new course that would culminate in the Nazi-Soviet Nonaggression Pact on the eve of World War II.

In defense of appeasement one can argue that the Royal Air Force and sophisticated air defense systems, especially radar screens, which helped Britain repel Germany's bomber offensive in 1940, could not have done so in 1938. Critics are quick to point out, however, that in 1938 the Wehrmacht was too weak to defeat Czechoslovakia, France, and Britain simultaneously. Moreover, several generals and diplomats, led by the recently retired Ludwig Beck, had informed London of their plans to arrest Hitler if Britain and France intervened on behalf of Czechoslovakia. The plot might not have succeeded in any event, but their conspiracy promptly collapsed when Chamberlain signed the Munich Agreement. Military action instead of appeasement in 1938 might have destroyed the Nazi regime at considerably less cost than the war that broke out a year later.[21]

Hitler never intended to abide by the terms of the Munich Agreement. On October 21, 1938, he directed the military to be prepared to liquidate "the remainder of the Czech state" and to occupy Memel (a German-speaking city ceded to Lithuania in 1919).[22] At the same time he announced, as he had done after the Austrian *Anschluss* and to Chamberlain after Munich, that the Reich had no further territorial demands. To add credibility to this promise, Foreign Minister Ribbentrop traveled to Paris in December 1938 to reaffirm Germany's abandonment of claims to Alsace-Lorraine. Nothing was said about Czechoslovakia, which Hitler had already decided to destroy. In January 1939 he pressured the Czech government to grant complete autonomy for the Slovaks and Ruthenians, a small minority group living in the extreme eastern part of the country. On March 14, 1939, with the Reich's backing, the Slovak government proclaimed an independent Slovakia. On the same day Czech president Emil Hacha, to preserve the integrity of what was left of the Czechoslovakian state, met with Hitler in Berlin. In a tirade reminiscent of that which Schussnigg had endured a year earlier, the Führer demanded the complete capitulation of Czechoslovakia. Resistance, the Czech president was told, would result in the annihilation of his country's army and the destruction of Prague by air. Hacha signed a prepared communiqué in which he "placed the fate of the Czech people and country in the hands of the Führer of the German Reich."[23]

The destruction of Czechoslovakia was complete on March 15, 1939, when German troops peacefully occupied Prague. Hitler and his entourage followed a few hours later. The last democratic state in eastern Europe had ceased to exist. The Nazis granted Slovakia satellite status and established the Reich Protectorate of Bohemia-Moravia in the western part of the country (roughly coterminous with the present Czech Republic). Former foreign minister Konstantin von Neurath was appointed Reich Protector. Hungary took over Ruthenia, but Hitler refused to cede any territory to Poland. On March 23, 1939, Lithuania agreed to Germany's annexation of Memel.

The Western powers did not protest the Reich's conquests, but the apparent victory was not without cost. Britain and France finally realized that Hitler was a liar who could not be trusted. He had not only swallowed up more territory, but, for the first time, he had broken his pledge to annex only lands inhabited by German-speaking peoples. The British and French, belatedly recognizing that their own security was threatened by Hitler's expansionism in eastern Europe, abandoned appeasement for diplomatic intervention. Their first test would soon come over Poland.

The Outbreak of War, 1939

In late March Hitler ordered Ribbentrop to begin negotiations with the Polish government over the return of German-speaking Danzig, which the Versailles treaty had converted to a free city to serve as a seaport for Poland, and unlimited access to East Prussia through the Polish Corridor. Chamberlain quite rightly suspected that "Herr Hitler" wanted more than Danzig and extraterritorial transportation rights. On March 31 Chamberlain, supported by his countrymen's public opinion and the French government, announced that Britain would guarantee Poland's territorial integrity if it was clearly threatened. Bolstered by Chamberlain's declaration, the Poles rejected the Reich's demands and refused Hitler's offer to extend

---

BOX 6.2 ■ HITLER'S DECISION ON WAR WITH POLAND,
MAY 23, 1939

This Nuremberg document, while much more explicit than the Hossbach Memorandum, played only a minor role in the trial. Speaking to his generals, Hitler hopes to avoid war with Britain and France while attacking Poland, but cautions that Germany must be prepared for a simultaneous conflict with the West. He does not yet envision Russia as an ally.

> Danzig is not the subject of the dispute at all. It is a question of expanding our living space in the East and of securing our food supplies. . . . If fate brings us into conflict with the West, possession of extensive areas in the East will be advantageous. . . . The Polish problem is inseparable from conflict with the West. There is therefore no question of sparing Poland, and we are left with the decision: *to attack Poland at the first suitable opportunity.* We cannot expect a repetition of the Czech affair. There will be war. Our task is to isolate Poland. The success of the isolation will be decisive. Therefore, the Führer must reserve the right to give the final order to attack. There must be no simultaneous conflict with the Western Powers.
>
> If it is not certain that a German-Polish conflict will not lead to war in the West then the fight must be primarily against England and France. . . . Economic relations with Russia are possible only if political relations have improved . . . . It is not impossible that Russia will show herself to be disinterested in the destruction of Poland. Should Russia take steps to oppose us, our relations with Japan may become closer. If there were an alliance of France, England, and Russia against Germany, Italy, and Japan, I should be constrained to attack England and France with a few annihilating blows. We must prepare ourselves for the conflict.

Snyder, *National Socialist Germany*, p. 146.

---

the 1934 German-Polish nonaggression pact for another twenty-five years. The stage was set for the final round of diplomatic brinksmanship between Germany and the western powers. For Hitler, the stakes had never been higher. He not only faced a more resolute Britain and France but his designs on Poland also drew its powerful eastern neighbor, the Soviet Union, into the diplomatic loop.

Hitler did not alter his Danzig–Polish Corridor demands throughout the spring and summer of 1939, but his true intentions were revealed in early April and again in late May. On April 3 he ordered plans for "Case White," an invasion of Poland to take place no later than September 1. His speech on May 23 (see text box) reiterated his *Lebensraum* policy, reaffirmed his intention to destroy Poland, and acknowledged the risk of war with Britain and France. Although unaware of the full extent of the Reich's military preparations, the western powers sensed that the crisis created by Poland's refusal to yield to Hitler's demands could easily plunge Europe into another world war. Hence there was much diplomatic maneuvering.

Both Germany and the western powers courted the Soviet Union, but neither was prepared to meet Stalin's demands for massive economic aid and a guarantee of Soviet territorial integrity. To strengthen his diplomatic position, Hitler sought to make Japan a partner in the Pact of Steel which he had negotiated with Italy in April, an agreement that would have obligated all three powers to fight against Britain, France, and the Soviet Union. The Japanese government, however, refused to commit itself.

The diplomatic impasse frustrated Hitler. Still smarting from the missed opportunity for war with Czechoslovakia, he was eager to demonstrate the Reich's military might by conquering Poland. Moreover, he was convinced that Germany needed a war to push rearmament ahead at an even faster pace. In August he told his generals: "Our economic situation is such that we can only hold out for a few more years."[24] The four-year plan had fallen short of its goals, and the increases in Germany's industrial capacity in 1938 and 1939 were due largely to the appropriation of Austrian and Czech facilities. For Hitler, the conquest of Poland was a key component in his strategy to gain resources and increase Germany's economic self-sufficiency by means of short, predatory wars. He feared that without a substantially expanded economic base his eastern empire would never materialize. Therefore, in late August he decided to come to terms with Stalin, whose negotiations with Britain and France had stalled. The communist dictator, worried about his own military security and convinced that the western powers were bent on directing Nazi Germany toward an invasion of the Soviet Union, had also decided to come to terms with Hitler.

On August 22, 1939, Hitler sent Ribbentrop to Moscow with an offer that Stalin could hardly refuse. In return for guarantees of nonintervention and massive shipments of raw materials, Germany would sanction the Soviet Union's occupation of eastern Poland and support its hegemony over the Baltic states of Lithuania, Latvia, Estonia, and Finland and the Romanian province of Bessarabia. These provisions were incorporated into the Nazi-Soviet Nonaggression Pact, signed the following day. The signatories revealed that the two powers, long at odds over ideological issues, had agreed not to attack each other in the event of war. They carefully concealed the cynical transfer of territories and the partitioning and conquest of nations. Much to the astonishment of the rest of the world, the two dictators had overcome ideological inhibitions and become de facto allies. Stalin gained territory and time to prepare his military forces for what he feared would be the inevitable Nazi invasion of his country. For Hitler, the benefits were immediate deliveries of food and raw materials and the assurance of Stalin's nonintervention in Poland.

The Nazi-Soviet Nonaggression Pact removed the last obstacle to war; diplomatic exchanges preceding the invasion of Poland were anticlimactic. On the afternoon of August 25 Hitler ordered the Wehrmacht to attack, but the Anglo-Polish alliance concluded the same day and reports of Mussolini's refusal to enter the war prompted him to rescind the order. Göring, the least hawkish among the Nazi hierarchy at that time, attempted

WONDER HOW LONG THE HONEYMOON WILL LAST?

This Clifford Berryman cartoon appeared in a London newspaper shortly after the signing of the Nazi-Soviet Nonaggression Pact.

to "reason" with Chamberlain through a Swedish intermediary, but the British prime minister was in no mood to negotiate. The French reaffirmed their support of the British position, and the Poles, who believed that their armed forces, backed by the western powers, could stop the Germans, refused to compromise. On August 31 an impatient Hitler ordered the invasion to begin on the following day.

With the Wehrmacht in attack positions on the border, Hitler and Goebbels decided that the German people, whose apathy was no less palpable than the previous year, needed an incident to arouse their patriotic passions. Heydrich ordered the local SS commander to stage a fake raid on a German radio station in the border city of Gleiwitz. Several SS men dressed condemned German prisoners in Polish uniforms, took them to the radio station, killed them with lethal injections, and machine-gunned the corpses. The bodies were photographed and portrayed in the German press as invading Polish soldiers. Unmoved by the Gleiwitz incident, most Germans greeted the news of the invasion with silence. Two days later, on September 3, 1939, when Britain and France reluctantly declared war on

---

BOX 6.3 ■ THE PEOPLE'S UNENTHUSIASTIC RESPONSE TO WAR

Bernt Engelmann, who was imprisoned in Dachau in 1944 for his anti-Nazi activities, was a young radio operator in the Luftwaffe at the outbreak of war in 1939. He describes the reaction to Hitler's announcement from Düsseldorf, where his unit was stationed:

> Since a radio blackout had been ordered, we had nothing to do but listen to news bulletins from morning till night. Now and then Pliechelko (a comrade) rode his motorcycle to nearby staff headquarters or into town on various official errands . . . . I of course went along with Pliechelko to guide him . . . around Düsseldorf. That meant that, in spite of all leaves being canceled, I got to see everyone again, my mother, Aunt Annie, Fräulein Bonse, and Herr Desch (all members of his anti-Nazi circle). This time they were certain that full-scale war was imminent.
>
> And indeed, on the morning of Friday, September 1, Hitler's decision was broadcast: "And so I have determined to speak with Poland in the same language Poland has been using toward us for months now. . . . My love of peace and my boundless patience must not be mistaken for weakness or cowardice. . . . Since early this morning . . . fire is being returned, and from now on each bomb will be answered with a bomb!"
>
> I rode into town with Pliechelko. No crowds had gathered. We saw no trace of rejoicing, certainly none of the wild enthusiasm that Germans had shown when war broke out in August 1914. Here and there small groups of people clustered around the newsstands, talking quietly among themselves, depressed and anxious. No one waved to us soldiers or pressed bouquets into our hands, as they did in 1914.

Bernt Engelmann, *In Hitler's Germany* (New York: Schocken Books, 1986), pp. 168–69.

Germany, their people's reaction was equally glum. Millions still had vivid memories of the horrors of the Great War.

"God help us if we lose this war," was Göring's response to the news from London and Paris on September 3. Hitler was much more optimistic. Publicly, he exuded confidence in the Wehrmacht's ability to crush Poland swiftly. Privately, he worried about Germany's powerful enemies and his own mortality. On the eve of the Nazi-Soviet Nonaggression Pact, the Führer told his generals that the current political and diplomatic situation favored the Reich: "There is no other choice left to us. In two or three years these fortunate circumstances will no longer exist. No one knows how long I may live. Therefore conflict [is] better now." He also revealed his genocidal intentions: "I have put my death's head formations in place with the command relentlessly and without compassion to . . . [murder] many women and children of Polish origin. . . . Poland will be depopulated and settled with Germans." The fate of Russia, he said, "will be exactly the same. . . after Stalin's death" (Hitler believed that the Russian dictator was seriously ill). His only fear was that "at the last moment some *Schweinehund* [a derogatory term] will present me with a mediation plan."[25] On August 25, 1939, that *Schweinehund*, presumably Neville Chamberlain, concluded a military alliance with Poland. The era of appeasement was over. This time there would be no mediation.

Conclusion

There is no doubt that Hitler wanted war with Poland. Most historians, however, hold that he did not want the world war that began when Britain and France refused to abandon their eastern ally—at least not at that time.[26] In the absence of explicit documentation, one can reasonably infer that Hitler expected Britain and France, who had so readily sacrificed Czechoslovakia for the sake of "peace in our time," to forsake another eastern European state in 1939 for the same reason. That they did not do so might have surprised the Führer, but it did not shake his determination to crush Poland and proceed with plans for building his Germanic empire in eastern Europe. The price for his "racial utopia" was a general war into which France and Britain would inevitably be drawn, but Hitler was prepared, even eager, to pay that price. Although he did not choose the moment of its beginning, he relished the prospect of war with the western powers, a war that he deemed essential to the fulfillment of his murderous goals. Britain and France made it official with their declaration, but Hitler unleashed the greatest war in human history.

INFOTRAC® COLLEGE EDITION SEARCH TERMS

For additional reading go to Infotrac College Edition, your online research library at http://www.infotrac-college.com.

Enter the search term "German history foreign policy" using Keywords.

Enter the search term "Hitler foreign policy" using Keywords.

Enter the search term "appeasement" using Keywords.

Enter the search term "Poland, World War, 1939–1945" using the Keywords.

Enter the search term "nonagression pact" using the Subject Guide.

Notes

1. Donald Cameron Watt, *How the War Came* (New York: Pantheon Books, 1989), p. 610.

2. A. J. P. Taylor, *Origins of the Second World War* (New York: Premier Books, 1961), p. 103.

3. Adolf Hitler, *Mein Kampf* (Boston: Houghton Mifflin, 1962), p. 688.

4. Norman Rich, *Hitler's War Aims* (New York: Norton, 1973), p. 4.

5. Ibid., p. 6.

6. Andreas Hillgruber, *Germany and Two World Wars* (Cambridge: Harvard University Press, 1981), p. 51.

7. Quoted in Fest, *Hitler* (New York: Harcourt Brace Jovanovich, 1973), p. 608.

8. John Hiden, *Germany and Europe, 1919–1939* (London: Longman, 1993), pp. 51, 211.

9. Ibid., p. 87; Gordon Craig, *Germany, 1866–1945* (New York: Oxford University Press, 1978), p. 679.

10. Quoted in Alan Bullock, *Hitler and Stalin: Parallel Lives* (New York: Alfred A. Knopf, 1992), pp. 531–532.

11. Ian Kershaw, *Hitler 1889–1945: Hubris* (New York: Norton, 1999), p. 590.

12. Hiden, p. 187.

13. David E. Kaiser, "Hitler and the Coming of the War," in Gordon Martel, ed., *Modern Germany Reconsidered, 1870–1945* (London: Routledge, 1992), pp. 182–83; Volker Berghahn, *Modern Germany* (New York: Cambridge University Press, 1982), p. 149.

14. Taylor, p. 131.

15. Kaiser, p. 185.

16. Hiden, p. 163.

17. Ibid., p. 163.

18. Quoted in Ian Kershaw, *Hitler 1936–1945: Nemesis* (New York: Norton, 2000), p. 164.

19. Gerhard L. Weinberg, *The Foreign Policy of Hitler's Germany: Starting World War II* (Chicago: University of Chicago Press, 1980), pp. 165–66.

20. Quoted in Alan Bullock, *Hitler: A Study in Tyranny* (New York: Harper & Row, 1964), p. 470.

21. Williamson Murray, *The Change in the Balance of Power, 1938–1939* (Princeton: Princeton University Press, 1984) p. 263.

22. Jeremy Noakes and Geoffrey Pridham, eds., *Documents on Nazism, 1919–1945* (New York: Viking Press, 1975), p. 551.

23. *Documents on German Foreign Policy,* Series D (Washington, DC, United States Government Printing Office, 1949–), Vol. 4, p. 270.

24. Kaiser, p. 188.

25. Quoted in Fest, p. 594; International Military Tribunal, *Trial of the Major War Criminals before the International Military Tribunal* (Nuremberg, 1947–1949), Vol. 26, 1014-PS.

26. Berghahn, p. 156; Fest, pp. 608–616.

CHAPTER SEVEN

Hitler's Limited War, 1939–1941

In his book *The Second World War*, British military historian John Keegan writes: "The Second World War is the largest single event in human history. . . . It killed fifty million human beings, left hundreds of millions of others wounded in mind or body, and materially devastated much of the heartland of civilization."[1] The war also ended European supremacy in world affairs, ushered in the atomic age, and ignited a "cold war" between the two giants among Germany's adversaries, the United States and the Soviet Union. World War II began as a series of short, limited campaigns by which Hitler mastered much of Europe. It escalated into a global conflict in 1941 when Germany invaded the Soviet Union and, four days after the Japanese bombed Pearl Harbor, declared war on the United States. Four years later, the belligerents laid down their arms and silenced their war machines, as Germany and Japan surrendered unconditionally.

More than half of the 50 million (the most recent estimates have been revised upward to 60 million) dead were noncombatants. Some perished as both sides used air power and other new weaponry in an attempt to cripple the enemy's war effort by destroying production facilities and attacking civilian targets. The majority of the defenseless victims died, however, because World War II was a new kind of war. In the spring of 1941, Hitler told his generals that the conflict was a "struggle of ideologies and racial differences and [would] have to be waged with unprecedented, unmerciful, and unrelenting hardness."[2] The Jews, a people without a state, could not retaliate, but Hitler's powerful enemies, particularly the Soviet Union, responded in kind. No one in 1918 could have imagined that, in less than a generation, a conflict combining advanced technology, new strategy, and murderous ideology would produce a death toll nearly six times greater than World War I.

In spite of the horror and futility of trench warfare, most generals and military planners before 1939 were still wedded to defensive tactics. Hitler, however, realized that his goals could be accomplished only by taking the offensive. He was quick to recognize the potential of new strategies formulated during the interwar period by English, French, and German thinkers, such as Basil Lidell Hart, Charles de Gaulle, and Heinz Guderian. Advanced technology, they argued, had made the stationary war of attrition obsolete and ushered in a new age of offensive warfare, spearheaded by tanks, motorized vehicles, and aircraft, which could cover hundreds of miles in several days and crush the enemy within a few weeks. The Germans were the first to practice the concept. They called it *Blitzkrieg* (lightning war), a term that first appeared in the Reich's military lexicon in 1939 and is now in common usage.

Colonel Heinz Guderian published a blueprint for Blitzkrieg in 1937, a year before he was promoted to general. It won Hitler's immediate, enthusiastic support. Fiercely opposed by conservative generals, Guderian's revolutionary theory of mechanized warfare would never have been practiced without the Führer's backing. The Luftwaffe was to be the "first-strike" arm of the invasion; it would cripple the enemy's air force; attack communication, transportation, and production centers; and bomb troop formations and civilian targets. The centerpiece of the Blitzkrieg would be the concentrated armored divisions of tanks, or *Panzers*, which would lead the ground attack. Motorized infantry traveling in trucks or tracked personnel carriers would follow the armor. Masses of regular foot soldiers would secure areas overrun by the mechanized units, thus allowing the motorized infantry to keep pace with the rapidly advancing tanks. If properly executed against an unprepared enemy, the Blitzkrieg would conquer whole countries, annihilate or capture entire armies, damage or destroy large cities, capture production facilities and war matériel, and subjugate civilian populations, all within weeks and without mobilizing the economy for total war.

Blitzkrieg in Poland

In September 1939 Germany was better prepared for the new style of warfare than any of its potential adversaries. Since the reintroduction of conscription in 1935, the Wehrmacht had grown to 105 divisions: 89 infantry, 10 motorized, and six armored, with over 3,000 tanks. Poland had only 40 divisions and 200 modern tanks. The French had as many troops as the Reich and, with their British ally, a comparable amount of armor, but their tanks were designed for infantry support rather than massed attack. Neither Britain, nor France, nor Poland had armored divisions or the defensive capability to stop the Blitzkrieg. Since nearly all of the Wehrmacht's combat-ready forces would be engaged in Poland, France, with over 60 divisions available for an assault on Germany, could have attacked the Reich's vulnerable western frontier. It was defended by only twenty-five weak reserve divisions and the West Wall (also known as the Siegfried Line), a defensive system that was still under construction. Nevertheless, Hitler had nothing to fear. The French remained strongly committed to the Maginot Line defensive strategy. Even if the high command had had a sudden change of mind and ordered French troops to attack Germany, they would have done so alone. Their British ally showed no interest in supporting an offensive operation in the first month of the war.

Germany also enjoyed superiority in the air. Evenly divided between fighters and light bombers, the Luftwaffe's 3,600 planes were ideally suited for tactical support of advancing ground forces in lightning campaigns. The Royal Air Force (RAF) could match the Luftwaffe in quality, but the British had neither enough bombers to conduct an air offensive nor fighters to defend against the Germans. With only 1000 first-line planes, the French air force was too weak to be effective on offense or defense.[3]

Divided into five armies attacking at specific points on the Polish-German frontier, the Wehrmacht broke through Polish defenses as early as September 4 and began rolling toward Warsaw. At the same time, the Luftwaffe bombed key military objectives and civilian targets. With a piercing siren-like sound as it descended to deliver its deadly payload, the German Stuka dive bomber was especially terrifying to Polish civilians. On September 25, ten days after the Wehrmacht had beaten back a Polish counterattack, hundreds of bombers destroyed much of Warsaw's inner city. Two days later, the city's commander surrendered to the Reich; all resistance ended on October 6. Meanwhile, Stalin, alarmed at the speed of the Reich's juggernaut, invaded eastern Poland on September 17. The Poles, who knew nothing of the territorial provisions of the Nazi-Soviet Nonaggression Pact, offered little resistance.

BUNDESARCHIV, KOBLENZ

This German photograph, not intended to arouse sympathy for the survivors, shows Warsaw after the bombardment in 1939. The Polish capital was the first major city in World War II to suffer the horrors of saturation bombing.

It was a crushing defeat for Germany's eastern neighbor. Poland lost nearly 200,000 men killed, wounded, or missing; more than 900,000 prisoners (700,000 to Germany, 200,000 to the Soviets); its entire air force; and its independence. Germany annexed the Polish Corridor and Danzig and occupied the central part of the country, including Warsaw. Hitler entrusted the rule of this area, designated as the General Government of the Occupied Polish Territories, to Hans Frank. The Soviets' share of the spoils in the east comprised nearly one-half of Poland's territory, one-third of its population, and a small but productive oil field in the southeastern part of the country. Inspecting his victorious troops near the front, a jubilant Hitler hailed the power, speed, and success of the first Blitzkrieg. It was an impressive performance, but the Wehrmacht's losses were far from negligible. Casualties totaled about 45,000 killed, wounded, or missing, while the Poles had destroyed or damaged several hundred planes and nearly one-fourth of the Panzer forces engaged—about 600 tanks. The Germans had used up 80 percent of their ammunition.[4] Replacing these losses would take at least eight months, which, despite Hitler's bravado, was a major reason for postponing offensive operations in the west until the spring of 1940.

Poland's agony had another dimension. Five weeks after the invasion, Himmler's SS Race and Settlement Office, which had existed since 1935, and a new subagency called the Reich Commissariat for the Strengthening of Germandom, began the Germanization of Poland. Assisted by the army, the SS arrested and executed thousands of the Polish intelligentsia, including teachers, writers, priests, and government officials; forcibly evacuated a million Poles and Jews from the annexed corridor to the General Government; and resettled the area with *Volksdeutsche*, ethnic Germans from various parts of eastern Europe. Heydrich's men drove hundreds of thousands of Jews from their homes and forced them to live in ghettos in the larger cities, such as Warsaw and Lodz. Although Hitler had not formulated the exact details of the new order in Europe, the outlines of Germanization were clear by the end of 1939. In Poland, whose Slavic and Jewish inhabitants were at the bottom of the Nazi racial hierarchy, thousands of noncombatants lost their lives within a few months of the German occupation. More thousands were uprooted, pauperized, and enslaved. The ghettoization of Polish Jews was the first step in the "Final Solution of the Jewish Question." Tragically, the horrors of Nazi racial policy were just beginning.

Germanization was central to Hitler's vision of the new order, but he rarely played a "hands-on" role in administering it. Directing the war effort was his top priority, and he became increasingly absorbed in it. Shortly after Poland's surrender, he made peace overtures to Britain and France, offering a cessation of hostilities in return for recognition of the division of Poland between Germany and the Soviet Union. He predicted death and destruction on a massive scale if the western powers should decline his offer. Hitler blamed the tense atmosphere on Jewish capitalism and hawkish elements in Britain led by Winston Churchill. If that view should prevail, he promised that Germany would fight, and vowed that a November 1918

BOX 7.1   ■   HIMMLER EXPLAINS GERMANIZATION

On May 25, 1940, Heinrich Himmler, the chief administrator of Germanization in Poland, wrote a memorandum to Hitler, titled "Reflections on the Treatment of the Peoples of Alien Races in the East." Nazi policies and their ultimate goal were made more explicit:

. . . . For the non-German population of the East there must be no higher school than the four-grade elementary school. The sole goal of this school is to be simple arithmetic—[being able to count] up to five hundred at the most; writing of one's name; the doctrine that it is a divine law to obey the Germans and to be honest, industrious, and good. I don't think that reading is necessary. Apart from this school there are to be no schools at all in the East.

. . . . The population of the General Government during the next ten years, by necessity and after a consistent carrying out these measures (which also included the deportation of racially fit Polish children to the Reich and their permanent adoption by German families), will be composed of the remaining inferior population supplemented by the population of the eastern provinces deported there. . . .

The population will, as a people of laborers without leaders, be at our disposal and will furnish Germany annually with migrant workers and with workers for special tasks (roads, quarries, buildings). . . . They will, under the strict, consistent, and just leadership of the German people, be called upon to help work on its everlasting cultural tasks and its buildings and perhaps, as far as the amount of heavy work is concerned, will be the ones who make the realization of these tasks possible.

A Nuremberg document published in Michael Berenbaum, ed., *Witness to the Holocaust* (New York: HarperCollins, 1997), pp. 75–76.

would never be repeated. Both countries rejected the offer, which one historian has called "an olive-branch clenched in a mailed fist."[5]

Within a week of the western powers' rejection, Hitler ordered the Wehrmacht to prepare for an invasion of western Europe on November 12. Several days earlier, Walther von Brauchitsch, the commander-in-chief of the army, advised Hitler to postpone the offensive because of bad weather and the need to train more troops in the art of mechanized warfare. A furious Hitler accused Brauchitsch and some of his colleagues on the General Staff of incompetence, cowardice, and disloyalty; nevertheless, he canceled the November 12 invasion. Lack of preparedness and bad weather forced the cancellation of four invasion dates in December and one in January 1940. Hitler reluctantly agreed to launch Operation Yellow, the code name for the invasion of western Europe, in May 1940.

Coinciding with, but unrelated to, Hitler's decision to postpone the November invasion were an assassination attempt and an officers' plot to overthrow the Nazi regime. The former was the work of Georg Elser, a Swabian carpenter, who had no connection with the military resistance. On the evening of November 8, 1939, Hitler visited Munich's Bürgerbräu

Cellar where he spoke to a group of old fighters and paid tribute to the fallen comrades of the Beer Hall Putsch. Because a heavy fog had grounded air traffic, he left the hall early so that he could return to Berlin by train. Had he adhered to his original schedule, a bomb that exploded near the speaker's podium, killing seven and injuring sixty-three, would almost certainly have ended the Führer's life. Elser was imprisoned and later executed at Dachau. The incident was the first of several in which Hitler would thwart the plans of assassins by altering his schedule, either accidentally or deliberately.

Among the leaders of the officers' plot were the retired general Ludwig Beck and his successor as chief-of-staff, Franz Halder; Admiral Wilhelm Canaris, head of the Abwehr, the Reich's military intelligence agency; and Colonel Hans Oster, Canaris's top aide. Two other high-ranking generals, Karl von Stülpnagel and Erwin von Witzleben, were also active participants. The conspirators' goal was to overthrow Hitler on the eve of the November 12 invasion and install a military government, but they were handicapped by poor planning, a lack of strong leadership, and the reluctance of Brauchitsch and other high-ranking generals to participate. The conspirators also disagreed on Hitler's fate. Some wanted to assassinate him, while others favored arresting him and administering psychological tests that would prove his unfitness to rule.[6] The plot was not detected, but the conspirators eventually disbanded without ever moving against Hitler. The resistance movement persisted, however. All the conspirators except Halder were involved in subsequent assassination plots, including the final and nearly successful attempt on July 20, 1944.

Had Hitler known of the conspiracy, it would have reinforced his contempt for many career officers, as well as an already exaggerated sense of his own indispensability. On November 23 he revealed to several generals how the assassination attempt two weeks earlier had affected his assessment of the war. He pointed out that Germany could oppose Russia only "when we are free in the West." He had "unalterably decided to attack France and England at the most favorable and earliest moment. . . . I consider it possible to end the war only by means of an attack. . . . The whole thing means the end of the World War, not just a single action. It is a matter of not just a single question but of the existence or non-existence of the nation."[7] As for the effect of the assassination attempt on his self-image, Hitler likened his position to that of his hero, Frederick the Great, whom he believed had saved Prussia during the Seven Years' War (1756–1763). The Führer was convinced that only he could save the Reich and lead it to victory:

> I must in all modesty describe my own person as irreplaceable. Neither a military nor a civilian personality could replace me. The attempts at assassination may be repeated. I am convinced of the strength of my brain and of my resolution. Wars will always be ended only by the annihilation of the opponent. . . . Time is working for the enemy. . . . If

the enemy will not make peace, then our position worsens. No compromises. Hardness toward ourselves. I shall attack and not capitulate.
The fate of the Reich depends upon me alone. I shall act accordingly.[8]

Success in Poland and another brush with death had magnified his self-
assurance to the point where he equated himself with Germany and linked
the fate of the nation to his own life, a "messianic sense run rampant."[9]
Hitler would still listen to suggestions, vacillate, and weigh options, but in
his own mind his destiny was clear: he alone could achieve his goals in his
lifetime, which, by the end of 1939, he had come to believe, would not be
long.

Blitzkrieg in Northern Europe

While Hitler and his military advisers planned the next round of offensive
operations in northern and western Europe, Britain and France focused on
defense. The French reinforced the Maginot Line, patrolled the Franco-
German border with light tanks, and braced themselves for the German invasion. The British increased appropriations for the air force, navy, and air
defense systems and engaged German submarines and warships on the high
seas. Both sides monitored the Winter War, in which Finland astounded the
world by beating back a powerful Soviet offensive in December 1939. Neither the Reich nor the western powers intervened. The Finns had won a
battle, but they could not win the war. Outnumbered nearly 50 to 1, they
surrendered to the Soviet Union on March 12, 1940. Finland retained its
sovereignty, but handed over more of its territory than Stalin originally demanded. Meanwhile, the principal belligerents scarcely fired at each other
on land—one of the many paradoxes of the most savage war in human history. This bizarre interlude of nearly eight months, from October 1939 to
April 1940, will be remembered as the "phony war" or *Sitzkrieg* (sitting
war), terms coined by contemporary journalists.

Hitler had always harbored doubts about Soviet military power, and
the Winter War convinced him that the Red Army was no match for the
Wehrmacht—a false assessment that played a critical role in Germany's defeat in the war against the Soviet Union. A more immediate effect of the
Winter War was a heightened awareness of Scandinavia's strategic importance. Hitler's war machine depended on Swedish iron ore, but the ore
could not be shipped from Swedish ports during the winter when the Gulf
of Bothnia, an arm of the Baltic, was frozen. During those months, the ore
had to be transported by rail to Norwegian ports and then by ship down
the Norwegian coast and on to Germany.

Hitler approved preliminary plans for the invasion of Denmark and
Norway in December 1939. At the same time, Britain's first lord of the ad-
miralty, Winston Churchill, proposed mining Norwegian coastal waters to
block the iron ore shipments, and landing British and French troops along
the coast to deny the Germans access to Norwegian port facilities. In early

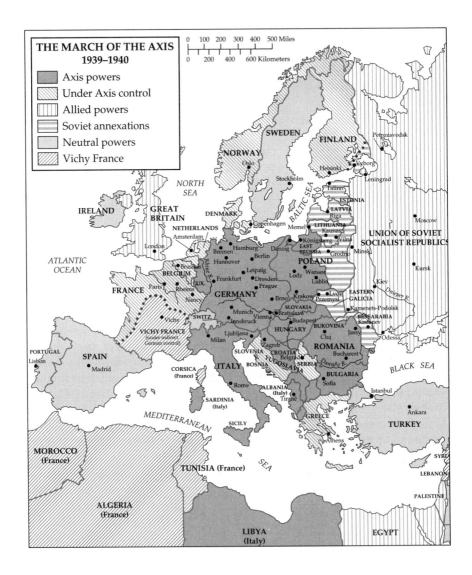

0   100 200 300 400 500 Miles

0   200   400   600 Kilometers

SWEDEN   FINLAND   Petrozavodsk

NORWAY   Helsinki   Vyborg
Oslo

NORTH
SEA   Stockholm   Leningrad

Tallinn

ESTONIA

IRELAND   GREAT   DENMARK   LATVIA   Moscow
BRITAIN   Riga

NETHERLANDS   Copenhagen Memel LITHUANIA
Amsterdam   Kaunas   UNION OF SOVIET
Königsberg Vilna   SOCIALIST REPUBLICS

London   Hamburg Danzig EAST Grodno Minsk
ATLANTIC   Bremen   PRUSSIA
OCEAN   BELGIUM   Hannover Berlin   POLAND   Kursk
BRUSSELS   Leipzig   Lodz   Warsaw

FRANCE   Paris Rheims   Frankfurt Dresden   Lublin   Kiev
Nancy   GERMANY   Prague   Brno Krakow Lvov   EASTERN
Przemysl GALICIA

Vichy   SWITZ.   Munich Vienna   SLOVAKIA   Kamenets-Podolsk
Innsbruck   Bratislava   BESSARABIA
VICHY FRANCE   Budapest   Kishinev
(under indirect   HUNGARY   BUKOVINA   Jassy
German control)   Ljubljana Milan   Cluj   Odessa

PORTUGAL   SLOVENIA   ZagrebCROATIA   ROMANIA
Lisbon   SPAIN   ITALY BOSNIA   Belgrade   Bucharest   BLACK SEA
Madrid   CORSICA   YUGOSLAVIA SERBIA   Danube R.
(France)   Rome   BULGARIA
Sofia   Istanbul

SARDINIA   ALBANIA
(Italy)   (Italy)   Ankara
Tirane

MEDITERRANEAN   SICILY   GREECE   TURKEY

SEA   Athens

MOROCCO   SYRIA
(France)

TUNISIA (France)   LEBANON

PALESTINE

ALGERIA
(France)

LIBYA   EGYPT
(Italy)

March 1940, just before German intelligence apprised him of the British
plan, Hitler ordered the Wehrmacht to invade during the first week of
April. Given the overwhelming strength of the Royal Navy, the invasion of
Norway was a risky undertaking; however, bad weather prevented British
ships from intercepting the German invasion fleet. The Wehrmacht's execution of its first and only amphibious operation was nearly flawless. Denmark, the land bridge to Norway, surrendered within hours after German
troops crossed the border on April 8. On the same day, the Reich launched
its invasion fleet, landing 10,000 troops at several sites in Norway, the most
important of which were the capital, Oslo, and the city of Narvik, which
was north of the Arctic Circle and the nearest Atlantic port to Swedish iron
mines. As reinforcements arrived on slower transports, Norwegian resis-

tance quickly collapsed. By April 14 the Germans controlled southern and central Norway.

The British managed to salvage something from "the ramshackle Norwegian campaign," as Churchill called it. The Royal Navy sank half of the Reich's twenty destroyers and two of its eight cruisers. Firing pre–World War I artillery as they guarded the Oslo fjord at its narrowest point, an additional German cruiser was sunk by the Norwegians. Two battle cruisers and a small battleship were disabled for months. For the first time in the war, Allied ground troops engaged their German counterparts. British forces at Narvik on April 14 enjoyed some success, but Anglo–French forces landing at other northern coastal locations suffered a humiliating defeat at the hands of German units, which the Allies often outnumbered. Moreover, the Wehrmacht seized the Norwegian ports with such speed that the British were forced to abandon their mining operation.

Hitler was pleased with the Scandinavian campaign. With the occupation of Denmark and Norway, his northern flank was secure, while Sweden, paying the price of a precarious neutrality, remained Germany's major supplier of iron ore throughout the war. During the winter months the ore was shipped by train to Narvik, from where it was transported on merchant ships down the Norwegian coast to Germany. The Norwegian coast also provided sites for submarine bases and airfields. The Germans used these bases to prey on British shipping and, later in the war, to attack Allied transport ships en route to the Soviet Union.[10] The German navy's heavy losses were not critical. The Reich's tiny surface fleet occasionally raided and harassed Allied shipping, but never during the war did it have the capacity to cripple the Royal Navy or to damage what was later to become Britain's lifeline to the United States. For the latter, the Reich would depend on its expanding submarine fleet, which was not involved in the Norwegian campaign.

Blitzkrieg in Western Europe

During the first year of the war, Hitler delegated the responsibility for tactics to his generals, but he laid down broad strategic aims and gave final approval to the plan of attack. In March 1940 he rejected Halder's proposal to secure Belgian airfields and North Sea ports before launching a major strike against France and Britain. This course of action, as Halder admitted, would postpone a decisive offensive against France until 1942. The Führer was much more enthusiastic about the ideas of General Erich von Manstein, one of the Reich's finest military minds.[11] Chief of staff for General Gerd von Rundstedt, the commander of Army Group A, one of three units designated for Operation Yellow, Manstein targeted the Ardennes region of southeastern Belgium as the main point of entry into France.

Generals on both sides judged the hilly, heavily wooded terrain of the Ardennes Forest to be virtually impassable for tanks. Manstein and Rundstedt disagreed. They argued that armored divisions breaking through the

Ardennes would separate the two main Allied armies and allow the Wehrmacht to overrun northern France. Hitler had been considering a similar approach. He claimed Manstein's Ardennes scheme, called "Sickle Stroke," as his own and made it the linchpin of Operation Yellow. It was to be executed by Rundstedt's Army Group A. To the north, Army Group B, commanded by General Fedor von Bock, would attack Allied forces in Belgium and the Netherlands, while south of the Ardennes a smaller Army Group C, led by General Ritter von Leeb, would engage the enemy opposite the Maginot Line.

Germany's adversaries—the French, British, Dutch, and Belgians—had a quantitative superiority in manpower, 156 divisions to 136, and tanks, over 4,000 to 2,750, but the Wehrmacht enjoyed the advantage in experience, organization, planning, and leadership. Britain and France had hastily assembled three or four mechanized groups, but they were no match for the Reich's ten powerful armored divisions, seven of which were assigned to Rundstedt's Army Group A. The Wehrmacht was a disciplined, highly motivated army, and its simple command structure—Hitler to the General Staff to the field commanders—ensured coordination between advancing ground troops, the Luftwaffe, and reserve and supply units. For the Allies, the situation was markedly different. Intelligent planning, strong leadership, effective use of equipment, coordinated troop movements, and basic communication were all lacking. The western powers were also handicapped by mutual suspicion between the British and French, a massive breakdown of morale among French soldiers and civilians, and the "Maginot Line mentality"—the vain hope that the line would stop, or at least slow, the German onslaught.

On May 10, the same day that Winston Churchill replaced Neville Chamberlain as prime minister, Hitler unleashed the Blitzkrieg in western Europe. In the north, the Allies were soon bogged down in a maze of Dutch and Belgian canals, dams, bridges, and twisted roads. Using airborne troops to capture fortresses and bridges behind enemy lines and air attacks to scatter and demoralize ground troops, Bock's Army Group B forced the Dutch's ten divisions to lay down their arms on May 14. While negotiations for a peace treaty were under way, Hitler ordered the Luftwaffe to bomb Rotterdam in order to terrorize the Dutch into unconditional surrender.[12] The raid killed nearly a thousand people and destroyed much of the city's center. The Netherlands surrendered the following day, May 15. The British portrayed the raid, the first of its kind in western Europe, as the wanton slaughter of defenseless civilians, and Rotterdam became a symbol of Nazi brutality throughout the world. The Rotterdam raid removed all restraints to the bombing of civilian targets, which both sides practiced with impunity throughout the war. Hiroshima and Nagasaki marked its horrifying climax.

Army Group B encountered more formidable resistance from Belgium's twenty-two divisions, but they could only briefly postpone the inevitable. The main body of Bock's army crossed the Meuse River and linked up with German paratroopers, who had captured fortresses behind Belgian lines. British and French reinforcements outnumbered the Germans, but they moved much too slowly and were ineptly led. These Allied forces, numbering over 300,000, were cut off from the main French army to the south when King Leopold surrendered the Belgian army on May 28. The Anglo-French troops retreated toward the port of Dunkirk, a town on the Channel coast in northern France.

Meanwhile, Army Group A in the Ardennes was executing Sickle Stroke to perfection. The Allies, expecting the heaviest German assault in Flanders, concentrated their air power and armor in northern Belgium. Hence, the 1,800 tanks of Rundstedt's Army Group A, led by Guderian's elite Panzer Corps of three armored divisions, faced light resistance. They negotiated the seventy-mile route through the "impassable" Ardennes into France in four days. French ground forces and British air attacks could not stop the subsequent drive through northern France. By mid-May the Germans clearly had the upper hand, but Hitler, overestimating France's staying power, ordered his armored columns to halt. Guderian and one of his divisional commanders, Erwin Rommel, whose reputation was greatly enhanced by the French campaign, persuaded the Führer to rescind the order. On May 20 Guderian's Panzer Corps reached Abbeville on the English Channel. In ten days Rundstedt's Army Group A had driven an impenetrable wedge between Allied forces in Belgium and the bulk of the French army to the south. Military experts around the world were stunned.

Upon reaching the Channel coast, Guderian turned north, hoping in one quick thrust to take Boulogne and Calais and destroy the Anglo-French army at Dunkirk. With Bock's forces closing in from the north, the only means of escape for the Allies was by boat across the Channel to England, but a rescue operation of that magnitude seemed to have little chance of success. On May 24 Rundstedt, with Hitler's approval, ordered Guderian's Panzers to stop fifteen miles south of Dunkirk. Bock's slower-moving Army Group B, the Führer believed, was in a better position to capture Dunkirk. Hitler and Rundstedt rightly believed that Guderian's tanks needed to pause for repairs and resupply, and that they could easily get bogged down in the canals and rivers around Dunkirk. On the other hand, Hitler and most of his military advisers wrongly believed that it would require the Reich's ten armored divisions at full strength to defeat the French. Moreover, they too readily accepted Göring's argument that precious manpower and armor would be wasted in a task that the Luftwaffe could easily accomplish.

Two days later Hitler changed his mind and ordered Guderian's Panzers to take Dunkirk. This decision clearly refutes the popular notion, which has always been speculative, that Hitler wanted to spare the British army so that he could reach an amicable agreement with the United Kingdom. Nevertheless, the two-day respite helped to save the vulnerable Allied

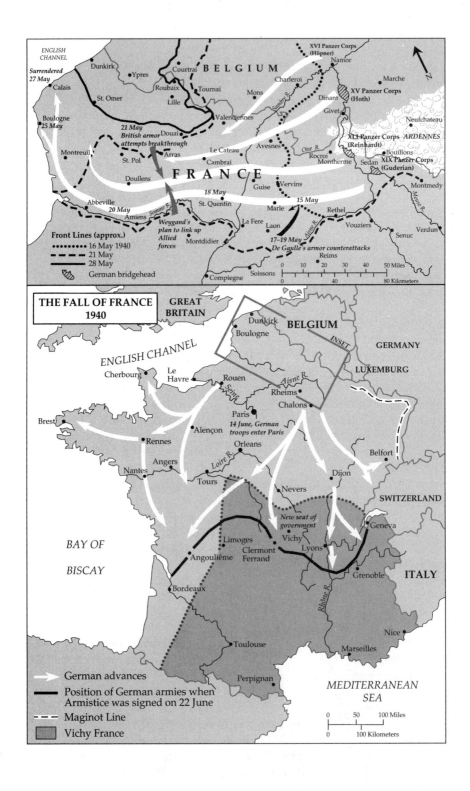

ENGLISH CHANNEL

Surrendered 27 May

Dunkirk · Ypres · Courtrai

BELGIUM

Calais

St. Omer · Roubaix · Tournai

Boulogne 25 May

Lille

Mons · Charleroi

Namor

XVI Panzer Corps (Höpner)

Marche

Valenciennes

Dinant

XV Panzer Corps (Hoth)

Givet

Neufchateau

21 May British armor attempts breakthrough · Douai · Arras

Le Cateau · Avesnes

Montreuil

St. Pol

Cambrai

F R A N C E

Rocroi

Montherme

Bouillons

XLI Panzer Corps (Reinhardt) ARDENNES

Doullens

Guise · Vervins

Sedan

XIX Panzer Corps (Guderian)

Montmedy

18 May

Abbeville

20 May · St. Quentin

Amiens · *Somme R.* · Marle

15 May

Rethel

Vouziers

Verdun

Senuc

Weygand's plan to link up Allied forces · Montdidier

La Fere

Laon · *Aisne R.*

17–19 May De Gaulle's armor counterattacks

Reims

Front Lines (approx.)
- ●●●● 16 May 1940
- --- 21 May
- — 28 May
- ◪ German bridgehead

Compiegne · Soissons

0 10 20 30 40 50 Miles
0   40   80 Kilometers

THE FALL OF FRANCE 1940

GREAT BRITAIN

Dunkirk

BELGIUM

Boulogne

INSET

GERMANY

ENGLISH CHANNEL

LUXEMBURG

Cherbourg · Le Havre · Rouen

Aisne R.

Seine R.

Rheims · Chalons

Brest

Paris

14 June, German troops enter Paris

Belfort

Rennes · Alençon

Orleans

Nantes · Angers

Loire R.

Nevers

Dijon

SWITZERLAND

Tours

Geneva

BAY OF BISCAY

Limoges

New seat of government

Vichy · Lyons

Clermont Ferrand

Angoulieme

Grenoble

ITALY

Bordeaux

Rhône R.

Nice

Toulouse

Marseilles

MEDITERRANEAN SEA

Perpignan

0   50   100 Miles
0   100 Kilometers

→ German advances

— Position of German armies when Armistice was signed on 22 June

--- Maginot Line

▨ Vichy France

forces. Protected by the canals that slowed Guderian's advance, the British began the evacuation on May 27. In spite of bad weather and the Luftwaffe, for which the Royal Air Force proved to be more than a match, the British completed the rescue operation by June 4; it will forever be known as the "miracle of Dunkirk." The Allied army had to leave its equipment on the beaches, but 338,000 troops were saved: 190,000 British, 109,000 French, and several thousand Belgians, Dutch, and Poles. (Polish officials who fled to England in 1939 and formed a government in exile were accompanied by remnants of the Polish army.) The Luftwaffe's performance fell far short of Göring's boast, and Guderian's tanks, which did not take Dunkirk until June 4, did not appreciably speed France's surrender.

Had Hitler not halted Guderian's armored columns on May 24, quite possibly they could have destroyed or captured the Allied forces at Dunkirk. The Führer's first major mistake was a costly one. With a powerful navy, an increasingly effective air force, loyal Commonwealth allies, and the promise of closer ties to the United States, Britain could have continued the war, but losing the European expeditionary force would have weakened the British will to resist and strengthened the hand of those in Churchill's government who wanted to make peace with Germany. A British withdrawal in June 1940 would have significantly altered the course of World War II.

There was more heavy fighting after Dunkirk, but the isolated, demoralized, and disorganized French army suffered one defeat after another. By mid-June all German forces, including Army Group C, which finally

A visibly elated Hitler on the occasion of his greatest triumph, the surrender of France on June 22, 1940.

breached the Maginot Line, converged on Paris. The French government rejected Churchill's proposal of an Anglo-French union and fled to Bordeaux on June 12, two days before the Germans took Paris. On June 16 Marshal Philippe Petain, the 85-year-old hero of World War I with strong right-wing sympathies, took over the government. He and his cabinet, which soon established itself in the resort city of Vichy, asked for an armistice. Hitler, intoxicated by the utter humiliation of Germany's "hereditary enemy," personally "stage-managed the armistice ceremony with pomp . . . [and] meticulous vindictiveness."[13] It took place on June 21 at Compiégne, near Paris, in the same railway car in which the Germans had received the terms of the armistice in 1918. As a gesture of contempt, Hitler left the car before the documents were signed. Motion-picture cameras recorded the Führer gleefully gesturing, almost dancing, as he savored the crowning achievement of his career. It is one of the most memorable images of World War II. When news of France's humiliation reached Berlin, Goebbels wrote: "The disgrace is now extinguished. It's a feeling of being born again."[14] Later Hitler toured Paris, seeing the city from the only car allowed to drive in the streets that day. What impressed him most was

---

BOX 7.2   ■   GERMAN TROOPS ARRIVE IN PARIS

Roger Langeron, prefect of police for seven and a half years (until he was imprisoned by the Gestapo in February 1941) describes the arrival of German troops in Paris:

> Paris awakened this morning—Tuesday, June 11—in a sort of dense cloud of black smoke. It is now nearly impossible to see in the streets. The crowds have gathered to ask questions of one another. Did the French troops burn their supplies before their retreat, or did the Germans destroy them as they advanced? The most severe problem for everyone is the mental anguish. What has happened to our armies? Where are they? The black sky only augments the uncertainty, the doubts.

> We have just learned that the oil storage tanks, located quite close to the city, were set afire during the night by the German bombardment. The exodus has increased considerably.

> From my windows on the Boulevard du Palais, I watch a sad and uninterrupted stream of horsecars, cattle, wagons, bicyclists, pedestrians, dogs, and farm animals. Mattresses are tied to the tops of cars, bags tied on behind, and the vehicles are filled with people and their most precious possessions, gathered hurriedly.

> At last, on Friday, the atrocious thing has come to pass. German troops have occupied Paris. Their headquarters have been set up at the Hotel Crillon.

> We wonder when and how they will confront us. Will they be cruel and violent? It seems to me most likely that I will be arrested right away and taken to Germany.

Tony March, ed., *Darkness over Europe: First-Person Accounts of Life in Europe during the War Years 1939–1945* (Chicago: Rand McNally, 1969), pp. 37–38.

Napoleon's grandiose tomb. Afterward he told Albert Speer, "It is magnificent. You must build me a bigger one in Berlin."[15]

Hitler's greatest victory was one of France's most devastating losses. French casualties totaled 125,000 killed, more than 200,000 wounded, and 1.5 million prisoners, as against the Wehrmacht's 45,000 killed or missing and 100,000 wounded. Britain lost 68,000 killed or wounded and all of its equipment. The Germans occupied about two-thirds of France, including the northern half of the country and the entire Atlantic coastline. Petain's regime in Vichy quickly became a Nazi satellite. The Wehrmacht governed Belgium, while Nazi civilian administrators ruled the Netherlands. The German occupation was brutal, but the Dutch, Belgians, and French were spared the horrors of Germanization as in Poland. There was no SS Race and Settlement Office or Reich Commissariat for the Strengthening of Germandom in western Europe.

Another consequence of Operation Yellow was Italy's declaration of war on France and Britain on June 10. Waiting until France's defeat was almost certain, Mussolini attacked the French-Italian border in the southeastern part of the country. "To make a people great," he told his son-in-law, Count Ciano, "it is necessary to send them into battle even if you have to kick them in the pants. That is what I shall do."[16] The Duce's reluctant warriors, outnumbering the French garrison at least 10 to 1, captured only a few hundred square yards of territory. Mussolini's rash decision expanded the war. Italian defeats at the hands of outnumbered British forces in Libya and an ill-advised invasion of Greece would lead to Germany's military involvement in North Africa and the Balkans in the spring of 1941.

The Battle of Britain

In an ostentatious public ceremony a few weeks after the fall of France, Hitler conferred the rank of field marshal on twelve generals. He boasted of his military prowess and took full credit for the Wehrmacht's brilliant performance in western Europe, but he knew that his victory was incomplete so long as the British remained in the war. Soon after France's surrender, the Führer set September 15 as the date for the invasion of Britain; its code name was Operation Sea Lion. The General Staff and Admiral Erich Raeder, the chief of naval operations, worked on a plan of attack, but they could not agree. The navy favored a massive assault at a single location on the southern coast, while the army preferred landings at several points.

Hitler, who admitted that he was "a coward on the sea," had no taste for an invasion of the United Kingdom with its powerful navy. He was also quite certain that his armed forces were unprepared for a large-scale amphibious operation. On the other hand, leaving Britain undefeated while he turned to his ultimate goal—the conquest of the Soviet Union—would necessitate fighting a two-front war, a crucial German error of World War I that he had vowed never to repeat. At this moment of indecision, he was receptive to Göring's boast that the Luftwaffe could bring Britain to its

---

BOX 7.3 ■ CHURCHILL'S "THEIR FINEST HOUR" SPEECH

On June 18, 1940, shortly before the French surrender, Winston Churchill delivered to the House of Commons one of World War II's most famous speeches. The excerpt below includes some of its most inspiring and memorable phrases:

> What General Weygand (commander of French armies at the time) called the "Battle of France" is over. I expect that the battle of Britain is about to begin. Upon this battle depends the survival of Christian civilisation. Upon it depends our own British life and the long continuity of our institutions and our Empire. The whole fury and might of the enemy must very soon be turned on us. Hitler knows that he will have to break us in this island or lose the war. If we can stand up to him all Europe may be free, and the life of the world may move forward into broad, sunlit uplands; but if we fail then the whole world, including the United States, and all that we have known and cared for, will sink into the abyss of a new dark age made more sinister, and perhaps more prolonged, by the lights of a perverted science. Let us therefore brace ourselves to our duty and so bear ourselves that if the British Commonwealth and Empire lasts for a thousand years men will still say, "This was their finest hour."

Brian L. Blakely and Jacqueline Collins, eds., *Documents in British History: Volume II, 1688 to the Present* (New York: McGraw-Hill, 1993), p. 242.

---

knees. Army and navy chiefs were skeptical, but they agreed that control of the skies was essential to the success of Operation Sea Lion. They supported Hitler's decision on August 8 to unleash the full might of the Luftwaffe against Britain, thus setting the stage for the first major air battle in the history of warfare.

Churchill's phrase—"Hitler will have to break us in this island or lose the war"—was an accurate assessment of the situation. In retrospect, it is clear that the Luftwaffe was not equipped to break either Britain's defenses or its morale. In August 1940 the Reich's two air fleets stationed in France had nearly 1000 ME 109 single-engine fighter planes, one of the best planes available during the early years of the war, and more than 1,000 medium-range bombers, which could also serve as dive bombers. These planes were poorly armed, however, making them vulnerable to British fighter attacks. British fighters also neutralized the dreaded Stuka dive bomber, which had terrorized and killed civilians in previous campaigns. Although the RAF had only 650 Hurricane and Spitfire fighters at the beginning of the battle, Britain's generously funded aircraft industry had increased its monthly output of new planes to 500 by the summer of 1940. Because Hitler had unaccountably ordered Messerschmitt and other German manufacturers to cut production to only 140 new fighters each month, the Luftwaffe could not easily replace lost aircraft. Churchill's memorable after-the-battle comment—"Never in the field of human conflict was so much owed by so many to so few"—reinforced his countrymen's belief (still widely accepted throughout the world) that the Germans had at least three times as many planes as the RAF. Recent research, however, shows that the British Fighter Command and the Luftwaffe fought the Battle of Britain on nearly numerically equal terms. The RAF kept 600 Hurricanes and Spitfires serviceable each day, while the Luftwaffe could never concentrate more than 800 ME 109s against them. Historian John Keegan writes: "These fighters, evenly matched in speed and firepower, were the cardinal weapons of the battle by which victory was to be decided."[17]

In addition to having almost as many planes as their enemy, the British enjoyed several other advantages. Although they had only 1,500 trained pilots—the few to whom so much was owed—versus the Luftwaffe's 10,000, imperiled RAF airmen bailed out over friendly territory and returned to action, whereas most Germans on downed aircraft either drowned or were taken prisoner. While British and German fighters had a comparable maximum range of 200 to 300 miles, the ME 109s had to fly 50 to 100 miles before encountering enemy aircraft. Home-based RAF fighters, which could engage the enemy as soon as they reached operational height, had more combat time in the air. The British had an effective detection and warning system, consisting of a ground observer corps and fifty radar stations. Radar, one of the many new technologies of the war, was a British invention that helped tip the balance against Germany. The British also benefited from the Luftwaffe's inconsistent execution and tactical errors, one of which occurred on August 12, before the first massive raids were launched. German bombers attacked several radar installations, but damaged only one. (The damage was quickly repaired.) Göring, who underestimated the effectiveness of this new technology, did not order follow-up raids for several weeks.

The defenders had gained yet another technological edge before the battle. Assisted by Polish intelligence officers, the British had begun to break the German military cipher.[18] Under the code name Ultra the cryptographers decoded information about Operation Sea Lion, the strength of the Luftwaffe, and the location of its bases. Still in its early stages, Ultra was helpful, but it sometimes failed to indicate the intended targets clearly or to pinpoint exact timetables of German bombers. Thus, decoding was of limited value during the Battle of Britain, but it would be more useful in the Battle of the Atlantic (Chapter 8) and for the Allied bombing offensive against the Reich (Chapter 11). The Germans never discovered that the British had broken their cipher.

From August 13 to September 7, intense aerial combat took place over Britain, as the Luftwaffe tried to gain control of the skies to smooth the way for the invasion on September 15. The principal targets were air installations, fighter bases, aircraft plants, and port facilities. Both sides suffered heavy losses, but the Germans gained an edge during the first week of

POPPERFOTO, LONDON

The human face of the Blitz. A rescue squad pulls a survivor from the rubble in Britain, November 1940. Some 40,000 British civilians were killed in the Blitz.

September when they disabled more planes than the British could replace. Had the Reich not changed tactics at this critical juncture, the Battle of Britain might have turned out differently. On September 7 Göring and Hitler, appalled by the Luftwaffe's heavy losses, abandoned the war on air bases in favor of massive attacks on London. Such raids, they believed, would

BOX 7.4 ■ THE BLITZ: TWO PERSPECTIVES

The Blitz, as described by an 9-year-old boy named Robin:

> After school they're teaching us how to put out fire bombs. We each get our own pump and our own bucket. There's a huge mountain of sandbags in the playground. When the gym teacher leaves we always stay to play war. The team that captures the sandbags wins. . . .

> Sometimes, in my bed, I can hear the buzzing of the German bombers. It's very soft and it comes in waves. It sounds as if they're growling: "We are very close, but from down there you can't see us." Those dirty cowards only dare come here after dark. But then at last, all at once you hear *pom, pom, pom* . . . very fast—and then you know that our anti-aircraft guns are going off. And then you hear the sirens howling and you have to run to the bomb shelter.

> . . . Joyce [his younger sister] doesn't seem too interested in biscuits tonight. She's just listening to the noise of the bombs and watching the flame of the paraffin lamp, which is flickering and keeps wanting to go out because of the shaking.

Kati David, *A Child's War: World War II through the Eyes of Children* (New York: Four Walls Eight Windows, 1989), pp. 31–32.

* * *

Excerpts from an Edward R. Murrow broadcast on September 10, 1940:

> We are told today that the Germans believe that Londoners . . . will rise up and demand a new government, one that will make peace with Germany. It's more probable that they'll rise up and murder a few German pilots who come down by parachute. . . .

> The politicians who called this a "people's war" were right. . . . I've seen some horrible sights in this city during these days and nights, but not once have I heard man, woman or child suggest that Britain should throw in her hand. These people are angry. How much they can stand, I don't know. The strain is very great. . . . After four days and nights of this air blitzkrieg, I think the people here are rapidly becoming veterans, even as their army was hardened at Dunkirk.

> Many people have already got over the panicky feeling that hit everyone in the nerve centers when they realized they were being bombed. Those people I talked to in long queues in front of the big public shelters tonight were cheerful and somewhat resigned. They'd been waiting in line for an hour or more, waiting for the shelters to open at the first wail of the sirens. . . . they carried blankets to throw over the chairs in this public underground shelter. . . .

> Of course, they don't like the situation, but most of them feel that even this underground existence is preferable to what they'd get under German domination.

Quoted in Stephen E. Ambrose, *American Heritage New History of World War II* (New York: Viking, 1997), p. 94.

undermine civilian morale and lure more British fighters into the sky, where they would be easier targets. Hitler also wanted retaliation for a British air raid over Berlin in early September.

The Luftwaffe's tactical shift eased the pressure on British fighter bases, but it did not reduce the number of planes needed to defend against the Germans, whose bombers attacked relentlessly and daily. During the "Blitz," as Londoners called it, thousands of civilians were killed, property damage was enormous, and many children were evacuated to the United States and Canada. By mid-September, after the largest single raid of the war, it was clear that German bombs were neither disabling the RAF nor breaking the people's morale. The Luftwaffe was simply not powerful enough to control the skies over Britain. Several weeks after the high point of the battle, the chief of the Luftwaffe's operational staff stated that an air fleet four times the size would have been needed to force Britain to its knees.[19] On September 17 Hitler postponed Operation Sea Lion indefinitely and ordered the Luftwaffe to shift to night raids. Called terror bombing, or saturation bombing, these raids were not aimed at strategic targets. They were intended solely to break civilian morale, which they clearly failed to do. In fact, the raids had the opposite effect; the British people were all the more determined to resist the Nazis. They were further encouraged by a decided shift in American public opinion in favor of the beleaguered island nation. A stronger pro-British stance in the U.S. was due in no small part to Edward R. Murrow, whose radio broadcasts on the CBS network vividly described the Blitz.[20]

London and other British cities were subjected to sporadic raids, some of them heavy, until May 1941, but for all practical purposes the Battle of Britain was over by the end of October 1940. Both sides claimed to have destroyed about 3,000 of the other's aircraft. Actual figures, however, were somewhat lower. From July 10, the first day of the lighter, preliminary raids, to the end of October, the Luftwaffe lost approximately a thousand fighters and 700 bombers, while the RAF lost just under 1,200 planes, mostly fighters.[21]

History's first air battle established precedents and taught lessons, most of which were ignored. More heavily armed four-engine bombers would have enhanced the Luftwaffe's offensive capability, but German industry unaccountably failed to mass produce such planes throughout the war. Both sides did improve ground-to-air defense systems and lengthened the range of fighters and bombers, but the Germans and, later in the war, the Allies, often failed to stage follow-up raids on strategic targets. From 1942 to 1945 the Allies routinely and relentlessly practiced saturation bombing of German cities in what was, until the last months of the war, a largely futile effort to break civilian morale. While under attack during the last two years of the war, the Germans made a critical tactical error. Despite the RAF's skillful use of air-to-air defensive aircraft during the Battle of Britain, the Luftwaffe failed to deploy large fleets of fighter planes to defend against Anglo-American bombers. Instead, Hitler ordered a disproportionate share of their limited resources to be spent on offensive aircraft in a futile effort to impede the progress of the Allied ground attack. It succeeded only in making German cities more vulnerable to enemy bombs. Air power was an awesome new weapon, but the basic lessons of the Battle of Britain—how to maximize its potential and to grasp its limitations—often went unheeded during the war. They have yet to be mastered.

The Mediterranean and the Balkans

Hitler reversed his no-two-front war policy on July 31, 1940, on the eve of the Battle of Britain, when he ordered Halder and the General Staff to draft a plan for the invasion of the Soviet Union. It was to be code-named Operation Fritz. Hitler assured his generals that the British were about to surrender, but that the loss of Russian support would hasten their demise: "With Russia smashed," the Führer declared, "Britain's last hope would be shattered. Germany will then be master of Europe."[22] Since it would be months before the Wehrmacht was prepared to "smash" Russia, Hitler's strategic options after the Battle of Britain were limited. He could neither invade Britain nor bomb it into submission, but he intensified submarine warfare on the Atlantic and sought to weaken the British presence in the Mediterranean. Hitler's immediate goal was to make shipping more hazardous for the British and to prevent them from occupying northwest Africa, which was nominally under French control. This strategy would not require a substantial military commitment if Spain and the Vichy regime would bear the main burden in the western Mediterranean and Mussolini would take the lead in North Africa and the eastern Mediterranean.

Hitler's Mediterranean partners proved inept or unreliable. Mussolini's invasion of Egypt in August 1940 started well but turned into a dismal failure. From bases in Libya, which had been part of their African empire since 1911, the Italians advanced into Egypt, where several well-equipped British divisions guarded the Suez Canal. Following a successful counterattack, a smaller British force routed the Italians and captured the Libyan port of Tobruk in January 1941. Nearly 50,000 Italian troops surrendered, while the remainder took refuge in eastern Libya. The British also crippled the Italian air force and navy, but they could not dislodge Hitler's Axis partner from North Africa or the Mediterranean.

In October 1940 Hitler personally discussed his Mediterranean strategy with Petain and the Spanish Generalissimo Francisco Franco. Both were noncommittal. Petain agreed in principle to defend French territories in northwest Africa and to support an Axis takeover of Gibraltar, the British island fortress off the coast of Spain, but he made no specific commitments. After the meeting, Petain told a friend: "It will take six months to discuss this program, and another six to forget it."[23] In the meeting with Franco, Hitler demanded Spanish support for the German invasion of Gibraltar, which his general staff and navy had been planning for three

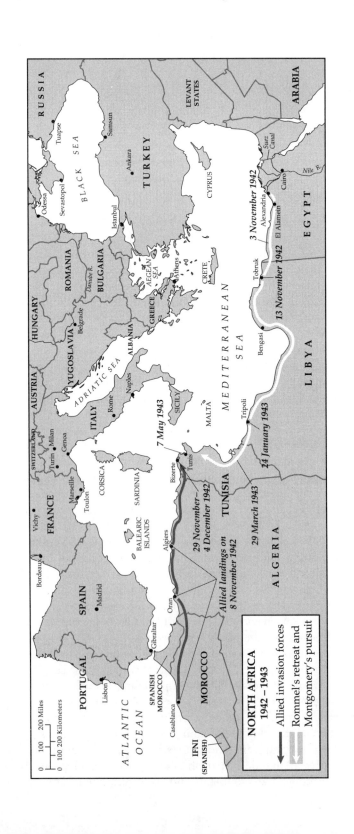

NORTH AFRICA
1942–1943

➡ Allied invasion forces

⇨ Rommel's retreat and
Montgomery's pursuit

months. Franco demurred, pointing out that Spain could not join the Axis powers until Germany had defeated Britain and taken its place as Spain's major trading partner. He also demanded extensive territorial compensation in French North Africa. Unaccustomed to brazen demands from the head of a lesser state, a furious Hitler broke off the talks with Franco, whom he referred to as "General Pip-Squeak." Later, he told Mussolini that he would prefer the extraction of four teeth to another meeting with Franco. Spain remained neutral throughout the war, and Hitler abandoned the Gibraltar project in December 1940.

On October 28, 1940, Mussolini compounded Hitler's Mediterranean dilemma with another ill-fated military venture. Boasting that Hitler "will find out from the newspapers that I have occupied Greece,"[24] the Duce ordered his forces to advance into the Greek hill country from Albania, which he had seized in 1939. The outnumbered Greeks stood their ground and pushed some of the invaders back into Albania. Hitler, whom Mussolini probably had alerted in advance, was not pleased. A substantial military commitment in the Balkans, he reluctantly concluded, might be the only way to salvage Mussolini's bungled initiative, deter British intervention in Greece, and secure his flank in southern Europe. Early in 1941 Hitler persuaded Bulgaria, Hungary, Romania, and Yugoslavia, all suppliers of valuable raw materials to the Reich, to join the Tripartite Pact, a mutual assistance agreement that also included Italy. (Japan became a signatory in September 1941.) The Belgrade government complied with Germany's request to transport troops to Greece on Yugoslavian railroads. Hitler directed his general staff to be prepared for an invasion of Greece no later than the second week of April 1941.

German troops first saw combat in the Mediterranean theater, not in Greece, but in North Africa. On February 17, 1941, Hitler dispatched two divisions, one light and one Panzer, to reinforce the Italian front in Libya. The commander of this small force was Erwin Rommel, characterized as an "obscure general" in a British intelligence report. Destined to become the Third Reich's most famous general, Rommel had mastered the art of armored warfare in the French campaign. In early March, before all his men and equipment had arrived, he ignored orders to remain on the defensive and launched an attack that drove the startled British back to the Egyptian border. Rommel's forces were too weak to take Tobruk or to invade Egypt, but the daring general had breathed new life into the Axis presence in North Africa. In late March, with a temporarily stable front in the Libyan desert, the British transferred nearly 60,000 troops to Greece. Hitler ordered an immediate attack.

Hitler had to alter his invasion plan, however, because of a coup in Yugoslavia. On March 25 anti-German army officers seized power in Belgrade and refused to allow the Wehrmacht to use Yugoslavian railroads. Hitler unleashed a hastily planned but superbly executed Blitzkrieg on April 6. Handicapped by a disorganized army, obsolete equipment, and hatred between Serbs and Croats, Yugoslavia fell in eleven days. It was divided

BOX 7.5 ■ GERMAN OCCUPATION OF GREECE

"You Greeks are in Paradise. . . . " These are excerpts from an account of the German conquest and occupation of Greece by Dr. Ruth Parmelee, director, and Emilie Willms, chief of the nursing division, of the American Women's Hospital in Athens:

On April 6, King George II of the Hellenes announced to his people that Germany had attacked Greece. . . . A brave fight was put up, but on April 19 Thessaloniki was taken, and on April 27 the enemy rolled down from the north into Athens (the same day on which the swastika flag was unfurled over the Acropolis); now Greece was to experience the "friendly" occupation of Germany.

Memories were still fresh of the three weeks' terrible struggle in the battle against the German forces, and the horrors of the Jannina Hospital (near Athens) bombardment on Good Friday. At that time doctors, nurses, and patients in the operating room were blown to pieces. Not forgotten were the dive-bombing and sinking of all the Greek hospital ships, the sinking of ships that carried British and Greek evacuees, and the direct attacks by Stukas on groups of demobilized, stranded soldiers struggling to get to their homes on foot. With these memories still so vivid before our eyes, it was not hard to understand the feeling of the Greek people. When the news spread of the German high command's saying to the mayor [of Athens], "We have brought you peace and quiet, and come as friends," it fell on deaf ears and heavy hearts.

The authors describe the immediate and acute shortage of food resulting from the "Germans' systematic seizure of all kinds of supplies":

When the mayor remonstrated with the German authorities for taking all the rice and begged them to leave some for the sick people and infants, the reply was: "You Greeks are in Paradise. No one is falling in the streets from hunger. In Poland one and a half million people are starving to death." And this was in the first weeks of the occupation!

Tony March, ed., *Darkness over Europe: First-Person Accounts of Life in Europe during the War Years 1939–1945* (Chicago: Rand McNally, 1969), pp. 51–52.

along ethnic boundaries. Slovenia, which had once belonged to the Austrian Empire, became a German protectorate, while German and Italian military officers, the SS, and local fascist collaborators governed Croatia, Serbia, and Montenegro.

The Germans encountered stubborn resistance as they moved south, but the Greeks, weakened by months of fighting against the Italians, and their undermanned British allies surrendered on April 27. The Germans, whose casualties were exceptionally light, captured or killed hundreds of thousands of Greek troops and installed a murderous government of occupation. "Years of desperate hunger, oppression and resistance, civil war and endless suffering, awaited the Greeks like their hapless northern neighbor."[25]

The British evacuated several divisions to Egypt and to the island of Crete, a hundred miles southeast of the mainland, but more than 10,000 troops and all of their equipment fell into German hands.

Germany's final campaign in the south was the invasion of Crete, launched on May 20. Hitler, whose deployment of ground troops and equipment had been remarkably successful, was initially reluctant to authorize an airborne assault on an island that he believed had little strategic value. However, airborne forces expert General Kurt Student and the persistent Göring, anxious to buttress the Luftwaffe's sagging reputation, convinced the Führer that the occupation of Crete was important. It would secure the Reich's southern flank of eastern Europe and prevent the British from using the Mediterranean island as a base for bombing Romanian oil fields. (The Ploesti oil fields in Romania had become the Reich's chief supplier of natural petroleum.) Hitler agreed. After a month of heavy fighting, the defenders surrendered. The Royal Navy evacuated 18,000 troops to Egypt, but 12,000 had been captured and nearly 2,000 killed in the fighting. It was a disastrous defeat for the British, but the Germans paid a high price for their victory. To take Crete, which proved to be less strategically significant than Student and Göring had predicted, the Wehrmacht sacrificed nearly 4,000 lives, a higher casualty rate than in any previous campaign. Hitler remained adamantly opposed to large-scale airborne invasions thereafter. Such operations might have been useful to the Reich, especially after airborne units had been re-formed and enlarged later in the war. Instead, it was the Allies, profiting from German mistakes in the Crete campaign, who would carry out successful airborne operations.

The British had lost Crete, but their power in the eastern Mediterranean was still formidable. They retained the island of Malta, which the Luftwaffe bombed relentlessly, and they thwarted the Reich's efforts to penetrate the Middle East. In Iraq, pro-German politicians seized the government in the spring of 1941. Hitler sent military aid to the new regime and, with the approval of Vichy France, landed planes in neighboring Syria to refuel before moving on to Iraq. But British troops dispatched from India and Palestine dislodged the pro-Axis regime in Iraq and restored a friendly government to power in Baghdad. Hitler, who the British thought might send troops into Syria, promptly withdrew German planes based there. On June 8 British and Free French troops attacked Syria, and after five weeks of heavy fighting the Vichy forces surrendered. With Britain firmly in control of the Middle East, the Reich had to abandon all hope of exploiting that region's oil resources.

Crete and the Middle East were only minor distractions for Hitler, who, throughout the spring of 1941, was preoccupied with Operation Barbarossa, the new code name for the invasion of the Soviet Union. During the campaign in Greece, he made one important change in the plan. The invasion, originally scheduled to begin on May 15, was postponed until June 22. The earlier invasion date would have given the Germans six additional weeks of favorable fighting weather on the Russian front in the late summer and early fall of 1941, which, as Guderian and other generals argued after the war, might have enabled the Wehrmacht to reach Moscow before the onset of the ferocious Russian winter. Hence, the Balkan campaign, if it was *the* principal reason for changing the invasion date, would have loomed large in Germany's defeat in the Second World War.

The Balkan Blitzkrieg was indeed a principal reason for postponing Barbarossa, but the weather was equally if not more important. Exceptionally heavy rainfall throughout the late spring left roads muddy and rivers swollen, slowing the movement of troops and equipment to the border of Soviet-occupied Poland, where the invasion would begin. To Hitler, this delay was of no great significance. He was supremely confident that the Blitzkrieg, which had made him master of Europe from the Arctic to the Mediterranean and from the English Channel to the Polish plain, would overwhelm the Red Army within months.

Conclusion

Hitler's confidence appeared well-founded. In less than two years, the Wehrmacht had extended Nazi rule far beyond the parameters of his immediate objectives. The German economy had not been overtaxed, and the resources of occupied territories were available. By the standards of twentieth-century bloodletting, Germany's losses in twenty-one months of war had been minimal. During the same period, the Wehrmacht's manpower and firepower had increased quantitatively and qualitatively, making Hitler's war machine on land one of the most formidable in European history.[26]

The prospect of fighting a two-front war—Britain on the west, Russia on the east—did not worry Hitler. He correctly assessed that Britain's success in North Africa and increased aid from the United States had strengthened its determination to fight on, but it still lacked the resources for offensive operations against Germany on land or in the air. Moreover, the Reich's growing submarine fleet in the North Atlantic was beginning to take a heavy toll on British shipping. Hence, Hitler saw an unobstructed path to quick victory over the Soviet Union. Few could have imagined that by the end of 1941 his powerful army would have suffered a major defeat at the outskirts of Moscow and that the Third Reich would be at war with the United States.

INFOTRAC® COLLEGE EDITION SEARCH TERMS

For additional reading go to Infotrac College Edition, your online research library at http://www.infotrac-college.com.

Enter the search term "World War, 1939–1945" using the Subject Guide.

Enter the search term "Blitzkrieg German" using Keywords.

Enter the search term "World War, 1939–1945, France" using Keywords.

Enter the search term "World War, 1939–1945, Italy" using Keywords.

Enter the search term "World War, 1939–1945, Greece" using Keywords.

Enter the search term "Battle of Ardennes" using the Subject Guide.

Enter the search term "Dunkirk, Battle of" using the Subject Guide.

Enter the search term "Rommel, Erwin" using the Subject Guide.

Enter the search term "Aerial Operations World War 1939–1945" using Keywords.

Enter the search term "Britain, Battle of, 1940" using the Subject Guide.

Notes

1. John Keegan, *The Second World War* (New York: Viking Penguin, 1989), p. 5.

2. "Commissar Decree, March 1941," in Louis L. Snyder, *National Socialist Germany* (Malibu, FL: Krieger, 1984) p. 165.

3. Gordon Wright, *The Ordeal of Total War* (New York: Harper & Row, 1968), p. 13.

4. M. K. Dziewanowski, *War at Any Price* (Englewood Cliffs, NJ: Prentice-Hall, 1991), p. 68; Keegan, p. 47.

5. Ian Kershaw, *Hitler 1936–1945: Nemesis* (New York: Norton, 2000), p. 265.

6. Harold C. Deutsch, *The Conspiracy Against Hitler in the Twilight War* (Minneapolis: University of Minnesota Press, 1968), p. 228; Joachim Fest, *Hitler* (New York: Harcourt Jovanovich, 1973), p. 628.

7. Quoted in Kershaw, pp. 276–77.

8. Quoted in Fest, pp. 612–13.

9. Sebastian Haffner, *The Meaning of Hitler* (New York: MacMillan, 1978), p. 108.

10. Gerhard L. Weinberg, *A World at Arms* (New York: Cambridge University Press, 1994), p. 120.

11. Keegan, p. 57.

12. Weinberg, p. 125; Stephen E. Ambrose, *American Heritage New History of World War II* (New York: Viking Press, 1997), p. 55.

13. Dziewanowski, p. 109.

14. Quoted in Kershaw, p. 299.

15. Quoted in Ambrose, p. 68.

16. Quoted in Wright, p. 28.

17. Keegan, pp. 93–94.

18. For the Polish-Ultra connection, see Weinberg, pp. 554–55.

19. Kershaw, p. 309.

10. Ambrose, p. 84.

21. Keegan, p. 102.

22. Quoted in Alan Bullock, *Hitler and Stalin: Parallel Lives* (New York: Alfred A. Knopf, 1992), p. 682.

23. Ibid., p. 684.

24. Quoted in Wright, p. 36.

25. Weinberg, p. 222.

26. Keegan, p. 173.

Hitler's Total War, 1941–1944

Quick victories over France and smaller European nations convinced Hitler that Blitzkrieg tactics would crush the Soviet Union in 4 to 6 months. The conquest of a nation with an area and population far greater than any European country would require a total war commitment of human and material resources, but only for a few months. The destruction of the Soviet state would enable the SS to Germanize the east and establish the economically self-sufficient continental empire that he had envisioned since *Mein Kampf*. Racial cleansing and empire-building would also be costly and brutal, but Hitler was certain that his goals could be achieved without converting the domestic economy to the kind of prolonged total war production that had crippled Imperial Germany in World War I. In less than two years, the Greater German Reich, he believed, could crush both Britain and the United States.

In retrospect, Hitler's hubris and miscalculation are obvious, but in the spring of 1941 his scenario was not entirely implausible. Although numerically superior to the Wehrmacht, the Red Army was handicapped by low morale, poorly trained and undisciplined recruits, and unqualified officers (Stalin had executed over half of his senior commanders in 1938). A British general predicted that "the Germans would go through them like a hot knife through butter."[1] Moreover, Stalin's eagerness to supply Germany with strategic materials, a provision of the Nazi-Soviet Nonaggression Pact, and his desperate attempts to maintain good relations in spite of Nazi aggression in the Balkans, suggest that he deeply feared Hitler. His inability to act when the attack occurred, and the Red Army's lack of preparedness, proved it.[2]

Although the British had proved their determination, as Churchill said, "to fight on unconquerable until the curse of Hitler is lifted from the brows of mankind,"[3] Britain lacked the resources to undertake offensive operations. American aid increased after March 1941 when the U.S. Congress passed the Lend Lease Act, which permitted the British to "borrow or lease" goods without paying for them. Delivery was difficult, however, because of the deadly efficiency of Germany's submarine offensive in the North Atlantic throughout 1941. Under President Franklin D. Roosevelt's prodding, U.S. public opinion and the Congress were gradually moving away from isolationism, but even with immediate congressional approval mobilization of the armed forces and the economy would take from two to three years. If there ever was to be a showdown with the United States, Hitler was confident that the Reich would be ready. But six months after launching Operation Barbarossa, one of the three Wehrmacht army groups barely escaped annihilation on the outskirts of Moscow, and Hitler declared war on the United States. The Third Reich was woefully unprepared for the prolonged war of attrition that followed.

Planning Barbarossa

On December 17, 1940, Hitler ordered his generals to prepare for a massive invasion of the Soviet Union. The military objectives of Operation Barbarossa, which took its name from Frederick Barbarossa, the legendary medieval emperor who died on a crusade to the east, were to abolish Stalin's regime, crush the Red Army, destroy or capture industrial centers, occupy and exploit agricultural and mineral-producing areas, and erect a defensive line from Archangel in the north to the Caspian Sea in the south. Hitler stressed the need for flawlessly executed troop movements that would rapidly encircle and either capture or annihilate the bulk of the Red Army. He promised to be much more involved in planning and directing the entire operation and to issue additional, more explicit, directives on political, military, and ideological aspects of the campaign.

Most military personnel and civilians were comfortable with Hitler's portrayal of the war in the east as an anti-Bolshevik crusade, but as head of Europe's most powerful state, he felt compelled to justify the gigantic military enterprise on strategic and diplomatic grounds. He may have no longer believed that "smashing Russia" would destroy Britain's last hope for survival, but the British refusal to capitulate was becoming increasingly bothersome. According to a study utilizing Soviet files released in 1990, Hitler was so concerned that he sent Deputy Führer Rudolf Hess on a quixotic flight to England in May 1941. Hess allegedly was the bearer of a serious peace offer that would have allowed Britain to retain its empire in return for supporting Germany's invasion of the Soviet Union. Publicly, Hitler denied prior knowledge of Hess's flight and attributed it to a "hallucination." The evidence that Hess was the Führer's messenger, or that he traveled with the "connivance of the British secret services and powerful elements in British society who wanted to make peace with Germany,"[4] is inconclusive. Two cabinet ministers visited him in prison, but Churchill never met with Hess.

Throughout the first months of 1941, Hitler claimed that the military buildup on the eastern front was an act of self-defense against Stalin's "imminent invasion" of German-held territory. There is no evidence to support Hitler's contention, but diplomatic relations between the two dictators had steadily deteriorated since the summer of 1940. Shortly after the fall of France, Stalin occupied the Baltic states—Lithuania, Latvia, and Estonia—and the Romanian provinces of Bessarabia and Northern Bukovina. Reports of Soviet troop concentrations in the latter, which did not belong to Stalin's sphere of influence under the terms of the 1939 Nonaggression Pact, worried Hitler and his generals. On the other hand, the Soviet dictator's suspicions were aroused by German aid to Finland, the presence of German troops in western Romania, Hitler's support of the Fascist General Ion Antonescu's regime in Romania, and the Tripartite Pact between the Reich, Italy, and Japan concluded in September 1940.

None of these issues were resolved when Soviet Foreign Minister Vyacheslav Molotov visited Berlin in November 1940. A heated exchange occurred. Hitler rebuffed Molotov's specific demands for concessions in Finland and the Balkans and spoke vaguely of a Russian sphere of influence "toward India and the far east." A subsequent discussion about the Soviet Union's role in the "liquidation of the British Empire" prompted Ribbentrop to insist that "Britain was finished," whereupon air raid sirens sounded and the entire party took cover in a bomb shelter. Molotov made his famous reply: "If this is so, why are we in this shelter, and whose bombs are these that are falling?"[5] The failure to reach an agreement heightened the atmosphere of tension and strengthened Hitler's argument that "preventive counter-measures" in Poland might be necessary to forestall a Soviet offensive.

Throughout the first months of 1941, both the strategy and tactics of Barbarossa became more specific. Although the German officers shared Hitler's low opinion of the Red Army, his senior generals, especially Brauchitsch, Halder, and Rundstedt, worried about the adverse effects of vast distances on logistics and movement.[6] Hitler minimized the space factor and insisted that, with Germany's resources and his army's combat experience, properly executed troop movements could simultaneously fulfill all his objectives along a 1,500-mile front.

In March 1941 Hitler laid out immediate tactical objectives: Army Group North under Field Marshal Ritter von Leeb would take the Baltic states and Leningrad; Field Marshal Bock's Army Group Center would overrun Soviet-occupied Poland and Belorussia and advance toward Moscow; Army Group South under Rundstedt's command would occupy Ukraine, the breadbasket of the Soviet Union, and drive eastward toward the mineral-rich Caucasus Mountains that lie between the Black and Caspian Seas. Hitler dismissed the suggestion that Moscow was strategically more important than Leningrad or Ukraine. He claimed that Stalin's regime could not survive without its major seaport, Leningrad, and the resources of the south, which were also vital to the Reich's war effort. He promised that Moscow would become a primary target after the northern and southern army groups had fulfilled their initial objectives.

In an address to his generals in March 1941, Hitler set forth the ideological objectives of the campaign:

> The war against Russia . . . is a war of annihilation. . . . [It] is a struggle of ideologies and racial differences and will have to be conducted with unprecedented, unmerciful and unrelenting harshness. . . . I know that . . . [this] is beyond the comprehension of you generals . . . but I insist that my orders must be executed without contradiction. The commissars are the bearers of ideologies directly opposed to National Socialism. Therefore the commissars will be liquidated.[7]

The army was to cooperate fully with four SS *Einsatzgruppen* (task forces), specially trained extermination squads of 500 to 900 men each, under the command of Reinhard Heydrich. His instructions from Hitler through Himmler were to liquidate Communist party functionaries, or commissars, "Jews in the service of the Party or the State," and "other extremist elements."[8] A few weeks before the invasion, Göring told the generals that millions of civilians in the industrial areas "will become redundant and will either die or have to emigrate to Siberia." He warned that efforts to feed the native population would "undermine Germany's war effort." Millions of civilians and prisoners of war under the army's jurisdiction would die as a result of this policy.[9] On June 6 Hitler issued the final draft of the "Commissar Order," which both the army and the SS implemented. Masses of nonbelligerents—and all Soviet Jews—would be the victims of this order, broadly interpreted and supplemented with more explicit directives.

Of the 3.8 million fighting men available to Hitler, 3.2 million were deployed on the eastern front. They were organized into 102 infantry, 19 armored, and 14 motorized divisions, with Army Group Center receiving the largest share. Total tank strength had risen from 2,700 in 1940 to 3,300, although the multiplication of armored divisions had been achieved by reducing the number of tanks contained in each. The Luftwaffe had 1,085 bombers and 920 fighters, a smaller total than at the outbreak of the Battle of Britain, although the quality was somewhat higher. With the addition of Romanian, Hungarian, Slovak, and Finnish contingents, Hitler had nearly 4 million men at his disposal. Soviet forces on the western front—170 infantry divisions, 6,000 planes, and nearly 10,000 tanks divided into fifty-four armored brigades—were numerically superior, but they lacked a coordinated defensive strategy. Hitler's invading force, the most powerful ever assembled in Europe, was superior in weapons, reserves, and operational skill.[10]

Operation Barbarossa, June–October 1941

Hitler's familiar comment, "when Barbarossa starts, the world will hold its breath and keep still," was an expression of his megalomania, but he also

OPERATION BARBAROSSA

- ————— 22 June 1941 border
- German drives
- Finnish and Romanian thrusts
- •••••••• Barbarossa Objective

voiced grave uncertainty before the invasion: "It is like pushing open the door into a dark room without knowing what lies beyond." On the evening of June 21, however, he had regained his confidence. He told Rundstedt: "You have only to kick in the door, and the whole rotten structure will come crashing down."[11] When he unleashed the invasion, which initially overwhelmed unsuspecting Soviet defenders, the structure, as he predicted, appeared to be "crashing down."

Stalin had received precise information from the British and his own excellent intelligence network, but it was not until noon on June 22, eight hours after the invasion had begun, that Molotov, speaking on behalf of Stalin, broadcast to the Russian people that the Soviet Union was at war with Germany. At this point, the Soviet dictator "removed himself from any public gaze and the Russian people heard not a sound from him until July 3."[12] Without precise directives from Moscow, frontline commanders could only react and improvise during the first days of the invasion. Why Stalin failed to prepare his defenses adequately is still a mystery. The fearful dictator, scrupulously honoring prewar trade agreements up to the moment of attack, obviously wanted to avoid military activity that might provoke the Germans. The suspicious dictator may have believed that British warnings were designed to undermine what was left of the Nazi-Soviet Nonaggression Pact, but this does not explain why he failed to act on information supplied by his own operatives. Stalin's temporary mental paralysis and the Red Army's lack of preparedness, for which he was directly responsible, cost the Soviets huge numbers of casualties during the first weeks of the invasion and contributed significantly to the Wehrmacht's early success.

The German offensive did not "smash the Red Army to splinters in seven short days," as the propaganda ministry boasted, but progress during the first four weeks was spectacular. Driving over 150 miles in five days, Army Group North overran Lithuania and Latvia and reached a point eighty miles south of Leningrad by July 10. In vast encircling movements covering 450 miles in twenty-three days, Army Group Center took Smolensk, about 200 miles west of Moscow, and captured nearly 500,000 prisoners. Encountering formidable Soviet resistance in Ukraine, Army Group South advanced more slowly. By the end of July the Wehrmacht had captured over a million prisoners, occupied thousands of square miles of territory, destroyed 1,500 Soviet tanks, and demolished thousands of planes. German casualties were only slightly higher than anticipated. All was proceeding on schedule, save that the Red Army's resistance had not collapsed and Stalin was still in power.

At the end of July Hitler halted offensive operations to discuss strategy with his generals. He stressed the need to close the gaps between rapidly advancing armor and slower-moving infantry divisions, through which many Russian troops had escaped. The strategic problem—how to utilize resources most effectively to achieve immediate objectives in the face of stubborn Soviet resistance—was more serious. Hitler assured his generals that the toughness of the Red Army was due to its numerical superiority and the Wehrmacht's tactical problems. He insisted that there was no need to worry over the fighting spirit and improved organization of some Soviet divisions, their excellent equipment (such as the mass-produced T-34 and KV tanks, which were superior to most German models), and the outbreak of partisan warfare behind German lines. These and other obstacles, he assured them, could be overcome by a shift in strategy.

Over the objections of Brauchitsch and Halder, who reiterated their "Moscow first" strategy, Hitler proposed that Army Group Center should temporarily halt offensive operations and allow its Panzer corps under Guderian and General Hermann Hoth to reinforce the drive to Leningrad in the north and to facilitate the capture of Kiev and much of the agriculturally rich Ukraine in the south. Guderian and Bock also objected, but Hitler pre-

BOX 8.1 ■ A YOUNG BOY EXPERIENCES THE SEIGE OF
LENINGRAD

The seige of Leningrad as experienced by Yuri, an 8- or 9-year-old boy:

Papa says people are eating rats. . . . That must be horrible. But Mama says, "It's
still better than dying from hunger." Who knows, maybe rats don't taste that bad.
And Mama could make anything delicious out of them, I'm sure. So you wouldn't
even know that you were eating a rat. As long as you didn't think about that long,
thin tail. . . . We are lucky that Mama can make anything taste wonderful. Today
we ate Papa's leather belt. First she soaked it for a very long time in water, and
then she cut it into tiny little pieces. It was just like minced meat. . . .

This is our second winter in Levinka (a small village on the outskirts of
Leningrad). We came here because we thought that there would be enough to eat
in a small village like this. But that isn't true at all. I feel hungry more here than at
home in Leningrad. . . . The other day I suddenly had to cry. I missed Papa so
much. He is still in Leningrad. But when I told Mama I wished I'd stayed with
him, she got mad and yelled, "Yuri! How can you say such a stupid thing? We were
nearly *dead!*"

"But there at least my belly left me alone. Here it's grumbling all the time."

"That's because there is still something in it. In Leningrad it was so empty that
you didn't feel anything anymore."

. . . So then, for the time being, my tummy won't leave me alone. Because all we
have left are blackened potatoes. The dandelions and the sorrel and the stinging
nettles won't come back until spring.

. . . If only the snow was gone, I could start searching for parsnips and turnips
again. . . . Oh, that parsnip I found last year! I stuffed myself. If I had taken it home
Mama could have cooked it. Then it would have tasted even better. But then I
would have had to share with the others.

Kati David, ed., *A Child's War: World War II through the Eyes of Children* (New York:
Four Walls Eight Windows, 1989), pp. 98–101.

vailed. Army Group North reached the outskirts of Leningrad by early September and laid siege to the city. The siege would last for nearly three years
and cause the death of over 1 million (at least 2 million by some estimates)
residents, but as Germany's economic priorities gradually shifted to southern
Russia, Leningrad lost much of its strategic value. Hitler never committed
enough resources to take the Soviet Union's second-largest city. Army Group
South fared better. On September 19, with perfectly executed pincers movements, the Germans captured Kiev and at least 600,000 prisoners. On September 26, when Hitler decided to resume the attack on Moscow, he reas-
signed Guderian and Hoth to Army Group Center and shifted armor from
the north to take part in the Moscow offensive. At the same time, the Führer
ordered Army Group South to advance beyond Kiev toward industrial centers in eastern Ukraine. Both offensives began at the end of September.

Ukrainian civilians greet smiling German troops.

NATIONAL ARCHIVES

Because Hitler postponed the drive on Moscow, Army Group Center lost six weeks of favorable fighting weather. According to Guderian's retrospective assessment, this mistake cost Germany the Russian campaign and, quite possibly, the war. Previous errors, however, were equally critical. The original Barbarossa directive, according to General Walther Warlimont, who recorded Hitler's meetings, "contained a large number of disconnected objectives with priority given to none."[13] There was an astonishing lack of intelligence about the high quality of Soviet armor and the depth of the Red Army's reserves. General Halder, who had thought the war to be won in early July, realized his mistake by August 11: "The whole situation makes it increasingly plain that we have underestimated the Russian colossus. . . . if we smash a dozen of [their divisions], they simply put up another dozen. . . . our troops, sprawled over an immense front line, without any depth, are subjected to the incessant attacks of the enemy."[14] Hitler and most of his generals had underestimated the resiliency of Soviet troops and the productive capacity of Russian industry, much of which was being disassembled and laboriously transported hundreds of miles east to the Ural Mountains, where the reassembled factories were relatively safe from the Luftwaffe. The Red Army

---

BOX 8.2 ■ CONSTRUCTION OF A WAR PLANT IN SIBERIA

The construction of a new factory in western Siberia is described in a September 18, 1942, article in *Pravda*, the party's newspaper and principal organ of propaganda. While the tone and manner of expression are clearly propagandistic, the extraordinary sacrifices and hard work of ordinary people made a vital contribution to the Soviet war effort:

> Winter had already come when Sverdlovsk received Comrade Stalin's order to erect two buildings for the plant evacuated from the south. . . . It was then that the people of the Urals came to this spot with shovels, bars and pickaxes: students, typists, accountants, shop assistants, housewives, artists, teachers. The earth was like stone, frozen hard by our fierce Siberian frost. Axes and pickaxes could not break the stony soil. In the light of arc-lamps people hacked at the earth all night. . . . Their feet and hands were swollen with frostbite, but they did not leave work. . . . On the twelfth day, into the new buildings with their glass roofs the machinery began to arrive. . . . And two days later, the war factory began production.

John Campbell, ed., *The Experience of World War II* (New York: Oxford University Press, 1989), p. 161.

---

was close to its own resources, while the Germans were moving farther away from their own. Spread over a 1,500-mile front, the army groups lacked sufficient resources to fulfill their objectives.

Another costly mistake, which had nothing to do with strategy or tactics, was Hitler's refusal to allow anti-Stalinist Ukrainian volunteers to fight with the Wehrmacht. The Ukrainians, who had initially greeted the Nazis as liberators, were eager to join the "crusade" against the hated Soviet dictator, who had exterminated millions of their compatriots in the early 1930s. Ignoring Goebbels's suggestion that military needs should supersede racial dogma, Hitler ordered the army and the SS to exterminate or enslave the Ukrainians, whom he dismissed as Slavic "*Untermenschen*" (subhumans), no different from or better than their ethnic cousins, the Poles and Russians. Nazi brutality drove thousands of Ukrainians to join the ranks of pro-Soviet guerrilla fighters. With weapons supplied by the Red Army, their hit-and-run tactics behind enemy lines did incalculable damage to the Wehrmacht.

The Moscow Offensive, October–December 1941

Despite tactical problems, Hitler's mistakes, and the recovery of the Red Army, the General Staff was guardedly optimistic when Bock unleashed the Moscow offensive on September 30. Soviet losses—prisoners, military and civilian casualties, industrial plant, and foodstuffs—were staggering, and the Red Army had yet to win a battle. Army Group Center, the Wehrmacht's most powerful striking force, had a precise objective and a plan. Panzer corps on its northern and southern flanks were to surround Moscow, while the bulk of the army was to attack the city head-on. By mid-October, the Germans had captured 600,000 prisoners, killed or wounded nearly a million soldiers and civilians, and reached a point less than 100 miles from the capital. Stalin, his army, and Muscovites feared the worst. Women and old men were conscripted to dig tank traps near the city, and some government offices were transferred to Kuibyshev, a city east of Moscow. Relocated Soviet industrial facilities were able to keep producing war matériel, but the Red Army still lacked heavy equipment. It seemed only a matter of time before swastika flags would be raised on Kremlin towers.

By the beginning of November, the weather, supply shortages, partisan activity, and the Red Army's stubborn resistance had slowed the German drive. Heavy rains turned dirt roads into quagmires, which slowed horse-drawn wagons and nearly immobilized wheeled vehicles. The Germans could not use their own freight cars and locomotives because Soviet railroad tracks had a broader gauge. As an unusually cold winter set in, trucks could traverse the frozen roads, but some German vehicles burned diesel fuel, which congealed at low temperatures. The engines would not run until the diesel was liquefied, a time-consuming process.

German troops found the lack of winter clothing, tough Soviet resistance, and the vastness of the terrain to be almost unbearable. The retreating

Exhausted German troops ride a tracked vehicle as it slowly traverses a muddy road on the vast Russian plain.

Russians fought fiercely, and their deadly T-34 tanks inflicted heavy casualties on the invaders. From the Romanians, German soldiers were infected with "disquieting sentiments," such as "You always had to kill a Russian twice over," and "No man who drew blood there ever left alive." A German soldier, amazed by the stoic behavior of wounded Russians, whom he could not hear cry out, groan, or curse, wrote: "There is something . . . inscrutable about their stern, stubborn silence."[15] Such demoralizing fears and "disquieting sentiments" would torment the Germans throughout the entire campaign.

The German offensive ground to a halt in early December, as temperatures dropped to -50 degrees Celsius. Nearly 25 percent of the Moscow attack force had been killed or wounded and over 30 percent of its armor disabled. Yet some of the half-frozen, exhausted, and hungry survivors managed to reach a point about thirty miles west of Moscow. On December 6, 1941, the Soviets launched a massive counterattack, spearheaded by thirty fresh, combat-tested divisions, fully equipped for winter warfare. These troops had previously been stationed in eastern Siberia to protect Soviet territory from a Japanese attack. At least one major battle had been fought between Russian and Japanese troops before their governments signed a nonaggression pact in April 1941.

Stalin did not transfer his far eastern reserves to Moscow until mid-September, when his master spy in Tokyo, a German Communist named Richard Sorge, convinced him that Japan had targeted resource-rich Southeast Asia, not the Soviet Union, for expansion. The Siberian divisions, together with the bloodied but still-formidable Moscow defenders under Marshal Georgi Zhukov (soon to become the Soviet Union's most successful general), stunned the invaders. Overruling Bock's plea for a full-scale retreat, Hitler ordered Army Group Center to hold its ground and fight to the last man. They withdrew 30 to 50 miles to the west, but their line did not break. Hitler took full credit for the heroic stand of his battered forces, and his no-retreat order would be repeated throughout the campaign, usually with disastrous results. He never realized that Army Group Center might have been destroyed if Stalin, thinking that the Germans were nearly finished, had not ordered a general offensive along the entire front on January 7, 1942. Zhukov and other generals had warned that such an attack would dissipate Russian strength over a wide front. They were right. Stalin's offensive failed to encircle and destroy German forces that had pulled back from Moscow.[16]

The power of the Soviet counteroffensive forced Hitler to re-assess Barbarossa. Characteristically, he blamed the failure of Blitzkrieg tactics on his generals, not on the power of the Soviet counterattack, the vastness of the terrain, or the weather. The war would be longer and costlier than he had anticipated, but under his "superior and indispensable leadership," it was still winnable. He dismissed Guderian and Hoth and forced Brauchitsch and the three army group commanders to resign. Hitler himself became the army's commander-in-chief. From establishing strategic objectives to the level of tactical planning, the war in the east became his war. "Revolving-door" field commanders would take orders directly from their Führer and warlord.

On December 11, 1941, Hitler announced to a stunned Reichstag that Germany had declared war on the United States. According to Ronald Lewin, one of Britain's leading World War II historians, it is difficult to decide which of Hitler's two greatest mistakes—the invasion of the Soviet Union and the declaration of war on the United States—was the more disastrous. "By engaging the Americans," Lewin writes, "he was responsible for his own coup de grâce."[17] Hitler's justification was not very convincing. He pointed out that German submarines would now be free to attack U.S. ships on the high seas—Britain's chief supplier—and that "our Japanese comrades-in-arms" deserved the Reich's support in their struggle against the British and Americans in Asia.

The timing of Hitler's decision, only five days after the Red Army's Moscow counteroffensive, and the reasons for that decision are puzzling but not entirely inexplicable. Several months earlier, Hitler had worried that Japan and the United States would negotiate a nonaggression pact—an agreement that would allow the United States to intervene in the European war—and had encouraged his Asian partner to attack U.S. bases in the Pacific. He assured Japan that Germany would reward such initiatives with a declaration of war against the United States. Though the Japanese attack on Pearl Harbor surprised Hitler, he unhesitatingly complied with Japan's request to honor his earlier pledge. In light of the setbacks on the eastern front, Hitler believed that a dramatic gesture was needed to show that he still controlled events. He was also convinced that Roosevelt was "itching" for a chance to enter the war in Europe. To wait for a declaration of war from the United States would, from Hitler's standpoint, have been viewed as a sign of weakness. Hence, the Führer, who in his speech to the Reichstag depicted Roosevelt as a warmonger backed by the "entire Satanic insidiousness" of Jews bent on Germany's destruction, took the initiative.[18] Hitler's rash decision committed his nation to war against a superpower, whose overwhelming superority in human and material resources would play a crucial role in the destruction of the Reich.

Historian and journalist Sebastian Haffner offers an intriguing but highly speculative psychological explanation. Hitler realized that he could not defeat the United States or establish a vast empire in the east, but if he could not be remembered as a great conqueror, "he would at least be the architect of a great catastrophe." The Reich's fall would trigger massive destruction throughout the world, creating "a world in flames," as he had earlier predicted. Hitler also prolonged an unwinnable war, according to Haffner, so that he could achieve his other cherished goal, the extermination of the Jews: "In December 1941 Hitler the politician finally abdicated in favor of Hitler the mass murderer."[19] Given the Führer's murderous anti-Semitism and his willingness to squander lives for the sake of his new racial order, Haffner's scenario is plausible.

The Russian Front, January 1942 to February 1943

Hitler's armies never recovered from the shock of their first major loss. There would be more than three years of bitter fighting, which would consume millions of lives, but the final outcome was no longer in doubt. Of Barbarossa's original objectives, only one was within reach in 1942. Since a long war would require abundant supplies of foodstuffs and minerals, Hitler decided to concentrate his limited resources in the south. After heavy fighting during the winter and early spring of 1942, Army Group South had secured the city of Kharkov and other industrial centers of eastern Ukraine. German forces had also captured, lost, and then recaptured Rostov, gateway to the Caucasus region. By May 1942 most of the Ukrainian "breadbasket" was under German occupation.

The primary objective of Hitler's 1942 summer offensive was the oil-rich Caucasus Mountains. After taking the Don River Basin and blocking the Volga River supply route near the city of Stalingrad, Army Group South, which had been divided into Army Groups A and B, was to attack the Caucasus region. The Wehrmacht, which suffered nearly a million casualties during the previous fall and winter, began its new offensive with human and material resources well below 1941 levels. The Red Army, on the other hand, was gaining strength. Despite the extremely high attrition rate of the first year of the war—4 million prisoners and nearly 4 million killed or missing—Soviet men and machines outnumbered the Germans nearly 3 to 1.

Hitler unleashed his offensive on June 28, 1942, against an army that had suffered heavy casualties in an abortive attempt to recapture Kharkov in May. Depleted Soviet forces fell back, as the Germans once again masterfully executed their pincers movements. They secured the Don River Basin, captured, killed, or wounded well over a million enemy troops, and slaughtered nonbelligerents with impunity. Pleased with the Wehrmacht's progress, Hitler issued a directive on July 23, 1942, that significantly altered the strategy he had outlined in April. The intention at that time was to advance on the Caucasus region following the encirclement and destruction of Soviet forces in the vicinity of Stalingrad. Against the advice of his generals, who were understandably concerned about the growing gap between Soviet and German resources, Hitler ordered his armies to take the Caucasus and Stalingrad simultaneously. "The strategy," writes Hitler biographer Ian Kershaw, "was sheer lunacy."[20]

To achieve his goals, Hitler ordered a Panzer group to abandon its drive on Stalingrad and reinforce Army Group A, which was advancing into the Caucasus. By August 9 German forces reached oil fields in the foothills and took the city of Maykop. The Soviets, however, had systematically destroyed that city's oil refineries. Even if the Germans could have held the Caucasus region, it would have taken months to repair the damaged facilities. The Reich never got a drop of oil from Soviet refineries or wells. Shortly after raising the swastika flag on the highest mountain in the Caucasus, Army Group A, which had taken heavy casualties, was forced to begin a retreat to the north, ultimately abandoning the coveted, mineral-rich territory that it had briefly held.

Meanwhile, General Friedrich Paulus' less mobile Sixth Army (which was part of Army Group B) with its preponderance of infantry had been assigned the unenviable task of taking Stalingrad. Progress was slow and casualties were high, but the Germans reached the suburbs by early September. A month later, Stalin poured reinforcements into the Stalingrad sector

---

BOX 8.3   ■   LAST LETTERS FROM STALINGRAD

In the introduction to *Last Letters from Stalingrad,* translated and published in 1961, retired American general S. L. A. Marshall writes:

> What men in combat write home . . . is rarely memorable. Yet there arises from these Stalingrad letters a dirge of melancholy . . . unlike any other chorus out of battle. It is the song of the doomed, the wail of a soldiery defeated and self-marked for death. . . . hope [had] already fled. They knew they had been failed and fooled . . . .

The letters were flown out on the last plane from Stalingrad; the army high command seized the letters and removed the addresses and senders' names. The first excerpt vividly describes the horrors of the last stages of the battle:

> You were supposed to die heroically, inspiringly, movingly, from inner conviction and for a great cause. But what is death in reality here? Here they croak, starve to death, freeze to death—it's nothing but a biological fact like eating and drinking. They drop like flies; nobody cares and nobody buries them. Without arms or legs and without eyes, with bellies torn open, they lie around everywhere.

An officer writes to his wife:

> I love you very much and you love me, so you will know the truth. . . . The truth is the knowledge that this is the grimmest of struggles in a hopeless situation. Misery, hunger, cold, renunciation, doubt, despair and horrible death. . . . what I wrote above is no complaint or lament but a statement of objective fact. I cannot deny my share of personal guilt in all this. . . . I am not cowardly, only sad that I cannot give greater proof of courage than to die for this useless, not to say criminal, cause.

Another soldier writes of his disillusionment with Hitler:

> The Führer made a firm promise to bail us out of here . . . and we (this soldier and many of his comrades had belonged to the Hitler Youth) believed it. . . . all my life, at least eight years of it, I believed in the Führer and his word. It is terrible how they doubt here, and shameful to listen to what they say . . . because they have the facts on their side. If what we were promised is not true, then Germany will be lost, for in that case no more promises can be kept."

Last Letters from Stalingrad, trans. by Franz Schneider and Charles Gullans (New York: New American Library, 1961), pp. 7, 46–47, 37–38, 50–51.

and appointed Marshal Zhukov, the "savior of Moscow," as commander-in-chief of the southern armies. Paulus and other generals urged Hitler to pull back from the city and reinforce Army Group A in the south, but the Führer's decision to take the city at all costs was unalterable. To the generals who held that the Caucasus was of much greater strategic and economic value (which accorded with his own view), Hitler argued that Stalingrad was an equally essential target because of its location: "There, 30 million tons of traffic on the Volga can be cut off, including 9 million of oil shipments," thus overnight paralyzing the Soviet war effort.[21] It was a specious argument. Hitler had become obsessed with taking the city named after his arch-enemy; to disengage his forces, he believed, would do irreparable harm to his prestige. The Führer's decision set the stage for the greatest single land battle of World War II in Europe and condemned over 250,000 German troops to death or captivity.

Despite powerful Soviet attacks that inflicted heavy casualties and blocked supplies and reinforcements, Paulus's battered Sixth Army had taken the center of the city by mid-November. Zhukov had deliberately left Stalingrad undermanned so that he could mass powerful armies to encircle it. On November 23 Soviet spearheads came together forty-five miles west of Stalingrad, sealing off the Sixth Army and one Panzer corps. Hitler denied Paulus' request to abandon the city and attempt to break through the gradually tightening encirclement. In early December, Hitler ordered Manstein's Panzer corps, which had been recalled from the north, to penetrate the Soviet ring, but it was much too strong. At the same time, Red Army divisions entered the city en masse, forcing Paulus' undersupplied, exhausted, and outnumbered troops to defend themselves, block by block and building by building. The Sixth Army was gradually being annihilated in the city that Hitler had ordered to be defended to the last man. Fortunately for the Wehrmacht, the troops in the Caucasus escaped the same fate. A powerful Soviet offensive in December threatened to cut off all German forces in southern Russia. If Hitler had not authorized a retreat, the still formidable Army Group A would have been destroyed.

The final days of the Sixth Army in Stalingrad were an unimaginable horror. The cold and hungry German troops fought furiously, but they could neither replace fallen comrades nor replenish diminishing supplies. The center of the city, littered with hundreds of thousands of corpses, was reduced to piles of rubble and crumbling buildings. Paulus begged Hitler to authorize a surrender, but the Führer refused to rescind his fight-to-the-last-man order. He promoted Paulus to field marshal on January 30, hoping that the honor of the army's highest rank would strengthen his will to resist and to commit suicide rather than surrender. The suffering and hopelessness of the Sixth Army, as well as the bungling of the Luftwaffe, were underscored on a clear day in January 1943, when a fleet of transports broke through the clouds to airlift supplies. Instead of food, medicine, and clothing, most of the cartons contained barbed wire and contraceptives! On February 3, 1943, Field Marshal Friedrich Paulus surrendered to the

German prisoners at Stalingrad nervously await their fate in the icy cold of another Russian winter.

Red Army. Stalingrad's death toll was well over a million people, including resident civilians and Russian, German, Italian, Hungarian, and Romanian combatants. Over half of Paulus' 300,000-man Sixth Army lay dead on the streets of Stalingrad. Despite its failure to supply the doomed army during the last stages of the battle, the Luftwaffe had earlier evacuated over 45,000 wounded. Only 90,000 survived to be taken captive. Most of them never saw Germany again.

After Stalingrad

Stalingrad was the greatest single military defeat in German history. Never before had an entire army been swallowed up in the vast wilderness of an alien land over 1,300 miles from Berlin. For soldier and civilian alike, it was the most traumatic event of the war.[22] Except for an abortive offensive in July 1943 at Kursk, about 400 miles northwest of Stalingrad in northern Ukraine, the Wehrmacht was on the defensive, retreating westward with ever-diminishing human and material resources until the end of the war. The Red Army, on the other hand, grew more powerful with each battle. Its morale, leadership, organization, and confidence were much improved, and it had access to huge reserves of manpower, increased Soviet war production, and large shipments of U.S. trucks and other four-wheel-drive vehicles.

In spite of all the difficulties, the retreating Germans made the Red Army pay dearly for every square mile of recaptured territory. They were

skillful and tenacious in defense and were able to stage an occasional counterattack. Shortly after Stalingrad, Hitler recalled Guderian to become in-
spector general of armored corps in the south, and appointed Manstein as
commander of Army Group B, renamed Army Group Don. In February
1943, Manstein's forces recaptured Kharkov and, by employing an elastic
defense, lured the advancing Russians, who were outrunning their supply
vehicles, into an overly aggressive pursuit. Following a successful attack
against an overexposed Soviet flank in the spring of 1943, Manstein proposed an orderly retreat to Kiev hundreds of miles to the west and coun-
terattacking what he assumed would be the Red Army's vulnerable flanks.
Hitler denied Manstein's request and reluctantly approved a plan to attack
the heavily fortified city of Kursk. Code-named Operation Citadel, it was
to be the last German offensive on the eastern front.

　　While Stalingrad was clearly the psychological turning point of the war,
most historians see Kursk as the decisive military turning point. It was the
largest tank battle of the entire war, with almost 3,000 tanks on the field at
the peak of the fighting. The Germans had seventeen armored divisions,
some of which were equipped with the new Panther and Tiger tanks.
Though they would become the most formidable armor in the European
theater after initial design flaws had been corrected, they were outnumbered
and eventually outfought by the Russian T-34 at Kursk. Taking advantage of
German delays, the Red Army fortified the area even more heavily and,
when the Wehrmacht attacked on July 5, the Soviets were well prepared.
Both sides suffered heavy losses in what became a battle of attrition. On July
12 Hitler ordered his generals to break off the attack, which had barely penetrated Kursk's defenses, and a few hours later the Soviets launched a massive
counteroffensive. If the Germans had not begun to withdraw at that point,
their entire army might have been destroyed. The Führer became even more
suspicious of his generals after the Kursk defeat and reverted to the rigid
"stand fast" mentality that led to the Stalingrad disaster. By January 1944 the
Red Army, in heavy fighting all the way, had driven the Wehrmacht into the
southeastern corner of prewar Poland and had lifted the siege of Leningrad.

　　The most remarkable aspect of the Russian campaign, after two-and-
a-half years of bloody fighting, was not the might of the Red Army's offensive, but the extent of the Wehrmacht's advance. Given its limited resources, its overextended supply lines, the simultaneous pursuit of multiple
objectives, and the enemy's vast reservoir of men and machines, the occupation of the remote Caucasus region, however brief, ranks as one of the
most amazing feats of military history. If Hitler had transferred most of his
forces from the Leningrad and Moscow sectors to the south for the 1942
summer offensive, let go of his Stalingrad obsession, and ordered the
Wehrmacht to enlist the support of the native population, Germany might
have been able to secure this vast area and exploit its resources. But such
rational policies were incompatible with Hitler's megalomania and his
murderous racial ideology.

BOX 8.4 ■   A "DEDICATED" GERMAN SOLDIER ON THE
EASTERN FRONT

While the excerpts from the diary of this German soldier, whose name was
Wilhelm Prüller, do not explicitly mention the murder of civilians, they provide insight into the thinking of a man so thoroughly indoctrinated with
Nazi ideology that he would do anything to destroy a people whom he believed to be a threat to the "superior race." He expresses such sentiments in
a letter to the wife of a fallen comrade, dated February 23, 1942.

"Believe me Fräulein Trunka, that I understand only too well how much
you miss your beloved fallen man. But you are a German girl; and as such
you are as enthusiastic about our fight for the life or death of our people as
all of us who are here on the front. Later in your life . . . you will . . . thank
the victims, who will have saved us and our children from a life of degrada-
tion and shame, of distress and desperation. . . . Just as we here are proud to
have taken part in this great fight, so you, Fräulein Trunka, must be proud to
have made such a heavy sacrifice for this fight. It was not in vain! Your Martin shall be avenged! The survival of our great Fatherland, our imperishable
people, and the victory over our accursed enemies shall have been accomplished through his death."

His signature reads: "Long live the Führer! Prüller!"

"Diary of a German Soldier," by Wilhelm Prüller, in Harold Elk Straubing, ed., *A
Taste of War: Eyewitness Accounts of World War II* (New York: Sterling Publishing Co.,
1992), pp. 158–159.

There is yet another side to the Wehrmacht's conduct of the war in the
east. A pattern of atrocities—the wanton slaughter of villagers, deportations,
starvation of prisoners, burning alive of school children, target practice on
civilian hospitals—was established early and continued throughout the campaign. Historian Alan Clark writes: "Atrocities were so commonplace that no
man coming fresh to the scene could stay sane without acquiring a protec-
tive veneer of brutalization."[23] While some German soldiers committed
atrocities only under duress, most were willing participants in what their officers called "a life-and-death struggle against the Jewish-Bolshevik system
and Asiatic barbarism." Generals not known as fanatical Nazis, such as
Manstein and Panzer commander Erich Höpner (who would be executed in
1944 for his part in the plot to kill Hitler), told their men several weeks before the invasion in 1941 that, as "carriers of a racial conception and . . .
avengers of all the atrocities [against] . . . the German people," they were to
demolish Russia in the defense of European culture against "the Muscovite-
Asiatic flood." The planning and execution of every battle was to be "dictated
by an iron will to bring about a merciless, total annihilation of the enemy."[24]

German troops, with or without official authorization, murdered hundreds of thousands of Russian nonbelligerents, whether commissars or ordinary civilians. They were motivated by anti-Semitism, fear and hatred of being overrun by "Slavic hordes" from the east, and most of all by a militant anti-Bolshevism. "Bolshevism was perceived as a deadly enemy which not only needed to be defeated in a traditional way, but also had to be completely and totally exterminated."[25] The army's most heinous crime was the treatment of Soviet prisoners. Of the 5,700,000 soldiers captured by the Germans, 58 percent (3,300,000) died, some in forced labor camps, but most in outdoor "holding pens" with little food and shelter. While the Wehrmacht did lack facilities to care for such a huge influx of prisoners, the evidence strongly suggests that it was "policy" to allow them to perish.

The Wehrmacht's slaughter of Soviet nonbelligerents was reflected in the ruthless treatment of its own troops. Whereas the Kaiser's army executed only forty-eight soldiers for desertion from 1914 to 1918, the Wehrmacht put to death between 16,000 and 18,000 of its own men for desertion alone. Other crimes, for which hundreds were executed, were cowardice, "dishonorable behavior," "subversion," and theft. (The memoirs of a commissioned officer record his reluctant execution of a soldier for stealing food for himself from a shipment sent to the entire company.)[26] Most of the executed soldiers were stationed on the Russian front. Ideology was the principal reason for the huge number of executions. In the Third Reich, a deserter was regarded not only as a disobedient soldier but also as a traitor to the national community. "Deserters were stigmatized as threats to the life of the community and as dangerous psychopathic outsiders—a status which, in accordance with the ideology and practice of Nazism, marked them out for liquidation."[27] Israeli historian Omer Bartov suggests that the high rate of capital punishment and the legalization of crimes toward the enemy "derived their legitimacy" from the same source, the "acceptance of the Nazi world view."[28] Thus, the high level of ideological commitment normally associated with the SS was also an essential feature of the Wehrmacht's behavior on the eastern front. This commitment helps to account for the motivation behind heroic performances in battle, as well as for the atrocities.

The War in the West, to January 1944

Even after the Allies escalated their bomber offensive against the Reich in 1943, to most German civilians "the war" was still the Russian campaign. The Battle of the Atlantic, Rommel's exploits in the Libyan desert, and the Allied invasion of North Africa and Italy were peripheral to the main event, where millions of fathers, husbands, and brothers were engaged day after day in a life-and-death struggle with the *Untermenschen* of the east. At least 80 percent of all German soldiers in World War II served on the Russian front. But Allied operations in the Atlantic and the Mediterranean,

BOX 8.5 ■   HORROR ON THE HIGH SEAS

Ordinary sailors fighting the Battle of the Atlantic experienced combat every bit as horrifying and deadly as ground troops. Hal Lawrence was a Canadian stationed on a corvette, a primitive warship assigned the task of seeking out submarines, discouraging or sinking them, and keeping straggling freighters in the convoy formation. The corvettes helped stave off a total disaster for the British in 1941 and early 1942. He describes what happened to several ships in an encounter with seven submarines in September 1941:

> Torpedo after torpedo tore into the ships' vitals. Despairing rockets begged for help, but little could be given. Burning ships glowed red and star shell drifting down cast an eerie white light. . . . Constantly came the rumble of depth charges exploding and, periodically, the thud of German torpedoes as the dogs of war harried the near-helpless flock. Wreckage littered the water: boats, floats, rafts, some with wildly waving men clinging to them, others empty. It's hard to say how many men were in the water, but the dull red flicker of the lights on their life belts seemed everywhere. Some men lolled limply, heads flopping. Some shouted weakly, hopefully, as an escort approached, and they yelled despairingly as she swept by. "The safe and timely arrival of the convoy" was the overriding consideration and an attack could not be broken off to rescue survivors.

Harold Elk Straubing, ed., *A Taste of War: Eyewitness Accounts of World War II* (New York: Sterling, 1992), p. 179.

where American manpower and matériel first had an impact, made possible the "second front"—that is, the invasion of France in June 1944, and heavier, more destructive bombing raids. Both would greatly expand the meaning of "the war" for the German people.

During the first months of 1942, Churchill, Roosevelt, and their military advisers formulated a second front strategy. Churchill, who had contemplated the bombing and invasion of Italy as early as March 1941,[29] pictured Axis-controlled Europe as an alligator, with France as the snout and the Mediterranean as the soft underbelly. Rejecting an immediate cross-Channel invasion of the snout as far too risky, the Allies adopted Churchill's plan to strike first at the soft underbelly. It would begin with the takeover of French North Africa, followed by the defeat of Rommel's Africa Corps and the invasion of the continent through Italy. If successful, this strategy would give the United States time to mobilize its vast reservoir of human and material resources, knock one of the Axis powers out of the war, provide air bases from which to bomb the Reich's defenses and industry, and divert German divisions from the Russian front. The latter would mollify Stalin, whose demand for an immediate cross-Channel invasion annoyed Allied leaders. Hitler's "fortress Europe" would be softened up, and a full-scale frontal assault on France would have a much better chance of success.

Allied planners believed that they would need a decisive edge in manpower and machines to dislodge the entrenched Axis forces. It was therefore essential to maintain a steady and continually expanding stream of human and material resources from the United States. Knowing little of Allied plans and having no other military options in the west, Hitler sought to sabotage Britain's lifeline to the United States. The result was the Battle of the Atlantic, which, from the British point of view, was the most crucial of the war. It raged most intensely from the summer of 1941 to spring of 1943.

At the beginning of 1941 the Germans had over 250 submarines, six cruisers and light battle ships, hundreds of torpedo planes, and thousands of magnetic mines. At year's end this combination of weapons had destroyed nearly 1,300 Allied vessels. Admiral Karl Dönitz's submarines, which accounted for most of the kills, attacked in groups called "wolf packs," which enabled the U-boats more effectively to penetrate the shield of warships escorting the convoys of vulnerable merchant ships. The German submarines embarked from concrete enclosures built along the coast of France; called "pens," they were virtually impervious to Allied bombs. The British reinforced the convoys, used sonar detection devices, and tried, with some success, to crack the Reich's coding system, but Dönitz could easily replace the submarines destroyed or damaged by the Royal Navy and the RAF. The most highly publicized incident of the Battle of the Atlantic in 1941 was the destruction of the new, state-of-the-art German battleship, the *Bismarck*, on its first raid. Although it was a spectacular victory for the Royal Navy, the Reich's few remaining surface ships continued to raid British commerce, occasionally with deadly accuracy.

The Battle of the Atlantic reached its most critical phase in 1942, when Hitler authorized a substantial increase in submarine production. The wolf packs accounted for more than 80 percent of all Allied losses at sea, totaling 1,664 ships, some of which were American. Despite an enormous increase in U.S. ship production, the Allies fell 1 million tons short of replacing the sunken vessels. Able to replace their losses, German U-boats reached Dönitz's goal of the monthly destruction of 700,000 tons of shipping in June and November. Moreover, the Germans were having more success in locating enemy ships and decoding messages.

By January 1943, two months after the Allied invasion of North Africa and four weeks before the surrender at Stalingrad, the Reich seemed to have gained the advantage in the Atlantic. It was short-lived. Within three months the Allies' shipping replacement rate rose to meet losses; convoys had more ships with more firepower, planes, and sophisticated detection devices; and British cryptographers had cracked the Germans' revised code. In May 1943, two months after Dönitz replaced Admiral Raeder as the navy's supreme commander, the Allies sank forty-one submarines. Unable to replace such heavy losses, Dönitz temporarily removed his wolf packs from the North Atlantic. There would be more action on the high seas in 1944 and 1945, but the Allies had won the Battle of the Atlantic by the spring of 1943.

Germany's success at sea in late 1942 coincided with a reversal of fortune in North Africa. After the retreat from Egypt in 1941, Rommel's Africa Corps dueled brilliantly with numerically superior British forces in the Libyan desert, took Tobruk in May 1942, entered Egypt in June, and reached El Alamein, only 60 miles west of Cairo and the Suez Canal, by early September. Here the "Desert Fox," the most admired and popular German general of the war, had to stop because of critical shortages of supplies, particularly fuel for his tanks. Hitler ordered Rommel to return to Germany for treatment of boils, a common ailment in the desert war. He wanted his successful general to be healthy for the next offensive, which aimed at capturing the Suez Canal, Britain's vital lifeline to India and the far east, and giving the Reich another opportunity to seize Middle Eastern oil fields. Given Hitler's reluctance to divert even small shipments of supplies earmarked for the Russian campaign, these objectives were totally unrealistic. Moreover, the British had gained complete air and naval mastery of the Mediterranean by spring 1942. They sank Italian supply ships at will and, determined to make a stand at El Alamein, heavily reinforced their Egyptian army.

In August the Eighth Army received a new commander, Bernard Montgomery, who would become Britain's most famous—and controversial—general of the war. He drew immediate criticism for postponing an attack until his forces had overwhelming numerical and (with the arrival of American Sherman and Grant tanks) qualitative superiority. When he unleashed the El Alamein offensive on October 23, 1942, Montgomery's army had 230,000 men and 1,200 tanks, as compared to the Axis' 80,000 and 500, respectively. Rommel returned to Egypt two days after the attack began, but the battle had already been decided. In the long retreat across the Libyan desert, his Africa Corps inflicted heavy casualties on Montgomery's forces and continually eluded capture. By February 1943 the Africa Corps was in Tunisia, nearly 1,300 miles from El Alamein. Rommel's defensive tactics were brilliant, but Churchill's retrospective assessment was correct: "Up till Alamein we survived. After Alamein we conquered."[30]

On November 8, 1942, Anglo-American forces launched Operation Torch, the invasion of North Africa. They landed on the coast of Morocco, near the city of Casablanca, and at two points farther east on the Algerian coast. The Allies quickly overcame fierce resistance from French forces under the jurisdiction of the Vichy government, established political control, and moved eastward toward Tunisia to link up with Montgomery's army pursuing Rommel. In February 1943 U.S. forces commanded by General Dwight D. Eisenhower had their first taste of combat with seasoned German troops at the Kasserine Pass in Tunisia. Rommel's tactical victory delayed the Allies, but his situation was hopeless. Anglo-American air and naval power blocked supply shipments, and on May 13, 1943, several weeks after Rommel had been evacuated to Italy, the Axis army surrendered. Hitler's dream of victory in Russia and the eastern Mediterranean had faded into the nightmare of Stalingrad, total expulsion from North Africa, and defeat in the Battle of the Atlantic. These reversals took place within a period of four months in 1943, from February to May.

The Allied victory in North Africa seemed assured when Roosevelt and Churchill met at Casablanca in January 1943. They agreed on the Italian island of Sicily as the initial landing site for the invasion of the continent. Other strategic issues were discussed, but the Casablanca meeting is most famous for FDR's announcement that the Allies would accept nothing less than unconditional surrender from the Axis powers. This policy was designed chiefly to convince Stalin, who was growing more suspicious of his western allies for delaying the second front, that Britain and the United States would not desert the Soviets and seek a separate peace with Germany. The unconditional surrender policy did not allay Stalin's suspicions, and Goebbels used it to stiffen his people's resistance in the face of impending doom after Stalingrad. He repeatedly cited the Casablanca declaration as evidence of the Allies' vindictiveness and their determination to "destroy the German people." Whether the unconditional surrender decree prolonged the war is debatable, but it unequivocally served notice on the Axis powers that nothing was negotiable.

Anglo-American forces invaded Sicily on July 9, 1943. The hilly terrain, the Germans' skillful defensive tactics, and wasteful competition between two "prima donnas," Montgomery and American tank commander George Patton, delayed capture of the island. When Patton's forces reached the city of Messina on August 17, 60,000 German defenders with all their equipment had escaped to the mainland. On July 25 the Fascist Grand Council dismissed and imprisoned Mussolini and asked King Victor Emanuel and Marshal Pietro Badoglio to form a new government. After negotiating with the Allies for several days, during which the Germans occupied and fortified southern Italy, the new government surrendered unconditionally. (The Italians did not sign the instrument of surrender until September 2.) The weakest of the three Axis powers had been defeated, but Italy now had to be wrested from the Germans. This long, arduous, and bloody campaign began with Anglo-American landings near the southern port city of Salerno in early September 1943. On September 12 Hitler dispatched an SS airborne force to rescue Mussolini from prison and install him as ruler of a puppet Fascist state in northern Italy. Entirely dependent on Hitler's support, the Duce's regime would have no effect on the outcome of the war.

The Italian campaign lasted until the end of the war. Everywhere the Allies landed or attacked, they encountered a skillful and stubborn defense. The capture of Rome in June 1944 coincided with the Normandy invasion, after which the Italian campaign was treated as little more than a

NATIONAL ARCHIVES

Stalin, Roosevelt, and Churchill pose for photographers at the Teheran Conference in November 1943. The frequent top-level wartime conferences of World War II were unprecedented in the history of warfare. To attend this conference in the Iranian capital Stalin had to leave the Soviet Union; it was the only time he did so.

diversion. Its impact on the war was minimal both for the Germans, who suffered 556,000 casualties, and the Allies, who lost 312,000 killed or wounded. It was a high price to pay for relatively meager results, but the campaign engaged twenty German divisions that might otherwise have opposed the Russians or strengthened the Reich's defenses in Normandy. In view of the appalling attrition rate on the eastern front and the awesome might of the Allied invasion armada in France, it is unlikely that German forces diverted from Italy would have significantly altered the outcome of either campaign.

The date for the invasion, May 1944, was announced at the first of two summit conferences of "the big three"—Roosevelt, Churchill, and Stalin—held in Teheran, Iran, from November 28 to December 1, 1943. The Soviet dictator, who appeared pleased that the second front was "imminent," promised to enter the war against Japan following the Reich's unconditional surrender. Swayed by Stalin's show of cooperation and moderation, Churchill abandoned his proposal to invade the Balkans, and both the British prime minister and the U.S. president agreed to shift their support to Marshal Tito's communist partisans in Yugoslavia. The big three also agreed to divide a defeated Germany into three zones of occupation. In a major concession to Stalin, the western leaders approved the transfer of the eastern third of Poland to the Soviet Union, for which the Poles were to be compensated with German territory. These decisions helped pave the way for the Soviet takeover of eastern Europe after the war.

Conclusion

By the end of 1943, Allied forces enjoyed the initiative on all fronts. The Red Army and Hitler's megalomania had turned his dream of living space in the east into the bloodiest nightmare in the history of warfare. In the western theater, the Reich had suffered defeats in North Africa and on the high seas; Anglo-American bombing raids on strategic targets and cities in Germany were becoming more frequent and destructive; and the enormous buildup of a cross-Channel invasion force was proceeding on schedule. The Third Reich faced certain defeat, yet Hitler seemed more determined than ever to continue the struggle. The Teheran Conference was followed by another eighteen months of bloody conflict that would consume the lives of millions of people. How Nazi Germany with its shrinking human and material resources was able to prolong the war against the two future superpowers and their British partner is a central theme of the next chapter.

INFOTRAC® COLLEGE EDITION SEARCH TERMS

For additional reading go to Infotrac College Edition, your online research library at http://www.infotrac-college.com.

Enter the search term "Barbarossa" using Keywords.

Enter the search term "Moscow, Battle of" using the Subject Guide.

Enter the search term "Stalingrad, 1942" using Keywords.

Enter the search term "Kursk" using the Subject Guide.

Enter the search term "Warsaw" using Keywords.

Enter the search term "Zhukov, Georgi" using Keywords.

Enter the search term "World War, 1939–1945, Africa" using Keywords.

Enter the search term "Montgomery, Bernard Law" using the Subject Guide.

Enter the search term "German U-Boats" using the Subject Guide.

Enter the search term "Naval operations World War 1939–1945" using Keywords.

Notes

1. Ronald Lewin, *Hitler's Mistakes* (New York: William Morrow, 1984), p. 117.

2. David Kaiser, *Politics and War* (Cambridge: Harvard University Press, 1990), p. 389.

3. Robert J. Rhodes, ed., *Winston S. Churchill: His Complete Speeches* (New York: R. P. Bowker, 1974), 2: 6231.

4. John Costello, *Ten Days to Destiny* (New York: William Morrow, 1991), pp. xiv–xvi.

5. Alan Bullock, *Hitler and Stalin: Parallel Lives* (New York: Alfred A. Knopf, 1992), p. 690.

6. Correlli Barnett, ed., *Hitler's Generals* (New York: Grove Weidenfeld, 1989), p. 10.

7. Quoted in Norman Rich, *Hitler's War Aims* (New York: Norton, 1974) pp. 212, 214; Franz Halder, *The Halder Diaries* (Boulder, Colo.: Westview Press, 1976), 2: 846.

8. Quoted in Ian Kershaw, *Hitler* (London: Longman, 1991), pp. 154–155.

9. International Military Tribunal (IMT), *Trial of the Major War Criminals* (Nuremberg, 1947–1949), 31: 84.

10. John Keegan, *The Second World War* (New York: Viking, 1989), p. 174; M. K. Dziewanowski, *War at Any Price* (Englewood Cliffs, NJ: Prentice-Hall, 1987), p. 170.

11. Quoted in Joachim Fest, *Hitler* (New York: Harcourt Brace Jovanovich, 1973), p. 648; Gordon Wright, *The Ordeal of Total War 1939–1945* (New York: Harper & Row, 1968), p. 38; Keegan, p. 174.

12. John Erickson, *The Road to Stalingrad: Stalin's War with Germany* (New Haven and London: Yale University Press, 1999), pp. 125–26.

13. Quoted in Lewin, p. 119.

14. Quoted in David M. Glantz and Jonathan M. House, *When Titans Clashed: How the Red Army Stopped Hitler* (Lawrence, KA: University Press of Kansas, 1995), p. 74.

15. Alan Clark, *Barbarossa* (New York: William Morrow, 1965), p. 146.

16. Glantz and House, p. 91.

17. Lewin, p. 117.

18. Ian Kershaw, *Hitler 1939–1945: Nemesis* (New York: Norton, 2000), pp. 445–46.

19. Sebastian Haffner, *The Meaning of Hitler* (New York: MacMillan, 1978), p. 120.

20. Kershaw, *Hitler: Nemesis*, p. 529.

21. Dziewanowski, p. 221.

22. William Craig, *Enemy at the Gates* (New York: Ballantine Books, 1973), p. xvii.

23. Clark, p. 193.

24. Quoted in Omer Bartov, *Hitler's Army* (New York: Oxford University Press, 1992), pp. 129–30.

25. Klaus-Jürgen Müller, "The Brutalisation of Warfare, Nazi Crimes, and the Wehrmacht," in John Erickson and David Dilks, eds., *Barbarossa: The Axis and the Allies* (Edinburgh: Edinburgh University Press, 1994), pp. 234–35.

26. Gottlob Herbert Bidermann, *In Deadly Combat: A German Soldier's Memoir of the Eastern Front* (Lawrence: University Press of Kansas, 2000), p. 176.

27. Steven R. Welch, "'Harsh but Just?' German Military Justice in the Second World War: A Comparative Study of the Court-Martialling of German and U.S. Deserters," in *German History: The Journal of the German Historical Society* (17: 3, 1999), p. 398.

28. Bartov, p. 95.

29. Gerhard L. Weinberg, *A World at Arms* (Cambridge: Cambridge University Press, 1994), p. 224.

30. Quoted in Martin Gilbert, *Winston S. Churchill* (Boston: Houghton Mifflin, 1988), 8:160.

The German People at War

On February 18, 1943, two weeks after the Stalingrad disaster, Joseph Goebbels warned Germany that it had only two choices, "victory or destruction." For two-and-a-half hours he harangued thousands of Nazi party faithful gathered at the Berlin Sports Palace, while millions more listened on the radio. Victory, he insisted, meant pursuing a war "more total and radical than we are capable of imagining today." He admitted that the regime had seriously underestimated the strength of the Soviet Union, which resulted from a mixture of "terroristic Jewry" and the "stupid toughness of the Russian race." He called upon workers to labor up to sixteen hours a day, while black marketeers and slackers would be summarily executed. Everyone, rich or poor, would carry the heavy burdens of total war with "grim determination." Goebbels concluded: "People, arise, and storm, break loose!" For twenty minutes a storm did break loose in the sports arena, as the loyal throng thundered its approval. The jubilant Goebbels, seven pounds lighter from his strenuous oratory, was also pleased with the response of radio listeners, most of whom, according to reports of local propaganda offices, were filled with renewed determination "to expend their last reserves of strength" in the struggle for survival.[1]

The audience was as startled as it was aroused. It was the first time in three-and-a-half years that Goebbels or any high-ranking official had portrayed the war in such bleak terms. The unpopularity of the war in September 1939 had given way to exhilaration, which peaked after the fall of France. Morale sagged slightly after the Battle of Britain, but rebounded when Hitler launched his "anti-Bolshevik crusade" in 1941. The failure of the Moscow offensive, Hitler's declaration of war on the United States, and the bloodletting of the 1942 offensives proved that the war would be a long one, but the majority still believed that Germany would win. After Stalingrad, that confidence waned. Goebbels could not eradicate "creeping defeatism," but his speech, buttressed by the ensuing victory-or-destruction propaganda campaign, strengthened the will to resist. For more than two years the German people endured a war "more total and radical," and more horrible, than even Goebbels imagined in February 1943.

Blitzkrieg Economics, 1939–1941

From 1939 to 1941 the Reich's economic policy, which some post-war historians called Blitzkrieg economics, was an expanded version of the 1936 four-year plan. Wage and price controls helped maintain economic stability, while arms production increased and the output of consumer goods declined. In September 1939 the government introduced rationing of clothes, shoes, and a wide range of foodstuffs, including butter, milk, meat, and eggs. Powdered milk and puddings and ersatz coffee and tea were usually available, and bread and potatoes were not rationed. Fresh fruits and vegetables were not rationed but were in short supply. While the grain-based diet was monotonous and not always appetizing,[2] there was enough food to nourish the body and hold discontent to a minimum. The SS Security Service, the SD, reported few complaints about the economy in 1940. Nor did Britain's refusal to surrender shatter confidence in the Führer. He spoke frequently in late 1940 and early 1941, assuring the people that victory without more deprivation or sacrifice was imminent.[3]

One of the most serious economic problems was a labor shortage created by the Wehrmacht's conscription of 7 million men during the first two-and-a-half years of the war. The regime expanded the compulsory labor service for young people but, adhering strictly to Nazi policy, the leadership refused to recruit more women into the workforce. Of the approximately 10 million women in employment at the beginning of 1942, only about 10 percent worked in war industries. The nearly 4 million foreign workers, among whom were Polish and French prisoners of war, did little to alleviate the labor shortage. Much factory machinery remained underutilized; the Reich's war production lagged well behind the output of Britain and the Soviet Union. Labor shortages would plague German industry throughout the war.

Blitzkrieg economics was driven by improvisation and opportunism, but underlying it all was Hitler's aversion to massive arms production for a long war. Such a policy of armament in depth, advocated by General Georg Thomas, head of the Wehrmacht's War Economy and Armaments Office, envisioned rigorous economic regulation, increased authority for the Wehrmacht's planning branch, and a steep decline in the production of consumer goods. The latter, Hitler believed, would lead to catastrophic shortages, reminiscent of World War I, and would destroy popular morale. The Führer preferred a flexible policy of armament in breadth, which would not require a major restructuring of the economy. Left free to improvise and adapt to specific situations, he could increase production of whatever was most needed for a particular campaign. Once the war had reached a successful conclusion, he could revert to normal production and supplement losses with the defeated enemy's equipment.

In March 1940 Hitler appointed Fritz Todt as the Reich's first minister of arms and munitions. The former supervisor of autobahn construction proved an able administrator. He established a central coordinating committee and subcommittees for each area of munitions production. These committees of factory managers and representatives of the Wehrmacht's War Economy and Armaments Office reduced red tape and duplication and made armaments production more cost-efficient. Todt's committees also laid the administrative groundwork for total war economics and armament in depth, which could be implemented if Blitzkrieg battle tactics failed. That failure became painfully obvious in December 1941.

In January 1942 Hitler approved a modification of Blitzkrieg economics. Besides substantial, across-the-board increases in weapons production, he authorized the call-up of an additional 500,000 men, 300,000 of them for the army. He agreed to tighter government controls, but would allow only a modest reduction in the manufacture of consumer goods. Todt's ministry and General Thomas, who had been lobbying for the arms-in-depth policy since December 1939, bid for administrative power over an expanded armaments program. Hitler decided in favor of his minister of arms and munitions. Several days after his appointment, Todt died in a plane crash. On the same day, February 8, 1942, Hitler appointed Albert Speer to be the Reich's new minister of arms and munitions. Speer enlarged Todt's administrative machinery and presided over the Third Reich's enormous armaments expansion.

Total War Economics, 1942–1944

Albert Speer, a 36-year-old architect with little administrative or political experience, seemed an unlikely candidate to head the ministry of arms and munitions. He was not an ardent Nazi and had no ties to anyone in the hierarchy except Hitler, who was genuinely fond of his young architect. Speer proved to be an able administrator and an extraordinarily astute, sometimes ruthless, politician, often outmaneuvering more experienced and fanatical Nazi leaders. He lost some political battles, but in most cases his policies, with Hitler's support, prevailed. Speer was the only insider to write a detailed wartime history of the regime. However one might judge his culpability—many feel that he should have been hanged at Nuremberg—students of Nazi history are indebted to him for insightful assessments of Hitler and his lieutenants, his discussion of the intense power struggles within the regime, and his detailed eyewitness account and analysis of Germany's war production.

Speer's task was a daunting one. Blitzkrieg economics had left Germany lagging behind its foes. In 1941 the Soviet Union and Britain produced armaments valued at $8.5 and $6.5 billion, respectively, while the

BILDARCHIV PREUSSISCHER KULTURBESITZ, BERLIN

Pictured in a prototype of a Tiger tank are Albert Speer (seated in the center) and Ferdinand Porsche (far right in civilian clothes), the automaker whose factory built the tank. One of the largest tanks deployed in the European theater, the Tiger sacrificed speed and maneuverability for heavy firepower and thick armor.

Reich produced only $6 billion worth of armaments. The United States, which entered the war on December 11, produced armaments worth $4.5 billion. Before Barbarossa, Hitler was not aware that the Soviets enjoyed a 2 to 1 superiority in tanks over the Germans. "Had I known they had as many tanks as that," he told Heinz Guderian, "I would have thought twice before invading."[4] Speer knew that the Reich could never match the Soviet output, but he believed that Germany's underutilized industrial plant could double or even triple its productive capacity. The enemy's numerical advantage would be reduced, and German know-how would ensure qualitative superiority.

The centerpiece of Speer's ministry was a central planning board, with subcommittees for each sector of war production staffed by industrialists, government officials, and representatives of the Wehrmacht and Luftwaffe. In April 1942 Hitler delegated broad powers to Speer's board in such areas as procurement of supplies, allocation of raw materials, production quotas, and the labor force. By February 1943, one year after Speer's appointment, the index of total production had doubled, rising to 207 from a base of 100 in February 1942. One year later, tank output had quadrupled and the index of total production registered 231. It was an impressive achievement, but Germany's $13.8 billion armament expenditure in 1943 was dwarfed by the U.S. outlay of $37.5 billion for the European theater alone. With Britain's $11.1 billion and the Soviets' $13.9 billion, the Allies' defense spending in 1943 totaled $62.5 billion.[5]

The pressure of the impending invasion of France in the spring of 1944 spurred Speer's committees and German industry to increase production by at least one-third. They succeeded. From the beginning of March to the end of July, the index of total production climbed from 231 to 322, a 39 percent increase. During Speer's tenure as minister of arms and munitions, annual production of aircraft rose from 15,000 to 40,000, while tank output increased from an annual 6,000 to 19,000. Though still far behind the Soviet Union and the United States, Germany outproduced Britain by 20 percent. It was a remarkable achievement in the face of formidable obstacles. British and American bombing forced Speer to assign thousands of workers to repair damaged facilities and to move industries underground, an expensive and laborious process. Allied bombing of coal gasification plants in Germany and oil fields in Romania led to critical fuel shortages, which mounted as the war progressed.

Speer also had to wrestle with political bottlenecks. Hitler gradually became less accessible, and sometimes supported Speer's enemies. Foremost among them were minister plenipotentiary of foreign labor Fritz Sauckel and Martin Bormann, who had become the de facto leader of the Nazi party in Hess's absence and had been appointed by the Führer to be his private secretary in 1943. Bormann defended the Gauleiters, the old fighter district leaders who resented the power of the industrialists on Speer's committees and feared that their own authority would be diminished if there were drastic cutbacks in consumer goods.

Speer delivered a threatening speech to the Gauleiters in October 1943. Citing "excessive" production of typewriters, radio receivers, refrigerators, and electric bedwarmers, he warned that the Gauleiters' efforts to obstruct the shutdown of consumer-goods production would no longer be tolerated: "If the districts do not respond to my requests within two weeks I shall myself order the shutdowns." Speer invoked the authority of the government and Himmler to "deal firmly with the districts that do not carry out these measures."[6] Consumer goods were gradually curtailed, but Speer believed that sharper cutbacks would have enabled German industry to raise war production to significantly higher levels in 1944. Bormann's opposition was unrelenting, and Himmler's SS, over which Speer had no jurisdiction, maintained its own massive industrial empire. Productivity was low in most SS facilities,[7] and they siphoned off vital raw materials that the more efficient industries under Speer's jurisdiction might have been able to convert into larger quantities of weapons, munitions, vehicles, and planes. Reflecting on the situation while in prison after the war, Speer wrote: "In the middle of 1941 Hitler could easily have had an army equipped twice as powerfully as it was . . . . We could even have mobilized approximately 3 million men of the younger age-groups before 1942 without losses in production."[8]

A principal reason for the failure to achieve higher levels of production and mobilization was the critical labor shortage. Over Speer's strong protests, the Wehrmacht continued to drain his pool of skilled workers to replace heavy losses on the Russian front. Despite double shifts, longer hours, and an influx of workers conscripted from western Europe, the shortage of all workers, whether skilled, semi-skilled, or unskilled, became steadily more acute. During his first year in office, Speer and the industrialists proposed conscripting women to work in war industries. Since Hitler was ideologically opposed to women working outside the home, he was inclined to agree with Sauckel, Göring, and the Gauleiters, who, for their own political reasons, urged him to reject female conscription. Engaged in a bureaucratic "turf war" with Speer over control of labor deployment, Sauckel and his supporters submitted a plan for a massive increase in the conscription of foreign workers, especially from eastern Europe. Hitler backed Speer's rivals.

As war production increased during the first eighteen months of Speer's tenure, shortages and deficiencies in the workforce continued to plague the regime. Speer believed that foreign workers would be more efficient if allowed to remain in their own countries, but Sauckel favored their employment within the borders of the Reich. With Hitler's approval he forcibly recruited civilians from eastern Europe and transported them to Germany, where they worked side-by-side with prisoners of war in agriculture and in the arms industries. By the middle of 1944, Sauckel's ministry had imported from 2.5 to 3 million additional foreign workers, mostly from the Soviet Union. Given the appalling conditions under which most of the *Ostarbeiter* (eastern workers) lived and worked, it is not surprising that overall productivity declined, but the sheer weight of numbers helped to prevent a sharp decline in total production. Unlike the Wehrmacht, which could not replace its losses, the foreign workforce never suffered from a shortage of fresh replacements.

Women remained largely underutilized until well into 1944. Speer, who continued to lobby for employing more women in war industries, found an unexpected ally in Josef Goebbels. The propaganda minister, who had consistently favored an all-out war effort, believed that compulsory labor service for all women would be popular. The SD reports confirmed his belief. Goebbels helped convince Hitler to sign, on January 13, 1943, the Decree on the General Mobilization of Men and Women for the Defense of the Reich. Two weeks later, Sauckel ordered all men between the ages of 16 and 65 and women between 17 and 45 to register for labor service unless they were in the armed forces, the civil service, or were employed for at least 48 hours a week. Registration was waived for pregnant women, mothers with children under 14, and all students.[9]

By the end of 1943, the number of women engaged in the production of war matériel increased, but most of those women had been employed in agriculture since 1940. The registration program, which was designed to

With the dark image of a grim-faced soldier in the background, this poster was meant to highlight the contributions of working women to the German war effort. The inscription reads, "You also help!"

attract the unemployed or underemployed, was not successful. Of the 3 million who had registered by the beginning of 1944, only 1.2 million were considered physically able to do factory work, and just over 50 percent of these could work only half time. Working-class women accounted for most of

---

BOX 9.1 ■ SPEER VISITS AN UNDERGROUND FACTORY

Speer describes his visit to a large underground rocket-production plant run by the SS:

> On December 10, 1943, I inspected the extensive underground installations where the V-2 was to be produced. In enormous long halls prisoners were busy setting machinery and shifting plumbing. Expressionlessly, they looked right through me, mechanically removing their prisoners' caps . . . until our group had passed them.
>
> . . . a professor of the Pasteur Institute in Paris . . . testified . . . at the Nuremberg Trial. He too was in the Central Works which I inspected that day. Objectively, without any dramatics, he explained the inhuman conditions in this inhuman factory. The memory is especially painful . . . because he made his charge without hatred, sadly and brokenly and also astonished at so much human degeneracy.
>
> The conditions for these prisoners were in fact barbarous, and a sense of profound involvement and personal guilt seizes me whenever I think of them. . . .
>
> The sanitary conditions were inadequate, disease rampant; the prisoners were quartered right there in the damp caves, and as a result the mortality among them was extraordinarily high.

Albert Speer, *Inside the Third Reich* (New York: MacMillan Company, 1970), pp. 370–71.

---

the increase, but some of them joined their middle-class counterparts—whom Hitler said were unfit for heavy work because they were "slenderly built with long legs"[10]—in finding ways to avoid employment or to be excused. Some pleaded physical or emotional disabilities, while others, without suffering immediate consequences, simply refused to register. By reducing the high benefits paid to soldiers' wives and widows if they worked, the government undercut many women's motivation to seek employment. Not wishing to offend Hitler's ideological sensibilities or to violate a central precept of the *Volksgemeinschaft*, the propaganda ministry continued to extol the virtues of young mothers who preferred to remain at home.[11] At the same time it urged women to join the workforce and praised them for doing so. Posters and slogans, however, did little to satisfy the grievances of women who worked in war industries, most of whom were from the working class. They resented the government's preferential treatment of middle-class women and complained bitterly at not receiving a wage packet comparable to the men whose jobs they were replacing. The regime did little to address these grievances, even though they represented cracks in the class solidarity of the *Volksgemeinschaft*.

The enslavement and mistreatment of foreign workers ranks as one of the most appalling Nazi atrocities. Sauckel, who aggressively conscripted them, was hanged at Nuremberg in 1946; Speer, who gratefully used them, escaped the gallows and served a twenty-year prison term. During the war at least 8 million foreigners were forced to work in German factories and mines and on farms and construction projects. By September 1944 they constituted nearly 25 percent of the total workforce. Workers from western Europe received more humane treatment because of their skills and higher standing in the Nazi racial hierarchy. The *Ostarbeiter*, from Poland and Russia, most of whom were unskilled or semi-skilled, provided the bulk of the foreign work force. Their hardships paralleled those of concentration-camp inmates or Russian prisoners of war, which some of them were.

Speer's inspection of an underground factory in 1943 did nothing to change the wretched conditions. Promises of better treatment from the factory managers and from the SS, which supplied the labor force, most of whom were prisoners of war, were not fulfilled. The recommendations of Speer's health inspectors were lost in the bureaucratic tangle. Not all foreign workers were treated so atrociously, but most were overworked, underfed, and housed in squalor; over 2 million perished inside the Reich during the war. Comtemporary SD reports cited few instances of protest from the German public. Like the Jews, foreign workers were isolated victims of indifference.

Public Opinion, Morale, and Propaganda

Even though many victims of the Reich's forced-labor policy were Russians or Ukrainians, Soviet prosecutors at Nuremberg interrogated Speer mostly about his accomplishments as minister of arms and munitions. Without a threefold increase in production under his jurisdiction, they charged, the war would have ended sooner and millions of Soviet lives would have been spared. Prolonging the war was not an indictable offense at Nuremberg, but the Soviet prosecutors' claim was correct. It was German civilians, however, who actually produced the matériel. Had they not worked longer hours, made greater sacrifices, and endured the hardships of Allied bombing, war production would not have tripled. After Stalingrad the German people knew that defeat was certain; yet morale and order did not break down until the last months of the war. The people persevered, sometimes in spite of their own government's propaganda and policies.

The SD reports monitored public opinion, morale, and propaganda. Since neither the controlled press nor the self-serving public opinion reports of the Gauleiters were reliable, SD chief Reinhard Heydrich required accurate and candid accounts of what the people were actually saying and doing. He obtained this information from biweekly reports submitted by SD specialists to the Main Security Office of the Reich in Berlin. Incorporating information furnished by thousands of agents, the reports rarely disguised public dissatisfaction with the conduct of the war, propaganda

films and speeches, shortages of consumer goods, and the privileges enjoyed by high party officials. The reports also recorded activities, statements,
rumors, and jokes judged to be suspicious. By the end of 1943, Bormann
and Himmler had denounced the reports, accusing the SD of "fostering
a defeatist mentality." In a conversation with Himmler's doctor, the operational head of the SD, Otto Ohlendorf, said that his staff could not be hon-
estly optimistic: "The more critical the situation becomes, the gloomier
become the reports." Ohlendorf was certain that Bormann withheld the
reports from Hitler.[12]

According to the SD, Stalingrad marked a decisive turning point in
public opinion. Before the battle, few doubted that the Reich would win
the war, although by the end of 1942 confidence had been shaken by re-
verses on the eastern front and North Africa, as well as by the increasing
frequency of Allied air raids. The public was also becoming skeptical about
the propaganda ministry's assurances that German casualties were relatively
light and that victory over the Bolshevik *Untermenschen* was imminent.
Long before Stalingrad, however, letters from soldiers on the Russian front
detailing the bloodbath contradicted official optimistic reports. The enthusiastic response to Goebbels' total-war speech eventually gave way to apathy and pessimism. According to one SD report, the change from falsely
optimistic coverage to "exceedingly somber reporting" of the war in the
east had created a "crisis of confidence" in the military and political leadership.[13] After Stalingrad, SD agents often used the terms "defeatism" and
"sense of futility" to characterize the public mood.

During the spring of 1944, Goebbels sought to divert attention from
catastrophe on the eastern front to the impending Allied invasion of
France. This shift in propaganda strategy coincided with the increased
tempo of the Anglo-American air offensive. Goebbels denounced the
"needless" bombing of civilians and nonstrategic targets and cited it as evidence that the Western powers were "no better than the Russians." He portrayed Churchill and the British as particularly villainous and assured the
people that the Wehrmacht would repulse the Anglo-American invaders
with the aid of "secret weapons." According to SD reports, Goebbels' efforts were not entirely in vain, but pessimism prevailed as the Allies
marched through northern France and liberated Paris in August 1944. At
the same time, the skies over Germany were becoming crowded with
British and American bombers. Appointed minister plenipotentiary for total war in July 1944, Goebbels was the only member of Hitler's top command to inspect bomb-damaged cities. He could do little more than encourage the residents to endure for the sake of the fatherland.

Documentary films show Goebbels listening to dazed victims of a
bombing raid amidst piles of rubble. One of the victims has raised a banner
on which are printed the words "Our walls may break, but our hearts never
will." Excellent footage for a propaganda film, to be sure, but it is by no
means a misleading image of the spirit of the German people as they were
relentlessly pounded by 2.7 million tons of bombs during the war. More

BOX 9.2 ■ A TEENAGER WITNESSES THE FIREBOMBING
OF HAMBURG

Seventeen-year-old Wolf Solhége was an eyewitness to the firebombing of
Hamburg:

[The wounded] . . . were so badly burned that we had to put them on stretchers.
When the phosphorous canisters hit the houses, this phosphorous stuff ran down
the stairs and out into the street. . . . The people ran out of these houses like living torches, and the flames on their bodies were put out by whoever could help
them. The badly burned had to be taken away in trucks or ambulances. . . . the
drivers had to be careful that the phosphorous didn't get under their tires—the
rubber burned immediately. . . . The local hospitals, were of course, quickly filled
with burn victims. . . . Most of the people died; it was impossible for so many injured to get the proper treatment. There was no option but to bury them in mass
graves.

We had to see to it that the corpses were removed as quickly as possible to prevent
epidemics from spreading. The bodies were often so badly mutilated that it was impossible to identify them. Many of them had died under collapsed buildings. We
dug out the ones we knew or suspected were still trapped in their cellars. . . .
Although we did all we could, many people suffocated from smoke inhalation, carbon monoxide poisoning. At one point I found a basement shelter that was full of
smoke. The people sat totally still against the wall, no one made a peep. I thought
my eyes were deceiving me, but they were all dead.

Johannes Steinhoff, Peter Pechel, and Dennis Showalter, *Voices from the Third Reich:
An Oral History* (Washington, DC: Regnery Gateway, 1989), pp. 215–16.

than 70 percent of that total fell after July 1, 1944. Regular air strikes
against civilian targets began early in 1942, when the British abandoned
strategic bombing by day, which was as costly for them as it had been for
the Luftwaffe in 1940, in favor of terror bombing by night. Churchill's
Ministry of Information was supremely confident—and totally incorrect—
in assessing the effects: "All the evidence goes to prove that the Germans,
for all their present . . . cockiness, will not stand a quarter of the bombing
that the British have shown they can take."[14]

Although Cologne and other cities of the Rhineland had been
bombed extensively in 1942, Hamburg was the first to experience the horrors of fire bombing. Between July 24 and August 2, 1943, huge fleets of
British Lancasters and U.S. B-17 Flying Fortresses dropped thousands of
tons of explosives on Germany's major seaport and second largest city. The
incendiary bombs caused a firestorm in which flames spread wildly, feeding
on themselves by consuming all available oxygen. The heat from the fire
reached approximately 1,000 degrees centigrade, creating deadly winds of
up to 150 miles per hour, uprooting trees, destroying buildings, and throw-
ing people into the flames.[15] The raid destroyed most of the city's center and

BILDARCHIV PREUSSISCHER KULTURBESITZ, BERLIN

Residents of Dresden pick up rubble after the February 1945 air raid.

killed nearly 50,000 residents. Many were unable to breathe in the oxygen-depleted atmosphere and died of suffocation. Not until the Dresden raid in February 1945, which produced approximately the same death toll as that on Hamburg, would a German city be so devastated by a firestorm. Following the Hamburg raid, the government strengthened air defenses, built more bomb shelters, and began evacuating urban children to rural areas. These measures helped maintain morale, but more fighter planes and anti-aircraft guns could not slow the momentum of the Allied air offensive. From early 1944 to the end of the war, raids occurred on a daily basis.

For millions of civilians, the air raids, which took an estimated 600,000 lives, were the most terrifying experience of the war. Every day the wailing air raid sirens sent masses of people scurrying to shelters, many of which were simply basements of houses or businesses. Some people were killed by shrapnel or burned by the phosphorous bombs before they could reach safety; others were crushed to death when shelters experienced direct hits. The SD reported that many victims felt anger toward party officials who had access to safer, more comfortable bomb shelters. The SD agents, quick to criticize the old guard of the NSDAP, commended the people's courage and self-control during the raids. Morale was shaken, but it crumbled only during the last months of the war.

Sustaining Morale

Faith and trust in the Führer helped sustain public morale. The SD reported that the bond between Hitler and the German people remained strong throughout the war, but there were periods of doubt. One of his lowest "approval ratings" occurred in the summer of 1943, following Italy's surrender; not that Germans were particularly fond of their erstwhile ally, but Mussolini's demise, along with more bombing and military defeats, symbolized the hopelessness of the war. The Duce's overthrow also sparked rumors about mental or physical disabilities that would make Hitler vulnerable to a military coup. There were jokes about the Führer's "new book," titled "My Mistake," and his flight from Germany in a submarine with Goebbels. Several weeks after Mussolini's overthrow, Hitler broadcast a speech about Italy's capitulation. An SD agent reported: ". . . . the calm voice of the Führer, who delivered his arguments with an unshakable confidence in victory, . . . communicated [peace] to many citizens. People exclaimed that 'as long as the Führer keeps his nerve, everything is OK with us.' "[16]

Hitler's self-imposed isolation did not shake the public trust. From mid-1943 to November 1944, he rarely left his East Prussian headquarters, which he named "Wolf's Lair." The charismatic leader, who once reveled in the adulation of the masses, limited his communication to an occasional radio address by which he sought to reassure the nation that he was still in charge. Instead of the Führer, the people blamed the generals and party officials for the defeats, shortages, and inadequate bomb shelters. Nevertheless, Hitler did not escape criticism and ridicule. The SD recorded the comment of a woman with two small children in an air raid shelter: "The Führer has it easy. He doesn't have to look after a family. If worst comes to worst in the war, he'll leave us all in this mess and put a bullet through his head! He's always said that he won't experience defeat!"[17] Hitler was sometimes the butt of popular jokes: "To be a good Nazi you must be as prolific as Hitler, as modest as Göring, as quiet as Goebbels, and as patriotic as Hess."[18] (Many felt that Hess's flight to England was an act of treason.)

The failure of the conspirators to assassinate Hitler on July 20, 1944, strengthened the bond between the Führer and his people. The SD reported that "even elements of the population which are not out-and-out supporters of National Socialism detest the attempted assassination." Another agent sensed a general sigh of relief, as if the people were saying "Thank God, the Führer is alive."[19] His brief radio address after the plot was one of his last. In the last months of the war, Goebbels found it increasingly difficult to keep the Hitler myth alive and persuade people that he was still the wise, self-sacrificing, hard-working Führer. The bond might have snapped if people had known how little Hitler actually cared for them; this was illustrated by a particularly damning incident in the spring of 1944. A train crammed full of wounded soldiers was sidetracked in the Munich railway station to allow the Führer's train to pass. For a few moments Hitler's private car was immediately adjacent to the troop train.

Aides suggested that he might wish to wave at them or salute through the window of his car. Hitler ordered the shades to be drawn and the train to exit the station as quickly as possible. He rarely visited wounded soldiers— the victims of bombing raids, never.

During the last years of the war, Bormann screened virtually every-thing that Hitler read or heard. The secretary withheld or edited bad news about the home front, but Hitler was pleased to hear Bormann's exagger-ated reports that his mandate to keep the people well-fed was being carried out. There were no "turnip winters" during World War II, but complaints about unequal distribution of food and clothing, the limited variety and quantity of food, and the tastelessness of ersatz products became more fre-quent and bitter as the war dragged on. As rationing became more restric-tive, black marketeers prospered despite harsh penalties for those who were caught. People who could not afford to buy abundant, high-quality, black-market items wondered why party "big shots" who lived in the "lap of luxury" did not make these goods available to the public. The SD also heard complaints that farmers and distributors were hoarding food.[20] Nev-ertheless, shortages did not become acute and widespread until the last year of the war. The availability of food, however monotonous and unappetiz-ing, helped sustain morale.

Nazi propaganda sought to convince the people that meatless days and the consumption of ersatz products were patriotic, but it could not eliminate ordinary people's resentment toward the privileged. Such hatred undermined the solidarity of the *Volksgemeinschaft*, which the regime sought to strengthen by means of ceremonies and rituals. In 1940 the Main Cultural Office of the Propaganda Ministry issued a manual titled *Die Neue Gemeinschaft* containing rubrics for ceremonies marking birth, Youth Pledge Day, marriage, and death. These occasions were to be "divested of all *völkisch* clichés, sentimentality, and cheap patriotism," and to focus on the solidarity of the *Volksgemeinschaft* and obedience to Hitler. Since mem-bership in the Hitler Youth was mandatory, Youth Pledge Day, the cere-mony marking the induction of 14-year-old boys into the Hitler Youth and girls into the League of German Girls, had a captive audience. Birth, mar-riage, and death ceremonies were not well attended. SD agents criticized party officials for their "sloppy handling" of the ceremonies, and even the Gauleiters conceded that Youth Pledge Day had "not yet succeeded in re-placing confirmation as the most significant ceremony in the life of a youth."[21]

While Youth Pledge Day may have failed to provide an "ideological high," recent studies show that the majority of young people remained loyal to the regime. Late in the war, teenagers manned anti-aircraft guns and thousands of young boys joined the *Volkssturm*, a home guard that also included old men. Survivors testify that many Hitler Youth members con-templated suicide when they heard of their Führer's demise. The regime abused their loyalty and "exploited and misled millions of them" in the name of perverted ideals.[22]

BOX 9.3 ■ A BARONESS WORKS IN A HOSPITAL

Baroness Irmela von Fölkersamb was drafted into the Labor Service and worked as a nurse's aide. There was nothing "pleasant" about her workplace:

> When I returned to the Rhine, toward the end of 1943, I immediately received another assignment. I could either work in a munitions factory or a hospital, and I chose the hospital. It was very trying. The hospital was in Ahrweiler, so we received the wounded soldiers from the Western front. Later, of course, we also treated many civilians who were wounded in the air raids. There were always between 200 and 300 patients, all of them surgical cases.

> I was in a big butcher shop. The days the hospital trains arrived were especially bad. We often spent ten hours at a time among moaning, wounded soldiers. There were amputations, and of course many shrapnel injuries, all of them patched up with horrible, filthy casts. . . .

> At first I did feel pity for these poor young men, who arrived badly wounded and screaming for their parents, and who were dead inside two hours or so. Your heart was breaking constantly. You cannot weep along with the soldiers for a year and a half at a hospital. You must become hardened. This actually happened to me quite quickly—there was just too much suffering. . . . The ones that really got to me were the ones who mutilated themselves. Soldiers . . . were poking around at their wounds with something they had concealed under their bed sheets. They did this out of sheer terror of being sent back to the front. In my opinion, these men were always the worst off.

Steinhoff, Pechel, and Showalter, *Voices from the Third Reich*, p. 461.

The Propaganda Ministry commended women as morale builders. Goebbels simultaneously extolled motherhood and domesticity on the one hand and women's new role as "working and fighting comrades" of men on the other. As more women joined the workforce or were drafted into the labor service to work in munitions factories and hospitals, the regime sought to make the workplace more pleasant by establishing day care centers for children, providing free soup for lunch, allowing time off for doing household chores, and permitting slacks to be worn instead of dresses. Women were rarely drafted into the army, but they performed military functions such as operating searchlights in anti-aircraft installations. Some women expressed moral indignation against Himmler's eugenics schemes and his glorification of mothers without husbands, while others were alienated by the regime's attacks against the church. Nevertheless, like the general population, most women remained loyal. They worked, sacrificed, risked their lives, and struggled courageously to hold fatherless families together.

The Nazi regime accelerated the tempo and pace of terror on the home front during the war. The Gestapo and other branches of the police arrested and incarcerated far more civilians than in the prewar years. The concentration camp population rose from approximately 20,000 in 1939 to nearly 600,000 at the beginning of 1945. New concentration camps were opened, and the authorities, who sought to conceal the camps' brutality during the first years of the regime, made no attempt to do so during the war. Executions increased substantially, as did the number of capital offenses, from three before 1939 to more than forty during the war. Before 1940, civil courts handed down approximately 16,000 death sentences, of which three-quarters were carried out. From 1940 to 1945, the Peoples' Court and the Special Courts, whose verdicts could not be appealed (the civil courts were stripped of most of their authority during the war), handed down 15,000 death sentences. Even when these courts did not impose the death penalty, the prisoners (no precise statistics are available, but there were probably thousands of them) were usually "handed over to the police," which meant that they were likely to be murdered outright by the SS and Gestapo, or sent to forced labor camps where they were literally worked to death.[23]

A dramatic increase in the number of anonymous civilian informers who were eager to betray their fellow citizens—whether for envy, jealousy, spite, greed, or ideological fervor—heightened the atmosphere of terror. Such popular cooperation enabled the Gestapo and SS to claim that they were acting "in the name of the people."[24] Historian Robert Gellately, whose most recent work is devoted entirely to the *modus operandi* of the Gestapo from 1933 to 1945, claims that, especially during the war years, the "Gestapo side of Hitler's dictatorship" was driven by the denunciations of ordinary citizens, most of whom were not even members of the Nazi party. The Gestapo itself, and other branches of the police network, according to Gellately, identified only 10 to 15 percent of all suspects who were subsequently arrested. An army of willing civilian informants turned in the rest.[25] Nevertheless, Gestapo agents remained the chief enforcers of terror. They arrested the victims and charged them with offenses ranging from the general (behavior violating the racial solidarity of the *Volksgemeinschaft*, subversive or treasonous activities, and defamation of government and party officials) to the specific (circulating jokes or rumors, initiating work slowdowns or stoppages, listening to German-language BBC newscasts on short-wave radio, black marketeering, and hoarding).

The regime used terror more liberally during the war to enforce the compliance of a society suffering unprecedented hardships. Hitler's government could no longer guarantee the *Volksgemeinschaft* a brighter future characterized by greater prosperity, expanded social benefits, and a vast European empire. With the gradual disappearance of the "carrot," Nazi officials felt compelled to rely more heavily on the "stick." The increase of terror on the home front was consistent with the wartime radicalization of the regime in other areas—the Wehrmachts' indiscriminate slaughter of Soviet civilians, the unprecedented increase in the rate of court martial executions of frontline soldiers, the euthanasia program, and the beginning of the Final Solution of the Jewish Question—to name a few disparate examples. The regime's brutal treatment of its own shook the people's morale, but did not break it.

Resistance

Resistance in Nazi Germany ranged from small acts of passive disobedience in everyday life to active participation in the anti-Hitler conspiracy. As the Gestapo and its helpers tightened their grip, any expression of disapproval, or association with a group under surveillance, became riskier. One might escape arrest, but no one could shut off Goebbels's ubiquitous propaganda machine, which condemned even the mildest form of disobedience, such as telling an anti-Nazi joke, as a crime against the *Volksgemeinschaft* and a betrayal of the brave fighting men at the front. Ironically, as the regime sought to strengthen the bonds of the racial community, its elaborate network of informants and spies fostered suspicion and isolation, precisely what the racial community was supposed to eliminate. Isolation and fear were powerful deterrents to disobedience, protest, and resistance. From the regime's point of view, the incidence of disloyal or subversive acts was alarmingly high, but in fact the relatively small number of perpetrators operated in isolation and, with the exception of the military conspirators, did not threaten the Hitler state.

The SD agents saw the church as a center of disloyalty, subversion, and defeatism. Whether Catholic bishops were protesting the confiscation of monastic properties and the removal of crucifixes from schools or boldly criticizing Himmler's eugenics program—which paid "racially fit" unmarried women to bear the children of SS fathers—the SD was equally suspicious. The euthanasia program, however, triggered more and bolder protests from Catholic and Protestant clergy than any other Nazi program. It began in August 1939 when Hitler authorized Dr. Karl Brandt (the written order has survived), a member of his personal medical staff, and Philipp Bouhler, the head of the Führer chancellery, to carry out mercy killing of *"unwertes Leben"* (literally, unfit life) and "useless eaters." Brandt and Bouhler quickly and efficiently set up the bureaucratic and medical structures to run a euthanasia campaign—at first, for "malformed infants." Eventually, up to 6,000 infants and children with a variety of congenital defects and incurable illnesses were killed in this phase of the program.

By the end of 1940, Brandt and Bouhler had greatly expanded the pool of medical and psychiatric personnel eager to participate in a project designed to "decimate the adult asylum population."[26] It became known as the T-4 Action, named after the location of its headquarters, Tiergartenstrasse 4 in Berlin. A group of SS technicians had erected six special killing centers, complete with gas chambers and crematoria, in various locations in Germany. Members of the medical community who willingly participated were not necessarily fanatical Nazis, but all favored elimination of "unfit life," mostly through sterilization, as a means to strengthen and purify the race. Few found it difficult to adjust to the Nazi regime's more radical solution. Although the total number of victims—approximately 70,000 (not including the children) by August 1941—was small by World War II standards, this wanton slaughter of innocents by people trained to be guardians of human life will always rank as one of the most loathsome of Nazi atrocities.

Most of the 70,000 adults were euthanized from the spring of 1940 to August 1941. The physicians selected the victims—initially, inmates of mental institutions and Jewish patients in psychiatric wards of regular hospitals. Later, the senile and patients who were chronically ill with tuberculosis, epilepsy, and cerebral palsy were added. The victims were seized by SS men and transported in buses and trains to the killing centers, where doctors and their assistants locked them in sealed chambers disguised as showers and activated the mechanism that administered the fatal dose of gas. "Death came in the dark, as the terrified victims rolled off benches or collapsed on the floor, or beat their hands against the doors when they realized what was happening to them."[27] After the gold teeth had been removed, a few of the bodies were sent to research facilities, but most were burned in the crematoria. The ashes were either dumped in nearby rivers or placed in urns. Survivors received death notices, which also informed them that the urns containing the ashes of their loved ones would be delivered for a stipulated price. The SS meticulously recorded expenses and income; "mercy killings" turned a profit. Although the killers did not realize it at the time, the euthanasia program would serve as a "dress rehearsal" for the Final Solution of the Jewish Question.

Despite the regime's efforts to maintain secrecy, the euthanasia program aroused the suspicions of the survivors, who often received two or three death notices listing different causes of death, and people who lived near the killing centers, who were offended by the noxious odors of thick black smoke reeking with the stench of burning flesh. In July 1940 the Protestant bishop of Württemberg, Theophil Wurm, wrote Minister of the Interior Frick that many people in his district had become suspicious of the smoke rising from the crematoria, the puzzling death notices, and the "air of mystery" that prompted people to think what was happening was "contrary to justice and ethics and cannot therefore be defended publicly like other necessary war measures."[28] Wurm's letter, along with protests from several other Protestant clergymen, was ignored.

What could not be ignored was a sermon on August 3, 1941, delivered by Clemens von Galen, the bishop of Münster in Westphalia, a region of northwestern Germany with a predominantly Catholic population. The outspoken bishop, whose protest a few weeks earlier against the regime's confiscation of monastic properties had made him a popular religious hero, was rumored to be preparing a sermon in which he would spare none of the gruesome details of the euthanasia program. The overflow audience in the Münster cathedral was not disappointed. Galen vividly described the selection, transportation, and liquidation of the victims, as well as the reaction of the survivors to the patently contrived death notices. He identified the killers as SS men and medical professionals, and charged the regime with breaking God's law of the sanctity of all human life and with undermining the morale of civilians and servicemen. A few severely wounded fighting men, he suggested, might have been euthanized. (There is no evidence that the regime ever resorted to such a practice.) Copies of the sermon were mimeographed and distributed throughout the country, to soldiers at the front, and even to some occupied territories. The Gestapo ordered all copies to be destroyed and arrested hundreds of people who were caught with a copy of the sermon. Galen was placed under house arrest.[29]

Goebbels and Bormann hastily convened a meeting to discuss the Galen situation. An official from the propaganda ministry pointed out that if the Bishop of Münster was not immediately hanged, other clergymen would be encouraged to attack the regime. "A martyred priest," said Goebbels, a native of the Rhineland who understood "the German Catholic mentality," would be far more dangerous than a living bishop. His execution would probably "set the majority of Catholic Westphalians against the regime." Bormann also favored death for the bishop, but was certain that Hitler, who felt a particularly pressing need for a population united in support of the armed forces at a critical juncture in the Russian campaign, would never sign the popular bishop's death warrant.[30] A few weeks later a furious Hitler, who vowed to "settle accounts" with Galen after the war, ordered the Gestapo to lift the bishop's house arrest. He also directed Dr. Brandt to suspend the mass gassing phase of the euthanasia program, which, he claimed, was no longer necessary because the "targeted figure of 70,000" had been reached. By claiming to have reached a previously established targeted figure, the existence of which is not supported by the evidence, Hitler was seeking to discount Galen's role in ending euthanasia. With the extermination apparatus in place and working smoothly, there is no reason to doubt that the regime intended to continue the program. In any case, Hitler ordered Dr. Brandt to continue liquidation of the "unfit" by means of starvation or lethal injection in a larger number of extermination centers located within several asylums.[31] Little is known of the "post-Galen" phase of euthanasia, but the death toll was almost certainly much smaller. Galen resumed his duties as a bishop and remained an unwavering supporter of the regime's crusade against Communism. He died in 1946, not long after the pope had elevated him to cardinal status. Clemens von Galen is honored as Münster's greatest hero to this day.

Galen's sermon was the church's most celebrated and effective protest; unfortunately, it was the only one to pressure Hitler to abandon one of his most cherished programs of racial murder. The Führer and his top command always viewed Protestant clergymen as less troublesome than Catholic priests. The handful who protested against euthanasia were either imprisoned or ignored. The SD did not mention the Confessing Church, which met infrequently during the war and issued cautious statements protesting euthanasia and the treatment of Jews. Church services for the war dead, which were well attended and "more impressive than the party's memorial ceremonies," made the SD suspicious. Moreover, pastors and priests, who were in contact with chaplains at the front, were usually the first to notify the family of a loved one killed in action. An SD agent, convinced that clergymen used the tragedies of war to undermine the *Volksge-meinschaft*, wrote: "A clergyman who can speak of a heavenly reunion with loved ones enjoys a tremendous advantage over a party official who can speak only of the beauty and joy of sacrifice for the Reich."[32]

Although some restrictions were placed on the clergy, many were able to function more or less normally. The Gestapo arrested hundreds of clergymen during the war, the Reich Press Chamber banned most church publications in 1941, and the Ministry of Education abolished religious instruction in public schools beyond the eighth year. Thousands of Protestant seminarians and pastors who were eligible for military service were drafted; often deliberately placed in the front lines, they suffered heavy casualties. Catholic seminarians were drafted, but most priests were not. With some restrictions, the Wehrmacht permitted Protestant and Catholic chaplains to minister to combat troops; the Luftwaffe banned chaplains. The government continued to collect the church tax and did not interfere with regular worship services. Most clergymen were not ardent Nazis, but neither were they potential "revolutionaries," as one SD agent observed. Many pastors prayed publicly for peace instead of victory, but with the exception of the handful who were involved in the anti-Hitler conspiracy, all supported their country's war effort.

The few young people who refused to join the Hitler Youth for religious reasons were either given long terms in the compulsory labor service or drafted into the army before they were of age. Some disaffected youths, however, banded together into gangs or clubs with no particular religious or political orientation. The largest of these groups was the Edelweiss Pirates, whose teenage members of both genders came from working-class families in industrial cities of the Rhineland, such as Cologne and Düsseldorf. Most had been, or still were, members of the Hitler Youth and employed in the Reich Labor Service. The regimentation of life in wartime Germany and the constant surveillance of the Hitler Youth Patrol, as well as the extended work week (sometimes up to 72 hours), food shortages, and the dearth of public entertainment, had become particularly onerous to these young people. They showed their contempt for the racial community's norms of behavior by wearing pirate insignia, skipping work to go on long hikes, and writing their own lyrics to popular tunes and folk songs. A quotation from one of their songs gives the flavor of their dissent: "Hitler's power may lay us low, and keep us locked in chains, but we will smash the chains . . . and the Hitler Youth in twain. One day we'll be free again." The Gestapo dissolved the Edelweiss Pirates in the summer and fall of 1944. Most members were sent to labor camps, drafted, or imprisoned. Several leaders were hanged.[33]

A different kind of nonconformist youth group, identified as the "swing kids," flourished in the early 1940s in Berlin, Hamburg, and other large cities. They had no connection with the Edelweiss Pirates. Coming from middle- and upper-class families, these teenagers could afford to buy English clothes and records, meet in night clubs, and indulge their passion for English and American jazz and swing music. They danced to the "enemy's decadent music" and practiced "liberated" sexual behavior, which the Hitler Youth Patrol denounced as "moral depravity." Himmler wanted to put the ringleaders into concentration camps for two or three years of beatings and forced labor, but the actual punishments—short prison terms, labor camps, and military service—were less harsh.[34]

At their peak, the Edelweiss Pirates numbered between 2,000 and 3,000, while there were never more than 1,000 swing kids. The only group of anti-Nazi young people with strong political convictions, the White Rose, originally consisted of five students and one professor at the University of Munich. Their leader was Hans Scholl, a medical student and veteran of the Russian front. What he had seen and heard of the lethal consequences of Nazi racialism had convinced him of the moral depravity and criminality of the Hitler regime. With Scholl's sister Sophie as co-leader, the White Rose issued flyers in the summer and fall of 1942, denouncing the war, "our spiritual and economic enslavement," and the destruction of "all moral and religious values."[35] The White Rose urged its readers to engage in passive resistance but suggested no specific course of action. By the end of 1942, the White Rose had established contact with universities in Hamburg, Berlin, and Vienna, but in February 1943 the Scholls and four others were arrested while distributing leaflets on the Munich campus. All six were tried before the People's Court, sentenced to death, and beheaded. With the arrest of fourteen others, the White Rose was crushed. Students at Munich and other universities did not protest as the Scholls had hoped.

The Plot to Kill Hitler

Members of the anti-Hitler conspiracy had several things in common with the White Rose. They were plagued by constant Gestapo surveillance, the arrest of key members, difficulties in communication and travel, and lack of popular support. In occupied countries, partisan fighters and members of the underground were national heroes; in Germany they were traitors, even to people who were not ardent Nazis. The conspiracy also had internal problems, such as the lack of forceful leadership, the split between the proponents of assassination and the advocates of a nonviolent overthrow of the regime, and disagreements over the kind of government that should replace the Nazi regime. Retired general Ludwig Beck and former mayor of Leipzig Carl Goerdeler led the conservative wing of the conspirators. They favored, somewhat reluctantly, the assassination of Hitler and the formation of an authoritarian government that would rule Germany proper and neighboring territories, such as Austria, the Sudetenland, Alsace-Lorraine, and the Polish Corridor. On the opposite end of the political spectrum were members of the idealistic, high-minded Kreisau Circle, named after the Silesian estate of its leader, Helmut James Count von Moltke, the great-grand nephew of Bismarck's field marshal. Moltke's group, which included a Jesuit priest and a Protestant pastor (the only active member who shared

Dietrich Bonhoeffer's pro-assassination view) favored Hitler's removal by nonviolent means and the establishment of a democratic, social reform-oriented Germany that would be an equal partner in a voluntary federation of European nations.

The Allied policy of unconditional surrender presented the conspirators with another divisive issue. The Beck/Goerdeler group and most of the military officers who had previously belonged to the conspiracy, as well as those who joined in 1943, advocated continuing the war if the Allies should refuse to make peace with a post-Hitler regime. The Kreisau Circle, which gradually moderated its strict nonviolent position without openly advocating Hitler's assassination, did not take a stand on the unconditional surrender issue. Dietrich Bonhoeffer, who met frequently with the Kreisau Circle and shared many of their Christian ideals, sought in vain to convince them that Hitler's assassination was the only way to rid the world of the festering evil of Nazism. Although Bonhoeffer was arrested in the spring of 1943 and spent the last two years of his life in prison, his influence was still felt among the conspirators. Few, if any, of Bonhoeffer's admirers supported his radical position on the war: he prayed for Germany's defeat, even if it meant unconditional surrender. Most of his co-conspirators favored a continuation of the war if the Allies should refuse to negotiate with an anti-Nazi regime.

The leadership problem was partly solved in the fall of 1943 when Colonel Claus von Stauffenberg was appointed chief of staff of the home army in Berlin. Stauffenberg had been severely wounded in North Africa, losing an eye, his right hand, and two fingers on his left hand. Though he was in constant pain, he proved to be the forceful leader the movement needed. He believed that Hitler was evil incarnate and that his assassination was the only way to stop the atrocities and end the war. Politically, Stauffenberg favored the establishment of a social democracy with co-conspirator and Socialist leader Julius Leber as chancellor, but he insisted that the conspirators postpone debates over the nature of the post-Hitler regime, as well as the unconditional surrender issue, and give their full attention to planning the assassination and the subsequent coup. It would not be easy. Several attempts to assassinate Hitler had been thwarted by his extremely tight security, his unpredictable schedules, and even by bombs that failed to explode.

Stauffenberg proposed that Operation Valkyrie—the home army's existing plan for establishing a military government in Berlin in the event of internal revolt—should be implemented throughout Germany and in the occupied territories following Hitler's death. The plan called for the army to arrest SS personnel and others who resisted. It was a feasible plan, but its success depended on the cooperation of the majority of generals on both fronts and throughout the Reich proper, an assassin who could pass through several security checks at the Wolf's Lair and place a lethal explosive in Hitler's conference room, the interruption of all communications from the Wolf's Lair, forceful and timely leadership to direct Operation Valkyrie in Berlin after the Führer had been dispatched, and (something

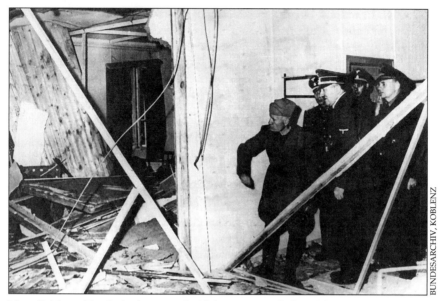

Mussolini (crouching in the foreground with his arm extended) paid his last visit to Hitler on July 20, 1944. This picture was taken in the Wolf's Lair barracks immediately after Stauffenberg's bomb exploded.

that had always eluded the conspirators) good luck. If any one of these conditions was not fulfilled—and in the end all five were not—the entire operation would be doomed. Although he was needed to direct operations in Berlin, Stauffenberg insisted that, as chief of staff of the home army, he was the ideal assassin. While reporting to Hitler at the Wolf's Lair on the status of Operation Valkyrie, he would plant the bomb. Amazingly, the Führer, whose survival instincts had become extremely acute, overlooked the potential for his own destruction in the home army's plan. A few months before July 20, 1944, he casually approved Operation Valkyrie.

Things went wrong from the moment Stauffenberg arrived at the Wolf's Lair on July 20, 1944, an exceptionally hot day. Hitler decided to hold his daily conference in a flimsily built, well-ventilated barracks building. Briefing sessions normally took place in his concrete bunker, where a powerful explosive would almost certainly have killed everyone. Because Mussolini was scheduled to arrive at Wolf's Lair that afternoon, Hitler cut the meeting short. Stauffenberg had to hurry the arming of the bomb and its transfer from his aide's briefcase to his own. His aide, Lieutenant Werner von Haeften, carried another bomb, but Stauffenberg either felt that he did not have time to arm it or that a second bomb was not necessary. In any case, the conspiracy's leader entered the meeting room with one bomb set to explode in ten minutes. Certain that the open doors and windows would weaken the blast, he placed the bomb under the table as close to Hitler as possible. Stauffenberg and Haeften quickly left the room and saw the explosion as they were driving through the last checkpoint of the compound.

Luck, or, as Hitler firmly believed, Providence, was once again on his side. The extreme heat changed the venue of the meeting, but that in itself did not save him. An aide accidentally kicked the briefcase and moved it to the other side of a heavy wooden table leg, away from the Führer, which was a move that saved his life. The explosion killed the aide and three others; Hitler suffered a punctured eardrum and a temporarily paralyzed right arm. Co-conspirator General Fellgiebel was able to disrupt communications from the Wolf's Lair only temporarily. There was yet another factor. If Stauffenberg had put the unarmed second bomb in his briefcase, it would have been detonated by the armed bomb, magnifying "the power of the blast not twofold but many times, killing everyone in the room outright."[36] Hitler told Mussolini that Providence had saved him to carry out his principal mission, the destruction of Bolshevism. Following the deposed Italian dictator's departure, a raging Hitler vowed revenge against the military officers whom he held responsible. He would "wipe out and eradicate the lot of them. These criminals . . . must hang immediately, without mercy."[37] He was as good as his word.

Meanwhile, Stauffenberg's plane landed in Berlin after a three-hour flight. He was dismayed to learn that his fellow conspirators, who were supposed to have implemented Operation Valkyrie at the moment of the explosion, had done almost nothing. They were waiting for confirmation of the Führer's death. Certain that no one had survived the explosion, Stauffenberg assumed command of the operation, but it was already too late. The three-hour interval between the explosion of the bomb and Stauffenberg's arrival in Berlin was critical. Had he been present to lead (and that was impossible since he was the only one who had access to Hitler) or if the conspirators in Berlin had initiated the military takeover of the government in Berlin immediately after the explosion at the Wolf's Lair, Operation Valkyrie might have succeeded, at least temporarily. Defenders of the Third Reich, stunned by rumors of Hitler's death, had time to recover before Stauffenberg mobilized his cautious conspirators late in the afternoon. His forces met resistance as they tried to seize communications facilities and arrest Gestapo and SS personnel. Outside the city, Panzer units loyal to the conspiracy waited too long to move into Berlin and fortify the home army's headquarters, where retired general Ludwig Beck was supposed to become head of the new government.

The conspirators' most astonishing oversight was to confine Goebbels to a room with a telephone. He contacted the Wolf's Lair (communications had been restored), spoke to Hitler, and asked him to order Major Otto Remer, who had entered the room to arrest Goebbels, to lead the counterattack against the conspirators. Later that evening, a Berlin radio station reported to the nation that the conspiracy was over and that Hitler had survived. At that point, the pro-Stauffenberg generals' takeover in Vienna, Prague, and Paris collapsed, and fence-sitting generals at home and abroad promptly reaffirmed their loyalty to Hitler. One of these, home army commander Friedrich Fromm (whom Hitler later had executed for cowardice),

assumed command of the troops loyal to the regime, now the overwhelming majority. Stauffenberg, General Friedrich Olbricht, one of the highest-
ranking anti-Hitler activists, Haeften, Olbricht's aide, and General Beck
were arrested, tried, and sentenced to death. Beck committed suicide, and
shortly after midnight on July 21 a firing squad executed Stauffenberg
(whose last words were "Long live our beloved Germany") and his three
co-conspirators.

Hitler's revenge was frightful. More than 5,000 people were executed
between August 1944 and the end of the war. Among the victims were
members of the Kreisau Circle, even though they were not directly implicated in the plot, and several members of the conspirators' families. Some,
including Field Marshal Erwin von Witzleben, were tried by the People's
Court, where Judge Roland Freisler humiliated and harangued them
before sentencing them to death. Hitler ordered the victims to be hanged
with piano wire and suspended from meat hooks. Some died instantly;
others writhed in agony for at least twenty minutes. These grisly scenes
were filmed, and Hitler took great delight in viewing the executions,
especially of aristocratic generals and officers whom he had always despised. General Henning von Treschkow, a high-ranking conspirator
who had directed at least two assassination attempts on the eastern front,
committed suicide on July 21. Two field marshals who were marginally
involved, Günther von Kluge and Rommel, also took their own lives.
The Gestapo hanged General Karl von Stülpnagel, a leader of the coup in
Paris.

A few days before July 20, General von Treschkow confided to a
friend that "in all likelihood everything will go wrong"; asked if the action
was necessary, he replied "Yes, even so." Shortly before his suicide he told a
friend: "I am convinced that we did the right thing. Hitler is the arch-
enemy not only of Germany but of the world. . . . I hope for our sake God
will not destroy Germany. . . . A human being's moral integrity begins
when he is prepared to sacrifice his life for his convictions."[38] While some
of the conspirators did not share his noble motivation, nearly all believed
that the assassination attempt had almost no chance to succeed. Its failure
had no effect on the outcome of the war. Except for Stauffenberg and
Goerdeler, who clung to the vain hope that the Allies would negotiate
with a military government that had overthrown Hitler, the men of July 20
were certain that the unconditional-surrender policy would remain in
place. They were right; the conspirators received no support whatsoever
from the Allies. (The pleas of Switzerland-based American OSS official
Allen Dulles to support, or at least encourage, the resistance movement fell
on deaf ears.) The failure of the plot not only stimulated Hitler's bloodlust
but it also energized his weakening body and reinforced his determination
to continue the war. It compounded the war's tragic consequences for the
conspirators' beloved homeland: more Germans died in the last nine
months of the war than in the previous fifty-nine months.

BOX 9.4 ■ A POSTWAR INTERVIEW WITH STAUFFENBERG'S SON

One of Stauffenberg's sons was interviewed some forty years after the war:

> I was one of four children. At the end of the war, I was seven years old; during the war, I had no idea of my father's involvement in the resistance. Although my mother was aware that he was a member of the resistance group, she did not know that he was the key figure in the plan to overthrow the regime. . . .

> Two days after (the assassination attempt), the Gestapo found out where we were and assigned two men to guard our house. The next day we were told that my mother (she survived) and my great uncle . . . had been taken away. A few days thereafter, the news came that my grandmother and her sister had suffered a similar fate. Two cousins were executed. We were taken to a home in Lower Saxony that had been established for . . . housing the children of resistance members. I remember a village pastor telling us that we would be taken away . . . but whatever happened, we were to remember that our parents had been outstanding, wonderful people. This preacher risked his neck in saying this; anyone could have reported him. . . . Later there were rumors of plans to donate this "worthwhile genetic potential"—we children and others in a similar position—to childless SS couples, but . . . the matron of the home . . . kept us protected. . . .

> The conspirators, including my father, realized that regardless of whether the attempt succeeded, something significant would happen. This is important for the leaders of the Federal Republic (before reunification in 1990) to remember. I am not sure whether they understand it.

Steinhoff, Pechel, and Showalter, *Voices from the Third Reich*, pp. 389–91.

The Germans (as well as individuals from other countries) who defied the regime and risked death to save Jewish lives have for decades been recognized and honored for their courage. The conspirators, who risked all to kill the man who condemned millions of Jews and other defenseless souls to death, saved no lives, but the July 20 plot symbolized "a recognition of the need to challenge a system that perverted every value it touched. For the participants in the uprising, success was less important than honor."[39] Most of their fellow citizens, while admiring their courage, regarded them for decades as traitors and murderers. Today most Germans, especially those who reached their maturity in the 1970s and 1980s, no longer hold the July 20 conspirators in contempt. On the other hand, there is little evidence to suggest that they have become national heroes. A monument dedicated to the conspirators stands in the Plötzensee prison in Berlin where several were hanged from the still-visible meat hooks, but only a sprinkling of monuments, streets, parks, and squares throughout the country bear the names Stauffenberg, Beck, Olbricht, or Bonhoeffer.

Conclusion

The Nazis owed their success to a judicious blending of terror, propaganda, the promise of the *Volksgemeinschaft*, material rewards, and the charisma of Hitler. As the regime converted to total-war economics, the prospect of a brighter future was overshadowed by the austerity and sacrifice required to increase war production. As Stalingrad and more Allied bombs put victory out of reach, propaganda about the *Volksgemeinschaft* and a vast continental empire ruled by the master race rang hollow. Goebbels's victory-or-destruction campaign emphasized continuing the struggle for the fatherland and the Führer against savage enemies on both fronts. The government simultaneously maintained the flow of consumer goods and tightened its repressive grip. The German people, whether civilian or military, produced and performed until it became impossible to do so.

Terror, dedication to Hitler, anti-Semitism, love of the fatherland, fear of the enemy, and the government's ability to keep the wheels of an industrial society moving all played a role in motivating the nation to fight on against overwhelming odds. Another factor was the loyalty among the general population, perhaps more widespread and deeply rooted than previously supposed, as indicated by the army of willing Gestapo informants. The regime also gained support, if not always enthusiasm, from the common German belief that one owes obedience to duly constituted authorities, even if their criminality is the rule rather than the exception. As Eberhard Bethge, friend and biographer of Dietrich Bonhoeffer, wrote: "To attack your own state . . . was and is not really acknowledged to be a civic right or duty, even when that state rides rough-shod over all morals and human rights."[40] Many decent, morally upright Germans, whether in the military or on the home front, reluctantly compromised their standards and obeyed their government—a criminal regime. Some forty years after the end of the war, Freya von Moltke, a woman with impeccable anti-Nazi credentials, admitted to an American interviewer: "I say that no one who survived in Germany is guiltless. . . . People who lived through the Nazi time and still live, who did not lose their lives because they were opposed, all had to make compromises at whatever point. And among them, I also count myself."[41] Her husband was Count Helmut James von Moltke, leader of the Kreisau Circle whom the Nazis executed for high treason in January 1945.

INFOTRAC® COLLEGE EDITION SEARCH TERMS

For additional reading go to Infotrac College Edition, your online research library at http://www.infotrac-college.com.

Enter the search term "Casablanca Conference" using the Subject Guide.

Enter the search term "Speer, Albert" using the Subject Guide.

Enter the search term "Hitler Youth" using Keywords.

Enter the search term "underground movements, World War, 1939–1945" using Keywords.

Enter the search term "anti-Nazi movement" using the Subject Guide.

Enter the search term "anti-Hitler plot" using Keywords.

Enter the search term "plotting Hitler's death" using Keywords.

Enter the search term "Stauffenberg" using the Subject Guide.

Notes

1. Ralf Georg Reuth, *Goebbels* (New York: Harcourt Brace Jovanovich, 1993), pp. 316–17; Martin Kitchen, *Nazi Germany at War* (London and New York: Longman, 1995), p. 51.

2. R. J. Overy, *War and Economy in the Third Reich* (Oxford: Clarendon Press, 1994), p. 284.

3. Ian Kershaw, *The "Hitler Myth": Image and Reality in the Third Reich* (New York: Oxford University Press, 1987), p. 157.

4. Quoted in John Keegan, *The Second World War* (New York: Viking, 1989), p. 215.

5. Alan S. Milward, *The German Economy at War* (London: Athlone Press, 1965), pp. 192–93; Paul Kennedy, *The Rise and Fall of the Great Powers* (New York: Random House, 1987), p. 355.

6. Albert Speer, *Inside the Third Reich* (New York: MacMillan, 1970), p. 312.

7. Milward, p. 157.

8. Albert Speer, *Spandau: The Secret Diaries* (New York: MacMillan, 1976), p. 51.

9. Kitchen, *Nazi Germany at War*, p. 141.

10. Ibid., p. 142.

11. Claudia Koonz, "The Fascist Solution to the Women Question in Italy and Germany," in Renate Bridenthal, Claudia Koonz, and Susan Stuard, eds., *Becoming Visible: Women in European History* (Boston: Houghton Mifflin, 1987), p. 562.

12. Felix Kersten, *The Kersten Memoirs, 1940–1945* (London: Hutchinson, 1956), pp. 212–13.

13. Marlis G. Steinert, *Hitler's War and the Germans* (Athens, OH: Ohio University Press, 1977), p. 191.

14. Quoted in Gordon Wright, *The Ordeal of Total War, 1939–1945* (New York: Harper & Row, 1968), pp. 176–77.

15. Kitchen, p. 91.

16. Steinert, pp. 217, 225.

17. Quoted in Kershaw, *The "Hitler Myth,"* pp. 205–206.

18. Quoted in Donald D. Wall, "The Reports of the *Sicherheitsdienst* on the Church and Religious Affairs in Germany, 1939–1944," *Church History* (December 1971): 450.

19. Steinert, p. 267.

20. Jill Stephenson, "War and Society in Württemberg, 1939–1945: Beating the System," *German Studies Review* (February 1985): 91.

21. NSDAP, *Hauptkulturamt der Reichspropagandaleitung, Die neue Gemeinschaft*, March 1940, pp. 3–4.

22. Gerhard Rempel, *Hitler's Children: The Hitler Youth and the SS* (Chapel Hill: University of North Carolina Press, 1989), p. 262.

23. Kitchen, p. 176; Christian Zenter and Friedemann Bedüftig, *Encyclopedia of the Third Reich* (New York: Macmillan, 1991), p. 160.

24. Ibid., p. 186.

25. Robert Gellately, *Backing Hitler: Consent and Coercion in Nazi Germany* (Oxford and New York: Oxford University Press, 2001), p. 188.

26. Michael Burleigh, *The Third Reich: A New History* (New York: Hill & Wang, 2000), pp. 383–84.

27. Ibid., p. 393.

28. Office of the United States Chief Counsel for Prosecution of Axis Criminality, *Nazi Conspiracy and Aggression* (Washington: U.S. Government Printing Office, 1946), Supplement A, pp. 1218, 1050.

29. John S. Conway, *The Nazi Persecution of the Churches* (London: Weidenfeld & Nicolson, 1968), pp. 280–81.

30. *Nazi Conspiracy and Aggression*, Vol. VI, pp. 405, 406, 410.

31. Burleigh, p. 402.

32. U.S. National Archives, *Records of the Reich Leader SS and Chief of the German Police*, Microcopy T-175, Roll 262. (Like most Nazi documents captured and catalogued after the war, the title of this collection is in English. The documents on each roll of microfilm, however, are in the original German.)

33. Detlev Peukert, *Inside Nazi Germany* (New Haven: Yale University Press, 1987), pp. 158–62.

34. Ibid., pp. 167–68.

35. Quoted in Inge Scholl, *Students Against Tyranny* (Middletown, CT: Wesleyan University Press, 1970), pp. 83–84.

36. Joachim Fest, *Plotting Hitler's Death: The Story of the German Resistance* (New York: Metropolitan Books, 1994), p. 257.

37. Quoted in Ian Kershaw, *Hitler 1936–1949: Nemesis* (New York: Norton, 2000), p. 688.

38. Quoted in Fest, pp. 289–90, 340.

39. Johannes Steinhoff, Peter Pechel, and Dennis Showalter, *Voices from the Third Reich: An Oral History* (Washington, DC: Regnery Gateway, 1989), p. 375 [the editors' own words].

40. Eberhard Bethge, "Troubled Self-Interpretation and Uncertain Reception in the Church Struggle," in Franklin H. Littell and Hubert G. Locke, eds., *The German Church Struggle and the Holocaust* (Detroit: Wayne State University Press, 1974), p. 181.

41. Quoted in Alison Owings, *Frauen: German Women Recall the Third Reich* (New Brunswick, NJ: Rutgers University Press, 1994), p. 25.

CHAPTER TEN

The Holocaust and Other Nazi Atrocities

Following a tour of death camp sites in Poland in 1979, Auschwitz survivor and Nobel Prize–winning author Elie Wiesel wrote: "As we evoke the Jewish martyrdom, we also recall the sufferings and death of the non-Jewish victims."[1] There were 9 to 10 million human beings—Gypsies, the mentally retarded, the incurably ill, the criminally insane, homosexuals, and multitudes of Poles and Russians—who were gassed, shot, burned, starved, worked to death, or allowed to die in concentration or prisoner-of-war camps, but only the Jews were marked for total extermination. Ethnic massacres have a long and bloody history, but they took on an unprecedented scale and rigor under the Nazi regime. Unlike Stalin, who liquidated millions of his own countrymen because he imagined them to be a threat to his absolute power, the Nazis were not motivated primarily by territorial, political, economic, or military concerns. Indeed, such factors were of secondary importance; Hitler and his lieutenants killed many of their non-Jewish victims, and all Jews, solely because of race.

In memoranda and meetings, Nazi officials rarely referred to their mission as liquidation, extermination, or annihilation. They preferred bureaucratic euphemisms, such as deportation, resettlement, and the "Final Solution of the Jewish Question." The prosecutors' staff at Nuremberg used the word *genocide* to define the policy of a government to liquidate an entire race of people. (The word *genocide* was first used to describe the Turkish massacre of the Armenians during World War I.) In the 1950s, survivors and Israeli scholars introduced the term *holocaust*, meaning whole or great destruction, especially by fire, or a burnt offering or sacrifice. As a proper noun, Holocaust has entered common usage. Since extermination of the Jews was essential to Hitler's vision of establishing a new racial order in Europe, a discussion of Nazi occupation policies is an appropriate introduction to one of the darkest chapters in the history of humankind.

Patterns of Nazi Occupation

Nazi-occupied Europe was a patchwork of conflicting jurisdictions and a cauldron of intense bureaucratic infighting involving the Wehrmacht, party officials, the foreign ministry, Göring's four-year plan, and the most powerful of all, Himmler's SS. The Nazis allowed limited self-rule to local fascist collaborators in Slovakia, Norway, the Netherlands, and France, but building a base of popular support for the new order was never a high priority. The war demanded the ruthless exploitation of human and material resources and rule by terror, neither of which were compatible with voluntary cooperation. "Smash, grab, and exploit," a principle reputedly enunciated by Göring, was scrupulously followed by Nazi occupation forces. The war also provided the opportunity, as Hitler said in 1943, to "liquidate the rubbish" and to create a unified Europe over which "the Reich [would] be the master." When that has been accomplished, according to Hitler, "the way to world domination is practically certain."[2]

Although Hitler did not develop specific long-range plans for permanent Nazi rule of Europe, a few general guidelines can be inferred from his monologues and discussions with his lieutenants. The continent would be ruled from its core, the Greater German Reich, which would include the annexed territories of Austria, the Sudetenland, and western Poland. Nazi planners were anxious to absorb other Germanic areas, such as the Netherlands, Denmark, Norway, and Flemish-speaking Belgium. Himmler believed that some Frenchmen and Walloons (French-speaking Belgians) would be worthy members of the greater Reich's *Volksgemeinschaft* if their true Germanic qualities could be restored. In parts of southern Europe, the Wehrmacht and Waffen SS would buttress the limited power of local fascist administrators. Poland and the Soviet Union were targeted for unmitigated colonial exploitation.[3]

Because of their higher ranking in Hitler's racial hierarchy, Scandinavians, Belgians, Dutch, and French nationals fared better under Nazi rule than Slavic peoples. The occupiers killed hostages, tortured and executed underground fighters, and conscripted laborers, but the non-Jewish population was spared mass extermination, resettlement, and deportation. Underground groups in western Europe committed acts of sabotage, spread anti-German newspapers, hid fugitives, evaded Sauckel's forced labor roundups later in the war, and sent information on German military movements to the Allies before and after D-Day. However, the resistance cells were too small and, especially in France, ideologically divided between Communist and non-Communist, to pose a serious threat to German authorities. Moreover, freedom fighters were often turned over to the Gestapo by collaborators, who also helped the Nazis to find, arrest, and deport Jews. The story of Anne Frank's family, which is not untypical, shows conquered peoples at their best and worst. For over two years a handful of courageous Amsterdam residents helped conceal Frank's family, smuggling

The High Tide of Nazi Rule 1942

- German-Italian Axis – 1939
- Axis satellite or ally – 1941
- Axis conquest – 1939-1942
- Allied power or under allied control – 1939
- Neutral nation
- Farthest Axis advance – 1942

0 ___ 500 Miles

food and other necessities to their attic hiding place, but it was a Dutch informer who betrayed them. The majority of western Europeans, however, were neither collaborators nor underground fighters. They made whatever political and moral compromises were necessary to hold the Nazis at bay.

Although a Slavic country, Czechoslovakia experienced less severe repression than Poland or Russia. Josef Tiso, the Fascist priest whom the Nazis installed as the puppet ruler of Slovakia in 1939, proved to be one of the most shameless collaborators in occupied Europe, while some Czechs of Bohemia and Moravia benefited from their captors' view that they were the most Germanized of all Slavic peoples. Reinhard Heydrich, who replaced former foreign minister Konstantin von Neurath as Reich Protector in the fall of 1941, believed that thousands of Czechs who "looked and acted Germanic," could, with the proper training, become bona fide members of the Greater German Reich's *Volksgemeinschaft*. While few Czech and Slovakian Jews escaped deportation to Polish ghettos and death camps, the Nazis did preserve the medieval ghetto of Prague as a "museum" of Jewish life in eastern Europe. Theresienstadt, a concentration camp that housed "privileged" Jews, such as artists, authors, physicians, professors, wealthy businessmen, and decorated veterans of World War I, was located in the Protectorate. Initially, the inmates of Theresienstadt did receive better treatment than those elsewhere, but by mid-1943 conditions had deteriorated drastically, as Theresienstadt became a holding camp for prisoners destined for Auschwitz.

One of the most highly publicized acts of Nazi terror occurred on the outskirts of Prague. In May 1942 Czech partisans bombed the car in which Heydrich was riding. In one of the few instances of poetic justice under the Third Reich, one of the most powerful, feared, and ruthless Nazi chiefs died a slow and agonizing death from the fragments of shrapnel and glass that had pierced his body. Following Heydrich's state funeral, Hitler ordered the arrest of hundreds of hostages and the destruction of the village of Lidice, whose residents were accused of aiding and abetting the assassins on their way to Prague. All the men of the village were executed, and the women and children were sent to concentration camps. Like Rotterdam, Lidice became a name synonymous with Nazi brutality throughout the world. The occupiers applied terror more liberally after Heydrich's death, but the Czechs were never brutalized as consistently as the Poles or Russians.

Fierce partisan warfare dominated the occupation of Yugoslavia and Greece. Nazi terror in Serbia, Croatia, and Montenegro resembled Germanization in Poland, but it was less thorough because the invaders were forced to defend themselves against the two largest partisan armies in Europe, Marshal Tito's Communists and the Chetniks under the conservative General Draza Mihailovic. The Germans slaughtered over a million civilians and partisans, and hundreds of thousands were killed as ancient ethnic hatred between Serbs and Croats erupted into civil war. German forces suffered heavier casualties than in any other Nazi-occupied country in Europe. With Allied support after 1943, Tito's Communists crushed the Chetniks and, with little assistance from the Red Army, drove the Germans out of Yugoslavia. Communist and monarchist guerrilla forces in Greece also warred on each other while fighting German and Italian occupiers, and their stubborn resistance and fierce partisan warfare provoked savage German reprisals. Greeks were shown no mercy despite their slightly higher ranking in the Nazi racial hierarchy. The Nazis deported and exterminated most of the Yugoslavian and Greek Jewish population, but Jews living under Italian rule were relatively safe until Italy's surrender in 1943. To their credit, the Italians, whose lack of anti-Semitic fervor infuriated the Nazis, either blocked or slowed deportations, not only from Greece but also from their own country.

Despised by the Nazis as the lowest form of non-Jewish humanity, the Poles were at the mercy of their occupiers for nearly five years, longer than any other conquered European people. Despite bureaucratic infighting and

Himmler's preoccupation with the extermination of the Jews, the Nazis liquidated the Polish intelligentsia, resettled nearly a million ethnic Germans in annexed western Poland from which Poles and Jews had been evicted, and conscripted millions of laborers. The insatiable demands of war saved the lives of millions of Polish peasants. Initially marked for extermination to make room for more ethnic Germans, they were drafted into the Reich's army of forced laborers. The few children who "looked Aryan" were raised by German families. The rest, dismissed by Himmler as "stupid and backward,"[4] were to be taught only simple arithmetic, how to write their own name, and absolute obedience to their German masters. Estimates of the death toll of non-Jewish Poles range from 1.5 to 2 million. This figure does not include slave laborers who perished in the Reich or the tens of thousands of underground fighters of the home army, whose efforts to free their homeland from Nazi rule were brutally crushed by the SS and Wehrmacht.

Hitler envisioned the Soviet Union as a vast colony that would support a hundred million Germans. Creating an imperial domain in the east would require social engineering on a grand scale: the enslavement, deportation, or extermination of millions of Poles, Russians, Ukrainians, Lithuanians, and Latvians; the transfer of healthy German stock to serve as colonial masters; and the establishment of "breeding stations" for SS men and their racially screened mates. One of Hitler's favorite fantasies was an autobahn stretching from Bavaria to the Crimea, which would then be settled by Germanic Tyroleans who lived in northern Italy. He believed that the climate of the Tyrol was similar to that of the Black Sea peninsula.

The Reich would reap rich economic rewards from the colonization of the Soviet Union, but the principal goal was the realization of Hitler's *Lebensraum* vision. In 1943 Himmler told a group of SS officers that 30 million Slavs might have to be sacrificed to achieve this goal: "Whether nations live in prosperity or starve to death interests me only insofar as we need them as slaves for our culture."[5] Several months after the invasion of the Soviet Union, an SS officer in Ukraine asked his superior: "If we shoot the Jews, liquidate the war prisoners, starve . . . the big cities, and reduce . . . the peasants through famine, . . . who will produce the economic goods?"[6] This question illustrates the contradictions between the Reich's economic needs and racial dogmas, as well as the sadistic brutality that typified Nazi behavior in eastern Europe.

The Red Army shattered Hitler's dream, but the reality was grim enough. According to postwar Soviet estimates, the Nazis killed from 10 to 15 million nonbelligerents, nearly half of Himmler's projection. Scholars who have studied documents made available since the collapse of the Soviet Union in 1991 estimate that doubling the original death toll—thus equaling or even exceeding Himmler's projection—would not be an exaggeration.[7] This estimate includes civilians and partisans who were shot, starved, or burned by the Wehrmacht and the Waffen SS, prisoners of war, and slave laborers, but not Soviet Jews. Long after most Nazi leaders had privately conceded defeat in the Soviet Union, Himmler still clung to the fantasy of an eastern racial empire. In August 1944 he spoke at a meeting of Gauleiters: "It is irrevocable that we shall found a Germanic Reich in the wonderful east, that we shall increase our blood base to 120 million, that we shall found the seedbed of German blood in the east."[8]

The Jews: Resettlement And Ghettoization 1939–1940

Despite Hitler's prediction that a European war would result in the annihilation of the Jews, Germany invaded Poland, whose Jewish population of 3.2 million was the largest west of the Soviet Union, without a blueprint for making Europe *Judenfrei*. As a first step, Himmler and Heydrich ordered Polish Jews to be transferred to large urban centers, from which they would gradually be resettled in the "Lublin Reservation," an area south of Warsaw near the Soviet zone. In the fall and winter of 1939–1940, tens of thousands of Jews were deported to labor camps in the Lublin district or crowded into ghettos, the largest of which were in Lodz and Warsaw. By appointing councils of elders, Heydrich then claimed that the ghettos were self-governing. In fact, the councils were little more than puppets for their SS masters, who charged them with the unenviable task of selecting residents for deportation. At first the destination was labor camps. Later, the unfortunates were packed into boxcars bound for the death camps.

The resettlement of Polish Jews was not a smooth, orderly, or thorough process. Because of overcrowded ghettos and labor camps, transportion difficulties, and bureacratic tangles, many Jewish communities were still intact as late as March 1942.[9] Though they suffered terrible deprivations and would eventually be murdered, they fared slightly better than fellow Jews who had been uprooted during the first two years of the war. The ghettos were supposed to be economically self-sufficient, but inadequate sanitation facilities and acute shortages of food and medical supplies resulted in the outbreak of typhus and diseases aggravated by malnutrition. Some starved to death. Conditions were especially bad in the labor camps, where the death toll, either from overwork or execution, was particularly high. In April 1940 Heydrich abandoned the Lublin Reservation as the ultimate destination for Polish Jews. The head of the General Government of Occupied Poland, Hans Frank, protested the "dumping" of Jews in his territory, and local SS officials complained that they could not handle the huge influx of deportees. Himmler and Heydrich needed a more efficient plan to remove all Jews from the General Government, the Greater German Reich, and western Europe.

Shortly after the fall of France, Himmler proposed the deportation of European Jews to "specified territories overseas." By the end of July 1940 senior SS officials had selected Madagascar, a French-owned island off the coast of southeastern Africa thousands of miles from Poland. A few weeks later SS officer Adolf Eichmann, who was destined to play a major role in the Final Solution and had distinguished himself by organizing the efficient transfer of Austrian Jews to Vienna for later shipment to the east, drafted the Madagascar plan. Eichmann, who was head of the Gestapo's Jewish Affairs Division, calculated that, with 120 ships carrying 1500 passengers each, it would take four years to relocate 4 million Jews from the General Government, the Greater Reich, Czechoslovakia, France, and the Low Countries. The project was to be financed by confiscated Jewish wealth. It was a fantastic and totally unworkable scheme, but Himmler, Heydrich, and even Hitler expressed interest and encouraged discussion of the Madagascar solution among SS leaders, most of whom wanted the Jews under their jurisdiction deported from Europe.[10] By the end of 1940, as the death toll continued to rise in the densely populated ghettos and labor camps in Poland, SS officers were still waiting for orders from their superiors. They were told that the Reich's shortage of surface ships and the power of the British navy all but ruled out Eichmann's Madagascar plan. An SS doctor proposed the mass sterilization of Jews as an alternative solution, but Himmler, who was not opposed to the idea on principle, rejected it as impractical because of limited manpower and inadequate financial resources.

Meanwhile the SS in western Europe, with the cooperation of French, Belgian, and Dutch authorities, was implementing anti-Jewish policies. Jewish property was "Aryanized" (sold to Aryans for much less than market value), and Jews were being arrested *en masse* and held in detention centers, from which many would eventually be transported to Polish death camps. According to Felix Kersten (Himmler's personal physician, whose massage therapy relieved the severe pain of the SS chief's stomach cramps), Hitler told Himmler in November 1940 that the SS would be responsible for exterminating Polish Jews.[11] Kersten is not always a credible witness, but there is no reason to doubt that Himmler and Hitler were thinking in terms of mass extermination at that point. If Himmler actually received such an order from Hitler, he did not mention it to his senior commanders, with the possible exception of Heydrich. What was clear by early 1941 was that measures unprecedented in scope and brutality were under consideration and that the SS would be responsible for carrying them out.

The *Einsatzgruppen*

Early in 1941 the Madagascar Plan was quietly dropped, as Hitler, Himmler, and Heydrich considered a more radical solution in the context of Barbarossa. The conquest of Russia would open a huge area for deportation and resettlement, and it would give the Nazis jurisdiction over 4.5 million Soviet Jews and at least 1.5 million Polish Jews, who either lived in or had fled to the eastern third of the country that was under Soviet occupation. Hitler's "war of annihilation" speech to his generals in March, from which the June 6 commissar order evolved, signaled his intention (so Himmler and Heydrich believed) to exterminate not only "Bolshevist-Jewish" com-

The activities of the mobile killing units known as *Einsatzgruppen* were the first stage in the mass killings of the Holocaust. This picture shows the execution of a Jew by a member of one of these SS killing squads. When it became apparent that this method of killing was inefficient, it was replaced by the death camps.

missars, but other Jews as well. Heydrich had already begun to train the four *Einsatzgruppen*, or task forces (the German term is commonly used), which would be entrusted with the ultimate responsibility for executing the order. In April, Field Marshal Walther von Brauchitsch, then commander-in-chief of the Wehrmacht, promised Heydrich that the army would respect the autonomy of the *Einsatzgruppen* and support their efforts to combat "anti-Reich tendencies" behind the front lines. Heydrich agreed to keep army group commanders "fully informed."[12]

On June 17, 1941, five days before the invasion of Russia, Heydrich summoned *Einsatzgruppen* commanders and officers, about forty in all, to a meeting in Berlin. If there was a written record, it has been lost. According to surviving participants, Heydrich told the group that Eastern Jewry provided the "reservoir of intellectuals for Bolshevism," and that the Führer wanted it destroyed. Heydrich instructed his officers to carry out their duties faithfully and to be "harsh but not brutal." One of the *Einsatzgruppen* leaders testified after the war that they had heard a direct "Führer order" from two high-ranking officials of the Reich Main Security Office (the administrative agency headed by Heydrich that coordinated all police work in Germany and occupied countries) on the eve of Barbarossa: "The Führer has ordered the liquidation of all Jews, Gypsies, and Communist functionaries in the entire area of the Soviet Union in order to secure the territory."[13] The newly formed task forces knew exactly what was expected of them.

The commanders of the four *Einsatzgruppen,* which varied in size from 500 to 1000 men, were senior members of the Security Police and the SD. Most were well-trained, highly motivated "ideological warriors." The rank and file consisted of combat-trained Waffen SS troops plus the two branches of the Order Police, or *Ordnungspolizei*, which consisted of career professionals with some military training and the reservists, men who were too old or physically unfit for combat and trained only for routine police duties in occupied territories. They were organized into reserve police battalions. Most were not party members, and they lacked the rigorous racial indoctrination of the SD and Security Police. What is known of "their numbers and their institution suggests that they were not part of a political-ideological elite."[14] By 1941 there were about eighteen reserve—and roughly the same number of militarized—battalions of Order Police, each with roughly 500 men, available for quick deployment in recently conquered territories. These "ordinary men" (Christopher Browning's designation), virtually ignored in earlier Holocaust studies, played a key role in the extermination process. They directly murdered, or helped others to murder, hundreds of thousands of Jews. The Order Policemen were under the command of Kurt Daluege, who reported to three regional Higher SS and Police Leaders, high-ranking SS officers appointed by and responsible to Himmler. They helped plan the Final Solution and, though their power in theory was considerable, Daluege and the three Higher SS and Police Leaders were subordinate to Heydrich.

> ### BOX 10.1 ■ THE TESTIMONY OF AN *EINSATZGRUPPE* LEADER
>
> Otto Ohlendorf, head of the SD reporting service and leader of *Einsatzgruppe D* for one year, testified at the Nuremberg Trials in 1945 and his own trial in 1947:
>
> > When the German Army invaded Russia, I was leader of *Einsatzgruppe D* in the southern sector, and in the course of a year, during which I was the leader . . . , it liquidated approximately 90,000 men, women and children. The majority of those liquidated were Jews, but there [were] among them some Communist functionaries. . . .
> >
> > When the kommandos . . . came into a town . . . they generally solved the Jewish question first. . . . A Jewish Council of Elders . . . [registered] the Jews and [assembled] them. Those Jews were told that they would be resettled in another area. (The Elders compiled a list of names and presented it to the Germans.) After the roll call the victims were taken via trucks to the place of execution . . . then shot standing or kneeling and buried at the place of execution. The personal property, valuables . . . and clothing . . . were confiscated . . . and went to the Reich Minister of Finance or were turned over to German Welfare Organizations.
> >
> > An additional method of execution was inaugurated in the *Einsatzgruppen* . . . in the spring of 1942 when it was determined that women and children were to be [gassed] in motorized gas vans. Again, the victims were told that they were being moved for . . . resettlement and thus induced to enter the vans. . . . [which would] accommodate 15 to 30 persons at a time. Approximately ten minutes treatment was enough to produce fatal results . . . The vans were loaded with the victims and driven to the place of burial, which usually was the same as that used for the mass executions. The time needed for the transportation was sufficient to ensure the death of the victims.
>
> U.S. National Archives, *Nuremberg War Crimes Trials, Records of Case IX, U.S. v. Otto Ohlendorf, et al.* (Nuremberg, 1949), Roll 29, Frames 237–38.

The first sweep of the four *Einsatzgruppen,* which included several militarized battalions of the Order Police, began on June 22, 1941. In the wake of the Wehrmacht's juggernaut, the four *Gruppen*—A in the north, B in the center, and C and D in the south—converted sections of eastern Poland, the Baltic states, White Russia, and Ukraine into killing fields. Jews were herded into the countryside, forced to undress and dig their own mass graves, and shot to death. Bodies were thrown into graves by fellow Jews awaiting execution, or by local laborers. Ukrainians and Lithuanians were often the most eager to help. Many corpses remained unburied and were left in heaps to rot on the ground. The Wehrmacht, as Brauchitsch had promised, helped supply the SS murder squads with whatever they needed, but relatively few ordinary soldiers actually participated in the mass killings. The bloodiest single massacre took place outside of Kiev in late September. In retaliation for Russian partisans' destruction of German army headquarters and much of the city's center, *Einsatzgruppe C* ordered the "resettlement" of 33,000 Jews. They were taken to Babi Yar, a nearby ravine, and slaughtered over the course of two days. According to the German report, "there were no incidents. . . . Thanks to the outstandingly efficient organization," the Jews believed up to the last moment that they were being taken to their new home.[15] Deception was a technique of crowd control which the Nazis successfully practiced throughout the Holocaust.

More Jews died during the first five weeks of Barbarossa than in the previous eight years of Nazi rule. Most *Einsatzgruppen* commanders and officers had a professional background, among them academics, civil servants, and lawyers. They were meticulous about body counts, and some of their statistical reports have survived. From June 22 to December 31, 1941, Heydrich's task forces reported the murder of 439,826 Jews.[16] In 1942 a second sweep of the *Einsatzgruppen*, reinforced by reserve battalions of the Order Police and Ukrainian and Lithuanian volunteers, added an estimated 400,000 to the death toll on the eastern front. Some of the victims were murdered in the urban ghettos of White Russia, the Baltic States, and Ukraine. By the fall of 1942 the *Einsatzgruppen* had killed over 1 million Soviet Jews.

While the *Einsatzgruppen* were destroying entire Jewish communities in the summer and fall of 1941, the death toll in the ghettos continued to rise. The number of new deportees increased substantially following the invasion of Russia, as the SS established new ghettos in eastern Poland, the Baltic States, and White Russia. An SS officer in the Warsaw ghetto reported: "The Jewish quarter extends over about 1,016 acres. Occupancy therefore works out at 15.1 persons per apartment and six to seven persons per room."[17] To dramatize the "proper treatment of Jewish vermin" in the ghettos, an SS camera crew produced a documentary film on daily life in the Warsaw ghetto in the fall of 1941. Surviving fragments show guards confiscating carrots and potatoes hidden under a boy's coat, a small girl on a filthy bed picking lice from a younger brother's hair, a staged meeting of the Jewish council, and a mother holding her baby walking on a street littered with bodies of the sick and dying. Goebbels previewed the film and, suspecting that it might generate a wave of sympathy for the Jews, declared it "unsuitable" for German audiences. It was never shown. An estimated 500,000 Jews perished in the ghettos from 1939 to early 1944. By that time the SS had completed the "liquidation" of the ghettos, a euphemism for destroying their living quarters and either shooting the survivors or transporting them to death camps.

Final Plans for the Final Solution

Despite the efficient work of the SS task forces, Himmler and Heydrich were not satisfied with the *Einsatzgruppen* solution to the Jewish question. It was appropriate for the Russian front, where the Wehrmacht was waging Hitler's war of annihilation, but it did not seem suitable for the liquidation of Jews

AP/WIDE WORLD PHOTOS

Hitler's two most evil henchmen, Henrich Himmler (left) and Reinhard Heydrich, stride confidently from a meeting in 1941. Hitler initiated the Final Solution, Himmler was the architect of the project, and Heydrich the builder.

from territories already under Nazi occupation. Moreover, by late summer 1941, problems had arisen. The mass shooting of the Jews was expensive and inefficient, and at times it required the shooters to look their victims in the face, which proved difficult even for some of Heydrich's hardened killers. By the fall of 1941, *Einsatzgruppen* commanders were successfully using mobile gassing vans, in which deadly fumes were piped into enclosed chambers on wheels. While many of the murderers preferred this more impersonal method of killing, it too was slow and inefficient. Nevertheless, it suggested to Himmler and Heydrich that mass gassing in permanent facilities might be the key to carrying out what would become the Final Solution, that is, the systematic annihilation of the entire Jewish population in Nazi-occupied Europe in death camps specially constructed for that purpose.

In mid-July 1941, Himmler met with SS officer Rudolf Höss, who had been commandant of the Auschwitz concentration camp since May 1940. According to Höss's recollection five years later, Himmler said: "The Führer has ordered that the Jewish question be solved once and for all and that we, the SS, are to implement that order." Since existing extermination centers in the east were not equipped "to carry out the large actions which [were] anticipated," the Reichsführer had designated Auschwitz as a major killing center. Located forty miles west of Cracow in annexed Upper Silesia, it was in an area that could be "easily isolated and camouflaged." Himmler had chosen Höss to supervise the construction of extermination facilities at Auschwitz because of his "complete devotion." As head of the Gestapo's Jewish Affairs Division and a member of Heydrich's inner circle, Eichmann, who was gradually being given more responsibilities and power, was to be the Auschwitz commandant's immediate superior. Himmler concluded the meeting with his customary anti-Jewish diatribe, which Höss had heard before, but this time the SS chief added something new: "Every Jew that we can lay our hands on is to be destroyed now during the war without exception." Himmler did not mention the *Einsatzgruppen,* nor did he elaborate on "existing extermination centers in the East," which might have been a reference to the unrealized plans of Daluege and the Higher SS and Police Leaders to build stationary gas chambers and crematoria to liquidate Soviet Jews.[18] In any case, it is Himmler's first explicit order to construct a permanent killing facility. At his trial in Jerusalem in 1961, Eichmann recalled a meeting in mid-July at which Heydrich also spoke of Hitler's order to exterminate the Jews of Europe.

A memorandum dated July 31, 1941, signed by Göring, addressed to Heydrich, and used by the prosecution at Nuremberg, discusses the "Final Solution of the Jewish Question," the first time that this euphemism appeared in official correspondence. The use of the term *final solution* implied that other options, such as the Madagascar plan and resettlement of the Jews to labor camps in the Soviet Union, had been abandoned in favor of the most radical solution of all, mass extermination. It reads:

> . . . I herewith commission you to carry out all necessary preparations with regard to organizational, substantive, and financial matters for a total solution of the Jewish question within the area of German influence in Europe. . . . I instruct you further to submit to me as soon as possible an overall plan showing the preliminary organizational, substantive, and financial measures for the execution of the intended final solution of the Jewish question.[19]

Göring acknowledged signing the memorandum at his Nuremberg trial, but he almost certainly did not write it. Since the Reich Marshal had already given Heydrich administrative authority to solve the Jewish question shortly after the outbreak of war in 1939, the July 1941 memorandum, though a bit more explicit, would appear to be redundant. But much had changed since the invasion of Poland. Barbarossa and the *Einsatzgruppen* had radicalized Nazi policy to a degree unimaginable in 1939; thus Göring might have felt compelled to reassert his authority as the still-unofficial, but widely acknowledged, second-in-command of the Third Reich. Most historians believe that Himmler and Heydrich, who ordered Eichmann to draft the memorandum, found Göring to be a willing signatory.[20] The memorandum served Heydrich's purposes at a critical period in the evolution of the Final Solution. His and Himmler's foes and rivals in the Nazi hierarchy were more likely to believe that a memorandum signed by Göring was an expression of Hitler's will. It validated what the SS had already done and confirmed Heydrich's authority to organize the Final Solution.

Most historians agree that, without Hitler's explicit directives, the Final Solution could never have taken place and that the absence of a written order, or orders, given his style of leadership and his wish to avoid an incriminating paper trail, was not unusual. Most scholars now believe that Hitler probably issued several orders, or what SS chiefs interpreted to be his orders, at various times throughout 1941, beginning with his "war of annihilation" speech to his generals in March. It is still uncertain, however, exactly when, in what form, and how often the Führer issued extermination directives. A small group of historians believe that Hitler never gave an order to exterminate the Jews. They contend that the radicalization of Nazi racial policy after the invasion of the Soviet Union and the administrative chaos created by the massive influx of Jews into Poland and Soviet territory, prompted local SS leaders and civilian administrators to resort to mass extermination. Hitler approved of their ruthless efficiency, which evolved into the methodical destruction of European Jewry.[21] Local SS leaders did initiate individual "actions," which cost the lives of thousands of Jews, but evidence to prove that these actions evolved into the systematic extermination of European Jews without Hitler's express order is lacking.

Hitler's speech to the Reichstag on January 30, 1939, in which he "prophesied" that a world war would result in the annihilation of European Jewry, has been interpreted as a signal that he intended before the outbreak of war to exterminate the Jews. While this argument is not without merit, it is clear that Hitler could not initiate a systematic extermination plan before the SS was organizationally and ideologically prepared to commit genocide, and the war of annihilation in the east had provided an effective cover for the mass slaughter of the Nazis' most despised minority. Before Barbarossa, Hitler ordered the *Einsatzgruppen* to liquidate Jewish commissars and, by implication, other Soviet Jews. Buoyed by victories during the first weeks of the Russian campaign, he solicited a more comprehensive plan of destruction, documented in Himmler's conversation with Höss, a similar discussion between Heydrich and Eichmann, and Göring's "commission" to Heydrich, all in July 1941. By October 1941 Heydrich had completed the preliminary draft of a comprehensive plan—deportation to camps in Poland equipped with gassing facilities—which Hitler presumably approved.[22] His approval at this time is a plausible inference based on several events: the use of mobile gas vans by the *Einsatzgruppen*, the construction of the first Polish death camps at Chelmno and Belzec in November 1941, and the transfer to the eastern front of SS officers whose participation in the euthanasia program had given them experience in gassing victims in stationary facilities. One of these was SS Major Christian Wirth, formerly of the euthanasia institute in Brandenburg near Berlin, where he had learned to liquidate mental patients "quickly and quietly" by piping diesel engine exhaust into a sealed chamber (sometimes bottled carbon monoxide was used) and to retrieve gold-filled teeth from the corpses.[23] Wirth helped design and supervise the construction of gas chambers at the death camps. The first gassing of Jews in one of the permanent facilities took place on December 8, 1941, at Chelmno in western Poland.

The flood of Jewish deportees and the slow advance of the Moscow offensive in the fall of 1941 prompted Heydrich to confer with SS, party, and state officials on the progress of the Final Solution. His meeting, originally scheduled for December 9, was postponed because of the Soviet counteroffensive at Moscow on December 6, the Japanese attack on Pearl Harbor, and the declaration of war on the United States on December 11. How these events affected Hitler's earlier tentative approval of Heydrich's plans was clarified during the next few days. On December 12 the Führer addressed an audience of about fifty senior party officials in Berlin. In discussing the consequences of Pearl Harbor, he promised that the war was still winnable and that Germany's "glorious future in the east" was inevitable. He also spoke of the Jews and referred to his 1939 prophecy. Goebbels summarized Hitler's comment: "With regard to the Jewish question the Führer is determined to make a clear sweep . . . He prophesied that, if they brought about another world war, they would experience their annihilation. That was no empty talk. The world war is there. The annihilation of Jewry must be the necessary consequence."[24] The following week Hitler expressed similar sentiments in meetings and conversations with Hans Frank, Alfred Rosenberg, and Himmler, who summarized Hitler's comment as "exterminate Jews as partisans." The Führer had reaffirmed his commitment to the systematic extermination of the entire Jewish population of Europe. It is also significant that Hitler, for the first time since the outbreak of war, called the conflict a "world war," which, as he had predicted in 1939, would bring about the destruction of European Jewry. That war had finally become reality. Heydrich was pleased. He could now use Hitler's blanket authorization of the concept of total annihilation "to expand the killing operations into an overall program of European-wide genocide."[25]

The long-awaited conference on the Final Solution was finally held on January 20, 1942, in a villa located near the Wannsee, a large lake in the western suburbs of Berlin. The delegation consisted of representatives from seven state ministries, including Justice, the Interior, and the Foreign Office, and six high-ranking SS officers. The SS *Obergruppenführer* (a rank roughly equivalent to an army general) Reinhard Heydrich was at the peak of his power and influence. Using artful persuasion and subtle intimidation, he convinced the delegates that Hitler, Göring, and Himmler had given him complete authority to organize and preside over the implementation of the Final Solution of the Jewish Question. Heydrich announced: "Emigration has now been replaced by evacuation of the Jews to the east as a further possible solution, with the appropriate prior authorization of the Führer." Evacuation to the east is on ongoing "provisional option," he continued, but it is already providing practical experience of "great significance in view of the coming Final Solution of the Jewish Question." In the most-quoted passage of the Wannsee Protocol (Eichmann's minutes of the meeting), Heydrich said:

> Under appropriate direction the Jews are to be utilized for work in the East in an expedient manner in the course of the final solution. In large labor columns, with the sexes separated, Jews capable of work will be moved into these areas as they build roads, during which a large proportion will no doubt drop out through natural reduction. The remnant . . . will require special treatment (*Sonderbehandlung*); because it will . . . represent the physically resistant part, it consists of a natural selection that could, on its release, become the germ cell of a new Jewish revival. . . . Europe is to be combed through from West to East [for its 11 million Jews] in the course of the practical implementation of the final solution.

At his trial in Jerusalem in 1961, Eichmann testified that all of the delegates knew—and some of them objected—that "special treatment" meant extermination. Eventually they all promised their unqualified support and pledged to hold the proceedings of the meeting in the strictest confidence, as Heydrich had ordered. They also agreed with Hans Frank's representative that the Final Solution should begin in the General Government, where transport would play "no major role" because of its large Jewish population.[26] Though not reflected in the minutes, Eichmann told the Jerusalem court that such terms as "killing and eliminating and extermination" were discussed.[27] It would take several months before Heydrich's program of mass extermination could be fully implemented, but the Wannsee Conference had removed all ambiguity and uncertainty: the Nazi regime was committed to the extermination of all European Jews at specially selected sites in the General Government and the Reich's annexed Polish territories. Although not explicitly mentioned in the minutes, there was little doubt among the delegates to the conference, as well as the thirty

SS, government, and party officials who received copies of the Wannsee Protocol from Heydrich, that mass gassing, which was already underway on a relatively small scale, would be the method of extermination.

The Death Camps

By late spring 1942, private German firms had completed construction of six death camps in Poland, including living quarters, prisoners' barracks, rail terminals, gas chambers, and crematoria. Belzec, Maidanek, Sobibor, and Treblinka were situated in the General Government, while Chelmno and Birkenau, the extermination unit of the Auschwitz complex, were located in Polish territory annexed to the Reich. Tens of thousands of Gypsies and some Russian prisoners of war were gassed in the camps, but the vast majority of victims were Jews. They came from the Greater German Reich, Slovakia, Bohemia/Moravia, Romania, Yugoslavia, the Soviet Union, western Europe, Greece, and Hungary, but at least 3 of every 5 Jewish victims were Polish. The SS Order Police reservists were particularly active in Poland throughout 1942. They targeted villages and small towns throughout the General Government, where they found, and murdered, tens of thousands of Jews who had not yet been relocated. The reserve police battalions also assisted in the liquidation of the ghettos and helped capture tens of thousands of Jews and put them on trains bound for the death camps.

Heydrich proved to be a superb organizer. Each camp was efficiently run by the commandant and a staff of well-trained, loyal administrators, guards, and physicians, most of whom belonged to SS Death's Head units (the branch of the SS that had managed concentration camps since 1934). They supervised the non-German personnel; enforced regulations; unloaded the trains; made the selection for immediate extermination, medical experiments, or forced labor; salvaged hair, clothing, and shoes; herded the naked victims into the chambers; and released the deadly gas. After the victims were dead, Ukrainian, Lithuanian, or Jewish laborers pulled gold-filled teeth and salvaged other valuables, and removed corpses from the chamber, which they either burned in the crematoria or buried in mass graves. The Economic and Main Administrative Office of the SS, headed by Oswald Pohl, was in charge of the economic side of the extermination program. Carefully and thoroughly, Pohl's men collected the valuables seized from gassed inmates and sent them back to Germany, where they were melted down into ingots and deposited in a special SS account of the Reichsbank.

Thirty-eight-year-old Reinhard Heydrich—tall, blond, blue-eyed, and athletic—the only member of Hitler's top command with the ideal Aryan physique and the only one to die during the war, was neither mourned nor missed when cut down by Czech assassins just months after the Wannsee Conference. He was one of the most powerful figures in the Nazi hierarchy, and one of the most feared. Rumors persisted that, in his

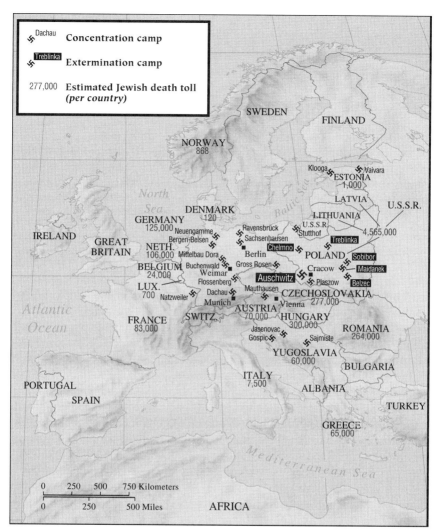

The Holocaust
Source: Jackson J. Spielvogel, *Western Civilization*, 4th ed., p. 835. Used by permission.

capacity as head of the SD, Heydrich possessed bulging files of incriminating evidence on Nazi leaders, which, given his ruthlessness and his thinly disguised ambition to become the supreme leader of the SS, he was prepared to use against any of them at any time. Heydrich's rivals, however, had a kind of "trump card" of their own; it was widely rumored that one of his grandmothers was Jewish, which, if true, would have been disastrous for the *Obergruppenführer*. He was well aware of the Jewish grandmother rumor and remained a loyal team player, but there is no reason to doubt that, if granted more time, he would have attempted a coup against Himmler. In any case, Heydrich had done his work well; the huge operation which was the Final Solution functioned like a well-oiled machine after his demise.

BOX 10.2 ■ **EXTERMINATION AT BELZEC**

Details from Kurt Gerstein's account of extermination at Belzec:

The train pulled in: 200 Ukrainians . . . tore open the doors and with their leather whips drove the Jews out of the cars. A loudspeaker issued instruction: to remove all clothing, even artificial limbs and eyeglasses; to tie their shoes together with small pieces of string, [and] to turn in all valuables, all money at the ticket window. . . . They approached. Wirth and I were standing on the ramp in front of the death chambers. Completely nude, men, women, young girls, children, babies, cripples, filed by. . . . They asked him what was going to happen and he answered: "The men will have to work, build houses and streets. The women . . . will be busy with housework." This was the last hope for some of these poor people, enough to make them march toward the death chambers without resistance. The majority knew everything—the smell betrayed it! They climbed a little wooden stairs and entered the death chambers, most of them silently, pushed by those behind them. . . .

Jewish workers opened the doors (after the gassing) . . . The men were still standing like columns of stone, with no room to fall or lean. Even in death you could tell the families, all holding hands. . . . The bodies were tossed out, blue, wet with sweat and urine, the legs smeared with excrement and menstrual blood. . . . Two dozen workers were busy checking mouths which they opened with iron hooks. . . . Others inspected anuses and genital organs, searching for money, diamonds, and gold. Dentists knocked out gold teeth, bridges, and crowns with hammers.

Captain Wirth . . . was in his element, and showing me a large can of teeth he said: "See the weight of the gold! Just from yesterday and the day before! You can't imagine what we find every day, dollars, diamonds, gold! You'll see!". . . .

[At a banquet that evening honoring all the participants, Doctor Pfannenstiel, Professor of Hygiene at the University of Marburg, said:] "Your work is a very great work and a very necessary duty. . . . When one sees the bodies of the Jews, one understands the greatness of your work."

Dawidowicz, Lucy S., ed., *A Holocaust Reader* (New York: Behrman House Publishers, 1976), pp. 107–109.

His lieutenants honored his memory by selecting the code name "Action Reinhard" for the liquidation process in the death camps of the General Government during the remainder of 1942.

Kurt Gerstein, an SS officer who played a dangerous double game—working at the death camps while trying to inform the outside world of the Final Solution—described a "typical day" of the liquidation at Belzec in 1942. French authorities, who imprisoned him after the war, discovered his written account in the cell where he committed suicide in July 1945. Gerstein recalled a train arriving with forty-five cars holding 6,700 people, of whom 1,450 were already dead. Ukrainian guards whipped the Jews, covered with excrement and vomit, out of the cars. A loudspeaker instructed all to undress and the women and girls to submit to the barber. As the naked victims were driven to the gas chambers disguised as showers, an SS man in a "pastoral voice" said: "No harm will come to you! Just breathe deeply to strengthen the lungs. Inhaling is a means of preventing contagious diseases." The officer in charge, Christian Wirth, ordered the chambers to be packed, "700–800 of them to every 75 square meters." Because of faulty diesel engines on that particular day, it took over three hours for the victims to die.[28]

The results at each camp were the same, but procedures differed slightly. At Treblinka, near Warsaw, the passengers were ushered into what appeared to be a normal railroad station, with a large clock, train schedules, ticket windows, and a waiting room. Assuming that it was a temporary stop on the way to their final destination, a labor camp farther east, the victims calmly walked out of the station to the platform where the selection was made. At that point, most realized that the train station was a cruel hoax, although some still hoped that what they heard about delousing and showers was true. The SS guards forced the Jews into the chambers amidst screams, cries, tears, and farewells. The few chosen for work duties knew that they would eventually die, but they clung to their horrible existence, which depended on the death of their comrades. Their worst job was to re-bury hundreds of thousands of corpses that had risen to the surface of shallow graves. The Jewish laborers finally rebelled in August 1943, forcing the SS to close Treblinka, where an estimated 700,000 Jews were exterminated in a thirteen-month period. Of the 600 escapees, only forty survived.

This Nazi photo shows a trainload of Jews arriving at the railroad station in the town of Auschwitz. The uniformed prisoners, who may also have been Jews, accompanied the victims on the last leg of their journey—to the Auschwitz/Birkenau death camp.

The others were killed by Polish peasants and partisans, Ukrainian guerrillas, Wehrmacht deserters, and the SS.[29]

By the end of 1943, the Nazis had closed or reduced operations in five of the six death camps. At Auschwitz/Birkenau, however, the SS operated the machinery of death until November 1944. Under Rudolf Höss's direction, twenty single-story brick buildings of a former Austrian artillery barracks near the town of Oswiecim, or Auschwitz, were converted into a prison camp. By 1943 it had grown into a huge complex of agricultural and industrial enterprises, living quarters for an army of laborers, medical facilities, railyards, and the Birkenau extermination center, which was also called Auschwitz II. (It was located at the tiny village of Brzezinka, Polish for birch trees, which in German are called *Birken*.) Nearly all non-Polish Jews and all Gypsies were murdered there, as were some Russian prisoners of war and Polish Christians. Life and death at Auschwitz were extensively documented, and most Holocaust survivors were interned there. After the war, Höss testified for the defendants at Nuremberg; he was hanged at Auschwitz in 1947.

In his testimony, Höss estimated that at least 2.5 million people perished at Auschwitz in approximately three years. Upon further reflection, he lowered his estimate to 1.3 million. When operating at peak efficiency, he claimed that the chambers killed 9,000 people daily. Höss boasted that his was the only camp to use Zyklon B, the commercial name for a pesticide of prussic acid crystals, which turned into gas when heated. It normally killed the victims in 5–20 minutes. The commandant and his staff created a surrealistic atmosphere of horror in what has aptly been called the "kingdom of Auschwitz." The sign over the main gate read *Arbeit Macht Frei* (work makes you free), but those selected for the work detail were told that "the only way out of here is through the chimney." Many of the victims walked to the gas chambers listening to the strains of Strauss waltzes and other "appropriate German music," played by an inmates' orchestra of accomplished musicians. Höss took particular pride in this "sophisticated method" of crowd control, which was not normally used in the other death camps. The musicians, who would eventually be gassed, also performed for the commandant and his family and camp personnel.

The Birkenau facilities were taxed to the limit in May 1944, as thousands of Hungarian Jews began arriving daily, but Höss and his technicians were prepared. One of the survivors of the last mass shipment of Jews to the last remaining death camp was Dr. Miklos Nyiszli, whom the "angel of death," Dr. Josef Mengele, chose to be his pathologist. In a 1946 memoir, Nyiszli recalled that at least half the victims, denied food and water for days in the sealed boxcars, were dead on arrival. The workers had to drag the other half, who were nearly comatose, into the chambers. Twenty minutes later, after electric ventilators evacuated the gas, the doors were opened. Dr. Nyiszli writes:

The bodies were not lying throughout the room, but piled in a mass to the ceiling. This was because the gas first inundated the lower layers of air and rose slowly toward the ceiling. This forced the victims to trample one another in a frantic effort to escape the gas. . . . The bodies of women, children, and the aged, covered with scratches and bruises from the struggle, were at the bottom. Blood oozed from their noses and mouth; their faces, bloated and blue, were so deformed as to be almost unrecognizable. . . . The [workers] lined up around the hill of bodies and flooded it with powerful jets of water . . . because the final act of those who die by drowning or by gas is an involuntary defecation.[30]

Höss lived comfortably near the killing center with his wife and five children.

Many of those selected for work died slowly and painfully. Ill-fed, subjected to beatings and other tortures, and often forced to assemble outdoors for interminable roll calls, they lived in overcrowded, unheated, filthy barracks and performed back-breaking toil for twelve hours a day. One of Auschwitz's major construction projects was a huge synthetic rubber plant

---

BOX 10.3 ■ ELIE WIESEL BEARS WITNESS

The Holocaust's most eloquent survivor, Elie Wiesel, writes of his first night at Auschwitz in the spring of 1944, following a long and torturous train ride from Hungary. He was 14 years old at the time:

> We did not yet know which was the better side, right or left; which road led to prison and which to the crematory. But for the moment I was happy. I was near my father. [His mother and sisters were gassed on arrival; his father survived the death march to Buchenwald in January 1945, but died shortly thereafter.]

> Another prisoner came up to us: "Poor devils, you're going to the crematory."

> He seemed to be telling the truth. Not far from us the flames were leaping up from a ditch, gigantic flames. They were burning something. A lorry drew up at the pit and delivered its load—little children. Babies! Yes, I saw it—saw it with my own eyes . . . those children in the flames. . . .

> I pinched my face. Was I still alive? Was I awake? I could not believe it. How could it be possible for them to burn people, children, and for the world to keep silent? No, none of this could be true. It was a nightmare. . . . Soon I should wake with a start, my heart pounding and find myself back in the bedroom of my childhood, among my books. . . .

> Never shall I forget that night, the first night in camp, . . . Never shall I forget the little faces of the children whose bodies I saw turned into wreaths of smoke beneath a silent blue sky.

> Never shall I forget those flames which consumed my faith forever.

Elie Wiesel, *Night* (New York: Hill & Wang, 1960), pp. 41–43.

(called Buna, or Auschwitz III), which cost the lives of at least 25,000 inmates. Shortly after completion, the Allies bombed the factory, which never produced a single ounce of rubber. One of the most insidious ways to dehumanize the prisoners was the "excremental assault."[31] The inmates, many of whom suffered from diarrhea, were allowed to relieve themselves only once or twice a day and had only one barrel of water per barracks for washing their filthy bodies and clothing.

A horrible fate awaited those selected for medical experiments. Most were lethal and utterly pointless, such as the request from a professor at the University of Strasbourg that the heads of 150 "Jewish-Bolshevist commissars, who embody a repulsive but characteristic subhumanity," be cut off and sent to Strasbourg for study. Dr. Josef Mengele, one of the most elusive Nazi fugitives after the war, assisted in the selection of arriving inmates and specialized in the "study" of twins. His ghoulish experiments on hundreds of Jewish and Gypsy twins, such as injecting dark eyeballs with blue dye, were designed to find ways of increasing the German birthrate. To discover more efficient methods of sterilization, SS doctors irradiated the genitals of men and women for fifteen minutes, castrated the men, and, after execution, sent the women's sexual organs to Berlin for analysis. Professor Carl Clauberg, who ran a clinic for the treatment of sterile women at the University of Königsberg, injected women's fallopian tubes with various chemicals, which stopped menstruation. He boasted to Himmler that his method would enable one doctor with ten assistants to sterilize several hundred women a day. Nearly all the subjects were gassed after the experiments.[32]

In November 1944 the Red Army's imminent takeover of southwestern Poland forced Himmler to shut down extermination facilities at Auschwitz. When Soviet troops occupied the camp in January 1945, some of the inmates were on their way to concentration camps in the Reich, such as Bergen-Belsen near Hanover, Buchenwald, and Dachau, which Allied troops liberated in April 1945. Thousands perished on these forced marches, and thousands more died of typhus and extreme malnutrition after they had reached the camps. One of those was Anne Frank. She survived Auschwitz, but succumbed to typhus at Bergen-Belsen.

In a memorandum to Himmler in the fall of 1944, Eichmann estimated the death toll at 6 million. The prosecutors at Nuremberg reduced the estimate to 5.7 million, but most scholars today accept Eichmann's count. Approximately 500,000 perished in the ghettos, 60 to 65 percent were exterminated in the six Polish death camps, at least 1.5 million were victims of the *Einsatzgruppen* and special actions of the Order Police battalions, and hundreds of thousands were starved, tortured, and murdered in forced labor camps. Based on fragmentary German records, Jewish sources, and various prewar and postwar census data, one of the most accurate estimates of both minimum and maximum losses was compiled in the late 1980s. Over half the victims were from Poland and the Soviet Union, with 3 million and 1.1 million, respectively. The data show six nations with deaths ranging from 1 million to 100,000: Hungary 564,000; Romania 287,000; Czechoslovakia 277,000; Lithuania 143,000; Germany 142,000; and the Netherlands 106,000. At the top of the five-digit range is France with 83,000, followed by Latvia, Greece, Austria, Yugoslavia, and Belgium, in that order. Including the much smaller losses from other nations, the Nazi regime murdered a maximum of 6,010,900 Jews.[33] (Approximately 5.3 million is the minimum estimate.)

The Victims

While the image of millions of Jews going to their death like sheep to the slaughter is misleading, the majority did remain passive. Physical resistance was inhibited by Nazi brutality and terror, sickness and starvation, isolation, the hostility of surrounding communities, and the indifference of the outside world. Many refused to believe that the Germans intended to kill

---

BOX 10.4 ■ A PSYCHIATRIST AS CAMP INMATE

How physical deprivation and dehumanization affected the prisoners is described by the Austrian physician Viktor Frankl, who survived four concentration camps, one of which was Auschwitz. He became a professor of psychiatry after the war:

> When the last layers of subcutaneous fat had vanished, and we looked like skeletons disguised with skin and rags, we could watch our bodies beginning to devour themselves. The organism digested its own protein, and the muscles disappeared. Then the body had no powers of resistance left. One after another the members of the little community in our hut died. Each of us could calculate with fair accuracy whose turn would be next, and when his own would come. After many observations we knew the symptoms well, which made the correctness of our prognoses quite certain. "He won't last long," or, "This is the next one," we whispered to each other, and when, during our daily search for lice, we saw our own naked bodies in the evening, we thought alike: This body here, my body, is really a corpse already. What has become of me? I am but a small portion of a great mass of human flesh . . . of a mass behind barbed wire, crowded into a few earthen huts; a mass of which daily a certain portion begins to rot because it has become lifeless. . . .

> Perhaps it can be understood, then, that even the strongest of us was longing for the time when he would have fairly good food again, not for the sake of good food itself, but for the sake of knowing that the sub-human existence, which had made us unable to think of anything other than food, would at last cease.

> Those who have not gone through a similar experience can hardly conceive of the soul-destroying mental conflict and clashes of will power which a famished man experiences.

Viktor Frankl, *Man's Search for Meaning: An Introduction to Logotherapy* (New York: Simon & Schuster, 1984), pp. 42–43.

every Jew in Europe. Even after the horrors of the "trains of death," in which the victims were packed tightly into boxcars—sometimes for days— with little ventilation, almost no food or water, and a bucket or two for excrement and urine, victims clung to the vain hope that Auschwitz or Treblinka was a temporary stop on the way to resettlement further east, or that the showerheads on the ceiling would spray them with water. For the growing minority of inmates who gradually realized what was actually happening, the odds against successful resistance were enormous. Terror had disarmed them emotionally, and deprivation had weakened them phys- ically. An escapee's chance of survival was slim at best, given the relentless pursuit of the captors and the virulent anti-Semitism of the local popula- tion—and the Nazis punished no crime more savagely than attempted escape.

Despite the obstacles, there were at least thirty documented cases of armed resistance in the ghettos, villages, and camps of Poland. Several un- derground organizations were formed in Lithuania and the Soviet Union, and many of those who managed to escape into forested areas were able to link up with partisan groups.[34] The most celebrated rebellion occurred in Warsaw in the spring of 1943, by which time the Nazis had liquidated most of the largest ghetto in eastern Europe. All but 50,000 of the original 400,000 inhabitants had been sent to the death camps. With few weapons, those remaining held off a superior force for several days, killing hundreds of Wehrmacht and SS troopers. Having quickly exhausted their meager supplies of ammunition, the rebels were forced to surrender. The Nazis de- stroyed the buildings, executed the rebels, and shipped the survivors to death camps.

The odds against successful resistance in the camps were greater than in the ghettos; yet there were three rebellions in concentration camps in the Soviet Union, and three in the Polish death camps. In October 1943, two months after the Treblinka uprising, 300 inmates at Sobibor attempted a mass escape. The thirty survivors joined Soviet partisan fighters, and the SS closed the camp. In September 1944 a resistance group in Auschwitz managed to blow up one of the crematoria and kill several Germans. Reprisals were savage, but nearly 650 were able to escape; of these, 450 were hunted down and killed by SS camp personnel. While the incidence of resistance was highest in eastern Europe, thousands of western European Jews rebelled against their Nazi captors. Holocaust historian Yehuda Bauer estimates that Jewish armed resistance was proportionately higher than that of any other captive people in Europe.

There were also many forms of passive resistance in the ghettos and camps. Bauer recounts the story of three members of the Jewish Council of Kosów, a small town in eastern Poland. When the Gestapo announced that it would come into the ghetto on Passover 1942, the Council, believ- ing that it was the signal for liquidation, told all the residents to hide or flee. Of the twenty-four members of the *Judenrat,* four decided to offer themselves as sacrificial victims—"to deflect the wrath of the Gestapo." As they waited for their executioners, one of them fled. "The three men of Kosów prepared to meet the Nazis on Passover 1942. Was their act less than firing a gun?"[35] Most remarkable is the fact that thousands of Jews survived the horrors of Nazi captivity and lived to bear witness to the rest of the world. Some testified against their tormenters, who failed in their mission to destroy all the Jews of Europe. The survivors represent one of the greatest triumphs of the human spirit.

The Murderers and the German People

The Final Solution of the Jewish Question was a massive operation in which tens of thousands of men participated, including several branches of the SS and police of various ranks who managed the death, labor, concentration, and transit camps, Nazi party officials, businessmen, engineers, contractors, workmen (many of whom were not prisoners), civil servants representing several government ministries, Lithuanian, Latvian, and Ukrainian volunteers and conscripts, and railroad personnel. It also required tons of equipment, machinery, and supplies, all of which had to be transported by train and processed by camp personnel. Of all the equipment needed to carry out the Final Solution, none was more important than the trains, which, of course, were also indispensable for the troops fighting their losing battle on the Russian front. Besides the hundreds of boxcars making daily deliveries of piteous human cargo for the gas chambers, trains also carried the dead victims' valuables and thousands of workers, non-Jews as well as Jews, on the return trip to Germany. The Final Solution nearly always took precedence over the needs of war, even well into 1944 when the Red Army launched its powerful offensive into Poland. On several occasions in that year Himmler ordered most of the Jewish workers, whose skills were useful in the Reich's defense-related industries, to be sent back to Auschwitz on the same trains that had carried them to the Reich. Boxcars carrying supplies and men to the Russian front were usually sidetracked to make room for the "trains of death." On at least one occasion, however, hospital cars filled with wounded soldiers had orders to use the main track back to Germany. The orders were lost, and the Auschwitz station master, assuming that the voices from the cars crying out for food and water in perfect German were German-speaking Jews, ordered the hospital train to be sidetracked and the cars to remain sealed.

The death factories functioned smoothly after Heydrich's assassination, but Himmler, the camp commandants, and other high-ranking SS officials, such as Adolf Eichmann, assumed a more direct supervisory role. Though the SS chief was a busy man—strengthening his position in the Nazi hierarchy, administering his ever-expanding, far-flung economic enterprises, and acting out the role of the commander-in-chief of numerous Waffen SS divisions—he reserved ample time for what he regarded as his

This photo shows a "shipment" of Hungarian Jews and the boxcar into which they had been crammed arriving at Auschwitz in the late spring of 1944. Within twenty-four hours most, if not all, of these people would be dead.

most important task: supervising the Final Solution and encouraging its perpetrators. Himmler met with SS leaders in the field and even witnessed a mass gassing at Auschwitz in 1942. Accounts of his reaction vary—some eyewitnesses claimed that he became physically ill and vomited—but all agree he was visibly upset by what he saw. He urged his men to be thorough and, without letting any victims "slip through the net," to speed up the process. Himmler was pleased with their performance, as evidenced in a speech delivered to SS leaders in western Poland in October 1943:

> . . . Let me, in all frankness, mention a terribly hard chapter to you. Among ourselves, we can openly talk about it, though we will never speak a word of it in public. . . . I am speaking about the . . . extermination of the Jews. . . . Most of you will know what it means to have seen 100 corpses together, or 500, or 1000. To have made one's way through that, and . . . to have remained a decent person throughout, that is what has made us hard. That is a page of glory in our history that never has been and never will be written. . . . We had the moral right, and the duty toward our nation to kill this people which wished to kill us. But we do not have the right to enrich ourselves with a single fur or a watch. . . . We do not, because we were exterminating a bacillus, wish to be infected by that bacillus in the end and die. . . . we fulfilled this heaviest of tasks in love to our people. And we suffered no harm in our essence, in our soul, in our character. . . . [36]

Himmler had become the second most powerful leader of the Third Reich because he shared Hitler's vision of a racial empire in the east, and his speech shows that he knew exactly how to transform his Führer's "nightmarish vision into reality."[37] Both Himmler and Hitler remained convinced to the end that the Final Solution was the Third Reich's greatest achievement.

Himmler's speech also sheds light on the murderers' motivation and the mechanisms that bound them together—a twisted sense of duty, a perverted love of country, and ideological commitment. In self-serving interviews and testimony after the war, surviving SS officers claimed that they were dedicated professionals whose top priority was to obey orders. They denied being pathological anti-Semites or sadistic killers. An *Einsatz* officer testified: "I was continually hearing myself and my men accused of barbarity and sadism when all I was doing was my duty."[38] In a similar vein, *Einsatzgruppe* commander Otto Ohlendorf testified at his own trial in 1947 that he was ordered to kill the Jews "for the reason that they were considered as endangering the security of the German Reich." He added that "none of us examined whether these persons (including Jewish and Gypsy children) at the moment, or in the future, would actually constitute danger, because this was outside our knowledge, and not a part of our task."[39] Like Ohlendorf, defendant Adolf Eichmann insisted that he bore no particular malice toward the Jews, but firmly believed that they posed a serious threat to the German *Volk*. Thus "he proved to be a model of bureaucratic industriousness and icy determination in carrying out his responsibilities . . . . His zeal expressed itself in his constant complaints about obstacles in the fulfillment of death-camp quotas."[40] Studies based on interviews and testimony of SS doctors reveal emotional disorders and self-deception, but not the psychosis of mass murderers. Psychologist Robert Jay Lifton and historian Michael Kater conclude that Dr. Josef Mengele and his Auschwitz colleagues, who selected the hardiest few for labor and the rest for immediate gassing, and who performed gruesome medical experiments, were "amoral racists," but not clinically psychotic. Along with hundreds of other German physicians, they believed that the ethical codes of their profession did not apply to "racial engineering."[41]

The testimony of death camp commandants and their SS assistants reveal a strong conviction that, as dedicated and determined enemies of the German people, the Jews had to be eliminated. They took great pride in their work, and some of them even enjoyed it. Auschwitz commandant Rudolf Höss boasted of his "superb job performance" and his conduct as a "sternly incorruptible soldier," and gave detailed descriptions of daily life, labor, and death at the "kingdom of Auschwitz." Survivors, however, testify that Höss was corrupt. Those who worked as household servants were ordered to steal food and home furnishings designated for camp personnel. "Höss settled down in such a well-appointed and magnificent home that his wife remarked, 'I want to live here till I die.'" He also impregnated an Italian prisoner, whom the SS killed in the last days of the war.[42] Another death camp commandant, Franz Stangl of Treblinka, who died in a West German prison in the early 1970s, kept an album titled "The Good Old Days," which was found after the war. It contains photographs, diaries, letters, and confidential reports written by the executioners and sympathetic German observers at the Treblinka death camp. As their work achieved a more "depraved efficiency," they had more leisure time. Snapshots show camp personnel at social gatherings, where they listened to music, drank, and laughed together after a day's work.[43]

Few scholars today would challenge the proposition that members of the SS Order Police, both career professionals and reservists, who were deployed for carrying out deportations, ghetto-clearing operations, and massacres, were major players in the Final Solution. Whether the behavior and motivation of these loosely trained, low-ranking SS men accurately reflected the attitudes of ordinary Germans has become the focus of several recent works on the Final Solution. Two American specialists, historian Christopher Browning and political scientist Daniel Jonah Goldhagen, are at the center of what has become a major controversy in Holocaust studies. Browning, in his 1992 study of Reserve Police Battalion 101, asserts that the behavior of these "ordinary men," when ordered to shoot down thousands of Jewish men, women, and children in Poland in 1942 and 1943, was not exactly ordinary. On the first action, the commanding officer did not mandate murder; from 10 to 20 percent of his men chose not to take part. Those who did participate, however, adjusted to their grisly assignment; they became cold-blooded killers, a bit reluctantly at first, but more enthusiastically with each action. Some of them survived and testified at hearings in West Germany in the 1960s. Based on a careful reading of their testimonies, Browning believes that their behavior and motivation can be explained by such factors as peer pressure, the habit and duty of obedience to superiors, and being products of a society infected with racism and caught up in the "siege mentality" of war. He concludes that highly bureaucratized and specialized modern societies "reduce the sense of personal responsibility of those implementing official policy . . . . the peer group exerts tremendous pressure on behavior and sets moral norms. . . . If the men of Reserve Police Battalion 101 could become killers under such circumstances, what group of men cannot?"[44]

In his *Hitler's Willing Executioners*, published in 1996, Goldhagen agrees that the Order Police were among the principal perpetrators of the Final Solution, but his emphasis is on how thoroughly and enthusiastically the reserve police battalions murdered Jews, not only in the killing fields of eastern Europe but also in the labor camps and on the "death marches" of Auschwitz survivors into Germany toward the end of the war. What sets his study apart from the others is his controversial explanation of the reservists' motivation. Goldhagen argues that German society before Hitler's takeover had become thoroughly infected with "eliminationist anti-Semitism," which he defines as the type of anti-Semitism that led ordinary Germans to believe "that Jews ought to die." The Nazi regime had only to harness it. Goldhagen concludes: "The inescapable truth is that, regarding Jews, German political culture had evolved to the point where an enormous number of ordinary Germans," as represented by members of the reserve police battalions, became—"and most of the rest of their fellow Germans were fit to be—Hitler's willing executioners."[45] It should be pointed out that, in light of new evidence, Browning acknowledges that he originally underestimated the number of ideologically motivated reservists who were ready to kill Jews from the start. "On the local level, they formed a crucial nucleus for the killing process, . . . [but] their influence was far out of proportion to their numbers in German society."[46]

With extensive documentation, Browning and Goldhagen resolve issues about the numbers of ordinary Germans involved in the Final Solution, but they cannot so easily answer a more difficult question: To what extent did civilians on the home front support the Holocaust? Browning's statement in the preceding paragraph, that the influence of the anti-Semitic Order Police who were ready to kill Jews from the start, "was far out of proportion to their numbers in German society," could be interpreted to mean that, while many Germans were probably enthusiastic supporters of the Holocaust, others were either indifferent to it or—and this group was probably smaller—deplored the harsh treatment of Jews. The implications of Goldhagen's thesis, however, are clear: ordinary Germans, as thoroughly infected with "eliminationist anti-Semitism" as members of the reserve police battalions, enthusiastically supported the Final Solution and, if given the opportunity, would have become willing executioners for the Führer. Moreover, like Hitler and Himmler, the vast majority of Germans may well have regarded the Holocaust as the greatest achievement of the Nazi regime.

Richard Breitman, the first American historian to have studied recently declassified British decodes of messages from the Reich Main Security Office to Order Police battalions in eastern Europe (this information was not available to Browning or Goldhagen) disagrees with Goldhagen, not on the extent of their participation but on their motivation. This new material shows that "Nazi authorities did not find the Order Police executioners quite so willing or easy to employ," and that they tried to manipulate and replace those assigned "to carry out the messiest tasks" of the Final Solution. Some historians share Goldhagen's view that the Holocaust had become an open secret by 1943 because the regime did not try very hard to conceal it from the German people. Breitman disagrees. He finds substantial evidence in the decodes that Nazi authorities, uncertain about the reliability of the Order Police and the support of the German people, took great pains to keep the Final Solution secret from the German public as well as from the outside world.[47] Breitman does not deny that anti-Semitism ran deep in German society, but he argues that, if Nazi authorities were confident of widespread public support of the Holocaust, they would not have tried so hard to conceal it from their own citizens.

How much ordinary Germans actually knew about the Holocaust remains an open question. Just as popular anti-Semitism had some influence on the behavior of the Order Police, it also had, in Breitman's words, "some influence on the German public reaction to the influx of information about genocide."[48] But how great was this influx of information? In *The Terrible Secret*, a 1980 study of the suppression of the truth about the Final Solution, Walter Laqueur argues that millions of civilians had heard enough from eyewitness accounts of soldiers, *Einsatz* troopers, and civilian employees to know that Jews were being killed *en masse* and to suspect that the regime's solution to the Jewish question was far more radical than resettlement.[49] To this list of informants can now be added the accounts of the Order Police, whose involvement had not been extensively documented when Laqueur published *The Terrible Secret*. But one can only estimate how many civilians heard the stories of mass murder, how much they were told, and how they responded to what they heard. Moreover, it is quite possible that some of the murderers themselves did not know in detail that their government was carrying out a program of systematic extermination of Europe's Jewish population. In any case, most German survivors of the Nazi period, responding to what they call American interviewers' "inevitable question" (that is, How much did you know about the Holocaust?), admit that they knew of mass deportations to labor camps and heard rumors of mass killings in the east, but insist that they did not know the "details" of the regime's program of deliberate, systematic extermination. Incredibly, Göring, Speer, and other Nuremberg defendants expected the court to believe that they, too, did not know the details, although Speer later admitted that he could have become fully informed if he had made appropriate inquiries.

Since there were fewer eyewitness accounts and reports of gas chambers in the death camps, it was easier to ignore the ugly rumors of systematic extermination. "Things I could not have stomached in 1935," Speer writes, "were palatable a few years later. This happened in one way or another to all of us in Germany. As the Nazi environment enveloped us, its evils grew invisible—because we were a part of them."[50] It was not difficult for the regime to conceal genocide from the many Germans whose indifference to the fate of the Jews was greater than their fear of the regime. Even those who might have, or should have, cared, insist that, while mass deportations and killings were common knowledge, their government's program of systematic extermination was not. "We did not know the details," was the answer of five retired clergymen, none of them Nazi sympathizers, who were interviewed in 1977. When asked if the flood of information about the Final Solution after the war shocked them, they answered no.[51] The majority of those who lived under the Nazi regime and survived stand by their stories, and probably always will. Nevertheless, a sense of guilt continues to haunt many of them and, to a lesser extent, their descendants. In light of current research and new evidence, most outsiders have become more skeptical than ever of what has become the inevitable question's stock answer: "We did not know the details."

Bystanders and Rescuers

While news of massacres reached the outside world shortly after the invasion of the Soviet Union, it was not until June 1942 that a British newspaper printed a story about the mass gassing of Jews in eastern Europe. There were also reports from the Polish underground, escaped prisoners, and ghetto radio transmissions. Some people dismissed these reports as propaganda or unsubstantiated rumors. Others believed that if massacres had taken place they were either unorganized pogroms or civilian casualties of Hitler's war of annihilation.

In August 1942 Eduard Schulte, a German businessman who had access to confidential Nazi sources, delivered a detailed account of the Final Solution to Gerhard Riegner, the representative of the World Jewish Congress in Geneva. He gave the document to officials at the American embassy in Bern, who telegraphed what they termed an "authentic account" of the Nazi plan to London and Washington. The U.S. State Department, convinced that Jews were being deported for labor purposes, judged the report to be "unbelievable, . . . a war rumor inspired by fear." Yet the Associated Press carried Riegner's story, which was published on November 25, 1942, by the New York *Herald Tribune* under the headline: "Wise (Rabbi Wise was a prominent American Jewish advocate) Says Hitler Has Ordered 4,000,000 Jews Slain." Also in November 1942, a Polish underground courier code-named Karski arrived in London with a story that corroborated Riegner's report. It, too, was published in Britain and shared with American authorities. Britain's decoders continued to intercept messages about the extermination of the Jews, but their government's need for military information had a much higher priority. British authorities gave Jewish matters little attention and never released the Order Police decodes to the United States.[52] Clearly, enough information was available on both sides of the Atlantic to conclude that the Nazis were systematically exterminating European Jewry, but Allied policymaking individuals or agencies never processed what they saw as bits of disparate information into a body of knowledge upon which they could have acted, or at least made recommendations to authorities at the highest levels of government.

Throughout 1943, U.S. foreign service officers continued to receive reports, mostly from Polish sources, that tens of thousands of Jews were being gassed at Auschwitz. Even skeptical U.S. State Department officials were forced to acknowledge that something more sinister than vast armies of slave laborers being worked to death was taking place at Auschwitz. Even though the fate of Jews in eastern Europe quite properly fell under the State Department's jurisdiction, none of its personnel submitted a report or made a recommendation to President Roosevelt or the military.

Toward the end of 1943, however, Secretary of the Treasury Henry Morgenthau finally converted bits of information into knowledge of the details. He was the first high-ranking U.S. official to conclude that the Nazis were systematically exterminating the Jews, and to take action. In January 1944 he persuaded Roosevelt to establish the War Refugee Board, whose principal purpose was to rescue as many Jews as possible.

In April 1944 two Auschwitz escapees, Rudolf Vrba and Alfred Wetzler, delivered a detailed eyewitness account to the Jewish underground of their native Slovakia. Added to their report, which reached Riegner in June, was information about the impending deportation of Hungarian Jews and a recommendation that the Allies bomb rail facilities and gas chambers at Auschwitz. Upon receiving the report from Riegner, the War Refugee Board intensified efforts to save Jews and endorsed the recommendation to bomb Auschwitz.

From early July to December 1944, American planes bombed synthetic fuel plants at Buna-Monowitz, or Auschwitz III, several times. On one of the runs several bombs accidentally fell near the Birkenau gas chambers (which were located about five miles from Buna), but British and American military chiefs vetoed bombing the extermination facilities as well as the camp's rail lines, which at that time were transporting Hungarian Jews to their death. They insisted that their principal job was to win the war and that military resources should not be diverted to nonmilitary objectives. American historian David Wyman, one the harshest critics of Allied policy toward the Jews, contends in his 1984 study titled *The Abandonment of the Jews*, that nonmilitary objectives were sometimes bombed and that U.S. planes could easily have destroyed or damaged the Auschwitz death factory in the summer of 1944, possibly saving the lives of 200,000 Jews. "The real reason [for the refusal]," he writes, "was the War Department's prior decision that rescue was not part of its mission. . . . To the American military, Europe's Jews represented an extraneous problem and an unwanted burden."[53]

A symposium on the bombing of Auschwitz was held in 1993 to mark the opening of the United States Holocaust Memorial Museum in Washington, D.C. Some of the contributors were sharply critical of Wyman's views, and even those who supported his thesis about the War Department's decision pointed out that the precision bombing technology required to destroy or easily damage the Auschwitz death factory was simply not available in 1944. In his introduction to the book of the contributors' essays, titled *The Bombing of Auschwitz: Should the Allies Have Attempted It?*, editor Michael J. Neufeld writes that, despite the Allies' extensive information about extermination at Auschwitz, genocide against the Jews was regarded with widespread apathy: "The Holocaust simply was not an important issue on the public or military agenda of World War II . . . . For the supreme Allied leadership in the West (not to mention the East), there were many more urgent priorities, such as doing everything possible to win the war as soon as possible; rescuing refugees, Jewish or otherwise, just got in the way."[54]

A bizarre plan to ransom Hungarian Jews in April added further confusion to the issue of Allied rescue efforts. As the Vrba report was being circulated in May 1944, Joel Brand of the Jewish Rescue Committee in Budapest delivered a proposal from Adolf Eichmann to Jewish officials in Istanbul: if the British would supply the Reich with 10,000 trucks for use exclusively on the eastern front, as well as large quantities of tea, coffee, cocoa, and soap, Eichmann would allow Hungary's 800,000 Jews to live. Their lives had been spared largely because Admiral Nicholas Horthy, the head of Hungary's satellite regime, had been loyal to the Reich and had made substantial contributions of men and matériel to the Russian front. Horthy's support wavered, however, as Soviet troops neared the Hungarian border in the spring of 1944. The Germans responded by occupying the country, thus giving Eichmann more authority over the largest and only remaining unmolested Jewish community in Europe. The incredulous SS officer believed that the British would seriously consider his "generous offer." Not surprisingly, they arrested Brand in Syria and sent him to their intelligence headquarters in Cairo for interrogation. Suspicious of a Nazi offer to trade Jews for trucks that would be used against an ally, the British rejected the proposal. This incident provides further insight into the "fantasy world" mentality of Nazi murderers. On the other hand, it also illustrates that Allied governments, which might at least have used this incident to give widespread publicity to Eichmann's plan and what was known about the "Hungarian Holocaust," were still largely indifferent to the fate of the Jews. Unfazed by the failure to convert his victims into "something of value" for the war effort, Eichmann continued to send them to their death. From the last shipment of Hungarian Jews in mid-July (Admiral Horthy halted the deportation of Jews shortly after the Allies bombed Budapest) to the closing of Auschwitz in November, over 100,000 Jews were gassed.

The Allies did not become involved in rescue operations until it was too late, while governments of smaller nations could protect only the Jews living within their borders. The U.S. War Refugee Board helped rescue 200,000 Jews in 1944, and the British granted temporary asylum to 100,000 refugees. In July 1944, Churchill wrote to Foreign Secretary Anthony Eden: "There is no doubt that this [the Final Solution] is probably the greatest and most horrible crime ever committed in the whole history of the world."[55] He favored bombing Auschwitz, but refused to lift the 1939 ban on Jewish immigration to Palestine. Neutral Spain, Turkey, and Sweden provided sanctuary, but the Swiss, fearing retaliation from their northern neighbor, interned some Jewish refugees and turned others over to Nazi authorities. The Bulgarian government managed to protect most of its Jews, and Danish citizens, many of whom defiantly wore the star of David when their Jewish countrymen were ordered to do so, smuggled 8,000 Jews into Sweden.

Like governments, international organizations and institutions did not act decisively until 1944. The most active among Jewish organizations, the World Jewish Congress, helped save thousands in Hungary and rescue the few who were still prisoners in camps throughout the Reich in 1945. The Vatican was well-informed, but Pius XII, fearing retaliation against German Catholics and, as some have charged, lacking sympathy for the plight of the Jews, decided not to protest.[56] However, the pope did help to protect thousands of Jews in Rome and encouraged his representatives in Budapest to forge Vatican passports for 2,500 Jews in the summer of 1944.

Red Cross officials claimed that they could do little to help because the Jews were not prisoners of war, but the Nazis granted them permission to inspect the Theresienstadt concentration camp in the summer of 1944. By this time, the camp for "privileged Jews" had become a nightmare, no different from other concentration camps. What the Red Cross saw on the tidy main street was a Potemkin village of freshly painted barracks, newly planted trees, shrubbery, and flowers, and healthy inmates. The rest of the camp, which they were not allowed to see, was crowded with the sick and dying housed in squalid barracks. Although not entirely convinced, the visitors issued a cautiously optimistic report about conditions in Nazi concentration camps. The Red Cross did act shortly before the end of the war, when a Swedish delegation and the organization's international president, Karl Burkhardt, met with Himmler's representative, Ernst Kaltenbrunner, and later with Himmler himself. These meetings helped secure the release of several thousand prisoners in Theresienstadt and other camps in the Reich.

The heroic rescue efforts of extraordinary individuals brighten this particularly dark chapter in the history of human cruelty. In the summer and fall of 1944, following the Hungarian government's adopting a policy to recognize preferred status for Jews holding passports from neutral countries, two diplomats, Charles Lutz of Switzerland and Raoul Wallenberg of Sweden, forged papers for over 30,000 Jews. Both had studied in the United States and spent time in Palestine, where they learned to admire and respect Jewish culture. They had also been involved in humanitarian causes before and during the war. Wallenberg is the more famous because of the tragic conclusion of his mission. Arrested by the Soviets in January 1945, he was never seen again.[57] Religious beliefs inspired Andre Trocmé, pastor of a Protestant church in the French village of Le Chambon, Corrie Ten Boom, one of the daughters of a devoutly Christian family in the Netherlands, and Dietrich Bonhoeffer to shelter Jews and help them to escape from Nazi-occupied territory. Corrie Ten Boom was the only member of her family to survive the horrors of internment in the Reich.[58] Bonhoeffer was arrested for helping to smuggle Jews out of Germany, but was executed for his involvement in the anti-Hitler conspiracy.

Since the release of Steven Spielberg's academy award–winning film, *Schindler's List*, German businessman Oskar Schindler has become the most famous rescuer of Jews. He is also the most curious, according to Australian novelist Thomas Keneally, author of the book on which the film is based, for no one knows what drove him to perform his cunning and dangerous feats "to salvage. . . a cross section of a condemned race." Keneally describes Schindler as a "*bon vivant*, speculator, charmer, and sign of contradiction."[59] The novel is based on the true story of a Sudeten German whose success as a war profiteer in Cracow, some forty miles east of Auschwitz, was made possible by cheap Jewish labor and extravagant gifts to SS officials. As Schindler came to realize what the Nazis were doing, he bribed, bluffed, and gambled to add more names to his list. He was penniless at the end of the war, but 1,100 Jews had been spared from the fires of Auschwitz. A half-century later, 6,000 *Schindlerjuden* and their descendants were alive. Schindler was one of a handful of rescuers who risked everything to fight against what appeared to be an invincible system of evil—and saved lives. The vast majority of people were bystanders.

Conclusion

The Final Solution and the war were inextricably linked. Hitler's war of annihilation on the eastern front provided the perfect opportunity for the systematic extermination of millions of Jews, and only Germany's imminent defeat ended the Holocaust. By late summer 1944, the Reich no longer had sufficient human and material resources to slow the Red Army's offensive, which would have given Himmler more time to kill more Jews, and simultaneously operate the Auschwitz/Birkenau killing machinery. On the other side, Allied leaders may have been skeptical that the Nazi extermination was systematic and deliberate, but they knew that their enemy was slaughtering unarmed civilians on an unprecedented scale. Meeting in Moscow in October 1943, the Big Three foreign ministers issued the "Declaration on German Atrocities in Occupied Europe," calling for postwar trials of Nazi war criminals. The Third Reich's war of annihilation against the Jews, Slavs, and other "racially unfit groups" was counterproductive. For the Allies, it converted World War II into a crusade against Hitler's regime and helped inspire more punitive policies toward the Reich, such as the massive bombardment of civilian targets, the refusal to negotiate with or encourage anti-Hitler conspirators, and insisting on unconditional surrender, which would inevitably result in the victors' postwar occupation of a devastated Germany.

The universal significance of the Holocaust is enormous. It proves that human beings are capable of committing every evil that the mind can conceive. It demonstrates that John Calvin's Reformation doctrine of the total depravity of man is still alive in an age of unprecedented scientific and technological progress and institutionalized humanitarianism. When plans for the establishment of a Holocaust memorial museum as a branch of the Smithsonian Institution were announced, President Jimmy Carter's commission on the Holocaust wrote a perceptive, eloquent, and sobering response to critics of the project:

> If the present branches of the Smithsonian represent the accomplishments of civilization, the Holocaust illuminates an alternative dimension of human experience. . . . The fact that this process of destruction was committed by one of the most cultured and technologically advanced societies adds a sober dimension to the progress celebrated by the Smithsonian. . . . The memorial/museum would allow the presentation of a more complete picture of civilization, a greater vision of its promises and dangers.[60]

The museum graphically and movingly exhibits those dangers, which still exist. Since World War II the demons that drove the Nazis to commit genocide—racial hatred, blind loyalty to a charismatic dictator, and ideological fanaticism—have been unleashed in such disparate parts of the world as Cambodia, Rwanda, and Bosnia. While millions have died, the survivors have not been entirely ignored by the outside world. Rescue efforts, humanitarian aid, and even military action (against the Serbs' "ethnic cleansing" in Kosovo in the late 1990s), have in small ways helped to alleviate the suffering of the victims. The Holocaust will always serve as a grim reminder of humankind's seemingly limitless capacity for evil, but it will also touch the collective conscience of humanity and, one hopes, inspire the more fortunate to come to the aid of the helpless.

INFOTRAC® COLLEGE EDITION SEARCH TERMS

For additional reading go to InfoTrac College Edition, your online research library at http://www.infotrac-college.com.

Enter the search term "Holocaust" using the Subject Guide.

Enter the search term "concentration camps" using Keywords.

Enter the search term "Jewish ghetto" using Keywords.

Enter the search term "Himmler, Heinrich" using the Subject Guide.

Enter the search term "Heydrich, Reinhard" using the Subject Guide.

Enter the search term "Nazi resistance" using Keywords.

Notes

1. Quoted in R. Miller, "Pilgrimage to the Country of Night," *New York Times Magazine*, November 4, 1979, p. 39.

2. Norman Cameron and R. H. Stevens, eds. *Hitler's Conversations, 1941–1944* (New York: New American Library, 1961), p. 125.

3. Dietrich Orlow, *A History of Modern Germany, 1871 to the Present* (Upper Saddle River, NJ: Prentice-Hall, 1999), p. 193.

4. International Military Tribunal (IMT), *Trial of the Major War Criminals* (Nuremberg, 1947–1949), 22: 480.

5. Ibid., 39: 428.

6. Gordon Wright, *The Ordeal of Total War, 1939–1945* (New York: Harper & Row, 1968), p. 123.

7. John Erickson, "Soviet War Losses and Calculations," in John Erickson and David Dilks, eds., *Barbarossa: The Axis and the Allies* (Edinburgh: Edinburgh University Press, 1994), pp. 257–58.

8. Quoted in Karl D. Bracher, *The German Dictatorship: The Origins, Structure, and Effects of National Socialism* (New York: Praeger, 1970), p. 413.

9. Christopher Browning, *Ordinary Men: Reserve Police Battalion 101 and the Final Solution in Poland* (New York: HarperCollins Publishers, 1992), p. xv.

10. Richard Breitman, *The Architect of Genocide: Himmler and the Final Solution* (New York: Alfred A. Knopf, 1991), pp. 130–31.

11. Felix Kersten, *The Kersten Memoirs, 1940–1945* (London: Hutchinson, 1956), p. 52.

12. Leni Yahil, *The Holocaust* (New York: Oxford University Press, 1990), p. 249.

13. Quoted in Breitman, *The Architect of Genocide,* p. 164.

14. Richard Breitman, *Official Secrets: What the Nazis Planned, What the British and Americans Knew* (New York: Hill and Wang, 1998), p. 41.

15. Yahil, pp. 257, 259, 280.

16. Ibid., p. 270.

17. Quoted in Yehuda Bauer, *A History of the Holocaust* (New York: Franklin Watts, 1982), p. 153.

18. Himmler's directives to Höss are quoted in Breitman, *Architect of Genocide,* p. 189; Breitman refers to the plans of the Higher SS and Police Leaders in his *Official Secrets,* p. 226.

19. Lucy S. Dawidowicz, ed., *Holocaust Reader* (New York: Behrman House, 1976), p. 73.

20. Breitman, *Architect of Genocide,* p. 193; Ian Kershaw, *Hitler 1939–1945: Nemesis* (New York: Norton, 2000), p. 471.

21. Mary Fulbrook, *The Divided Nation: A History of Germany, 1918–1990* (New York: Oxford University Press, 1992), pp. 115–16.

22. Richard Breitman, "Auschwitz and the Archives," *Central European History* (September/December 1985): pp. 373–76; Christopher Browning, *Nazi Policy, Jewish Workers, German Killers* (Cambridge: Cambridge University Press, 2000), p. 39.

23. Gerald Fleming, *Hitler and the Final Solution* (Berkeley: University of California Press, 1984), p. 24.

24. Quoted in Kershaw, *Hitler: Nemesis,* p. 490.

25. Ibid., p. 494; Himmler's summary of Hitler's comment is quoted in Breitman, *Official Secrets*, p. 86; for a detailed interpretation of the significance of Hitler's remarks in December 1941 see Browning, *Nazi Policy, Jewish Workers, German Killers*, pp. 53–57.

26. Direct quotations from the Wannsee Protocol are taken from Rita Steinhardt Botwinick, ed., *A Holocaust Reader: From Ideology to Annihilation* (Upper Saddle River, NJ: Prentice-Hall, 1998), pp. 166, 168–69.

27. Kershaw, *Hitler: Nemesis*, p. 493.

28. Dawidowicz, pp. 107–108.

29. Jean-Francois Steiner, *Treblinka* (New York: New American Library, 1968), p. 303.

30. Quoted in Otto Friedrich, "The Kingdom of Auschwitz," *The Atlantic* (September 1981), p. 53.

31. Terrence De Pres, *The Survivor: Anatomy of Life in the Death Camps* (New York: Oxford University Press, 1977), pp. 51–71.

32. Friedrich, pp. 46–47.

33. Donald L. Niewyk, ed., *The Holocaust* (Boston: Houghton Mifflin, 1997), p. xv.

34. Jackson J. Spielvogel, *Hitler and Nazi Germany* (Upper Saddle River, NJ: Prentice-Hall, 2001), p. 293.

35. Yehuda Bauer, "Forms of Jewish Resistance," in Niewyk, p. 125, 132.

36. *Office of the United States Chief Council for Prosecution Axis Criminality, Nazi Conspiracy and Aggression* (Washington: U.S. Government Printing Office, 1946), 4: 563–64.

37. Browning, *Nazi Policy, Jewish Workers, German Killers*, p. 172.

38. Quoted in Heinz Höhne, *Order of the Death's Head* (New York: Ballantine Books, 1971), p. 371.

39. U.S. National Archives, *Nuernberg War Crimes Trials, Records of Case IX, U.S. vs. Otto Ohlendorf, et al.* (Nuremberg, 1949), Roll 29, Frames 229–30. (A digest of Ohlendorf's trial and that of other *Einsatzgruppen* commanders has been published in book form.)

40. Robert S. Wistrich, *Who's Who in Nazi Germany* (New York: Routledge, 1995), p. 50.

41. Gitta Sereny, *Into That Darkness* (New York: Vintage Books, 1974), p. 22; Michael H. Kater, *Doctors under Hitler* (Chapel Hill: University of North Carolina Press, 1989), pp. 234–35.

42. Friedrich, p. 13.

43. Ernst Klee, Willi Dressen, and Volker Riess, eds., *"The Good Old Days," The Holocaust as Seen by Its Perpetrators and Bystanders* (New York: Free Press, 1991), p. xii.

44. Browning, *Ordinary Men*, pp. 188–89.

45. Daniel Jonah Goldhagen, *Hitler's Willing Executioners: Ordinary Germans and the Holocaust* (New York: Alfred A. Knoff, 1996), pp. 14, 454.

46. Browning, *Nazi Policy, Jewish Workers, German Killers,* p. 175.

47. Breitman, *Official Secrets*, p. 7.

48. Ibid., p. 226.

49. Walter Laqueur, *The Terrible Secret* (New York: Penguin Books, 1980), pp. 31–32.

50. Interview with Albert Speer, *Playboy,* June 1971, p. 43.

51. The interviews are discussed in Donald D. Wall, "The Confessing Church and the Second World War," *Journal of Church and State* (Winter 1981): 27–28.

52. Breitman, *Official Secrets*, p. 145.

53. David S. Wyman, *The Abandonment of the Jews* (New York: Pantheon Books, 1984), p. 307.

54. Michael J. Neufeld and Michael Berenbaum, eds., *The Bombing of Auschwitz: Should the Allies Have Attempted It?* (New York: St. Martin's Press, 2000), p. 9.

55. Quoted in Martin Gilbert, *Auschwitz and the Allies* (New York: Holt, Rinehart and Winston, 1981), p. 341.

56. Two works extremely critical of Pope Pius XII's response to the Holocaust are Guenter Lewy, *The Catholic Church and Nazi Germany* (New York: McGraw-Hill, 1964) and the more recent John Cornwell, *Hitler's Pope: The Secret History of Pius XII* (New York: Viking, 1999).

57. Yahil, pp. 642–43.

58. Philip Hallie, *Lest Innocent Blood Be Shed* (New York: Harper Colophon Books, 1979); Corrie Ten Boom, *The Hiding Place* (Old Tappen, NJ: Spire Books, 1971).

59. Thomas Keneally, *Schindler's List* (New York: Simon and Schuster, 1982), p. 9.

60. Quoted in Michael J. Neufeld and Michael Berenbaum, p. ix.

CHAPTER ELEVEN

Collapse of the Third Reich

On November 3, 1943, four weeks before the Teheran Conference, Hitler told his generals that the struggle against Bolshevism had "demanded extreme exertions" and still threatened the Reich, but "a greater danger now appears in the west: an Anglo-Saxon landing." The loss of more territory in the east, he said, would not strike a "fatal blow to the nervous system of Germany," but if the enemy breached the Atlantic Wall (coastal defenses in France and Belgium) "the immediate consequences would be unpredictable." Hitler sensed that the Allies would "launch a major offensive against Western Europe, at the latest in the spring." He had therefore decided to reinforce coastal defenses, "particularly those places from which long-range bombardment of England [with missiles] will begin."[1]

Within days after the conclusion of the Teheran Conference, reinforcements began arriving on the French coast. Hitler transferred Field Marshal Rommel from Italy to France to improve coastal defenses and to command an army group. Rommel and his immediate superior, Field Marshal Gerd von Rundstedt, were pessimistic about the Reich's chances of victory, but Rommel clung to the hope that if the Wehrmacht could beat back an Allied invasion of France and reinforce the eastern front, a strategic stalemate and peace with the west might be possible.[2] Germany's most celebrated general accepted his new post eagerly and set about his task with characteristic energy, skill, and thoroughness.

On the other side of the English Channel the buildup of the largest invasion armada in history was proceeding on schedule. By the end of 1943, German submarines could do little to impede the progress of convoys transporting troops and huge stocks of planes, tanks, vehicles, arms, foodstuffs, and medical supplies from the United States. According to a popular joke, only barrage balloons kept the British Isles from sinking into the ocean under the weight of weapons and supplies.[3] Allied bombers continued to blast

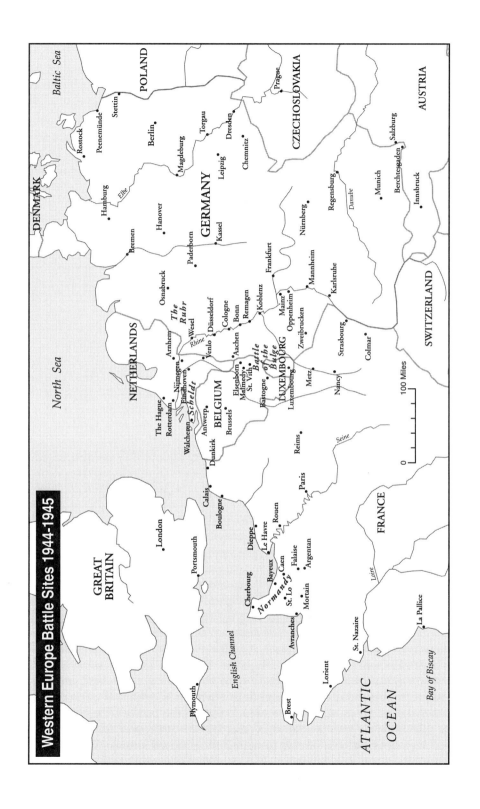

Western Europe Battle Sites 1944-1945

Baltic Sea

POLAND

DENMARK

Stettin
Peenemünde
Rostock
Berlin
Magdeburg
Torgau
Dresden
Prague
CZECHOSLOVAKIA
AUSTRIA
Salzburg
Berchtesgaden
Innsbruck
Munich
Regensburg
Nürnberg
Leipzig
Chemnitz
Hamburg
Hanover
Elbe
GERMANY
Kassel
Bremen
Paderborn
Osnabruck
The Ruhr
Frankfurt
Mannheim
Karlsruhe
Düsseldorf
Wesel
Rhine
Cologne
Bonn
Koblenz
Remagen
Venlo
Aachen
Mainz
Oppenheim
Zweibrucken
Strasbourg
Colmar
SWITZERLAND
Arnhem
Nijmegen
Eindhoven
Battle of the Bulge
LUXEMBOURG
Luxembourg
Metz
Nancy
Elsenborn
Malmédy
St. Vith
Bastogne
NETHERLANDS
Scheldt
The Hague
Rotterdam
Walcheren
Antwerp
BELGIUM
Brussels
Dunkirk

North Sea

Reims
Seine
100 Miles
0
Calais
Boulogne
Paris
London
Portsmouth
Dieppe
Le Havre
Rouen
FRANCE
GREAT BRITAIN
Cherbourg
Bayeux
Caen
Falaise
Argentan
St. Lo
Mortain
Avranches
Normandy
Loire
St. Nazaire
La Pallice
Plymouth
English Channel
Lorient
Brest
ATLANTIC OCEAN
Bay of Biscay

Germany, and the Red Army recaptured Kiev and most of Ukraine in November 1943. At the same time, a defiant Joseph Goebbels, who had no illusions about the enormous odds against the Reich, wrote in his diary: "We have burned the bridges behind us. We no longer can turn back, but we also no longer want to. We are forced to extremes, and therefore are also ready for extremes. We will go down in history either as the greatest statesmen or as the greatest criminals."[4] Goebbels did not live to see the second half of his prediction come true.

The Bombing of Germany

In the interwar period, military thinkers had established two objectives of strategic bombing: to inflict material damage by striking at industrial and military targets, and to undermine the enemy's morale by terrorizing and killing civilians. During the early years of the war, the British sought to achieve both objectives simultaneously, but the effort was too costly. In early 1942 they decided to concentrate on terror bombing by night. Destructive raids in the Rhineland in 1942 were followed by the fire-bombing of Hamburg, Kassel, and Magdeburg in the summer and fall of 1943. Aided by "Window," the code name for dropping bundles of tin foil to jam German radar, British bombers hit Berlin in sixteen major raids from November 1943 to March 1944. Firestorms did little damage to the capital city's more solidly constructed buildings and shelters, but 6,000 Berliners perished, and over a million were left homeless.

American strategists decided on precision bombing of industrial and military targets in daylight hours. United States commanders were convinced that their durable B–24 Liberator and the heavily armed B–17 Flying Fortress would be less vulnerable to German fighters and anti-aircraft guns. The newly developed Norden bombsight, they believed, would enable crews to locate strategic targets more precisely and drop their loads more accurately. These theories were practiced in 1943, as thousands of U.S. planes attacked factories, air installations, and transportation facilities. Like the British before them, the Americans discovered that daylight precision bombing was costly and did less damage than expected. Unlike their ally, the USAF (United States Army Air Force) persisted.

Among the many U.S. raids in the second half of 1943, two were particularly significant. In August, B–17s hit the rocket research station on the Baltic island of Peenemünde, where the Germans were constructing V–2 ballistic missile rockets. Partly because of bomb damage, the deployment of V–2 rockets had to be postponed until September 1944, two months after the Normandy invasion.[5] An October raid on the ball-bearings factory at Schweinfurt in central Germany had less fortunate results. With more fighter planes and anti-aircraft guns and an improved airborne radar device that could not be jammed by Window, the Germans shot down 60 U.S. bombers and damaged 140. Recognizing the need for more effective long-range fighter escorts, the USAF scaled back the number of daylight missions. Less than 10 percent of the Reich's productive capacity was damaged in 1943.

In early March 1944, the USAF resumed regular daylight raids with larger fleets of bombers escorted by the newly developed P-51 Mustang, one of the best long-range fighters of the war. Flying Fortresses and Liberators blasted aircraft factories, synthetic fuel plants, and transportation centers, while the British continued their relentless assault on civilians and cities. At the same time, Anglo-American raids on the French coast disrupted the Reich's communication and transportation facilities and helped soften Rommel's defenses for the Normandy invasion. When the Allies landed on June 6, 1944, the Luftwaffe's fleet of 300 planes was short of fuel, and the Wehrmacht found it difficult to move tanks, troops, and supplies where they were most needed. Following the establishment of beachheads in France, the Allies intensified their air assault on Germany. Between March and September, oil production declined from 316,000 to 17,000 tons; by the end of 1944, bombs had destroyed over 700,000 railroad cars. The Wehrmacht could not take full advantage of increased production in the summer of 1944 because of critical fuel shortages and clogged transportation arteries. Moreover, the heavy bombing forced a sharp increase in the production of anti-aircraft guns at the expense of field artillery, which significantly reduced the army's firepower. In 1944 Allied air raids damaged nearly 20 percent of Germany's manufacturing facilities.

As the Germans fell further behind in the production of conventional armaments in 1944, Hitler and his generals looked to new weapons that would stop or at least impede the progress of Anglo-American air and ground offensives. The most promising was the world's first jet-propelled aircraft, the Messerschmitt 262 (ME 262), ready for mass production in the fall of 1943. If Hitler had not insisted on converting these planes into fighter-bombers equipped to attack the cross-Channel invasion force and to bomb British cities, there might have been enough ME 262 fighters— whose top speed of 500 miles per hour was faster than any British or American aircraft—to stop or curtail the Allied air offensive in late 1943. Because of delays in the conversion process, only a few fighter-bombers could engage the enemy on D-Day. In September 1944 Hitler allowed several hundred ME 262s to be used as fighters, but they were overwhelmed by thousands of Spitfires and Mustangs. Moreover, a shortage of fuel and trained pilots grounded many of the jets. This revolutionary plane, which could have turned the tide in favor of the Reich, or at least prolonged the war, had little impact.

In mid-June 1944, Hitler unleashed the first of the *Vergeltung* (vengeance) weapons, the V-1, a pilotless jet-propelled plane. Throughout the summer thousands of "buzz bombs," as the British called them, were fired from sites along the Channel coast, targeting London and other British cities. Each one carried a one-ton warhead and flew up to 400 miles an hour. Thanks to a faulty guidance system and the relative ease with which they could be shot down, 75 percent of the V-1s never reached their targets, but the 25 percent that exploded on impact killed nearly 9,000 British civilians. In September the first V-2 rockets, also carrying one-ton warheads but flying nine times faster than the V-1, were launched. The Allies had no defense against these forerunners of modern medium-range ballistic missiles. They killed 2,700 people, mostly civilians. Fortunately for the British, most of the rockets missed their targets because of faulty launching mechanisms. As the Allied armies advanced, the Germans moved their launching sites further inland and aimed most of the missiles at Antwerp, the Belgian city that had become the Allies' major port of entry by the end of 1944. The V-2s inflicted only minor damage. Under constant bombardment, the Germans had neither the time nor the facilities to correct deficiencies and mass produce the vengeance missiles.

The Reich's dazzling technological feats had little effect on the outcome of the war. There were not enough new weapons, they were deployed too late, and the jet fighter's awesome defensive potential was wasted. In his memoirs, Speer blames the failure on Hitler and the bureaucratic tangle created by Himmler's bid for SS control of "miracle weapons" production. The massive expenditure of time and resources on the V-2s was wasted, according to Speer, because they "proved to be . . . an almost total failure." He writes that a lighter and more easily controlled ground-to-air

MARGARET BOURKE-WHITE

The picturesque center of Nuremberg, devastated by Allied bombs, suffered the same fate as many other German cities. The judicial complex where the post-war trials were held escaped damage.

BOX 11.1 ■ THE DRESDEN RAID: AN EYEWITNESS ACCOUNT

The Dresden raid, as eloquently described by an anonymous Swiss wartime municipal employee:

It sounded as if hell had erupted, because amid the ear-piercing roar of the low-flying bombers came an increasing number of explosions. It was a noise beyond the grasp of the senses, and all I remember is that I thought: Hell has broken loose! And then I saw the rising of a flaming sea which, within a few minutes, inundated the entire city in one huge glowing wave. . . . Huge red and yellow tongues of fire were roaring toward the sky. Streaming, trembling, madly onrushing clouds—dark brown, grayish yellow, red and white masses of smoke, which the storm whipped past the burning town only to have them replaced by new ones—intermingled with brilliant white, red, and yellow explosions out of which the big bombers seemed to rise like flocks of giant birds on their flight from hell. But they did not flee. . . . The most agonizing nightmare could not approach this . . . fascinating and horrible spectacle of Dresden's eclipse that took place before my eyes.

When the second attack came, there was no warning from any sirens because the entire power system had broken down. . . . still more fire and still more bombs rained down on the already doomed city. . . . This time there were at least five hundred four-motor planes at work. Again the attack lasted only twenty minutes. . . . Again, not a single anti-aircraft gun was firing, not a single night fighter had taken off to attempt a counterattack. . . .

The non-explosive bombs did not penetrate the paved or asphalted streets; the fire had wrought the destruction. . . . Even the victims in the Grosser Garten (a park) were not torn to pieces by explosive bombs, but were slain by a million incendiary sticks which had been thrown down over that park.

Ten days after the attack, the mountains of bodies had not been disposed of, in spite of the fact that big trucks had been put into service to carry the dead as quickly as possible to the mass graves. No one was taking the trouble to identify the bodies. They were simply loaded into these trucks, often together with debris and ashes.

Tony March, ed., *Darkness over Europe: First-Person Accounts of Life in Europe during the War Years 1939–1945* (Chicago: Rand McNally, 1987), pp. 188–90.

defensive rocket, successfully tested and developed in 1942, would have been a more effective weapon. This rocket, code-named Waterfall, in conjunction with the ME 262 used exclusively in a defensive capacity, "would have significantly weakened the Anglo-American air offensive."[6]

Whether any German weapon, machine, or strategy could have blunted the Allied air offensive in the last eight months of the war is questionable. Daily raids of 5,000 planes or more were normal from September 1944 to the end of the war. At least a million Germans, some of whom were fit for combat duty, manned anti-aircraft guns, while another million were engaged in the increasingly formidable task of repairing bomb-damaged facilities. By the beginning of 1945, U.S. planes had destroyed or damaged nearly all synthetic fuel plants, and the Soviets had captured the Ploesti oilfields in Romania. Communication and transportation centers had been crippled, and intensive bombing had reduced huge sections of Germany's great cities—Berlin, Cologne, Mannheim, Stuttgart, Munich, Nuremberg, Hanover, and Bremen—to piles of rubble.

One of the most destructive raids of the war occurred in mid-February 1945. Incendiary bombs from British and U.S. planes set off a gigantic firestorm in Dresden, a picturesque city in eastern Germany, whose population of 630,000 had been swelled by a flood of refugees. Having never been subjected to heavy air raids, Dresden was virtually defenseless. Modern scholars have shown that earlier estimates of 135,000 fatalities were exaggerated. The actual death toll was between 40,000 and 50,000, roughly the same as that of the Hamburg raid in 1943. The debate over the purpose of the raid, however, continues: why was a city with no strategic value, located in the path of advancing Soviet armies, attacked at all? A plausible answer is that Churchill ordered the raid to impress Stalin with the might of the Allied air offensive and to show that his western Allies were prepared to "take the war" to a part of eastern Germany that would fall under Soviet jurisdiction after the war.

Allied bombs did not win the war, but precision bombing of industrial and military targets may have shortened it. Damage to transportation and communication facilities and synthetic fuel plants helped ground the Luftwaffe, block the flow of war matériel and supplies, and reduce the effectiveness of "miracle weapons." Air strikes on military targets in France and the Low Countries contributed to the success of the Normandy invasion and subsequent campaigns. If some of the 2 million men needed at home to serve in anti-aircraft crews and civil defense roles could have been transferred to the front, they might have helped slow Russian and Allied offensives. Area bombing damaged 30 to 80 percent of fifty German cities, but it failed to undermine morale. The air attacks did, however, create an atmosphere of "great sorrow and insecurity among German civilians."[7] Whatever the benefits of strategic bombing, the cost for the Allies was high. The Germans destroyed or irreparably damaged 22,000 British and 18,000 U.S. aircraft and killed 160,000 Allied airmen. The entire operation cost the United States $43 billion. Despite tactical errors, heavy casualties, and disappointing results, the bombing of Germany established the importance of air power in modern warfare. Since 1945 few victories have been won without aerial supremacy.

Pre-Invasion Strategies

The bombardment of Belgium and northern France throughout the spring of 1944 was a dramatic demonstration of Allied superiority in human and material resources. It convinced Rommel that Germany's only chance for victory, and a slim one at best, was to crush the invaders on the beaches. Rundstedt believed that the Wehrmacht had a better chance of winning an inland battle of maneuvers, while Hitler felt that his most celebrated general was too pessimistic. Odds against the success of any German strategy were enormous. By June 1944 the Reich had 58 infantry divisions (up from 48 in 1943) and ten armored divisions, but most were down in strength at least 50 percent compared to 1940. Rommel's shore line defenses—mines, concrete stakes, steel spikes, barbed wire, bunkers, and gun shelters—were formidable, but he had neither the time nor the resources to fortify the entire 200-mile coastline from Calais to Normandy. Anticipating a landing at the Channel's narrowest point, Rommel made the level beaches of Calais, only twenty miles from England, the most impregnable stretch of the French coast.

Hitler sensed that the Allies might do the unexpected. Although Normandy was seventy-five miles from Britain and sections of its narrow beaches were closed off from the interior by high cliffs, he told Rundstedt a few weeks before D-Day that he "attached particular importance to Normandy."[8] Defending Calais still had the highest priority, but Hitler ordered the Atlantic Wall on the Normandy coast to be strengthened. Armored reinforcements, without which Rommel's plan could not possibly succeed, were stationed along the Seine River west of Paris. From this location, these tanks, which were forbidden to start their engines without a Führer order, could move either toward Calais or Normandy.

On the other side of the Channel, the Reich's adversaries staged one of the most elaborate deceptions in military history. The Allies bombed the Calais landing site more extensively than Normandy, sent false radio messages, and set up a vast dummy invasion force in southeastern England, directly across the Channel from Calais. Captured German agents in Britain who had secretly defected sent photographs of this bogus buildup and informed Berlin that General George Patton, whom Wehrmacht officers feared more than any other Allied general, would command the Calais invasion force. So effective was the deception that German generals four weeks after the Normandy landing were still expecting the main landing at Calais. Even Hitler was deceived.

Heavy storms in early June convinced Hitler and his generals that the Allies would not invade until the weather cleared. Rommel went home to Stuttgart on June 4 to celebrate his wife's birthday. Before retiring at 5:00 A.M. on June 6, Hitler left strict orders that he was not to be awakened before mid-afternoon. On the evening of June 5, General Dwight D. Eisenhower, whom Roosevelt had appointed supreme commander of Allied forces at the Teheran Conference, decided to take advantage of a break in the weather. With the words "OK, let's go!" Ike (his commonly used nickname) launched the massive invasion armada, code-named Operation Overlord. The first wave of twelve divisions was transported in 600 warships and over 4,000 transports and landing craft. Overhead were 12,000 planes.

From Normandy to Arnhem

Eisenhower planned to execute Operation Overlord in three stages. The break-in, during which the first wave of airborne and infantry troops would establish beachheads, would be followed by the buildup, the expansion of the invasion forces and the beachheads. Thereafter, the Allies were to break out toward Paris and the German border. Of the 150,000 troops landed on the first day on five separate beaches—the British and Canadians on Gold, Juneau, and Sword, and the Americans on Omaha and Utah, nearly 10,000 were killed or wounded. Omaha Beach, which was defended by combat-hardened German troops manning entrenched gun emplacements on bluffs overlooking the beach, accounted for half of the D-Day casualties. General Omar Bradley, operational commander of American forces, assured the Omaha-bound troops that naval gunfire and air bombardment would severely weaken German defenses and that paratroopers landing behind enemy lines would finish the job. He made a prediction that the soldiers would long remember and he would deeply regret: "You men should consider yourselves lucky. You are going to have ringside seats

NATIONAL ARCHIVES

Omaha Beach on June 7, showing the Allies' overwhelming superiority in manpower and matériel, looked quite different twenty-four hours earlier. Though almost everything that could go wrong did go wrong, costing 2500 American lives, the single most important thing succeeded: the landing.

BOX 11.2 ■ **AMERICAN OVERCONFIDENCE AT OMAHA BEACH**

Overconfidence at Omaha Beach, in the words of American soldiers.

From the 115th Infantry Regiment:

It came as quite a shock to many when, just prior to going ashore, the men assembled on the decks of the landingcraft had heard that they might have land fighting. Briefing had stressed the fact that the landing itself would be relatively simple; that the troops would merely walk ashore, make for the high ground, and then walk until the objective was reached. Many of the men had put on clean socks the night before in anticipation of a long hike their day ashore.

A private wrote:

I was dumb enough not to feel the slightest trepidation. We really thought that at any moment the whole Reich was going to collapse. We saw what we had, heard what they didn't have. We really thought that we only had to step off that beach and all the krauts would put up their hands.

Two veterans of the Sicilian campaign, a Captain Reed and General James Gavin, spoke of underestimating the Germans and overestimating air power.

Reed: "We have got to stop belittling the fighting ability of the German. The enemy is vicious, clever, and ruthless." Gavin wrote retrospectively in 1979: "For years we had been told that our weapons were superior to any we would encounter. After all, we were soldiers from the most highly industrialized and richest nation on earth. But the very preoccupation with our advanced technology caused many to assume technology alone would win battles—more emphasis was placed upon victory through air power than better infantry."

General Leonard Gerow, commander of the V Corps at Omaha, was supremely overconfident in his pre-invasion proclamation:

. . . . the Hun has been driven from the sea, annihilated by the Russians, kicked out of Africa, bombed from the air and is now nervously and hopelessly waiting for you to deliver the knockout blow. . . . No troops have ever entered battle better trained or more magnificently equipped. Supporting us will be the tremendous resources of the Allied Naval and Air Forces. Success is assured. With victory will come the eternal gratitude of freedom loving nations the world over."

Quoted in Adrian R. Lewis, *Omaha Beach: A Flawed Victory* (Chapel Hill: University of North Carolina Press, 2001), pp. 296–97.

for the greatest show on earth."[9] It was, instead, the greatest carnage of D-Day. The German defenses were nearly impregnable to naval and air attacks, and most of the paratroopers accidentally landed prematurely or in the wrong places. Despite the terrific pounding, the men on the spot were able to regroup, improvise, and eventually secure Omaha Beach by late afternoon of D-Day.

The outnumbered German defenders fought with their usual skill and tenacity, and the armor, which Hitler belatedly ordered to attack the beachheads, helped the Wehrmacht contain the Allies near the Normandy landing sites. Nevertheless, by June 27 the buildup phase of Overlord was complete. A million troops had landed, and U.S. forces had captured the port city of Cherbourg. After three weeks of heavy fighting over relatively short distances, during which U.S. troops were slowed by hedgerows (high earthen banks topped by thick hedges that were well-suited to defensive warfare), Anglo-American forces captured Caen and Saint-Lo, two strategically located Norman towns. In seven weeks the Allies, still only a few miles from the landing sites, but finally in a position to begin the breakout, had suffered 117,000 casualties, all of which were quickly replaced. The Wehrmacht could replace only 10 percent of its 113,000 casualties.[10]

When the breakout began on July 25, the Allied High Command had divided its armies into two groups. Montgomery commanded the 21st Army Group, mostly British and Canadian, while Bradley led the U.S. 12th Army Group, which included Patton's Third Army. On the German side, Hitler replaced Rundstedt with Field Marshal Günther von Kluge. Rommel suffered a fractured skull and other serious injuries when British aircraft attacked his staff car on July 17, only three days before the anti-Hitler conspirators' assassination attempt, in which he was marginally implicated. Both Rundstedt and Rommel had told Hitler that the Wehrmacht's position on the western front was hopeless. The change in command had little effect on German strategy. On August 2, Hitler foolishly ordered a counterattack: "We must strike like lightning. When we reach the sea the American spearheads will be cut off. . . . We might even be able to cut off their entire beachhead."[11] The plan nearly destroyed his entire western front.

The final battle for Normandy took place near the town of Falaise. The Allies easily repulsed the counterattack and forced the Wehrmacht into a partly enclosed valley, called the Falaise pocket or gap. Hitler replaced Kluge, who had led the retreat into the Falaise pocket, with the steadfastly loyal Field Marshal Walter Model. A few days later, Kluge committed suicide. With the bulk of the Reich's western army trapped, Bradley sought to close their narrow escape route by linking U.S. forces moving north with British and Canadian troops advancing south from Caen. Bradley's troops reached the linkup point, but the progress of their counterparts from the north had been slowed by Montgomery's delay in sending reinforcements and by unexpectedly heavy German resistance. Thus, the British and Canadians did not close the gap. The U.S. Third Army was in an excellent position to seal off the Germans' escape route, but Bradley ordered Patton's army to advance eastward toward Paris. The failure to close the pincers movement allowed the Waffen SS Hitler Youth Division, stationed at the neck of the Falaise pocket, to hold it open until August 19. As a result 35,000 German troops escaped, salvaging 25,000 vehicles.

The Allies had missed a golden opportunity to annihilate the bulk of the German army in France, but it was still a stunning victory. The Germans left behind 50,000 prisoners, 10,000 dead, and the wreckage of nearly a thousand tanks. On August 20, Hitler ordered his Fifteenth Army, which was still waiting for the invasion at Calais, to help stabilize the front on the Seine west of Paris. It was too late. The Wehrmacht was powerless to stop Patton's Third Army rolling toward the Reich's border south of Paris. North of the French capital, Allied forces driving eastward from Falaise encountered little resistance.

The Allies had not planned to capture Paris, but at General de Gaulle's request, Eisenhower sent American troops to reinforce the French general's army and resistance fighters in the city. Together, American and French forces liberated Paris on August 25. Casualties were light, and like Rome, the City of Light escaped serious damage. There might have been more destruction if the German commander, Dietrich von Choltitz, had obeyed Hitler's order to turn Paris into a western Stalingrad. Soon after the liberation, Montgomery's army group swung north into Belgium and Luxembourg, while Patton's forces continued their drive through eastern France toward the German border. By September 15, British and American armies had captured most of Belgium, placing them only a few miles from the Reich. To the south, Patton's Third Army was in Lorraine close to the Franco-German border. The Germans offered only light resistance.

At the end of August, as Allied armies had outrun their supply lines, Eisenhower discussed future strategy with Montgomery and Patton. Both generals proposed a massive single strike directly into Germany, knowing that only one of them could make the assault; the other would have to halt in order to conserve supplies. From Belgium, Montgomery believed that he could take the Rhineland and the Ruhr in a matter of weeks, while Patton was certain that the Wehrmacht could not stop his Third Army driving from eastern France directly into the Reich and reaching the Rhine south of the Ruhr by October 1. Eisenhower overruled both proposals. Either plan, he argued, ran the risk of Allied forces being outflanked by the Wehrmacht, which could then launch a counterattack. His more cautious approach called for an advance along a broad front stretching from the Netherlands to the Swiss border. The broad-front strategy dictated the slower movement of men and supplies, but it would allow Allied forces to destroy all pockets of resistance west of the Rhine and advance toward Berlin virtually unimpeded. No strategy could succeed, however, until Allied forces had been sufficiently resupplied.

A principal reason for the supply problem was that Hitler ordered his troops on the Channel coast, whom the Allies had separated from the rest of the Wehrmacht, to hold the French ports of Le Havre, Boulogne, Dunkirk, and Calais, as well as the Scheldt estuary in Belgium. It was a decision which, in the words of John Keegan, "demonstrated once again his uncanny ability . . . to avoid the worst consequences of his acts of operational folly."[12] Wehrmacht demolition experts had previously destroyed the docks at Brest and severely damaged port facilities at Cherbourg. They were not repaired until late October.

Anglo-American troops captured Antwerp in early September, but the Belgian seaport located on the Scheldt River nearly sixty miles from the sea was blocked by fierce German resistance along the estuary. The

Allies could not use Antwerp's docks until they had cleared the waterway in late November 1944. Eisenhower's broad-front strategy remains controversial to this day. Most military historians agree that Allied armies might have reached the Rhine by late fall 1944, but could have advanced no farther until multiple supply routes had opened.[13] That did not happen until early 1945.

Overruled in the broad-front/narrow-front dispute, the usually cautious Montgomery proposed a daring plan, code-named Operation Market-Garden: The Allies would cross the Rhine in the Netherlands with airborne troops acting as a spearhead for infantry and armored divisions on the ground. The paratroopers were to capture five bridges in the Rhine delta, the most important of which was at Arnhem, located at the farthest end of the drop zone. With this site firmly secured, ground troops supplied from the air would have a clear path into northwest Germany. Along the way they could take out the Reich's V-2 rocket launching pads. The odds favored the Allies if they encountered only light resistance at the landing sites or on the road traveled by ground forces. According to Stephen Ambrose, Eisenhower enthusiastically endorsed Market-Garden; two decades after the war he told the historian: "I not only approved of Market-Garden, I insisted on it." Eisenhower had an "irresistible impulse to keep attacking," writes Ambrose, and he also hoped, as did Montgomery, that Market-Garden would overrun V-2 launching sites.[14] (The first V-2 rockets hit London on September 8.)

Montgomery launched Market-Garden on September 17. Despite unexpectedly heavy resistance, the Allies took four of the sites in a few days. The British First Airborne Division, assigned the unenviable task of taking the "bridge too far" at Arnhem, was mauled by German ground troops and two SS Panzer divisions that happened to be in the Dutch city for repairs and refitting.[15] The Dutch underground and Ultra, the code name for British cryptographers who had cracked the German code, knew the precise location of the SS armor, but Montgomery ignored their warning. The Allies suffered 12,000 casualties, at least 2,000 more than on D-Day. Had Market-Garden's forces been deployed to clear the Scheldt estuary, the supply routes to the German border by way of Antwerp might have been open in late September. After the Arnhem debacle, Eisenhower, who had been appointed the supreme field commander in early September (much to the chagrin of Montgomery), finally ordered the British general to attack the well-defended Scheldt estuary. It was not cleared until December.

Market-Garden marked the end of a period of solid Allied victories and forward momentum. Anglo-American forces were near the German border, but limited supplies, the increasing number of inexperienced replacements, and exceptionally cold and wet weather kept them from launching a major offensive. The Germans enjoyed a brief respite, during which they strengthened the "West Wall," a term designating their defenses along the Franco-Belgian border. To the Siegfried Line, a stationary fortification that paralleled the Maginot Line in places, they added land mines, barbed wire, gun emplacements, and tank traps. Making the West Wall even more formidable was the arrival of hundreds of heavy tanks and over 100,000 men. The source of this additional manpower and armor was the home army commanded by Himmler, who had replaced the disgraced General Fromm following the July 20 plot. Himmler was also responsible for recruiting and training young teenagers and middle-aged men for the *Volkssturm*, a new home guard to be used as the last line of defense inside the Reich.

Though the odds were heavily against a breakthrough, Eisenhower ordered an attack. General Courtney Hodges's First Army crossed the German border in October, penetrated the Siegfried Line, and after intensive street-by-street combat in which both sides suffered heavy casualties, took the city of Aachen. It was the first city inside the Reich to fall to the Allies. Aachen had little strategic value, but as the medieval emperor Charlemagne's capital city, it had some symbolic importance. The First Army, intending to close on the Rhine, then moved south through a densely wooded area called the Hürtgen Forest. They took the forest, but did not reach the Rhine. Fighting "under conditions as bad as American soldiers ever had to face," the First Army suffered 24,000 combat casualties and lost another 9,000 soldiers to trench foot, disease, or combat exhaustion. To the south, Patton's Third Army encountered stiff resistance while slowly advancing through the hilly countryside of Lorraine. It did not reach the West Wall until mid-December. Battle casualties numbered 47,039.[16] Though U.S. forces were just inside or very near the German border by early December 1944, they had lost tens of thousands of men, and supply shortages persisted. At its most vulnerable time since Omaha Beach, the U.S. army was about to face Hitler's last desperate offensive in the west and to fight the largest battle in its history, the Battle of the Bulge.

The Eastern Front

Hitler launched Operation Barbarossa on a broad front in June 1941. Three years later his battered legions, outnumbered 4 to 1, were defending themselves on a broad front from northeastern Romania in the south to Finland and the Baltic states in the north. By the end of 1943, the Soviets had the numbers and equipment to destroy German forces using the conventional massive frontal assault, but they had become practiced at maneuver, surprise, and initiative, which were far more effective, and less costly, than the "sledgehammer approach" of the first years of the war. The Germans, on the other hand, had lost so many men and so much equipment that they could no longer blunt Soviet offensives with the quick, sharp counterattacks that had been so effective in 1943. Moreover, fighting partisans in the rear had also taken its toll.[17] The Soviets took full advantage of the Wehrmacht's vulnerability. During the first months of 1944, the Red Army drove the Germans out of the Ukraine, occupied the Romanian province of Bessarabia, and invaded Finland and the Baltic states. Stalin had assured Roosevelt and Churchill that his June offensive, coinciding with the Allied invasion of France, would prevent Hitler from reinforcing the Atlantic Wall.

The Germans knew that Stalin was planning a major offensive, but deceptive maneuvers kept them guessing as to its precise location. Facing the awesome power of a 5,000,000-man army spearheaded by 5,200 tanks with an air cover of 6,000 planes, the Germans had to reckon with the heaviest concentration of forces striking either the Baltic region, White Russia and eastern Poland in the center, or Romania and Hungary in the south. Soviet forces attacked all three areas, but the most powerful offensive—118 divisions supported by 43 tank brigades—was unleashed in the center on June 23, 1944. By the beginning of July, they had driven the enemy from White Russia, torn a 250-mile gap in the German line, killed or captured nearly 200,000 men, and destroyed 900 tanks. The magnitude of the Wehrmacht's defeat, which matched the Stalingrad and Kursk disasters, allowed the Soviets to overrun eastern Poland. They reached the outskirts of Warsaw by the end of July, triggering one of the greatest massacres of the war.

Expecting Soviet reinforcements, the Polish home army rebelled on August 1, 1944. They managed to hold out during several weeks of heavy fighting, but received no Soviet aid despite an urgent appeal to Stalin from Roosevelt and Churchill "to drop supplies and ammunition to the patriot Poles of Warsaw." When the Germans finally suppressed the rebellion, Hitler ordered Erich von dem Bach-Zelewski, general of the Higher SS and Police Leader Corps and a specialist in anti-partisan operations, to destroy the city and deport its inhabitants. His methods were exceptionally cruel even by SS standards: wounded insurgents were drenched with gasoline and burned alive, women and children were chained to tanks to silence Polish anti-tank weapons, and crowded hospitals were set on fire. When the Poles surrendered in early October, the Germans had slaughtered nearly 250,000 people, deported over 700,000 to concentration camps or forced-labor facilities, and destroyed virtually every building in the city. Soviet forces had outrun their supply lines, but if Stalin had given the order, they could have aided the Polish insurgents. The Red Army received no such order, resulting in a great political victory for the Soviet dictator. The Germans saved him the trouble of liquidating the nationalist home army, which would have presented a formidable obstacle to the establishment of communist rule in Poland.[18]

The Red Army was uniformly successful throughout eastern Europe in the fall of 1944. Finland surrendered, but retained its independence. A Soviet sweep through the Baltic region in September and October resulted in the recapture of Estonia, northern Latvia, and Lithuania. The collapse of the German front in the south led to the defection of several satellite states. In Romania, anti-German forces overthrew General Ion Antonescu's Fascist regime and surrendered to the Soviets. The Red Army occupied Bulgaria and helped Marshal Tito's Communist partisans capture Belgrade on October 20. At the same time, a revolt of Slovakian partisans, even with Soviet

NORTH SEA

DENMARK

NETHERLANDS

Amsterdam

Hamburg

Elbe R.

BALTIC SEA

Danzig

Rastenburg

Third White
Russian Front
(Chernyakovsky)

EAST
PRUSSIA

Stettin

Second White
Russian
Front (Rokossovsky)

Vistula R.

Berlin

Potsdam

Oder R.

Lodz

Warsaw

POLAND

Antwerp

GERMANY

Torgau

Dresden

BELGIUM

Rhine R.

Remagen

Frankfurt

Prague

First
Ukrainian Front
(Petrov)

LUX.

Rheims

Strasbourg

Colmar

20 January

Pilsen

Stuttgart

Danube R.

"West Wall"
German
defences

Vienna

Fourth
Ukrainian Front
(Petrov)

SWITZ.

AUSTRIA

Budapest

HUNGARY

Second
Ukrainian Front
(Malinovsky)

FRANCE

Milan

Dongo

Trieste

Turin

ITALY

Venice

Genoa

Bologna

Ravenna

15 January

ROMANIA

Third
Ukrainian
Front
(Tolbukhin)

YUGOSLAVIA

BULGARIA

CORSICA

SARDINIA

0   125   250 Miles

0   125   250 Kilometers

COLLAPSE ON THE EASTERN FRONT

Front line, 19 August 1944
Front line, 26 September
Front line, 31 December
Front line, 11 January 1945
Front line, 8 February
Front line, 20 February

reinforcements, was overcome by tenacious German resistance in the Carpathian Mountains. In Hungary, a new Fascist regime and German reinforcements could not stop the Soviet juggernaut, which reached the outskirts of Budapest in early November. By January 1945 southern Latvia, the western half of Poland, parts of Hungary, and the northern fringes of the Balkans were all that remained of Hitler's eastern empire. Soviet forces had also occupied the eastern part of East Prussia, the first penetration of pre-war German territory. Like the Allies in western Europe, however, the Red Army had to be resupplied before mounting a massive attack against the Reich.

War and Diplomacy, December 1944–April 1945

In late August 1944, Hitler decided to use his last reserves in the west for an offensive through the Ardennes, the site of the Wehrmacht's spectacular breakthrough in 1940. However, his objectives for what would become the

Reich's second Ardennes offensive were quite different. A breakthrough on the western front, he told Speer, "will lead to a collapse and panic among the Americans. . . . [When] we take Antwerp . . . they'll have lost their supply harbor. . . . And there'll be a huge encirclement of the entire English army with hundreds of thousands of prisoners. Like it was in Russia!"[19] Rundstedt, whom Hitler reappointed as western commander-in-chief in early September, and General Model were skeptical, but they had to obey the Führer, who had assumed operational command for the Reich's last offensive of the war. In early November, Rundstedt and Model received specific details: reinforced with seventeen infantry and ten armored divisions—a larger force than Guderian had in 1940—Rundstedt's army was to strike the Ardennes line, which was defended by only four U.S. divisions. The objectives were to cut off Allied armies holding eastern Belgium north of the Ardennes and block the main supply route by capturing Antwerp. Hitler believed that he could split the enemy coalition and force the British to leave the war. Despite the U.S. Army's impressive performance in July and August, he still had a low opinion of the combat capabilities of American troops. Hitler assured his generals that a German victory in Belgium would seriously demoralize the American home front and enable him to reconstruct the eastern front, which had been robbed of some of its finest divisions for the Ardennes. Hitler was prepared to gamble his last reserves on an offensive that, given the Allies' overwhelming superiority in human and material resources, his generals knew, and he must have known, had almost no chance to succeed.

The Wehrmacht's progress during the first few days of "Operation Autumn Fog," launched on December 16, seemed to justify Hitler's confidence. For reasons not entirely clear, he insisted that the radio should not be used to communicate the most sensitive information regarding the offensive. Thus, Ultra was unable to intercept any messages indicating specifically that German forces were massed at the Belgian border for an attack—an attack which came as a complete tactical surprise. Ultra did detect the transfer of tanks and troops from the east to the west, but Eisenhower and Bradley, certain that the enemy lacked strength for an assault, attached little importance to its troop movements. With its four U.S. divisions, the Ardennes was the weakest point in the Allied line. Two of the three infantry divisions had suffered heavy casualties in the Hürtgen Forest; the third, made up mostly of men under age twenty, was entirely new to combat, and the single armored division was inexperienced.[20] The Germans enjoyed yet another advantage: heavy cloud cover grounded Allied combat and reconnaissance aircraft.

The Wehrmacht's reinforced armored and infantry divisions quickly overran the badly outnumbered American defenders during the first days of the offensive. The Germans benefited from the absence of Allied air cover and the delay in sending reinforcements, which was due largely to Eisenhower's initial belief that the attack was not a major offensive. Nevertheless, he did move armored divisions from the north closer to the Ardennes and

> **BOX 11.3 ■   THE BATTLE OF THE BULGE: INTERVIEWS WITH SURVIVORS**
>
> Based on interviews with survivors, Stephen Ambrose describes the bitter cold of the Ardennes in December 1944 and its effects on the soldiers in the foxholes:
>
> > . . . . the men got directives on how to prevent trench foot. They were ordered to massage their feet and change their socks every day. Sergeant Lick recalled, "We would remove our wet socks, hang them around our neck to dry, massage our feet and then put on the dry socks from around our neck that we had put there the day before.
> >
> > The best way to avoid trench foot (which some senior officers thought to be malingering) was to lace the boots lightly and take them off before climbing into a sleeping bag. . . . But, Lick said, "we couldn't take our boots off when we slept because they would freeze solid and we couldn't get them on again in the morning."
> >
> > Men wrapped their feet in burlap sacks, when available, but the burlap soaked up the snow, [making] the boots soggy and the socks wet. Sergeant Lick lost all his toenails but through regular massages and a rotation of his socks he avoided trench foot. Trench foot put more men out of action than German 88s, mortars, or machine-gun fire. During the winter of 1944–45, some 45,000 men had to be pulled out of the front line because of trench foot—the equivalent of three divisions.
> >
> > First a man lost his toenails. His feet turned white, then purple, finally black. A serious case of trench foot made walking impossible. Many men lost their toes, some had to have their feet amputated. If gangrene set in, the doctors had to amputate the lower leg. It has to be doubted that many men did this deliberately. A shot in the foot was much quicker, less dangerous, and nearly impossible to prove that it hadn't been an accident.
>
> Stephen E. Ambrose, *Citizen Soldiers*, pp. 259–60.

ordered Patton's Third Army on the southern flank to reinforce the Ardennes if the attack should develop into a full-scale offensive. During the first week, the Wehrmacht had created a bulge in the Allied line 65 miles deep and 45 miles wide, from which the battle took its name. Both sides sustained heavy losses in some of the bloodiest and most intensive combat experienced by any army in World War II. The horror of combat was compounded by the bitter cold of one of the worst winters in a century. The snow was waist-deep in places, and thousands of soldiers had to be evacuated from the front because of frostbite, frozen extremities, and trench foot. The latter was particularly common among American troops, who spent long, agonizing hours in foxholes with light jackets and wet socks. For reasons not entirely clear, U.S. frontline troops during the first days of the Battle of the Bulge had not been supplied with winter clothing.

By December 25, German armor and infantry had completely sur-rounded the strategically located city of Bastogne, but no further advance was possible. They had launched the offensive with a critical fuel shortage, and their failure to capture Allied fuel storage tanks compounded the shortage. While a few German divisions were at full strength, most were undermanned and, in the words of SS Panzer general Sepp Dietrich, were "made up chiefly of kids and sick old men."[21] Momentum began shifting to the Allies on December 23 when the skies cleared. Fighter bombers im-mobilized the German armor that still had fuel and inflicted heavy casual-ties on ground troops. When Eisenhower and Bradley finally realized that Operation Autumn Fog was a full-blown offensive, they dispatched rein-forcements, which, along with the stubborn defense of the besieged troops, kept the Germans from taking Bastogne. On December 26, Patton's Third Army arrived and forced the attackers to abandon the siege and begin a tactical withdrawal. When Montgomery's army moved on the bulge from the north on January 3, the Wehrmacht was in retreat.

By January 16 the battle was over, but not before more heavy fight-ing. The retreating Germans fought tenaciously against mostly American troops, who had finally been resupplied. In retrospect it appears that they could have simply bypassed the bulge and isolated what was left of the original attack force. Some of Eisenhower's generals actually suggested that approach, but the cautious Supreme Commander ordered his armies to clear the bulge area of all pockets of German resistance. It was a costly ef-fort for the Allies, but it may have helped to weaken the Reich's Rhineland defense force. In any case, it was at the time, and remains to this day, an-other controversial decision. For the Allies, the Battle of the Bulge was by far the largest and costliest single battle of the war in Europe. They suffered 81,000 casualties, all but 4,000 American. From December 16 to January 16, the Germans killed over 19,000 Americans and took another 15,000 prisoner. The Wehrmacht's losses—100,000 men, 800 tanks, and 1000 planes—were greater, and irreplaceable. The Battle of the Bulge briefly de-layed the Allied drive into the Rhineland, but the Wehrmacht never re-gained the offensive in the west, and its defensive capability in the east was further weakened. At best, Hitler's last gamble "bought a little time at great cost."[22]

In late January 1945, Allied armies, more powerful than ever, invaded the Rhineland. The anticipated crossing of the river in one to two weeks, however, did not materialize. The depleted, battered remnants of the Wehrmacht resisted stubbornly and flooded the terrain with water released by blowing up dams on the Roer River, a tributary of the Rhine. Progress was slow, and casualties were greater than expected, but by the beginning of March the invaders had secured the west bank of the Rhine from north of Cologne and the Ruhr south to Mainz, a distance of over 100 miles. Ger-man demolition crews had destroyed bridges along this stretch of the river, but inexplicably failed to blow up a railroad bridge at Remagen, about twenty miles below Cologne. On March 7, U.S. forces captured the bridge, and within twenty-four hours 8,000 men had crossed the Rhine. Thousands more, with equipment and vehicles, followed during the next few days.

The Allied crossing of the Rhine infuriated Hitler. He convened a special court martial to try the Remagen demolition crew and had four of them executed. For the third time he dismissed Rundstedt—who had strongly objected to Hitler's insistence on defending the west bank of the Rhine—as supreme commander on the western front. The old warrior's replacement was Field Marshal Albert Kesselring, who had gained experience in defensive warfare in Italy. The new commander, however, could not slow the Allied juggernaut, especially after Patton's Third Army established a bridgehead south of Mainz using assault boats and then rapidly building a pontoon bridge. The path to the Reich's heartland lay open.

By early January 1945, over 5 million Soviet troops were deployed on the eastern front from East Prussia to the outskirts of Budapest, a distance of over 500 miles. Marshal Zhukov and General Ivan Konev, commanders of the twin spearheads of the main attack launched on January 12, had at their disposal over 2 million men, 3,500 tanks, 28,000 heavy guns, and 10,000 planes. Their objectives were to drive the Germans out of western Poland, occupy eastern Germany, and take Berlin, about 450 miles due west. The Wehrmacht could deploy only 600,000 men, 700 tanks, 8,000 guns, and 1,300 planes. Stalin ordered another army group to take Danzig and cut off East Prussia, while a force to the south was to complete the conquest of Hungary and advance toward Czechoslovakia.

After a month of heavy fighting, Zhukov's army had established two bridgeheads on the Oder River, only thirty-three miles from Berlin's eastern suburbs. Konev's army group had also crossed the Oder in Silesia, sixty miles southeast of Berlin. The northern group had reached Danzig and cut off the defenders of East Prussia. Battling reinforced divisions in Hungary, and the Red Army captured Budapest on February 14. Still-formidable German defenses and overextended Russian supply lines, however, forced Stalin to halt offensive operations at the Oder River, inside Germany's pre-war borders.

When the Big Three met at Yalta in the Crimea from February 4 to 11, 1945, the Red Army had driven 300 miles in eighteen days and was about to cross the Oder River, the last natural barrier on the road to Berlin. The Allies were inside the Reich, but had not yet reached the Rhine. The positions of the two armies, however, had little effect on previous agreements. A joint advisory commission established at Teheran had drawn the borders for the division of Germany into three roughly equal zones of occupation. Roosevelt and Churchill proposed that the French should share in the governance of Germany. Stalin agreed on condition that the French zone would be taken from territory assigned to Britain and the United States. The Big Three decided on a similar four-power occupation of Berlin, 110 miles inside the Soviet zone.

Stalin renewed his demand for the cession of German territory east of the Oder-Neisse line to Poland; already German residents were fleeing or being expelled from that region. Roosevelt and Churchill tentatively approved. The Big Three reaffirmed the unconditional surrender policy, but agreed to leave tactical decisions to field commanders. They also agreed to try Nazi war criminals and to de-Nazify, demilitarize, and democratize German society, although they differed widely on the interpretation of the latter. All Yalta decisions, including the controversial questions of free elections in eastern Europe and incentives for Stalin's declaration of war on Japan, were based on the assumption that the anti-Nazi alliance would outlast the war. Stalin's refusal to hold free elections in Romania and Poland after Yalta signaled cracks in that alliance.

Within weeks after the Yalta Conference, Allied armies in the west and the Red Army in the east were closing in on what was left of the Third Reich. After establishing bridgeheads at several locations on the Rhine, armies under Eisenhower's command surrounded the Ruhr and captured several hundred thousand German troops. Allied troops encountered relatively light resistance as they drove into the heart of the Reich. By the end of March, a rapidly advancing U.S. force of approximately 50,000 men (a small fraction of the total) was less than 100 miles from Berlin. Its commander, General William Simpson, and Montgomery urged Eisenhower to allow these troops to march on Berlin—as did Churchill, who was growing increasingly suspicious of Stalin's intentions. The British prime minister felt strongly that the British and Americans "should shake hands with the Russians as far to the east as possible." Eisenhower decided against it. On March 31 he proposed to Stalin that the Elbe River, where Allied troops would link up with the Red Army, would become a temporary line of demarcation between the Soviet and Anglo-American armies. Stalin quickly agreed, claiming that Berlin, which lay to the east of the Elbe, no longer had much strategic significance. The Soviet dictator, who was eager to take Berlin, was lying. Alarmed at Eisenhower's rapid advance into central Germany, he advanced his timetable for the Berlin offensive.[23]

Eisenhower's decision, controversial at the time, probably saved the lives of thousands of Allied soldiers, who would almost certainly have perished in the battle for Berlin. He also knew that Roosevelt, Churchill, and Stalin had agreed to divide Germany into zones of occupation after the war and that Berlin would lie in the Soviet zone. Even if American forces had taken the city, the Yalta agreement would have required them to withdraw from what would become the Soviet sector of Berlin as well as all territory east of the Elbe. Certain that the Red Army would take the Reich's capital, Eisenhower targeted as important military objectives the Leipzig-Dresden area and the "National Redoubt" in the mountains of southern Germany, where it was believed that fanatical Nazi forces would make a last-ditch stand against the Allies, thus prolonging the war for months. Between April 20 and May 4, American troops dispatched to the south captured Nuremberg, Munich, and Hitler's mountain retreat at Berchtesgaden, but they discovered that the National Redoubt was a myth—a myth that Goebbels had cleverly fostered since the end of 1944. The National Redoubt had yet another important consequence. On April 25, before Eisenhower had learned that it did not exist, Patton's Third Army crossed the Czech border and was in an excellent position to take Prague. To avoid a clash with the Russians, Eisenhower ordered Patton's army to halt and take a sharp right turn into Austria, in the direction of the illusory redoubt. The outspoken American general and the British were furious. They believed, and most modern historians agree, that U.S. forces could easily have taken Prague, which might have kept the Soviets from occupying Czechoslovakia. The Czech capital fell to the Red Army on May 9.[24]

Stalin was pleased with Eisenhower's controversial decisions, but the Soviet dictator, who suspected that his Anglo-American allies might try to "beat him" to Berlin, ordered his two top generals to hurry their preparations, so that a final assault would begin no later than April 16. Zhukov's forces were to encircle the city from the north, while Konev's troops would swing around from the south. The two armies would then meet west of the city, which would be surrounded, and close in for the kill. The two Soviet marshals followed Stalin's orders to the letter. On the morning of April 16, 1945, 1.5 million Soviet troops, supported by an enormous mass of artillery and tanks, launched the final attack on the capital of the Third Reich. It would be the last battle of World War II in Europe.

The Last Days of the Third Reich

In November 1944, Hitler abandoned his headquarters in East Prussia in favor of the Reich Chancellery in Berlin. The frequency and intensity of Allied air raids gradually forced him to spend more time in the bunker underneath the Chancellery. By the beginning of March, he had taken up permanent residence in the bunker, which housed offices, communications facilities, meeting rooms, and living quarters. Hitler's declining health at age 55 was clearly visible—an "ashen complexion," stooped shoulders, tremors in his limbs, and a left foot that dragged when he walked. Already at the end of December 1944, when it was clear that the Ardennes offensive had failed, one of his generals was shocked by the Führer's "stooped figure with a pale and puffy face, hunched in his chair, his hands trembling, his left arm subject to a violent twitching which he did his best to conceal, a sick man apparently borne down by the burden of his responsibility."[25] According to his personal physician, Theodor Morrell, Hitler suffered from Parkinson's disease, high blood pressure, colitis and other painful digestive disorders, insomnia, and nervous exhaustion.

Although his colleagues regarded Morrell as a dishonest and greedy quack, Hitler trusted him implicitly. While it is still widely believed that the physician's injections and tonics did great harm to Hitler physically and psychologically, Morrell's diary and its editor, the controversial British historian David Irving, show that the Führer was given relatively small doses of

Berlin, May 1945. Two old survivors of World War I sit amidst the ruins of World War II.

vitamins and mild drugs during the last two years of the war to restore his flagging energy. Some of the ingredients were produced in Morrell's factory, from which he made a handsome profit, but as one of Hitler's most ardent admirers, he was genuinely trying to help his famous patient. Irving insists that Hitler never had a serious addiction problem and that Morrell's treatments did not significantly aggravate his physical or mental condition.[26] Two of Hitler's leading biographers, Ian Kershaw and Joachim Fest, agree that Morrell's medications and tonics were neither physically toxic nor addictive. Kershaw points out that his unhealthy life style seriously weakened his physical condition and that enormous mental strain and excessive stress aggravated pre-existing personality disorders, such as phobias, hypochondria, hysterical reactions, and paranoia. However sick and prematurely old he may have looked, what is most remarkable about Hitler during the last months of the war, Fest writes, is the "consistency . . . with which he took up and carried out his early obsessions. He was a person who continually needed artificial charging. In a sense Morrell's drugs and medicines replaced the old stimulus of mass ovations."[27]

It is indisputable that by January 1945 Hitler was a very sick man who needed Morrell's ministrations to stave off totally debilitating mental and physical conditions. Even as his body weakened, however, his indomitable will gave him the strength to direct defensive strategy and exercise absolute authority over his subordinates. As death and destruction escalated during the first months of 1945, Hitler angrily rejected the notion of a separate peace with either the Soviets or the West, as suggested by Goebbels, Göring, and Himmler. The Führer would consider negotiations only if there were a military success, and the chances of that were virtually nonexistent. Thus, he could speak of little else but "will overcoming adversity, of holding out until 'five minutes past midnight.' Meanwhile, Germany burned."[28] Hitler knew little and cared less about his people's misery outside the bunker. In the words of biographer Alan Bullock, "the underground bunker represented a closed world in which a separate drama," isolated from the tragedy of war outside, took place. "The link between the two," writes Bullock, "was the daily situation reports and conferences, which in the final weeks bore less and less relationship to what was happening in the real world."[29]

With much of its highly industrialized infrastructure destroyed in the last months of the war, Germany finally "ceased to work." Everywhere there were signs: once great cities reduced to rubble, administrative chaos, severe food and fuel shortages, multitudes of homeless people, roads

---

**BOX 11.4 ■ THE RUSSIANS ENTER BERLIN:
AN 11-YEAR-OLD'S ACCOUNT**

An eleven-year-old boy, who lived through the Russian conquest of Berlin, describes the horrors, which included SS men executing fellow Germans:

> The fighting got so bad that we could not leave our basement. When there was a lull, we went up and saw soldiers marching, carrying their weapons, and lines of horse-drawn wagons. There were endless lines of people walking or pushing carts with their belongings. You could hardly walk in the streets anymore because of dead horse, dead pigs, or dead people. . . .

> One morning we heard a terrible pounding on our steel door. My grandmother opened it, and there were two Russian soldiers with guns. We clung to our mother. The Russians searched our house looking, maybe, for soldiers. They took my mother's jewelry and her watch, then left. During the day more troops came. Women started to run away because of—I didn't know what sex was like until I saw it in the streets—rape. There was a lot of rape and looting going on, and people were being shot.

> The SS shot a lot of German soldiers because they were not interested in fighting anymore. They killed not only young boys who were crying that they wanted to go home, but many soldiers because they had lost their will to fight. They were even hanged from the lampposts as traitors. And I remember quite clearly when my brother and his friends went into the basement of a house that had been bombed: there were five German soldiers sitting there, all shot. Then the Russians did the same things, only much worse because the women had to run for their lives. . . . [His mother escaped, but many of their neighbors were raped and murdered.]

> [He concludes:]

> At the age of 11, I was already a man. . . . I had seen German soldiers hanged, children shot, women raped. I had seen everything. I was a man.

Steinhoff, Pechel, and Showalter, *Voices from the Third Reich*, pp. 437–39.

clogged with refugees, and streets and roads littered with unburied bodies. The fate of civilians in the path of the Red Army was especially hard. Thousands were killed in their homes or while attempting to flee to the west. Some of the victims were part of a vast stream of refugees—an estimated 12 million at the end of the war—expelled by Soviet, Polish, and Czech authorities from East Prussia, former German provinces east of the Oder-Neisse line, the Sudetenland, and German communities in the Soviet Union and elsewhere in eastern Europe.

Russian soldiers with vivid memories of Nazi atrocities in their country, looted, tortured, raped, and murdered with impunity. Refugees from East Prussia and other eastern provinces streamed into Berlin and cities to the west with horror stories that spread rapidly throughout the shrunken Reich. They told of vengeful soldiers of the Red Army, often drunk and frequently out of control, indulging in orgies of plunder, rape, torture, and murder. In studies written since the breakup of the Soviet Union, scholars estimate "that as many as 1.4 million women in the eastern territories were raped—some 18 percent of the female population of those regions. In East Prussia, the percentage may well have been much higher."[30] Not all Russians behaved brutally, as described by a 17-year-old German soldier in Berlin: "The first troops were friendly and gave us food. They had officers who spoke German very well and told us to be calm, that everything would be all right." Just forty-eight hours later, however, "the next wave of Russian troops arrived, and they settled in to stay. These Russians were really bad. Their main problem was liquor, and they were the ones who started the period of rape and destruction in Berlin."[31] Red Army soldiers from the more primitive areas of the Soviet Union were especially fascinated, and often puzzled, by the products of western technology. Terrified civilians witnessed these soldiers, whom they called "Mongolians," wearing enough wristwatches to cover both arms. Not knowing what to do when the watches stopped, they simply threw them away. Compared to the Wehrmacht's earlier wanton slaughter of defenseless Soviet citizens, the Russian rampage was of much shorter duration, and it was less systematic and ideologically motivated. Nevertheless, it was, in its own way, equally horrifying and lethal.

Allied ground troops were less vengeful than their Soviet counterparts, but, except for Dresden and Berlin, western Germany bore the brunt of air strikes from the beginning of January 1945 to the end of the war in May. Hundreds of thousands were killed, wounded, or left homeless, as British and American planes dropped nearly three times as many bombs as in all of 1942 and 1943. Since most military targets had been severely damaged or destroyed, German civilians were the principal target. While critics of the indiscriminate use of air power charged that these massive attacks on helpless civilians of a mortally wounded nation were morally indefensible, others believed that they were at least partly justified in light of Nazi atrocities. That was certainly the attitude of many Allied ground troops when they liberated the concentration camps at Dachau,

Buchenwald, Bergen-Belsen, and Mauthausen in Austria. Hardened veterans who had experienced the horrors of combat were sickened by heaps of skeletal corpses and the emaciated bodies of survivors. Consequently, many German civilians experienced, and many Allied soldiers felt that they deserved, harsher treatment from their captors. Still, most ordinary citizens preferred to surrender to U.S. or British soldiers rather than to take their chances with the Soviets. To discourage surrender, the SS hanged or shot thousands of Wehrmacht troops. Some SS men in Berlin, who may have acted under Hitler's order, blew up a rail tunnel under the Spree River that sheltered hundreds of people and four packed hospital trains. Thousands drowned. While wreaking vengeance on fellow Germans whom their Führer had accused of betrayal, the SS was simultaneously executing prisoners in their custody days, or even hours, before the arrival of Allied troops.

If the "Nero Order" had been carried out, the fate of millions in the path of Allied armies would have been even worse. On March 18, Speer addressed a memo to Hitler advising him that the economy would collapse in 4–8 weeks, after which the war could not be continued. Speer wrote: "We have no right . . . to undertake destruction which could affect the existence of the people . . . . We have the duty of leaving the people every possibility of establishing a reconstruction in the . . . future."[32] Speer hardly expected a positive response, but Hitler's reply at a military briefing that evening came as a shock. He ordered the military to clear the "western invasion areas of all inhabitants immediately, starting behind the main zone of military operations." The incredulous generals pointed out that transportation facilities had been destroyed and that food supplies were insufficient. "Let them march on foot," was Hitler's response.[33]

The next day he issued the order that historians later named after the Roman emperor Nero, who was suspected of putting the torch to Rome in the first century A.D. Hitler decreed the total destruction of "military, transport, communication, industrial, and supply facilities, as well as material assets which the enemy might use for continuing his struggle." When Speer objected, Hitler replied: "If the war is lost then the nation will also be lost. There is no need to show any consideration for the foundations which the nation needs for its most primitive survival." To Hitler, the Nero Order was a punishment for a people whose "weakness and cowardice," he believed, had betrayed him. The future, he said, "belongs exclusively to the stronger nation from the east. In any case, what remains after this struggle are only the inferior, for the good have died in battle."[34] By blocking the execution of this order, Speer helped spare the German people from the horrors of a scorched-earth policy.

The End and Immediate Aftermath

The Nero Order left no doubt that Hitler had always regarded the German people as his instrument—that he had never been motivated out of "love

ULLSTEIN, BILDERDIENST

Hitler's last photographed act outside the bunker was his review of teenage *Volkssturm* recruits on his fifty-sixth birthday, April 20, 1945. Ten days later he was dead.

and loyalty" to his people, as he would claim in his political testament. By early April, according to Speer, Hitler had separated himself completely from the human tragedy going on outside the bunker: "He no longer had any relationship to it. When he talked about the end, he meant his own and not that of the nation. He had reached the last station in his flight from [the ugly] reality" of the death throes of the Third Reich.[35] Yet he had not abandoned all hope that a miracle might save him, as demonstrated by his euphoric reaction to President Roosevelt's death on April 12. Goebbels assured him it was the miracle that would save the Reich, just as the death of the Russian empress Elizabeth in 1762 had spared Frederick the Great and Prussia from almost certain catastrophe in the Seven Years' War. "It is written in the stars," Goebbels said, "that the second half of April will be a turning point for us."[36] Hitler's euphoria was short-lived. On April 16, just four days after Roosevelt's death, Zhukov and Konev launched the final attack on Berlin. By April 20 both army groups were inside the city limits, fighting their way toward the center, street by street.

April 20 was Hitler's fifty-sixth birthday. The Führer observed the occasion by reviewing a group of Hitler Youth teenagers who were to participate in the battle for Berlin. Motion-picture cameras recorded the stooped, limping Führer patting the cheeks of boys in shabby uniforms who looked to be no older than fourteen. It is one of the most striking images of the last days of the Third Reich. On April 23, Göring sent Hitler a telegram suggesting that he, the still-unofficial successor, should "assume immediately the total leadership of the Reich, with complete freedom of action in domestic and foreign affairs."[37] The following day Bormann, who had eagerly delivered Göring's letter to Hitler, revealed that Himmler was trying to negotiate an end to the war through a Swedish intermediary, Count Bernadotte. Hitler was furious at the "betrayal" of two trusted lieutenants. The Führer's secretary, Martin Bormann, who believed that their fall from grace would give him more power, was elated. Bormann, the supreme "snitch" of Hitler's inner circle, had reached the pinnacle of his position as the most hated man in the Nazi hierarchy. (When asked at the Nuremberg trials if he knew where Bormann was, Göring replied, "I hope he is burning in hell.")

By the last week in April, Red Army artillery was shelling the courtyard of the Reich Chancellery. A motley group of German defenders was still fighting furiously and inflicting heavy casualties on the invaders (over 100,000 Soviet soldiers died in the battle for Berlin), but Hitler had finally accepted the inevitable. He would stay in Berlin and take his own life. Except for naming Admiral Karl Dönitz as his successor, there were no surprises in Hitler's political testament, which he dictated to Bormann on April 29. Göring and Himmler were expelled from the party and stripped of all their offices. Goebbels was appointed chancellor of the Reich, Alfred Seyss-Inquart, former governor of the Netherlands, replaced Ribbentrop as foreign minister, and—what must have been a disappointment for the Führer's obsequious secretary—Bormann's prize was party chancellor, a position he had held without formal appointment since Hess's flight to Britain in 1941. Though he was not expelled from the party, Speer's position was taken by Otto-Karl Saur.

By April 29, 1945, with the exception of a few die-hards like Joseph and Magda Goebbels and Martin Bormann, there was hardly anyone left, save Hitler himself, to believe in his lies. In his testament, the Führer claimed that he had always been solely motivated by "love and loyalty" to his people and that neither he nor anyone in Germany wanted war in 1939. The war was "instigated exclusively by those international statesmen who were either of Jewish descent or worked for Jewish interests." If there is to be another world war, these "international conspirators in money and finance . . . that race, Jewry, which is the real criminal of this murderous struggle, will be saddled with the responsibility." He concludes with a charge to the leaders of the nation to observe the laws of race scrupulously and to oppose mercilessly "the universal poisoner of all peoples, International Jewry."[38] Hitler's political testament is thoroughly consistent with long-established character traits: he accepts no personal responsibility for his monstrous crimes and blames others, notably the Jews, for the "murderous struggle" of World War II.

After signing his last will and testament on the afternoon of April 29, Hitler married his long-suffering mistress, Eva Braun. Of his once-powerful lieutenants, only Bormann and Goebbels remained in the bunker. Speer had left a few days earlier, offering in vain to take the Goebbels children and Eva Braun with him. Outside the bunker, Russian forces were in the ruins of the

BOX 11.5 ■ HITLER'S LAST WILL AND TESTAMENT

Excerpts from Hitler's last will and testament:

> In these three decades (since 1914) I have been actuated solely by love and loyalty to my people in all my thoughts, acts, and life. They gave me the strength to make the most difficult decisions which have ever confronted mortal man. In these three decades I have spent my time, my working strength, and my health.

> It is untrue that I or anyone else in Germany wanted the war in 1939. It was desired and instigated exclusively by those international statesmen who were either of Jewish descent or worked for Jewish interests. I have made too many offers for the control and limitation of armaments, which posterity will not for all time be able to disregard, for the responsibility for the outbreak of this war to be laid on me. I have . . . never wished that after the first fatal world war a second against England, or even America, should break out. Centuries will pass away, but out of the ruins of our towns and monuments hatred will grow for those finally responsible whom we have to thank for everything, International Jewry and its accomplices.

> I also made it quite plain that, if the nations of Europe are again to be regarded as mere shares to be bought and sold by these international conspirators in money and finance, then Jewry, the race which is the real criminal in this murderous struggle, will be saddled with the responsibility. I further left no one in doubt that this time millions of children of Europe's Aryan peoples would not die of hunger, millions of grown men would not suffer death, nor would hundreds of thousands of women and children be burnt and bombed to death in the towns without the real criminal having to atone for this guilt, even if by more humane means. . . .

> I die with a happy heart, conscious of the immeasurable deeds and achievements of our soldiers at the front, our women at home, the achievements of our farmers and workers, and the work, unique in history, of our Youth who bear my name. . . .

The measure of the man and what defined his political career are succinctly expressed in the conclusion of his testament. It is also his legacy: Adolf Hitler leaves nothing to posterity except his murderous hatred of the Jews:

> Above all I charge the leaders of the nation and those under them to scrupulous observance of the laws of race and to merciless opposition to the universal poisoner of all peoples, International Jewry.

Noakes and Pridham, *Documents on Nazism, 1919–1945*, pp. 678–80.

Reich Chancellery. When Hitler heard about the execution of Mussolini and his mistress and the public desecration of their bodies, he gave his aides explicit directions on how to dispose of his and Eva's bodies after their suicide. The next day, April 30, 1945, Hitler and Eva bid farewell to their staff and retired to his suite. Those waiting outside heard a single shot. Upon entering the room they found Hitler lying dead on the sofa, having shot himself through the temple.[39] Eva died by poison. Their bodies were taken outside to the courtyard, doused with gasoline, and burned. The Russians identified the charred remains but, inexplicably, the Soviet regime did not allow publication of the autopsy report until 1968.[40]

Once Hitler was dead, the spell over his subordinates was broken. In an appendix to his master's will, Goebbels wrote that he had made an "unalterable resolution . . . at the side of the Führer, to end a life which will have no further value if I cannot spend it" in his service.[41] On May 1 Joseph and Magda Goebbels gave their children poisoned candy and then had an SS orderly shoot them. Martin Bormann fled the bunker on the same day. Since his body was not found, the Allies assumed that he had escaped. He was tried in absentia at Nuremberg and sentenced to death. (In 1972, German authorities discovered and positively identified his remains in Berlin near the site of the bunker and pronounced him dead.) On May 2, the same day that German forces surrendered in Italy, Dönitz asked for a separate peace with the Allies and declared that the Reich intended to continue the war against the Soviets. Britain and the United States refused. On May 7, Dönitz and General Alfred Jodl surrendered unconditionally to Eisenhower in Reims, France. The Soviets received the instrument of surrender from Keitel the next day in Berlin. May 8, 1945, was celebrated as VE-Day, victory in Europe. The Third Reich had outlasted its founder by just one week.

Cooperation among the victors gave way to suspicion and fear after VE-Day, but two previously scheduled joint endeavors were held. In July 1945 the last wartime summit conference was held at Potsdam near Berlin.

NATIONAL ARCHIVES

Three of the more infamous Nazis at the Nuremberg trials. From left to right: Hermann Göring, Rudolf Hess, and Joachim von Ribbentrop.

Under pressure from Stalin, President Harry Truman and Churchill's successor, Clement Atlee, ratified the de facto transfer of former German territory east of the Oder–Neisse line to Poland. The territory was officially classified as "under Polish administration." In November, the trial of Nazi war criminals by the International Military Tribunal opened at Nuremberg's palace of justice. The four indictments were conspiracy, or planning to, wage war; fighting an aggressive war; war crimes, such as killing non-belligerents; and crimes against humanity, which included extermination of the Jews. Allied prosecutors built their case on the voluminous cache of captured Nazi documents. Responding to charges that the victors were more interested in vengeance than justice, the judges allotted two-thirds of the nine-month trial to defense attorneys.

At the end of September 1946 the judges handed down their verdicts: death by hanging for Göring (who poisoned himself hours before the execution), Ribbentrop, Sauckel, Frank, Frick, Seyss-Inquart, Rosenberg, Streicher, Ernst Kaltenbrunner (an SS officer who assumed some of Heydrich's responsibilities), and the two generals, Keitel and Jodl. Sentenced to life imprisonment were Hess, Walter Funk (Schacht's successor as minister of economics), and Admiral Raeder; Speer, Baldur von Schirach, Konstantin von Neurath, and Dönitz received shorter prison sentences. Franz von Papen, Hjalmar Schacht, and a radio commentator, Hans Fritsche, were acquitted. Critics charged that the sentences for some, especially Jodl and Hess, were too harsh, while others, particularly Speer, were too lenient. Military officers around the world argued that Dönitz and Raeder should never have been tried at all. While there was no lack of incriminating evidence against him, a few observers felt that the obscure Kaltenbrunner was a stand-in for Heinrich Himmler, who committed suicide in British custody on May 17, 1945. Perhaps the most positive outcome of the controversial trials was to document exhaustively, for the German people as well as the rest of the world, the atrocities of Hitler's regime.

Hitler's Legacy

Hitler's legacy abounds in ironies. Instead of an economically self-sufficient continental empire and a united Europe ruled by the "master race," Germany lost one-fifth of its prewar territory, and its four zones of occupation were governed by military officials of the victorious powers. The former Reich's population increased substantially, but not according to the Nazi plan. Millions of refugees from the east crowded into a shrunken, devastated country whose transportation, communication, and food-distribution systems had broken down. Hitler unleashed a war of annihilation against Communism, but the Soviet Union emerged as one of two superpowers in the world. Conquered or satellite states in eastern Europe—Poland, Czechoslovakia, Hungary, Yugoslavia, Romania, and Bulgaria—were under Communist rule by 1948.

The map legend reads:

ALLIED ZONES OF OCCUPATION
- British
- French
- United States
- Soviet
- Polish

The Third Reich dominated European diplomacy before and during the war, but within two years after VE-Day, Germany had become a pawn in the Cold War between the Soviet Union and the United States. In 1949 the French, British, and American zones merged into a new semi-sovereign state, the German Federal Republic, with its capital at Bonn on the Rhine. Weeks later, the Soviets countered with the conversion of their zone into the German Democratic Republic, with its capital in East Berlin. The three western powers clung to their sectors of the former capital, and West Berlin became an enclave of prosperity and democracy inside the economically austere East German police state. The most astonishing irony was the birth of the state of Israel in 1948. With strong moral support and generous financial aid from nations seeking to compensate Jews for the Holocaust, Israel has prospered and played a pivotal role in international affairs.

Hitler left an ambiguous legacy for German society. Inadvertently, the Nazis accelerated the pace of modernization by stripping the traditional elites of political power and partially leveling a hierarchical class structure. Democratic political institutions took root in the Federal Republic, but authoritarianism, Communist-style, flourished in East Germany. Traditional patriarchialism relaxed its hold over German society as the exigencies of war forced the Nazis to extend privileges and opportunities to women. Germans on both sides of the Iron Curtain (a phrase originated by Goebbels, but made famous by Churchill) recovered from the war's material devastation, but the trauma of war and a sense of guilt for Nazi atrocities left deep emotional scars.

The Communist rulers of the East German Republic conveniently blamed the Holocaust on Hitler's fascism, which they had resisted and which they claimed was still flourishing in the Federal Republic. The West Germans, on the other hand, paid reparations to Israel and investigated the causes and crimes of Nazism. By the end of the 1960s, state governments of the Federal Republic had passed laws requiring the Holocaust to be taught in public schools. Historians debated whether Nazism was an aberration from the German norm or a continuation of what had occurred earlier, and asked why Germany had succumbed so easily to Nazism. Answers varied, and millions would have preferred to "forget the whole business," but at least the "undigested past," however painful, was being discussed.

The debate among West German historians reached a new high in the mid-1980s in a highly publicized exchange, called the *Historikerstreit* (historians' dispute). The central issue, as it had always been, was how to interpret the Third Reich, whose "horrors still haunt the modern consciousness." Some felt that the time had come, some forty years after the end of the war, for a major reevaluation of the Nazi legacy. Seeking to mitigate guilt and restore an untainted patriotism, conservative historians "relativized" Nazi crimes by placing them in the context of twentieth-century massacres and the cruelty and terror increasingly characteristic of modern warfare. Others believed it was possible to "normalize" the Nazi past by calling attention to the regime's "positive aspects" and focusing on ordinary citizens who lived with "moral ambiguities" and experienced great suffering, especially during the last years of the war. Liberal historians held that one could not relativize or normalize Hitler's regime without minimizing the enormity of its atrocities. They argued that Auschwitz must always remain unique, and that the universal significance of the Third Reich as the paradigm of a highly civilized nation descending into barbarism must never be explained away.[42]

With the crumbling of the Berlin Wall, the collapse of communism in East Germany, and the reunification of the two Germanies in October 1990, the *Historikerstreit* itself had become history. Yet the debate over the German people's "burden of guilt" goes on. Hitler biographer Joachim Fest believes that, as survivors of the Third Reich disappear into history, public memory will fade and the Nazi experience will no longer trouble the German conscience.[43] Shortly before he was hanged at Nuremberg in 1946,

Hans Frank uttered a memorable phrase: "A thousand years shall pass and this guilt of Germany shall not have been erased."[44] Many agree with Frank's assessment and hope that the horrors of Nazism will remain indelibly impressed in the collective memory of succeeding generations of Germans—and for all humankind as well. "German history matters to all of us," writes American historian Allan Mitchell, "because it is human history; it is a part of everyone's past."[45] The darkest chapter of German history must always "be there" to serve as a grim reminder of what can happen, anytime, anywhere, when hatred, ideological fanaticism, and a charismatic leader run amok: ordinary people are converted into cold-blooded murderers of the defenseless.

INFOTRAC® COLLEGE EDITION SEARCH TERMS

For additional reading go to Infotrac College Edition, your online research library at http://www.infotrac-college.com.

Enter the search term "bombing Germany" using Keywords.

Enter the search term "Dresden" using Keywords.

Enter the search term "Hamburg, Germany" using the Subject Guide.

Enter the search term "strategic bombing" using Keywords.

Enter the search term "V-2 rockets" using Keywords.

Enter the search term "D-Day" using the Subject Guide.

Enter the search term "Eastern Front" using Keywords.

Enter the search term "Red Army" using Keywords.

Enter the search term "Braun, Eva" using Keywords.

Enter the search term "Battle of the Bulge" using the Subject Guide.

Enter the search term "Normandy Invasion" using the Subject Guide.

Enter the search term "Eisenhower, Dwight D." using the Subject Guide.

Enter the search term "Bradley, Omar" using the Subject Guide.

Enter the search term "Patton, George S." using the Subject Guide.

Enter the search term "peace, World War, 1939–1945" using Keywords.

Enter the search term "World War, 1939–1945, Reparations" using the Subject Guide.

Enter the search term "German reunification question" using the Subject Guide.

Notes

1. Quoted in John Keegan, *The Second World War* (New York: Viking, 1989), p. 370.

302

2. David Fraser, *Knight's Cross: A Life of Field Marshal Erwin Rommel* (New York: HarperCollins, 1993), p. 454.

3. Gerhard L. Weinberg, *A World at Arms* (Cambridge: Cambridge University Press, 1994), p. 660.

4. Louis Lochner, *The Goebbels Diaries, 1942–1943* (New York: Doubleday, 1948), p. 527.

5. Weinberg, p. 617.

6. Albert Speer, *Inside the Third Reich* (New York: MacMillan, 1970), pp. 365–66.

7. Michael J. Lyons, *World War II: A Short History* (Upper Saddle River, NJ: Prentice-Hall, 1999), p. 225.

8. Keegan, pp. 373–74.

9. Quoted in Adrian R. Lewis, *Omaha Beach: A Flawed Victory* (Chapel Hill and London: University of North Carolina Press, 2001), p. 296.

10. Weinberg, pp. 687–90.

11. Quoted in Keegan, p. 403.

12. Ibid., p. 411.

13. Weinberg, p. 699.

14. Stephen E. Ambrose, *Citizen Soldiers: The U.S. Army from the Normandy Beaches to the Bulge to the Surrender of Germany, June 7, 1944–May 7, 1945* (New York: Simon & Schuster, 1997), pp. 118–19.

15. Cornelius Ryan, *A Bridge Too Far* (New York: Simon & Schuster, 1974), p. 8. When Montgomery ordered the First Airborne Division to capture the bridge at Arnhem, Lt. General Frederick Browning, the deputy commander, replied: "But sir, I think we might be going a bridge too far."

16. Ambrose, pp. 165, 177.

17. David M. Glantz and Jonathan M. House, *When Titans Clashed: How the Red Army Stopped Hitler* (Lawrence: University Press of Kansas, 1995), pp. 180–81, 204.

18. Alan Bullock, *Hitler and Stalin: Parallel Lives* (New York: Knopf, 1992), pp. 852–54.

19. Quoted in Ian Kershaw, *Hitler 1936–1945: Nemesis* (New York: Norton, 2000), p. 731.

20. Keegan, pp. 444–45.

21. Ibid., p. 441.

22. Ibid., p. 447.

23. Glantz and House, pp. 262–63.

24. Lyons, p. 275.

25. Quoted in C. L. Sulzberger, *World War II* (Boston: Houghton Mifflin, 1985), pp. 264–65.

26. David Irving, *The Secret Diaries of Hitler's Doctor* (New York: MacMillan, 1983), pp. 63–72. In his *Hitler's War* (1977), Irving asserted that Hitler was not responsible for Nazi anti-Semitism and knew nothing about the Final Solution until late 1943. See Michael R. Marrus, *The Holocaust in History* (Hanover and London: University Press of New England, 1987), p. 34. More recently, Irving has joined the ranks of Holocaust deniers. His controversial position does not seem to have colored his interpretation of Morrell's diary.

27. Kershaw, p. 728; Joachim Fest, *Hitler* (New York: Harcourt Brace Jovanovich, 1973), p. 673.

28. Kershaw, p. 753.

29. Bullock, p. 877.

30. Kershaw, p. 763.

31. Johannes Steinhoff, Peter Pechel, and Dennis Showalter, eds., *Voices from the Third Reich: An Oral History* (Washington, DC: Regnery Gateway, 1989), pp. 429–30.

32. Quoted in Kershaw, p. 785.

33. Speer, pp. 438–39.

34. Ibid., p. 473.

35. Quoted in Bullock, p. 885.

36. Ibid., p. 885.

37. Louis L. Snyder, *National Socialist Germany: Twelve Years That Shook the World* (Malibur, FL: Krieger, 1984), p. 174.

38. Ibid., p. 178.

39. Hugh Trevor-Roper, *The Last Days of Hitler* (New York: Collier Books, 1962), pp. 259–61.

40. Lev Bezymenski, *The Death of Adolf Hitler* (New York: Harcourt Books, 1968).

41. Snyder, p. 179.

42. Peter Baldwin, ed., *Reworking the Past: Hitler, the Holocaust, and the Historians' Debate* (Boston: Beacon Press, 1990), pp. 10–13.

43. Ibid., p. 15.

44. Quoted in Eugene Davidson, *The Trial of the Germans* (New York: MacMillan, 1966), p. 439.

45. Allan Mitchell, "The Three Paradoxes of Nazism," in Allan Mitchell, ed., *The Nazi Revolution* (Boston: Houghton Mifflin, 1997), p. 23.

Suggestions for Further Reading

The bibliography below offers a tiny sampling of the vast and continually expanding body of literature on Nazi Germany. It is limited to English-language works that are accessible to the general reader. A wide variety of topics are covered, and recent, historiographically significant works are emphasized.

I. GENERAL

A. Documentary Collections

Documents on German Foreign Policy, 1918–1945. United States Department of State, 1949–1983.(a multi-volume collection from the archives of the German Foreign Ministry)

International Military Tribunal. *Trial of the Major War Criminals Before the International Military Tribunal, 42 vols.* Nuremberg, 1947–1949. (the trial proceedings provide a documentary history of Nazi Germany)

Office of the United States Chief Counsel for Prosecution of Axis Criminality. *Nazi Conspiracy and Aggression, 10 vols.* Washington: U.S. Government Printing Office, 1946. (the prosecution's voluminous evidence sheds light on the planning and execution of all phases of Nazi criminality)

B. Surveys

Berghahn, Volker. *Modern Germany: Society, Politics, and Economy in the Twentieth Century.* New York: Cambridge University Press, 1982. (detailed, analytical coverage of subtitle topics)

Bracher, Karl D. *The German Dictatorship:The Origins, Structure, and Effects of National Socialism.* New York: Praeger, 1970. (a critical survey with a political emphasis)

Burleigh, Michael. *The Third Reich: A New History.* New York: Hill and Wang, 2000. (detailed, interpretative work, analyzing particular themes in depth)

Craig, Gordon. *Germany 1866–1945.* New York: Oxford University Press, 1978. (extensively documented, detailed, and comprehensive; in the Oxford History of Modern Europe series)

Fischer, Klaus P. *Nazi Germany: A New History.* New York: Continuum, 1995. (comprehensive, detailed narrative and analysis)

Fulbrook, Mary. *The Divided Nation: A History of Germany 1918–1990.* New York: Oxford University Press, 1992. (interpretative overview with social and cultural emphasis)

Hildebrand, Klaus. *The Third Reich.* London: Allen & Unwin, 1984. (a concise narrative and a historiographical essay of approximately equal lengths)

Kershaw, Ian. *The Nazi Dictatorship: Problems and Perspectives of Interpretation.* London: Edward Arnold, 1987. (varying interpretations of specific topics)

Orlow, Dietrich. *A History of Modern Germany, 1871 to the Present.* Upper Saddle River, NJ: Prentice Hall, 1999. (balanced coverage from Bismarck to reunification; fourth edition)

Spielvogel, Jackson. *Hitler and Nazi Germany.* Upper Saddle River, NJ: Prentice Hall, 2001. (balanced, well-researched narrative and synthesis; fourth edition)

Wistrich, Robert S. *Who's Who in Nazi Germany.* New York: Routledge, 1995. (detailed coverage of a representative cross-section of German Society from 1933 to 1945)

C. Collections of Essays, Excerpts, and Primary Sources

Bessel, Richard, ed. *Life in the Third Reich.* New York: Oxford University Press, 1987. (eight social history essays from the journal *History Today*)

Domarus, Max, ed. *Hitler: Speeches, and Proclamations.* trans. by Mary Fran Gilbert. Wauconda, IL: Bolchazy-Carducci, 1990– (three of four volumes have been translated, covering the period from 1932–1940)

Martel, Gordon, ed. *Modern Germany Reconsidered 1870–1945.* London: Routledge, 1992. (essays analyzing historiographical issues on a variety of topics)

Mitchell, Allan, ed. *The Nazi Revolution.* Boston: Houghton Mifflin, 1997. (excerpts from full-length studies reflecting current research trends, mostly on the prewar years)

Mosse, George, ed. *Nazi Culture: Intellectual, Cultural, and Social Life in the Third Reich.* New York: Grosset & Dunlap, 1966. (a variety of primary sources on prewar Nazi culture)

Noakes, Jeremy and Geoffrey Pridham. *Nazism, 1919–1945: A Documentary Reader.* Exeter: University of Exeter Press, 1983–1994. (primary sources, narrative, and analysis, emphasizing the prewar years)

Remak, Joachim, ed. *The Nazi Years: A Documentary History*. Prospect Heights, IL: Waveland Press, 1990. (brief excerpts covering all twelve years of the Third Reich)

Snyder, Louis L. *National Socialist Germany: Twelve Years that Shook the World*. Malibur, FL: Krieger, 1984. (brief, documentary excerpts on politics, diplomacy, and war)

II. BIOGRAPHICAL

A. Hitler

Bullock, Alan. *Hitler: A Study in Tyranny*. New York: Harper & Row, 1964, revised edition. (the first full-length and still one of the best political biographies; first published in 1952)

———. *Hitler and Stalin: Parallel Lives*. New York: Alfred A. Knopf, 1992. (this longer work reflects recent research; comparison with Stalin is fascinating and revealing)

Fest, Joachim. *Hitler*. New York: Harcourt Brace Jovanovich, 1973. (lengthy, but always interesting, insightful, and well written)

Haffner, Sebastian. *The Meaning of Hitler*. New York: Macmillan, 1978. (provocative assessment of Hitler's historical significance)

Hitler, Adolf. *Mein Kampf*, trans. by Ralph Mannheim. Boston: Houghton Mifflin, 1962.

Jäckel, Eberhard. *Hitler in History*. Hanover, NH: University Press of New England, 1984.

———. *Hitler's Weltanschauung*. Middletown, CT: Wesleyan University Press, 1972. (Jäckel's works focus on the interaction between Hitler's ideology and charismatic leadership and the German people)

Kershaw, Ian. *Hitler*. London: Longman, 1991. (a concise study of the nature of Hitler's power)

———. *Hitler 1889–1936: Hubris*. New York: Norton, 1999; *Hitler 1936–1945: Nemesis*. New York: Norton, 2000. (this masterful two-volume biography—over 1,400 pages of text and 362 pages of notes, some from previously untapped sources, most in German—by a leading, if not *the* leading, historian of Nazi Germany, is a compelling narrative, with fascinating details, fresh insights, and provocative analysis; it is unlikely to be surpassed)

———. *The 'Hitler Myth': Image and Reality in the Third Reich*. New York: Oxford University Press, 1987. (analyzes Hitler's hold over the German people)

Smith, Bradley F. *Adolf Hitler: His Childhood, Family, and Youth*. Stanford, CA: Hoover Institution, 1967. (solid, thoroughly researched study that avoids psychological theorizing)

Waite, Robert G. L. *The Psychopathic God Adolf Hitler*. New York: Basic Books, 1977. (best of the "psycho-biographies")

B. Other Nazi Leaders

Deschner, Günther. *Reinhard Heydrich: A Biography*. New York: Stein & Day, 1981.

Fest, Joachim. *The Face of the Third Reich*. New York: Ace Books, 1970. (sketches of leading Nazis)

Irving, David. *Göring, A Biography*. New York: William Morrow, 1989. (sympathetic "reassessment," almost an apology, by the controversial British historian)

Lang, Jochen. *The Secretary, Martin Bormann*. New York: Random House, 1979.

Reuth, Ralf Georg. *Goebbels*. New York: Harcourt Brace, 1993.

Smelser, Ronald and Rainir Zitelmann, eds. *The Nazi Elite: 22 Biographical Sketches*. New York: New York University Press, 1993. (concise, "meaty" essays, mostly by German authors)

Speer, Albert. *Inside the Third Reich*. New York: MacMillan, 1970. (perceptive and informative; the best "insider's" account)

————. *Spandau: The Secret Diaries*. New York: MacMillan, 1976. (reflections based on notes jotted down while serving his 20-year prison sentence)

Smith, Bradley F. *Heinrich Himmler: A Nazi in the Making 1900–1926*. Stanford, CA: Hoover Institution, 1971. (based on Himmler's early diaries; the SS leader awaits a full-length scholarly biography)

III. BEFORE 1933

Allen, William S. *The Nazi Seizure of Power: The Experience of a Single Town, 1930–1935*. New York: Franklin Watts, 1984. (revised edition of Nazis working at the local level)

Childers, Thomas. *The Nazi Voter: The Social Foundations of Fascism in Germany, 1919–1933*. Chapel Hill: University of North Carolina Press, 1983. (quantitative analysis of Nazi electoral support)

Friedrich, Otto. *Before the Deluge: A Portrait of Berlin in the 1920s*. New York: Harper & Row, 1972. (popular history that interweaves cultural and political developments)

Fritzsche, Peter. *Germans into Nazis*. Cambridge: Harvard University Press, 1998. (politicized by the war and Weimar, ordinary Germans helped make Nazism a popular movement)

Gay, Peter. *Weimar Culture: The Outsider as Insider*. New York: Harper & Row, 1968.

Herwig, Holger, ed. *The Outbreak of World War I*. Lexington, MA: Heath, 1991. (recent interpretations of the controversy over the Fischer thesis and the 1914 war guilt question)

Kater, Michael H. *The Nazi Party: A Social Profile of Members and Leaders*. Cambridge, MA: Harvard University Press, 1983. (like Childers, Kater uses quantitative research methods)

Mosse, George L. *The Crisis of German Ideology*. New York: Grosset & Dunlap, 1964. (intellectual and cultural roots of Nazism in the late 19th and early 20th centuries)

Nicholls, A.P. *Weimar and the Rise of Hitler*. New York: St. Martin's, 1991. (now in its third edition, this concise survey emphasizes political history)

Orlow, Dietrich. *The History of the Nazi Party, 1919–1933*. Pittsburgh: University of Pittsburgh Press, 1969.

Peukert, Detlev. *The Weimar Republic: The Crisis Of Classical Modernity*. New York: Hill & Wang, 1991. (economic, neo-Marxist interpretation of Weimar's decline and fall)

Rosenbaum, Ron. *Explaining Hitler: The Search for the Origins of His Evil*. (New York: Random House, 1998. (discusses controversies over and theories about Hitler's psyche, his ancestry, his sexuality, the origins of his anti-Semitism, and the meaning of his evil)

Stachura, Peter, ed. *The Nazi Machtergreifung*. London: Allen & Unwin, 1983. (ten essays on how the dymanics of NSDAP social and political mobilization facilitated the *Machtergreifung*)

Turner, Henry Ashby Jr. *German Big Business and the Rise of Hitler*. New York: Oxford University Press, 1985. (the study of an uneasy relationship)

IV. THE THIRD REICH AND GERMAN SOCIETY, 1933–1939

A. Political and Economic (titles with an asterisk also cover the war years)

Broszat, Martin. *The Hitler State: Foundation and Development of the Internal Structure of the Third Reich*. London: Longmans, 1981.

Caplan, Jane. *Government Without Administration: State and Civil Service in Weimar and Nazi Germany*. Oxford: Clarendon Press, 1989. (broad coverage of the chaotic and inefficient nature of Nazi administration, exemplified by the ministry of the interior)

Gellately, Robert. *The Gestapo and German Society: Enforcing Racial Policy, 1933–1945*. New York: Oxford University Press, 1990. (Gestapo agents, in this revisionist, comprehensive study, were few in number and needed a host of voluntary citizen informers to be effective)*

————. *Backing Hitler: Consent and Coercion in Nazi Germany* (Oxford: Oxford University, 2001. (a well-documented, comprehensive study charging that most Germans were enthusiastic accomplices of the regime's racist and repressive campaigns against "enemies of the people")*

Höhne, Heinz. *The Order of the Death's Head*. New York: Coward McCann, 1969. (broader in scope than the title, this account covers the SS as a whole)*

Johnson, Eric A. *Nazi Terror: The Gestapo, Jews, and Ordinary Germans*. New York: Basic Books, 1999. (broad coverage of a lean Gestapo force that was the chief enforcer of terror, enjoyed popular support, and targeted small groups, especially the Jews)*

Koehl, Robert L. *The Black Corps: The Structure and Power Struggles of the Nazi SS*. Madison: University of Wisconsin Press, 1983.*

Kogon, Eugen. *The Theory and Practice of Hell: The German Concentration Camps and the System Behind Them*. London: Secker and Warburg, 1950. (a survivor's account that covers the concentration camp system)*

Krausnick, Helmut and Martin Broszat, eds. *Anatomy of the SS State*. New York: Walker, 1968. (four historians' essays written in December 1963 for trials of SS death camp personnel)*

Overy, Richard J. *The Nazi Economic Recovery, 1932–1938*. London: MacMillan, 1982. (fresh insights into the relationship between rearmament and economic recovery)

Peterson, Edward N. *The Limits of Hitler's Power*. Princeton: Princeton University Press, 1969. (how the bureaucracy limited the "total power" of the Nazi state)

Schweitzer, Arthur. *Big Business and the Third Reich*. Bloomington: Indiana University Press, 1964. (an economic history of the early years of the Third Reich)

B. Cultural, Intellectual, Social (titles with an asterisk also cover the war years)

Bentley, James. *Martin Niemöller*. New York: Free Press, 1984.

Beyerchen, Alan D. *Scientists Under Hitler: Politics and the Physics Community in the Third Reich*. New Haven, CT: Yale University Press, 1977.*

Bosanquet, Mary. *The Life and Death of Dietrich Bonhoeffer*. New York: Harper Colophon Books, 1968.*

Burden, Hamilton. *The Nuremberg Party Rallies: 1923–1939*. New York: Praeger, 1967.

Burleigh, Michael. *Death and Deliverance: "Euthanasia" in Germany, c. 1900–1945*. Cambridge: Cambridge University Press, 1994. (traces the origins of the idea, its support in the medical community, and its horrible culmination under the Nazi regime)*

Conway, John S. *The Nazi Persecution of the Churches*. London: Weidenfeld Nicolson, 1968. (utlilizing captured Nazi documents, this work emphasizes the regime's attitudes and policies)*

Engelmann, Bernt. *In Hitler's Germany: Daily Life in the Third Reich*. New York: Schocken Books, 1986. (a memoir, written like a novel, about ordinary Germans)*

Heck, Alfons. *The Burden of Hitler's Legacy*. Frederick, CO: Renaissance House, 1988. (a memoir about the Hitler Youth experience)*

Helmreich, Ernst C. *The German Churches Under Hitler: Background, Struggle, and Epilogue*. Detroit: Wayne State University Press, 1979. (detailed coverage of all religious groups)*

Hull, David S. *Film in the Third Reich: A Study of the German Cinema*. Berkeley: University of California Press, 1969.*

Kater, Michael H. *The Twisted Muse: Musicians and Their Music in the Third Reich*. New York: Oxford University Press, 1997.*

———. *Doctors Under Hitler*. Chapel Hill: University of North Carolina Press, 1989. (broad coverage of the medical profession and doctors' role in the Final Solution)*

Kershaw, Ian. *Popular Opinion and Political Dissent in the Third Reich: Bavaria, 1933–1945*. New York: Oxford University Press, 1985. (support and dissent at the "grass-roots" level)*

Koonz, Claudia. *Mothers in the Fatherland: Women, the Family, and Nazi Politics*. New York: St. Martin's Press, 1987. (emphasizes the contradictions of Nazi policy)*

Owings, Alison. *Frauen: German Women Recall the Third Reich*. New Brunswick: Rutgers University Press, 1994.(American journalist's account based on interviews with 29 women of diverse backgrounds)*

Peukert, Detlev. *Inside Nazi Germany: Conformity, Opposition, and Racism in Everyday Life*. New Haven: Yale University Press, 1987. (how Nazi ideology affected everyday life)*

Plant, Richard. *The Pink Triangle: The Nazi War Against Homosexuals*. (New York: Henry Holt, 1986.*

Proctor, Robert. *The Nazi War on Cancer*. Princeton: Princeton University Press, 1999. (covers German researchers' discovery of the link between cigarette smoking and lung cancer)

Rempel, Gerhard. *Hitler's Children: The Hitler Youth and the SS*. Chapel Hill: University of North Carolina Press, 1989. (broader than the title, this work is a history of the Hitler Youth)*

Schoenbaum, David. *Hitler's Social Revolution*. New York: Doubleday, 1966. (detailed study of social change to 1939)

Stephenson, Jill. *Women in Nazi Society*. New York: Harper & Row, 1981.*

Zeman, Zbynek. *Nazi Propaganda*. New York: Oxford University Press, 1964. (still one of the best works on Nazi propaganda and Goebbels's aims and methods)*

V. HITLER'S FOREIGN POLICY

Carr, William. *Arms, Autarky, and Aggression: German Foreign Policy, 1933–1939*. New York: Norton, 1973. (emphasizes the connection between economics and foreign policy)

Eubank, Keith. *World War II: Roots and Causes*. Lexington, MA: D.C. Heath, 1992. (excerpts from full length studies reflecting recent research)

Hiden, John. *Germany and Europe, 1919–1939*. London: Longman, 1993.

Hildebrand, Klaus. *The Foreign Policy of the Third Reich*. Berkeley: University of California Press, 1973. (focuses on the ideological basis of Hitler's foreign policy)

Hillgruber, Andreas. *Germany and Two World Wars*. Cambridge, MA: Harvard University Press, 1981. (emphasizes Hitler's expansionist program culminating in world domination)

Murray, Williamson. *The Change in the Balance of Power, 1938–1939*. Princeton, NJ: Princeton University Press, 1984. (detailed study, from the Anschluss to the outbreak of war)

Rich, Norman. *Hitler's War Aims: Vol. I, Ideology, the Nazi State, and the Course of Expansion*. New York: Norton, 1973. (covers Hitler's plan for conquest and the war to Dec. 1941)

Shirer, William L. *Twentieth Century Journey, Vol. II: The Nightmare Years, 1930–1940*. Boston: Little, Brown, 1984. (an American journalist's memoir on Nazi foreign policy and life in the Third Reich)

Taylor, A.J.P. *Origins of the Second World War*. New York: Premier Books, 1961.

Watt, Donald Cameron. *How the War Came: The Immediate Origins of the Second World War, 1938–1939*. New York: Pantheon Books, 1989. (detailed study stressing Hitler's desire for war)

Weinberg, Gerhard L. *The Foreign Policy of Hitler's Germany: Diplomatic Revolution In Europe 1933–1936*. Chicago: University of Chicago Press, 1970.

———. *The Foreign Policy of Hitler's Germany: Starting World War II, 1937–1939*. Chicago: University of Chicago Press, 1980. (Weinberg's works are definitive)

VI. WORLD WAR II

Abzug, Robert H. *Inside the Vicious Heart: Americans and the Liberation of Nazi Concentration Camps*. New York: Oxford University Press, 1985.

Ambrose, Stephen E. *D-Day June 6, 1944: The Climactic Battle of World War II*. New York: Simon & Schuster, 1994.

————. *Citizen Soldiers: The U.S. Army from the Normandy Beaches to the Bulge to the Surrender of Germany, June 7, 1944–May 7, 1945.* New York: Simon & Schuster, 1997. (both works cover the experiences of soldiers in their own words, as well as the bigger picture of strategy, tactics, and leadership; the Battle of the Bulge is the central event of *Citizen Soldiers*)

Barnett, Correlli, ed. *Hitler's Generals.* New York: Grove Weidenfeld, 1989. (a collection of scholarly essays)

Bartov, Omer. *The Eastern Front, 1941–1945: German Troops and the Barbarization of Warfare.* New York: St. Martin's, 1985.

————. *Hitler's Army: Soldiers, Nazis, and War in the Third Reich.* New York: Oxford University Press, 1992. (covers the brutalization of German soldiers on the eastern front and, as the author sees it, their ideologically motivated murders of Russian civilians)

Bezymenski, Lev. *The Death of Adolf Hitler.* New York: Harcourt Books, 1968. (autopsy reports of Hitler, Eva Braun, and the Goebbels family, published twenty-three years later)

Bidermann, Gottlob Herbert. *In Deadly Combat: A German Soldier's Memoir of the Eastern Front.* Lawrence: University Press of Kansas, 2000. (edited and translated by Derek S. Zumbro)

Boyne, Walter J. *Clash of Wings: World War II in the Air.* New York: Simon & Schuster, 1994.

Cameron, Norman and R.H. Stevens, eds. *Hitler's Secret Conversations 1941–1944.* New York: New American Library, 1961.

Clark, Alan. *Barbarossa: The Russian-German Conflict 1941–1945.* New York: William Morrow, 1965. (still one of the best single-volume accounts)

Corum, James. *The Luftwaffe.* Lawrence: University Press of Kansas, 1997.

Cowley, Robert, ed. *No End Save Victory: Perspectives on World War II.* New York: Putnam, 2001. (essays by specialists, such as Stephen Ambrose, John Keegan, and David Glantz, on topics ranging from Dunkirk, to Stalingrad, to Falaise, to Berlin)

Craig, William. *Enemy at the Gates: The Battle for Stalingrad.* New York: Ballantine Books, 1973.

Dupuy, Trevor N., David L. Bongard, and Richard C. Anderson, Jr. *Hitler's Last Gamble: The Battle of the Bulge, December 1944–January 1945.* New York: HarperCollins, 1994.

Edmonds, Robin. *The Big Three: Churchill, Roosevelt, and Stalin in Peace and War.* New York: Norton, 1991.

Erickson, John and David Kilks, eds. *Barbarossa: The Axis and the Allies.* Edinburgh: Edinburgh University Press, 1994. (essays by specialists on various aspects of the campaign)

Fraser, David. *Knight's Cross: A Life of Field Marshal Erwin Rommel*. New York: HarperCollins, 1993.

Glantz, David M. and Jonathan House. *When Titans Clashed: How the Red Army Stopped Hitler*. Lawrence: University Press of Kansas, 1995.

Goebbels, Joseph. *The Goebbels Diaries, 1939–1942*, trans. & ed. by Fred Taylor. London: H. Hamilton, 1982.

———. *The Goebbels Diaries, 1942–1943*, trans. & ed. by Louis Lochner. New York: Doubleday, 1948.

———. *Final Entries, 1945: The Diaries of Joseph Goebbels*, trans. & ed. by Hugh Trevor-Roper. New York: Putnam, 1978.

Irving, David. *The Secret Diaries of Hitler's Doctor*. New York: MacMillan, 1983. (the author translates and edits Morrell's diaries and writes a lengthy introduction)

———. *The Trail of the Fox*. New York: Dutton, 1977. (this biography of Rommel, written before the author became embroiled in Holocaust controversy, is a readable, solid work)

Keegan, John. *The Second World War*. New York: Viking, 1989. (a detailed, analytical, and readable narrative by a distinguished military historian)

Lewin, Ronald. *Hitler's Mistakes*. New York: William Morrow, 1984. (mostly the war years, but pre-war examples are also covered)

Lewis, Adrian R. *Omaha Beach: A Flawed Victory*. Chapel Hill & London: University of North Carolina Press, 2001), p. 296.

Lyons, Michael J. *World War II: A Short History*. Upper Saddle River, NJ: Prentice-Hall, 1999. (solid, relatively brief narrative and analysis in its third edition)

———. *Ultra Goes to War*. New York: McGraw-Hill, 1978. (instances in which Ultra reports made a difference)

Manstein, Erich von. *Lost Victories*. Chicago: Henry Regnery, 1958. (the general's memoirs cover the French and Russian campaigns in detail and blame Hitler for what went wrong)

Neillands, Robin. *The Bomber War: The Allied Air Offensive Against Nazi Germany*. Woodstock: Overlook Press, 2001.

Overy, Richard. *Why the Allies Won*. New York: Norton, 1995. (sees superior leadership, organization, and morale as important as the huge advantage in war materiél)

Petrova, Ada and Peter Watson. *The Death of Hitler*. New York: Norton, 1995. (using post-Soviet evidence, including a piece of Hitler's skull, the authors tell a the complete story of the suicides and what happened to the remains of Hitler, Goebbels, and the others)

Ryan, Cornelius. *A Bridge Too Far*. New York: Simon & Schuster, 1974. (popular history account of the ill-fated [for the Allies] Battle of Arnhem)

Read, Anthony, and David Fisher. *The Fall of Berlin*. New York: Norton, 1992.

Stein, George. *The Waffen SS: Hitler's Elite Guard at War*. Ithaca, NY: Cornell University Press, 1966.

Taylor, Telford. *March of Conquest: The German Victories in Western Europe, 1940*. New York: Simon & Schuster, 1958.

Trevor-Roper, Hugh R. *The Last Days of Hitler*. New York: Collier Books, 1962. (still one of the best accounts)

van der Vat, Dan. *The Atlantic Campaign: World War II's Great Struggle at Sea*. New York: Harper & Row, 1988.

Weigley, Russell F. *Eisenhower's Lieutenants: The Campaign of France and Germany*. Bloomington: Indiana University Press, 1981.

Weinberg, Gerhard L. *Germany, Hitler, and World War II: Essays in Modern German and World History*. New York: Cambridge University Press, 1995.

————. *Germany and The Soviet Union, 1939–1941*. Leyden: Brill, 1954, 1972.

————. *A World at Arms: A Global History of World War II*. Cambridge: Cambridge University Press, 1994. (this massive survey utilizes both primary and secondary sources)

Wright, Gordon. *The Ordeal of Total War, 1939–1945*. New York: Harper & Row, 1968. (one of the few surveys to cover only the European theater)

VII. NAZI GERMANY IN WARTIME

Baird, Jay W. *The Mythical World of Nazi Propaganda, 1939–1945*. Minneapolis: University of Minnesota Press, 1974. (examines the nature of Nazi propaganda, its successes and failures)

Beck, Earl R. *Under the Bombs: The German Home Front, 1942–1945*. Lexington: University Press of Kentucky, 1986.

Dallin, Alexander. *German Rule In Russia, 1941–1945*. Boulder, CO: Westview Press, 1981. (second edition of a journalist's work originally published in 1957)

Fest, Joachim. *Plotting Hitler's Death: The Story of the German Resistance*. New York: Henry Holt, 1996. (a leading Hitler biographer writes a compelling narrative and solid analysis of the resistance, emphasizing the July 20 plot)

Gill, Anthony. *An Honourable Defeat: A History of German Resistance to Hitler, 1933–1945*. New York: Henry Holt, 1994.

Herzstein, Robert E. *The War That Hitler Won: Goebbels and the Nazi Media Campaign*. New York: Paragon House, 1987.

Homze, Edward L. *Foreign Labor in Nazi Germany*. Princeton, NJ: Princeton University Press, 1967.

Kitchen, Martin. *Nazi Germany at War.* London and New York: Longman, 1995. (comprehensive coverage of a variety of topics, including war production, bombing raids, women, youth, the churches, and arts and entertainment)

Koehl, Robert. *RKFDV: German Resettlement and Population Policy.* Cambridge, MA: Harvard University Press, 1957.(account of Himmler's Reich Commissariat for the Strengthening of Germandom [RKFDV] in eastern Europe)

Kramarz, Joachim. *Stauffenberg: The Architect of the Famous July 20th Conspiracy to Assassinate Hitler.* New York: MacMillan, 1967. (in spite of the title, a solid biography)

Littell, Franklin H. and Hubert G. Locke, eds. *The German Church Struggle and the Holocaust.* Detroit: Wayne State University Press, 1974. (broader than the title, these essays discuss the protests of the Confessing Church, emphasizing the war years)

Lukas, Richard C. *The Forgotten Holocaust: The Poles Under German Occupation, 1939–1944.* Lexington, KY: University Press of Kentucky, 1986.

Macksey, Kenneth J. *The Partisans of World War II.* New York: Stein & Day, 1975.

Milward, Alan S. *The German Economy At War.* London: Athlone Press, 1965. (sees blitzkrieg, or limited-war, economics of the first two years evolving into a total war economy)

Overy, Richard J. *War and Economy in the Third Reich, 1938–1945.* Oxford: Clarendon Press, 1994. (challenges Milward's thesis of blitzkrieg economics evolving into a total war economy, but agrees that Germany substantially increased its war production from 1942 to 1944)

Rich, Norman. *Hitler's War Aims: Vol. II, The Establishment of the New Order.* New York: Norton, 1974. (a comprehensive account of Nazi rule over occupied Europe)

Rupp, Leila J. *Mobilizing Women for War: German and American Propaganda, 1939–1945.* Princeton, NJ: Princeton University Press, 1978. (an interesting "compare and contrast" study)

Scholl, Inge. *Students Against Tyranny.* Middletown, CT: Wesleyan University Press, 1983. (the surviving sister of Hans and Sophie Scholl tells the story of the White Rose)

Steinert, Marlis. *Hitler's War and the Germans.* Athens, OH: Ohio University Press, 1977. (insightful work on public opinion during the war, based largely on SD reports)

Steinhoff, Johannes, Peter Pechel, and Dennis Showalter. *Voices from the Third Reich: An Oral History.* Washington, DC: Regnery Gateway, 1989. (interviews with people from all walks of life, chiefly during the war years)

Vassiltchikov, Marie. *Berlin Diaries, 1940–1945.* New York: Random House, 1987. (unique perspective of a Russian aristocrat living in Berlin and surviving the war)

Whiting, Charles. *The Home Front: Germany.* Chicago: Time-Life Books, 1982. (popular history, richly illustrated)

VIII. THE HOLOCAUST

Bauer, Yehuda. *A History of the Holocaust.* New York: Franklin Watts, 1982.

Berenbaum, Michael, ed. *Witness to the Holocaust.* New York: HarperCollins, 1997. (an illustrated documentary history in the words of its victims, perpetrators, and bystanders)

Breitman, Richard. *The Architect of Genocide: Himmler and the Final Solution.* New York: Alfred A. Knopf, 1991. (covers Himmler's primary role)

———. *Official Secrets: What the Nazis Planned, What the British and Americans Knew.* New York: Hill and Wang, 1998. (the first study of recently declassified British intercepts of coded Nazi communications shows that the British were reluctant to share or act upon their extensive knowledge of the Final Solution)

Browning, Christopher. *Fateful Months: Essays on the Emergence of the Final Solution.* New York: Holmes and Meier, 1985. (covers stages of Hitler's orders for the Final Solution in 1941)

———. *Nazi Policy, Jewish Workers, German Killers.* Cambridge: Cambridge University Press, 2000. (recent lectures reassessing earlier works in light of current research)

———. *Ordinary Men: Reserve Police Battalion 101 and the Final Solution in Poland.* New York: HarperCollins, 1992. (how a battalion of the SS Order Police with little indoctrination or training became enthusiastic killers of Jews)

———. *The Path to Genocide: Essays on Launching the Final Solution.* New York: Cambridge University Press, 1992. (how Himmler, Heydrich, and other SS leaders interpreted and carried out Hitler's orders)

Cornwell, John. *Hitler's Pope: The Secret History of Pius XII.* New York: Viking, 1999. (broad, highly critical coverage of Eugenio Pacelli, whom the author sees as pro-German and anti-Semitic before and after he became Pius XII in 1939)

Dawidowicz, Lucy S., ed. *Holocaust Reader.* New York: Behrman House, 1976. (a comprehensive collection of documents)

———. *The War Against the Jews, 1933–1945.* Holt, Rinehart & Winston, 1975. (a detailed general history of the Holocaust)

De Pres, Terrence. *The Survivor: Anatomy of Life in the Death Camps.* New York: Oxford University Press, 1977. (analysis by a scholar who was not an inmate)

Fleming, Gerald. *Hitler and the Final Solution.* Berkeley: University of California, 1984. (detailed coverage of documentation showing that Hitler ordered the Final Solution)

Gilbert, Martin. *Auschwitz and the Allies.* New York: Holt, Rinehart and Winston, 1981. (explains why the Allies did not bomb Birkenau, the extermination center of Auschwitz)

_____. *The Holocaust: A History of the Jews of Europe During the Second World War.* New York: Holt, Rinehart and Winston, 1985. (narrative with excerpts from eye-witness accounts)

Goldhagen, Daniel Jonah. *Hitler's Willing Executioners: Ordinary Germans and the Holocaust.* New York: Alfred A. Knopf, 1996. (argues that "eliminationist anti-Semitism" had so permeated society that a large number ordinary Germans became—and most of the rest of their fellow Germans were fit to be—Hitler's willing executioners; a highly controversial work)

Gordon, Sarah. *Hitler, Germans, and the "Jewish Question."* Princeton, NJ: Princeton University Press, 1984. (covers Nazi policies before and during the war)

Hallie, Philip. *Lest Innocent Blood Be Shed: The Story of the Village of Le Chambon and How Goodness Happened There.* New York: Harper & Row, 1979. (rescue of Jews in southern France led by the village's Protestant pastor, Andre Trocmé)

Hilberg, Raul. *The Destruction of the European Jews.* rev. ed. New York: Holmes & Meier, 1985. (this detailed work, originally published in 1961, was the first general history)

————. *Documents of Destruction: Germany and Jewry, 1933–1945.* Chicago: Quadrangle Books, 1971. (another good documentary collection)

————. *Perpetrators, Victims, Bystanders: The Jewish Catastrophe, 1933–1945.* New York: HarperCollins, 1992. (analyzes motivation of the three groups named in the title)

Keneally, Thomas. *Schindler's List.* New York: Simon & Schuster, 1982. (Steven Spielberg's award-winning film is based on this book, written as a fact-based novel)

Kielar, Wieslaw. *Anus Mundi: 1500 Days in Auschwitz/Birkenau.* London/New York: Penguin Books, 1980. (one of the most detailed survivors' accounts)

Klee, Ernst, Willi Dressen, and Volker Riess, eds. *"The Good Old Days": The Holocaust as Seen by Its Perpetrators and Bystanders.* New York: Free Press, 1991. (excerpts from diaries, letters, and reports written by executioners and sympathetic observers)

Klemperer, Victor. *I Will Bear Witness: A Diary of the Nazi Years.* New York: Random House, 1998. (this two-volume work tells the story of the author's [married to an Aryan woman] survival living in Dresden under the Nazi regime)

Laqueur, Walter. *The Terrible Secret: Suppression of the Truth About Hitler's "Final Solution."* New York: Penguin Books, 1982. (discusses information available to the Allies through 1942)

Levi, Primo. *Survival in Auschwitz.* New York: Collier Books, 1961. (a survivor's account)

Lewy, Guenter. *The Catholic Church and Nazi Germany.* New York: McGraw-Hill, 1964. (highly critical study of the "accommodation" of the German bishops and Pius XII)

———. *The Nazi Persecution of the Gypsies.* New York: Oxford University Press, 2000. (one of the first studies of the Gypsies, most of whom were killed at Auschwitz)

Lifton, Robert Jay. *The Nazi Doctors: Medical Killing and the Psychology of Genocide.* New York: Basic Books, 1986.

Neufeld, Michael J. and Michael Berenbaum, eds., *The Bombing of Auschwitz: Should the Allies Have Attempted It?* New York: St. Martin's Press, 2000. (most of the essays in this anthology conclude that, given 1940s technology, bombing Birkenau would not have helped the Jews)

Niewyk, Donald L. *The Holocaust: Problems and Perspectives of Interpretation.* Boston: Houghton Mifflin, 1997. (excerpts from works on central themes of the Holocaust, reflecting current research and different points of view)

Segev, Tom. *Soldiers of Evil: The Commandants of the Nazi Concentration Camps.* New York: McGraw-Hill, 1987.

Sereny, Gitta. *Into That Darkness: An Examination of Conscience.* New York: McGraw-Hill, 1974. (interviews in the early 1970s with convicted Treblinka commandant, Franz Stangl)

Shermer, Michael, and Alex Grobman. *Denying History: Who Says the Holocaust Never Happened and Why Do They Say It?* Berkeley: University of California Press, 2000. (one of the first scholarly studies of Holocaust deniers and refutation of their claims)

Steiner, Jean-Francois. *Treblinka.* New York: Simon & Schuster, 1967. (factual account in novel form by a survivor's son)

Ten Boom, Corrie. *The Hiding Place.* Old Tappen, NJ: Spire Books, 1971. (moving account of a devoutly Christian Dutch family that hid Jews and suffered for it in Nazi concentration camps)

Wiesel, Elie. *Night.* New York: Bantam, 1982. (brief, deeply moving memoir by the Nobel Prize–winning Auschwitz survivor)

Wyman, David S. *The Abandonment of the Jews: America and the Holocaust 1941–1945.* New York: Pantheon Books, 1984. (highly critical of U.S. policy, especially the State Department)

Yahil, Leni. *The Holocaust: The Fate of European Jews.* New York: Oxford University Press, 1990. (detailed narrative and synthesis)

IX. HITLER'S LEGACY

Baldwin, Peter, ed. *Reworking the Past: Hitler, the Holocaust, and the Historians' Debate.* Boston: Beacon Press, 1990. (sixteen scholars examine the 1980's *Historikerstreit*)

Conot, Robert E. *Justice at Nuremberg*. New York: Harper & Row, 1983. (detailed account of the trials)

Davidson, Eugene. *The Trial of the Germans*. New York: MacMillan, 1966. (an account of the trial that includes biographical sketches of the defendants)

Peterson, Edward N. *The Many Faces of Defeat: The German People's Experience in 1945*. New York: Peter Lang, 1990. (reflections of a scholar who was in the U.S. army of occupation in 1945)

Smith, Bradley F. *Reaching Judgement at Nuremberg*. New York: Basic Books, 1977. (how the judges arrived at the verdicts)

Stern, Fritz. *Dreams and Delusions: The Drama of German History*. New York: Random House/Knopf, 1987. (analyzes the pivotal role of the Third Reich in German history)

Turner, Henry Ashby. *Germany from Partition to Unification*. New Haven: Yale University Press, 1992. (traces the path to re-unification in 1990)

Index

Photo Credits